Legal Protection for Computer-Implemented Inventions

Legal Protection for Computer-Implemented Inventions

A Practical Guide to Software-Related Patents

Sabine Kruspig

Claudia Schwarz

Wolters Kluwer

Published by:
Kluwer Law International B.V.
PO Box 316
2400 AH Alphen aan den Rijn
The Netherlands
Website: www.wolterskluwerlr.com

Sold and distributed in North, Central and South America by:
Wolters Kluwer Legal & Regulatory U.S.
7201 McKinney Circle
Frederick, MD 21704
United States of America
Email: customer.service@wolterskluwer.com

Sold and distributed in all other countries by:
Quadrant
Rockwood House
Haywards Heath
West Sussex
RH16 3DH
United Kingdom
Email: international-customerservice@wolterskluwer.com

ISBN 978-90-411-5229-9

e-Book: ISBN 978-90-411-5244-2
web-PDF: ISBN 978-90-411-9034-5

Table of Contents

Foreword

Whenever a new, commercially valuable, technology emerges, the following question has to be answered: how does it fit into systems of protection of intellectual property? Computers, or more generally programmable devices, have changed the world in the last seventy years, and among many other issues have raised the problem of how, whether and to what extent innovative software may be protected by patents. In some systems, such as the US, the relevant law was formulated before computers had any impact on everyday life; other systems, such as the European Patent Convention, were formalized after the importance of computers became apparent and make specific reference to them. Even in the latter case, the novelty of the technology at the time of the law's introduction and its continued (and continuing) evolution meant that it has had to be interpreted in the circumstances not anticipated by the legislators. Inevitably, this has also been an evolutionary process, as courts in the various jurisdictions have tried to develop a consistent approach to what is and is not patentable. Even if we suppose optimistically that this goal has been achieved in the major jurisdictions, the practitioner still faces a challenging task in formulating and prosecuting a patent application in this field: first the critical concepts (e.g., 'further technical effect' at the European Patent Office or 'abstract' in the US system) are difficult to understand and apply; second even in jurisdictions which are theoretically applying the same law, such as England, Germany and the EPO, different legal systems and traditions mean that different approaches are taken.

Software extends yearly into more and more fields of application; more and more patent practitioners are having to come to grips with the intricacies of patents relying on innovative software. The authors of this book provide a practical guide for this work, rather than an academic analysis. The second chapter explains some fundamentals of computer science in order to lay a foundation for understanding what may and may not be protected by a patent. After an introduction to the legal problems in a world context, subsequent chapters explain the relevant law and guidelines in different jurisdictions and explore how they have been applied through discussion of important cases, giving practical guidance for preparing and prosecuting patent applications in these different jurisdictions.

The authors are well qualified for their task: Claudia Schwarz has long experience as a patent attorney working in this field; Sabine Kruspig has the necessary insight into how patent applications will be read and guidelines applied by patent offices through her long experience as an examiner and director at the EPO. The views from 'both sides of the fence' make their guidance especially valuable.

Dai Rees
Retired Chairman of EPO Board of Appeal 3.5.06
July 2017

List of Abbreviations

Legal

ACM	Association of the Computing Machinery
AIA	America Invents Act
BGH	German Supreme Court (Bundesgerichtshof)
BoA	Board of Appeal
BPatG	German Federal Patent Court (Bundespatentgericht)
CA	Court of Appeal (Court d'Appel (France))
CBM	Covered Business Methods (USA)
CFR	Code of Federal Regulations
CII	Computer Implemented Invention
CN	WIPO Country Code for China
CP	Computer Program
CPC	Cooperative Patent Classification
CPP	Computer Program Product
CRI	Computer related inventions (India)
DE	WIPO Country Code for Germany
EBoA	Enlarged Board of Appeal (EPO)
EP	WIPO Country Code for European Patent Application/Patent
EPC	European Patent Convention
EPO	European Patent Office
EU	European Union
FI/F-term	File Index Term (Japan)
GAO	Government Accountability Office (US)
GL	Guidelines

ICT	Information and Communication Technology
IEEE	Institute of Electrical and Electronics Engineers
IN	WIPO Country Code for India
INPI	Institut national de la propriété industrielle (France)
IoT	Internet of Things
IP	Intellectual Property
IPAB	Intellectual Property Appelate Board (India)
IPC	International Patent Classification
IPHC	Intellectual Property High Court (Japan)
IPR	Intellectual Property Right
IPR	Inter Partes Review
ISO	International Organization for Standardization
JP	WIPO Country Code for Japan
JPO	Japan Patent Office
KIPO	Korean Intellectual Property Office
KR	WIPO Country Code for South Korea
MoPP	Manual of Patent Practise (GB)
OIN	Open Invention Network
OSI	Open Systems Interconnection
PatG	German Patentgesetz
PCT	Patent Cooperation Treaty
PHOSITA	Person Having Ordinary Skill In The Art (US)
PRB	Chinese Patent Re-examination Board
PTAB	Patent Trial and Appeal Board
SIPO	Chinese State Intellectual Property Office
TRIPS	Trade-Related Aspects of Intellectual Property Rights
TRIZ	Theory on Inventive Problem Solving
UKIPO	United Kingdom Intellectual Property Office
UP	Unitary Patent (Europe)
UPC	Unitary Patent Court (Europe)
UPCA	Unitary Patent Court Agreement (Europe)
US	WIPO Country Code for USA
USA	United States of America
USPTO	United States Patent and Trademark Office
WIPO	World Intellectual Property Organization

Computing

HPLs	Higher Programming Languages
IT	Information Technology
ICT	Information and Communication Technology
ISO/OSI	ISO/OSI Model in Communication Networks (International Standard Organization/ Open System Interconnection defines seven layers in a complete communication system)
Computational X	stands for various fields of study with a merge of computing; X can stand for established disciplines like biology, finance, chemistry, social siences ...
GUI	Graphical User Interface
HCI	Human Computer Interface
CPU	Central Processing Unit
IoT	Internet of Things
SWEBOK	Software Engineering Book of Knowledge
API	Application Programming Interface
SDLC	Software Development Life Cycle

List of Figures

List of Tables

Acknowledgements

The authors would like to thank all the people who supported the creation of this book from the initial ideas to completion. Without their assistance it wouldn't have been possible to write a book with information from several countries.

We are very grateful to have a group of excellent foreign colleagues who provided us with guidance through some difficult national information.

In particular Ms Kruspig would like to thank her former colleagues at the European Patent Office who inspired her during the daily work and during the work in project groups to contribute to a book on CII. Mr Dai Rees (former Chair of a Technical Board of Appeal (TBoA)) and Mr. Martin Müller (member of a TBoA) gave assistance and feedback on matters of patent law, computer science and language. Feedback on several facets of computer science was provided in particular by Professor Monika Heiner (TU Cottbus, Germany), Professor Matti Tedre (Professor at School of Computing, University of Eastern Finland) and Mrs Friederike Nickl, chairperson of the working group 'Software Engineering Live' at the German Informatics Society.

Further, we want to express our gratitude to Mrs Medha Rolvering, Global Head of Intellectual Property Software AG, Germany. She provided us with contacts in her home country, India. We are thankful to our colleague, patent attorney Mrs Ji Young (Bellina) Seo at Kim&Chang (Korea). She participated in our lecture, which we had given in Seoul, Korea 2014 and provided us with contacts to her colleagues Mr Stephen T Bang and Ho-Yeon Lee at Kim & Chang. Moreover, we want to express our thanks to Mr Jongmyun KIM, Patent Attorney at IAM Patent & Law Firm, Seoul, Korea.

Mr Fan Zhang, Patent Professional with Schindler, Switzerland, Inventio AG has participated in one of our seminars in Germany. He provided us with several actual legal texts and translations from Chinese into English.

We are thankful to all our colleagues in the patent departments of their respective companies, in the law firms and in Court for their support and helpful discussions.

Thanks also to Mr Steve Lambley, Netherlands and to Mrs Julia Flyng for reviewing the texts from a linguistic and editorial point of view.

Our special thanks go to our editor Ms Christine Robben at Wolters Kluwer and her team, who had so much patience with us. We would like to thank the team of

NewGen Knowledge Works for their excellent assistance in the preparation and management of the final production of the book.

This acknowledgement would not be complete without thanking our families and friends for their patience and their understanding when we did not participate in common activities but focused on the book.

Especially, Mrs Schwarz wants to thank her husband, Stefan Schwarz, for encouraging her activities and for his understanding. Without his support the book would not have been possible.

CHAPTER 1
Introduction

Software is everywhere. Nowadays most products are equipped with software: from accelerators in nuclear physics to software ecosystems to washing machines controlled by fuzzy logic. According to a recent WIPO press release, computer technology saw the highest percentage of published patent applications worldwide (7.9% of the total), followed by electrical machinery (7.3%) and digital communication (4.9%).[1]

There is a need for patent protection in order to safeguard a company's legal position. But is software development patent protectable?

The unsatisfactory answer is that it depends. It depends on the subject matter, on the national jurisdiction and on the drafting language. A 'one size fits all' approach is not feasible.

Clients want to have legal certainty and transparent criteria in order to be able to judge patentability on an objective basis.

However, software challenges patent law, due to a number of aspects.

Software is different. In contrast to other technical domains, computer science is non-tangible, is abstract, may even be virtualized and cloudified, and may be copied easily.

Software applications may be technical or non-technical. Computer-implemented inventions may be related to technical or non-technical subject matter. It would, however, be misleading to classify software apodictically to one of those categories. Thus, it is a mistake to generally consider software the same as a business method or as an abstract idea.

Software challenges patent law. Former criteria for assessing patentability may not apply to computer-implemented inventions. Therefore, the whole system is changing dynamically as new criteria are found and applied in case law.

1. *Global Patent Applications Rose to 2.9 Million in 2015 on Strong Growth from China; Demand Also Increased for Other Intellectual Property Rights*, WIPO Press Release PR/2016/802, Geneva (23 November 2016).

Enforceability and cost. How can enforceable software patent applications be competitively drafted and how can a patent portfolio for computer-implemented inventions be established in several countries without spending money unnecessarily on problematic examination proceedings?

The legal requirements in patent law differ from country to country. Therefore, this publication aims to provide an overview of the provisions for the protection of computer-implemented inventions in selected countries. It examines the major hurdles in each particular country and describes the best practice to be adopted.

Chapter 2 deals with fundamentals of computing. Later chapters will show the interpretation of some basic features in different jurisdictions. A computer program is neither a program as such nor an algorithm. The definition of software in computer science often differs from the definition in patent law. This can make the situation unclear and may lead to misunderstandings.

Chapter 3 refers to the key issues when dealing with the patent protection of software. This Chapter shows important issues as a kind of summary, which need to be considered in every jurisdiction and irrespective of the particular national law. How can we protect cloud software, which is distributed among several servers that are located in several countries? How should patent applications (claim categories, source code as part of the description) be drafted? In computing, virtualization refers to the act of generating a virtual (rather than a physical) version of physical object, including but not limited to a virtual computer hardware platform, virtual operating system, virtual storage device, or virtual computer network resources. So, for inventions based on the concept of virtualization, how should technical features, such as hardware related features, be highlighted? How detailed and on what layer in the abstraction model in computer science should we describe the invention?

Chapters 4–12 are the book's main chapters, concerned with the key countries and their legal situation for computer-implemented inventions in each country. If official guidelines for computer-implemented inventions are available, these are discussed. In the last section of each chapter, relevant decisions, if available in English, are discussed. These chapters have generally the same or a similar structure. Chapter 4 deals with decisions of the European Patent Office, Chapter 5 refers to German decisions, Chapter 6 to the United Kingdom, Chapter 7 to France, Chapter 8 to the USA, Chapter 9 to China, Chapter 10 to Korea, Chapter 11 to Japan, and Chapter 12 to India.

Chapters 13 and 14 refer to regulations in the context of the Patent Corporation Treaty (PCT) and with respect to future development, in particular to the Unified Patent System.

In Chapter 15, the core messages from the legal analyses in the national chapters are summarized and a checklist is provided for an international comparison, followed by an outlook on future developments.

The views expressed in this book are those of the authors and not necessarily the views of legal authorities.

CHAPTER 2

Basics of Computer Science and Protection of Software

§2.01 INTRODUCTION

The patent system is one major component of a complex legal system to protect Intellectual Property (IP). The law of IP protection according to the World Intellectual Property Organization (WIPO) generally 'aims at safeguarding creators and other producers of intellectual goods and services by granting them certain time-limited rights to control the use made of those productions'.[1] IP is traditionally divided into two branches, 'industrial property' and 'copyright'. With the appearance of the first modern digital computers at the end of the 1940s the question arose of how to protect creative ideas in the field of computer technology with existing or new IP systems. Legislators struggled with the means to protect software mainly due to the specific properties of software. These do not fit into the traditional understanding of technology in the patent system. Such an opinion was expressed by different people for years. One example is the article '*RESPONSE*: THE MODELS ARE BROKEN; THE MODELS ARE BROKEN!' authored by the computer scientist A. Newell in 1986.[2] It was a reaction to an article written by Professor Chisum. He criticized the negative view expressed after the *Gottschalk v. Benson* decision on patentability of algorithms in the US.

Chapter 2 will focus on the basics of computing and software development in order to explain general views and options in claim formulation for the filing of patent applications. Topics of enforcement will not be addressed. Discussions relate in particular to claim formulation, search and examination but not to litigation.

1. WIPO *Intellectual Property Handbook: Policy, Law and Use* 2004, Chapter 1, http://www.wipo.int/export/sites/www/about-ip/en/iprm/pdf/ch1.pdf (accessed 21 April 2017).
2. Newell, A. *Response: The Models Are Broken, the Models Are Broken* 47 U. Pitt. L. Rev. 1023, 1986.

§2.02 COMPUTER PROGRAM: ALGORITHM OR FINAL PROGRAM IN THE CLAIM?

In the 1960s discussions on protection of software mainly took place in the US. The interested circles discussed several proposals. According to the Association of Computing Machinery (ACM) computer professionals were 'appalled by the tremendous information gap between the law makers and enforcers and the industry's techniques and economics'.[3] One proposal suggested that the Patent Office should test the computer program. IBM indicated three investments in the production of a workable program:

- 'the development of concepts;
- the preparation of documentation and flowcharts;
- the actual writing, testing, and debugging of the program.'

It was pointed out that 'the concept, the detailed description, and the actual sequence of instructions would be treated in different ways'.[4]

At the end of the 1970s international discussions for a 'sui generis' law for the protection of software took place under the guidance of WIPO.[5] The model provisions identified were similar to the earlier IBM proposals:

> that computer software includes:
>
> i) Supporting material (flowcharts, written description of the program);
> ii) Documentation on how to use the program;
> iii) The program itself.
>
> Furthermore, the program is recognized as comprising two major elements, the underlying process, system of operation or algorithm and the set of instructions that explain the process in detail. (Emphasis added by the author).[6]

The model provisions were not accepted but they already indicated the facets of software that could be subject to protection. The patent system and the copyright protection became the major legal protection means for the protection of software despite ongoing debates.

The appearance of a separate software industry and the growing importance of software in all areas of professional and private life triggered the adaptation of IP law for, software protection. This process was and is connected with political and ideological questions. The free and open source movement was and is a major opponent to patents for software.[7] Main arguments of the latter against 'software patents' are based on freedom of information, the inhibitory character of the patent system which does

3. Duggan, M.A. *Patents and Programs: The ACM's Position*, Comm. of the ACM, Vol. 14, No. 4, April 1971.
4. Galbi, E.W. *Software and Patents: A Status Report*, Comm. of the ACM, Vol. 14, No. 4, April 1971.
5. WIPO *Mustervorschriften für den Schutz von Computersoftware* GRUR Int. 1978, 286.
6. *Software: An Emerging Industry* OECD, Paris 1985, ICCP Information, Computer and Communication Policy Series, 159.
7. Eimer, Th.R. *Arenen und Monopole: Softwarepatente in den USA und in Europa* Springer, 2010.

not fit with the incremental character of innovation in the software area, the expensive and lengthy procedures which seem not to correspond to a general shorter lifetime of software products and others.

§2.03 THE KNOWLEDGE GAP BETWEEN COMPUTER SCIENCE AND PATENT LAW

The focus of this book is on the protection of software by patents. The knowledge gap observed by ACM between law and computing technology in the 1960s has not really disappeared after nearly fifty years. An overview focussing on the European Union was given by Broman in his thesis. He points out that 'current legal protection of the Intellectual Property (IP) for "computer programs" and associated components is fractured and contains a gap that provides for legal uncertainty for the author/creator/inventor'.[8] In order to reduce the gap the next chapters describes some very basic terms of computing. The explanations cannot replace a deeper study of computing. Examples of the knowledge gap are:

(1) the use of the term 'software patent' disregarding the meaning of 'software';
(2) the inability to differentiate between the computer program itself (per se, as such) and the concept (or algorithm, process) underlying the program;
(3) the impressions given that business method patents and software patents are the same;
(4) a lack of understanding of the specifics of Computer Science (CS) and in particular of software compared to subjects of other sciences e.g.:
  (a) the high degree of modularity and abstraction in computing, in particular that completely different programs (games, text processing, video processing, tax calculation, ...) can run on the same hardware of a computer ('von Neumann computer' or stored program computer) or computer network;
  (b) the inability to distinguish between the technology of a data carrier and the digital information (binary bits) stored on a data carrier or transmitted by a data carrier.

It will be indicated that the patent system protects software based on the process, system of operation or algorithm underlying a computer program. Difficulties arise under some legislation when processes describe subject matter (rules of games, methods for doing business, presentation of information ...) excluded from patentability if claimed as such.

8. Broman, M. *Harmonised Intellectual Property Protection for Software Solutions Within EU – A Modest Proposal* 2014 http://lup.lub.lu.se/student-papers/record/4457090 (accessed 21 April 2017); Broman suggests a new term 'software solution' which is supposed to cover important aspects of 'computer programs' like source code and object code, Graphical User Interface – GUI, Application Programming Interface – API, functions and data and information.

A permanent challenge for the patent system is the application of its fundamental concepts, constructions and limitations to new technologies. Where to draw the line between topics eligible for patent protection and topics not eligible for patent protection? And even if an alleged invention is eligible, how to do a proper search for prior art and how to cope with the requirements of substantive examination and further possible procedures in the life of a patent? This is in particular the case in the area of Biotech and Computing.[9]

§2.04 THE PATENT SYSTEM AS PROMOTER OF TECHNOLOGICAL DEVELOPMENT

Some fundamental requirements for obtaining a patent exist all over the world despite differences in the patent system of nations and/or regions. The patent professional will be familiar with them and they will not be repeated in detail here. The general aim of the patent system consists among others in promoting the development of technology and in enabling the public to access the respective information.[10] As indicated by Bently: 'A patent is a limited monopoly that is granted in return for the disclosure of technical information.'[11] It follows that certain subject matter is not eligible to patent law because it does not represent technical information. Additionally, there might be political or economic reasons to exclude topics from protection even if regarded as technical.

The role of technology plays a crucial role in the context of the protection of computer programs by patents. Determination of eligibility to patent law is difficult under the implicit but long-standing role of technology in the patent system.

Some patent laws explicitly indicate a list of excluded subject matter. However, nowadays such excluded subject matter such as rules of games can be implemented by means of a computer program. The patent system is confronted with what are sometimes called 'mixed inventions'. In the area of computing this mainly refers to a combination of patentable computational features usually with non-patentable subject matter (e.g. in the area of graphical user interfaces the combination of aesthetic features with features of a program for the creation of such features on a display).

As in other technologies (e.g. physics, chemistry) theoretical concepts, scientific fundamentals of such technologies are usually excluded. However, in addition to the normal exclusions the problem exists with software processed by digital computers. Does all the software belong completely to technology? The answer to this question is closely related to the perception of computing in society. It has changed over the years (more in Chapter 2, §2.05, [C]). Furthermore, how could the daily practical work be done in the patent system?

9. Arezzo, E. & Ghidini, G. *Biotechnology and Software Patent Law*. Edward Elgar, 2011.
10. Gervais, D.J. *International Intellectual Property: A Handbook of Contemporary Research* Edward Elgar, 2015, 40.
11. Bently, L. et al. *Intellectual Property Law* 4th ed. Oxford University Press, 375.

[A] Pragmatic Reasons to Exclude 'Computer Programs Per Se'

It was already clear in the 1960s that **the program itself** (or as such) cannot be the subject of a patent claim for very pragmatic reasons. It can be part of the description. In the early days of the computer, many programs were written in **machine code** based on the machine code instructions of the computer. A typical computer program in machine code is indicated as a sequence of zeros and ones (binary bit patterns). As indicated by Currie machine code could:

> look like this
>
> 1001010010010010
>
> 0010100100001001
>
> 0010100010010010
>
> 1110010100101010
>
> etc.[12]

Such a program is understandable for the computer. It is based on an instruction set valid for a processor type. The machine code cannot be indicated in a patent claim, neither partly nor completely. Since this machine code is hard to create and to understand for a human being the assembler language was created. Binary sequences were replaced by more understandable little words:

> Thus an instruction to load the number 5 into a CPU register might look like
>
> LD 5
>
> instead of
>
> 0010010001001101.[13]

A program written in assembler language has to be translated into machine code by a special program called **assembler**. Even assembler languages are difficult to cope with. Higher Programming Languages (HPLs) with a higher level of abstraction were developed. Early ones were COBOL (Common Business Oriented Language), FORTRAN (FORmula TRANslation) and ALGOL (ALGOrithmic Language). The Encyclopedia of CS, fourth edition indicated about thousand HPLs in the year 2000 with about fifty HPLs with a broader use.[14]

If complete computer programs were the subject of a patent claim or of the description, patent professionals (e.g. examiners, patent attorneys, etc.) would need detailed skills to deal with all the different programming languages developed since the appearance of the modern digital computer. This knowledge could be limited to the fifteen current popular languages[15] in industry but even this would not make the whole topic any easier. Proponents of more patent standardization like Freilich et al. suggest

12. Currie, E. *Fundamentals of Programming Using Java* Cengage Learning EMEA, 2006, 2.
13. Currie *supra* n. 12, at 3.
14. Ralston, A. et al. *Encyclopedia of Computer Science* 4th ed., 2003, Appendix VI, key high-level languages.
15. Mashable, Inc., *15 programming languages you need to know in 2015, http://mashable.com/2015/01/18/programming-languages-2015/#K6GTuKRq4mqu* (accessed 7 February 2017).

the use of representational language like 'object-oriented languages, modelling languages, pseudocode, and knowledge representation'.[16] Pseudocode is used in descriptions. Not all other options might be realistic due to the lack of an overall acceptance for terminology and tools in the software community.

This limitation also has implications for the prior art search. Simplified, as indicated in rule 39.1 PCT – an International Searching Authority (ISA) has to do a search for a computer program only to the extent that the ISA is equipped to search prior art concerning such programs. Normally Patent Offices do not search in computer programs (source code or object code). The search is very often done in Non-Patent Literature such as books, journals ... that describe concepts of programs.

As pointed out by Zeidman, an expert in patent and copyright infringement cases for software, the search in code and comparison to other code is mainly done for copyright infringement cases or for important patent infringement cases.[17] This has to be done by experts. It is expensive and time consuming. Search and comparison of code is supported to a certain degree by software for analysing the code. Some tools also exist for reverse engineering with simplified means: extracting general structural information from machine code (running the software development process backwards).[18] Reverse engineering is also a matter for experts. Legal rules exist which forbid reverse engineering in certain situations.

Some open source communities recommend creating defensive publications e.g. in the IP.com databases. This should be done in order to avoid the granting of patents for solutions in open source software.[19] Patent examiners can find such publications.

Patent Offices do not examine the program itself. The respective rule for examination is rule 67.1 PCT.[20] No patent office systematically collects computer programs and other kind of digital data (computer games, digital media (sound, images ...).

It seems that this very fundamental constraint is sometimes forgotten in the current discussion on 'software patents' since the content of the claim is seen as identical to a computer program itself or as a material thing like a table. As indicated in The Agreement on Trade-Related Aspects of Intellectual Property Rights (TRIPS), Section 1, Article 10, (1):

---

16. Freilich, J. et al. *Towards Patent Standardization* Harvard Journal of Law and Technology, University of Illinois College of Law Legal Studies Research Paper No. 16–26, 27 May 2016.
17. Zeidman, B. *The Software IP Detective's Handbook: Measurement, Comparison, and Infringement Detection* Prentice Hall Professional, 2011.
18. Schweyer, F. *Die Rechtliche Bewertung des Reverse Engineering in Deutschland und Den USA: Eine Rechtsvergleichende Abgrenzung Zwischen Geistigem Eigentum und Gemeinfreiheit Bei der Analyse Von Konkurrenzprodukten* Mohr Siebeck, 2012.
19. Writing and Publishing Effective Defensive Publications, A White Paper by IP.com August 2014. Protecting your intellectual property and freedom to operate. By Mark O'Donnell, Vice President Client Solutions. The brochure can be downloaded after submission of some data here: http://ip.com/writing-and-publishing-effective-defensive-publications/.
20. WIPO *Regulations under the PCT as in force from July 1, 2015* http://www.wipo.int/pct/en/texts/ (accessed 21 April 2017).

> Computer programs, whether in source or object code, shall be protected as literary works under the Berne Convention (1971).[21]

The differences between various representations of a computer program during software development are explained in more detailed in Chapter 2, §2.07.

[B] Computer Programs as Implementation of 'Ineligible Subject Matter'

The fundamental nature of software imposes further limits on the current patent system. Mental processes can be implemented by means of a computer program. As indicated by D.M. Berry: '(1) … software allows the delegation of mental processes of high sophistication into computational systems' and furthermore '(2) networked software, in particular, encourages a communicative environment of rapidly changing feedback mechanisms …'.[22] The latter is possible due to '(3) … a greater use of embedded and quasi visible technologies … This turns life into quantifiable metrics that are now visible and amenable for computation and processing'. 'Digital humanities' – originally 'computing in humanities' – is an expression to indicate the increased use of computing in traditionally non-technological areas.[23]

Most patent systems exclude all kinds of mental and other non-technical processes from eligibility for patent protection. Thus, the general question is if, and when yes, under which circumstances are usually excluded mental processes (e.g. finding friends, promoting the staff member with the highest grade of competencies, creating a relationship with a customer) eligible for patent protection if implemented in software (e.g. partly located in different parts of a wide area network).

There is a plenty of critical literature on different aspects of 'software patents'. Criticism is given from different perspectives.

H.V.J. Moir provides a recent overview mainly from an economic perspective.[24] A comparison is made mainly between the examination practice of the Australian patent office, the USPTO and the EPO based on concrete patent applications. He underlines the **difficulties to find the relevant state of the art documents for business methods**. With and without software implementation they are not very well documented. State of the art can hardly ever be found in patent literature since patent documentation in the field of technology is primarily directed to the collection of patent documents. Objections are raised as to the economic value of granted patents directed to simple computerization of known business processes and to the combination of known processes.

From the historical perspective, the business area was one of the first important application areas of digital computers. In 1959, one of the first higher programming

21. WIPO *Trade-Related Aspects of Intellectual Property Rights*, 1994, https://www.wto.org/english/docs_e/legal_e/27-trips_01_e.htm (accessed 21 April 2017).
22. Berry, D.M. *The Philosophy of Software – Code and Mediation in the Digital Age* Springer, 2011.
23. Berry, D.M. *Understanding Digital Humanities* Springer, 2012.
24. Moir, H.V.J. *Patent Policy and Innovation – Do Legal Rules Deliver Effective Economic Outcomes?* 2013.

languages was created: COBOL (Common Business Oriented Language).[25] COBOL programs still run on computer systems in the business area, e.g. at banks or insurance companies.[26] However, details were kept secret and are kept secret. They are hardly ever published. Finally, fundamental business algorithms are usually not part of patent literature, the primary search documentation for many patent examiners.

Another perspective starts from the requirement to disclose the invention in a manner sufficiently clear and complete for the invention to be carried out by a **person skilled in the art** (or PHOSITA – person having ordinary skill in the art). Knowledge should be made available to the public. Some people require the disclosure of the source code.[27] Very often the claimed subject matter is seen as overbroad and without implementation details. However, applicants are reluctant to indicate details due to the rapid progress of technology (integrated circuits, communication protocols, display technology, user interfaces ...). Even if storage of programs would not be a problem today, dealing with thousands of lines of code remains a practical problem. Depending on the legislation it is difficult to find the correct level of disclosure to avoid the refusal of the application as 'mental act', 'abstract idea' or as 'computer program as such'.

[C] Education in Computer Science

The high pace of development of computing technology, its convergence with other areas of information technology (telecommunication, media) in recent years and the increased application of computing in many fields (interdisciplinary character)[28] makes determination of the patentability requirements not an easy task. While more and more people use a computer in professional and/or private life, according to Ensmenger:

> the work of computer specialists is opaque to outsiders. Their activities are often regarded by non-practitioners as being at once too difficult and technical to be understood by mere mortals, and too trivial and tedious to be worth the effort.[29]

He stresses that the public have no clear view on the work of computer professionals. Computer history is often explained based on hardware – computer generations but not on software. Scientists who made seminal contributions to

25. *COBOL: Introduction* Smithonian, The National Museum of American History http://americanhistory.si.edu/cobol/introduction (accessed 21 April 2017).
26. Coughlan, M. *Beginning COBOL for Programmers*, Apress, 2014.
27. Adams, S. *Law and Economics of Software Patent Disclosure* 2008 https://papers.ssrn.com/sol3/papers.cfm?abstract_id=1415722 (accessed 21 April 2017).
28. Computer Science Curricula 2013, Curriculum Guidelines for Undergraduate Degree Programs in Computer Science, 2013, The Association of Computing Machinery uses in the Computer Science Curricula 2013 the term 'Big Tent' view of Computer Science in order to show the cross-disciplinary work in areas like 'Computational Biology' or 'Computational X' for all other interdisciplinary work. http://ai.stanford.edu/users/sahami/CS2013/final-draft/CS2013-final-report.pdf (accessed 21 April 2017).
29. Ensmenger, N. *The Computer Boys Take Over – Computers, Programmers and the Politics of Technical Expertise* The MIT Press, 2010, 1–2.

informatics are not really known apart from some successful entrepreneurs like Bill Gates and Steve Jobs.

Without going into details, the public image of computing is ambivalent. Empirical data is indicated e.g. by A. L. Payne in her thesis which focuses on the knowledge of pupils and students in Anglophone countries.[30] The nature of CS is not understood, partly due to conflation with Information and Communication Technology (ICT). For many people 'to be good at computing' means 'to be good at using a computer', there is no theory only practical skill; computing is ubiquitous and easy to use. ICT at schools often means text processing, spreadsheets and presentation software. This knowledge is important. It can be achieved e.g. by the European Computer Driving Licence (ECDL), also known as International Computer Driving Licence (ICDL) in non-European countries.[31] However, this level of knowledge might not be sufficient for a deeper understanding of computing under patent law. Other people believe that computing is just coding. Education and qualification in computing remains an important topic in many countries/regions of the world.[32] As pointed out by Wing in 2006, education in **computational thinking** is required not only among computer scientists but also among all who use a computer to solve problems.[33] It is more than programming and it requires 'thinking at multiple levels of abstraction'.

According to a study in the US, a lack of qualification in more recently developed technologies like CS can be observed among patent examiners and patent attorneys/agents.[34] This leads to a decrease in quality because patent applications are filed which should not have been filed. Patents are granted for so called 'trivial patents'.[35] While the number of computing/software-related applications is growing enormously, the number of patent attorneys/agents with a background in computing is low. The US study indicates that in 2010 'approximately ninety percent of the patent bar is trained in chemical, mechanical, biological or electrical fields while less than five percent are trained directly in computer fields'.

In June 2016, the US Government Accountability Office (GAO) published the results of a survey among patent examiners at the USPTO. As a result, the USPTO has to meet several challenges. Clarity of patent applications, lack of time for doing a thorough search, availability of prior art are among the topics. The quality report indicates 'that most patent suits involve software-related patents and computer and communication technologies'. Stakeholders told GAO '...it is easy to unintentionally infringe on patents associated with these technologies because the patents can be

30. Payne, A.L. *Why Do Students Choose Computing?: Influences, Perceptions, Engagements* 2013; https://curve.coventry.ac.uk/open/file/e0ea7a3b-9a34-43e3-9018-582d56b3154e/1/paynecomb.pdf (accessed 21 April 2017).
31. ECDL Foundation *European Computer Driving License* http://ecdl.org (accessed 21 April 2017).
32. Informatics Europe *Informatics Education* http://www.informatics-europe.org/working-groups/informatics-education.html (accessed 21 April 2017).
33. Wing, J.M. *Computational Thinking*, Communications of the ACM, Vol. 49, No. 3, March 2006, 33.
34. Clifford, R.D. et al. *A Statistical Analysis of the Patent Bar: Where Are the Software-Savvy Patent Attorneys?* 11(2) N.C. J. L. & Tech., Spring 2010.
35. Zeidman, B. *The Software IP Detective's Handbook: Measurement, Comparison, and Infringement Detection* Prentice Hall Professional, 2011.

unclear and overly broad, which several stakeholders believe is a characteristic of low patent quality'.[36] In 2015, the EPO replaced the staff reporting system based on seniority and performance by a performance related system.[37] Production was increased by 14% in 2015. According to the user satisfaction survey of 2015, quality in search and examination at the EPO was highly appreciated by applicants.[38] The future will show if granted patents fulfil legal certainty requirements of the interested circles.

Knowledge of fundamentals of computer science is a prerequisite for patent professionals. It becomes increasingly important not only for people working in core fields of computing but also for other technologies that use computing for automation of processes in their fields.

[D] Multidisciplinary Character and Increased Network Character of Computing

As indicated earlier computing is becoming more and more multidisciplinary. The increased multidisciplinary character of computing results in questions like:

- Who is the person skilled in the art (PHOSITA), and what is obvious to that skilled person? Can it be a team?
- What is common general knowledge?

The application of general solutions of computing or ICT (e.g. wireless technology for the connection of devices over a certain distance like Bluetooth®) to several areas of technology has to be considered in order to avoid 'trivial' patents. The problems resulting from the multidisciplinary character are indicated e.g. with the 'Stupid Patent of the Month: A Drink Mixer Attacks the Internet of Things'.[39] The patent US8788090 was in fact granted in 2014, for a mixer to be connected to the Internet to allow customized ordering. The granted patent was used to attack a patent which allows 'customers to "remotely customize the operation" of a "thermostat"'. It was also selected as stupid patent of the month to show the problem of overbroad claims.

An additional challenge for the patent system is the territorial principle of patent protection on the one hand and the increased networked character of computing applications (cloud computing, Internet of Things ...) on the other.[40]

36. United States Government Accountability Office *Patent Office Should Define Quality, Reassess Incentives, and Improve Clarity, June 2016* http://www.gao.gov/assets/680/678247.pdf (accessed 21 April 2016).
37. EPO *EPO Annual Report 2015* https://www.epo.org/about-us/annual-reports-statistics/annual-report/2015.html (accessed 21 April 2017).
38. EPO *User satisfaction survey 2015 on search and examination services* http://documents.epo.org/projects/babylon/eponet.nsf/0/3865556CE6B8991AC1257F65005A5C03/$File/user_satisfaction_survey_2015_search_and_examination_en.pdf (accessed 21 April 2017).
39. *Daniel Nazer: Stupid Patent of the Month: A Drink Mixer Attacks the Internet of Things* IOT Council http://www.theinternetofthings.eu/daniel-nazer-stupid-patent-month-drink-mixer-attacks-internet-things (accessed 21 April 2017).
40. Trimble, M. *Global Patents: Limits of Transnational Enforcement* OUP USA, 2012.

[E] Summary

To sum up, difficulties in the legal practice concerning software-related patents result to a certain degree from a long-term knowledge gap between patent law and computing. It is necessary to make a distinction between the two basic elements of a computer program: the algorithm or process and the instructions that transform the algorithm into the final computer program. The concrete list of instructions of the computer program is protected under copyright.

First, the complete computer program itself (per se, as such) as a sequence of instructions or machine code cannot be indicated in a claim. Patent Offices do not collect computer programs. They usually do not search in computer programs (code) but in sources of information that describe general principles of such programs.

Second, the subject of a claim (in different claim forms) is more similar to the algorithm underlying a computer program. More details will be provided in Chapter 2, §2.06 [D].

Third, algorithms can describe internal processes of a computer/computer network but also processes of different sciences/technologies. Due to the rapid development of ICT and in particular of computing, algorithms of traditional technological fields *and* originally mental acts (e.g. organizational methods between companies and/or human beings) are implemented by means of a computer program. This is a challenge for the patent system.

Fourth, the three earlier points describe a general view for the sake of simplicity. In specific cases, boundaries can be blurred. Furthermore, media content encoded in binary form as a binary file (software) is disregarded here.

§2.05 INFORMATICS OR COMPUTER SCIENCE

[A] Computer Science and Informatics: Different Terms in Different Countries

The beginning of modern digital computing is generally considered to begin in the 1940s.[41] The term ‘informatics’ appeared in the 1960s. Nowadays, the term ‘computer science’ is mainly used in the international area.

In Europe both terms – ‘computer science’ and ‘informatics’- are used. Some differences exist in the view of some computer professionals in that ‘computer science’ is more oriented to theoretical fundamentals of computing.[42]

Informatics is an important part of information technology (IT) and ICT. The term ‘informatics’ exists in many European languages (e.g.’ Informatik’ in Germany, Switzerland, and Austria; ‘informatique’ in France; ...). In English speaking countries, the term ‘computer science’ is mainly used. Informatics Europe, an association of CS departments and research laboratories in Europe and neighbouring areas, explains

41. Cerruzzi, P.E. *Computing – A Concise History* The MIT Press essential knowledge series, 2012.
42. Hellige, H.D. *Geschichten der Informatik: Visionen, Paradigmen, Leitmotive* Springer, 2004.

differences in the meaning among different European countries.[43] Digitization – the transformation of information into digital data – allows the increased processing of such data by digital computers/computer networks. Former separated technologies like telecommunication and CS are converging.[44] However, this does not mean that CS will no longer exist as a science on its own.

Computers seem to be everywhere. According to Hennessy, there are five mainstream computing classes from the perspective of computer professionals. The recent classification comprises portable mobile devices (e.g. smartphone, tablet) and clusters/warehouse scale computers additionally to desktop, server and embedded systems.[45] The enormous amount of embedded systems, where the (micro-) processor in a system is invisible for the normal user, is very often forgotten in discussions on the use of computers.

According to Informatics Europe 'Computer science concerns itself not with computers but with computing: processing information using algorithmic techniques'.[46] Informatics Europe divides CS research into three major areas: Theory, Systems and Applications:

- '**Theory research'** concerns itself with conceptual frameworks for understanding computations, algorithms, data structures and other aspects of computing'. Mathematics is of major importance.
- '**Systems research'** is devoted to producing artefacts and assessing their properties.' It includes such specialties as: software engineering, ...; programming languages and their implementation (compilers, interpreters); human-computer interface and graphics; database research; networking and operating systems; security, which addresses the issue of maintaining integrity and privacy of information; and others.
- '**Applications research'** is devoted to the specifics of computing for a particular discipline, for example computational chemistry or computational finance. This area is sometimes called '**Computational X**'.

Theory and Systems Research are very often called '**Core Computer Science**'. Informatics Europe emphasizes the role of CS as an original discipline combining science and engineering. It has a set of seminal concepts and paradigms (e.g. the notion of algorithm, the notion of algorithmic complexity) which are important for computer scientists but very often scientists of other disciplines do not know them.

In German speaking areas of Europe, one can find the four subdivisions of informatics: applied, technical, practical and theoretical informatics.[47]

The focus on a certain facet of CS can result in misinterpretations:

43. Informatics Europe *Informatics Education in Europe: Institutions, Degrees, Students, Positions, Salaries Key Data 2008–2012* http://www.informatics-europe.org/images/documents/informatics-education-europe-data-2008-2012.pdf (accessed 21 April 2017).
44. Hacklin, F. *Management of Convergence in Innovation – Strategies and Capabilities for Value Creation Beyond Blurring Industry Boundaries* Physica – Verlag Heidelberg, 2008.
45. Hennessy, J.L. et al. *Computer Architecture: A Quantitative Approach*, 5th ed., Elsevier 2012, 5.
46. Informatics Europe *Research Evaluation for Computer Science* Draft, 2008 http://www.informatics-europe.org/images/documents/research_evaluation.pdf (accessed 21 April 2017).
47. Fischer, P. et al. *Lexikon der Informatik* Springer 2010, 430.

(1) CS has deep roots in mathematics. Like in other sciences, mathematics is used to express concepts and relationships. Pure mathematics is not patentable under any patent law. As a result, the proximity of CS to mathematics makes it sometimes difficult to draw the line between patentable and not patentable items. This is especially true for software-related patents. The appearance of the term 'algorithm' that has its roots in mathematics makes people believe that CS is mainly mathematics. However, the term 'algorithm' has a different meaning in CS. In his book 'Math you can't use' Klemens expressed the extreme view that software is just mathematics and mathematics is not patentable.[48] Thus, the engineering aspects of CS and of software development are disregarded. On the other side, there are articles/books which show the differences between CS and mathematics.[49,50]

(2) Specific characteristics of the CS create difficulties in the determination of patent eligible subject matter under all patent jurisdictions:
   (a) The fact that with one and the same hardware but different software the computer can become a different device e.g. for playing games, for financial calculations, for watching TV ...
   (b) The combination of visible, touchable hardware with intangible software creates difficulties in finding the right patent claim formulation.

As expressed by Willoughby 'patent law has been based on the common sense idea that patents should be issued for technologies'.[51] Years of discussions on software-related inventions show the difficulties to find the boundaries of patentable subject matter for computing under different national and international jurisdictions.

[B] End-User Programming

Many people all over the world use a computer at work and in private life. The knowledge on how to use a computer - computer literacy - is sometimes mixed up with knowledge in CS.

Modern tools and programming languages allow an apparently easy creation of computer programs by people without a background in computing. This is called 'end-user programming' in CS.[52] End-users programmers adapt a program to their needs, people developing web pages, creating macros. End-users like biologists, physicists can exhibit a high level of knowledge in programming in their field. Modern web technologies, scripting languages and other tools give end-users even more possibilities.

48. Klemens, B. *Math You Can't Use* Brookings Institution Press, 2006.
49. Rechenberg, P. *Was ist Informatik?* InformatikSpektrum, 2010, 54–60.
50. Colburn, T.R. *Philosophy and Computer Science* M.E. Sharpe, 2000.
51. Willoughby, K.W. *What Can Be Patented? Confronting the Confusion in Patent Law About Patent Eligible Subject Matter* Scholars' Press, 2014, 165.
52. Costabile, M.F. et al. *End Users as Unwitting Software Developers* WEUSE IV'08, 12 May 2008, Leipzig, Germany.

An overview on web related tools for end-users is given in the book 'No Code required'.[53] On the one hand it is an enormous progress to enable end-users to create software according to their wishes but on the other hand this approach simplifies the view on CS and software development. Under patent law, this can result in misleading evaluation of software-related patents.

[C] Views on Computing: What Is the Topic of Computing?

There is no simple definition of CS since it is a relatively young science. According to Schneider, there are a few one-sided views (misconceptions) about CS.[54] CS is not the study of computers or how to write computer programs. It is also not the study of the uses and applications of computers and software. Schneider explains that 'learning to use a software package is no more a part of CS than driver's education is a branch of automotive engineering. A more precise definition is the characterization of CS as the science of **algorithmic problem solving**. Before a computer can be used for solving a problem an algorithm has to be found which is suitable for this task and which can be the basis for a computational implementation in hardware or more often in software. The term 'algorithm' has a specific meaning in CS.[55] It is not equal to meaning of 'algorithm' in mathematics.

Since the appearance of CS discussions took and take place whether computing is a science. This was also a major topic during the ACM Ubiquity Conference in 2014. Denning described the history:

> Computing began as science, morphed into engineering for 30 years while it developed technology, and then entered a science renaissance about 20 years ago. Although computing had subfields that demonstrated the ideas of science, computing as a whole has only recently begun to embrace those ideals.[56]

Several authors describe the growing importance of computing and of software in the modern society. According to Meisel 'software is pervasive in our modern culture' and changes economy. The result is the 'software society'.[57] Difficulties with software patents in the US are described. The enormous influence of computing is also indicated by Kernighan.[58] Digitization of processes and products is the result. Software allows more flexibility than hardware. It is easier to change and cheaper. Algorithms as

53. Cypher, A. et al. *No Code Required: Giving Users Tools to Transform the Web* Morgan Kaufmann, 2010.
54. Schneider, G.M. et al. *Invitation to Computer Science* Cengage Learning 6th ed. 2013, 2.
55. Schneider, G.M. et al. *Invitation to Computer Science* Cengage Learning 6th ed. 2013, 11; Algorithm: a well-ordered collection of unambiguous and effectively computable operations that, when executed, produces a result and halts in a finite amount of time. Some problems are algorithmically unsolvable or their solution cannot be expressed algorithmically (e.g. correct step-by-step fashion). Furthermore, the solution might not be efficient (e.g. takes too much time).
56. Snodgrass, R. *Ubiquity Symposium* ACM, June 2014.
57. Meisel, W. *The Software Society: Cultural and Economic Impact* Trafford Publishing.
58. Kernighan *D is for Digital: What a Well-Informed Person Should Know About Computers and Communications* DisforDigital.net 2011.

fundamental components of software play a growing role and determine the functionality of devices and large systems.

Tedre gives a well-founded overview on different views on CS over the years in his book.[59] He describes the 'three different intellectual traditions: the logico-mathematical tradition, the engineering tradition, and the scientific tradition'. It is emphasized that 'drawing lines between them is very hard'. This fuzziness is the dilemma of patent law with software protection. Due to different developments in computing over the years, the one or the other tradition was seen as important.

Figure 2.1 shows the description of computing in 1968, 1989 and 2003. Smaller fields are not indicated. It can be seen that fundamental topics exist during all the years. Basic concepts might be created years ago. Their use or importance might change over the time influenced by progress in other fields like integrated circuits technology, communication technologies, new programming languages or display technologies.

Tedre emphasizes the importance to see computing as a discipline on its own. Furthermore, he underlines that 'Computing solves problems that are different from the problems of mathematics, natural sciences, and engineering. ... To facilitate the possibilities of computing to be used across the disciplines, the unique aspects of computing must be adequately explained to people from other disciplines.' This position has to be considered by the patent system. Explanations and rules have to be tailored to the language of computing. As already indicated in Chapter 2, §2.04 [D] professionals of other fields are often not aware of the universal nature of a computational concept. Thus, as soon as it was possible to connect a consumer device (e.g. mixer, toothbrush) over a specific wireless net to an app at a smartphone it is not really surprising if this concept is applied later e.g. to an electric shaver. The same is true e.g. for basic storage access methods or for a database structure which can be applied to collect data e.g. on prices or persons. Basic computational concepts used in other fields of technology cannot be disregarded in the determination of inventive step.

59. Tedre, M. *The Science of Computing – Shaping a Discipline* CRC Press 2015.

Figure 2.1 Descriptions of Computing in 1968, 1989, and 2003

1968 **Computer Science Subjects** Zadeh	**1989** **Subareas of Computing** Denning	***2003*** ***Core Technologies*** ***Denning***
Models of computation Finite state systems Programming systems	**Algorithms** **Data structures**	
Automata theory Formal languages and grammars	**Programming languages**	***Compilers***
Switching theory Computer design and organisation	**Architecture**	***Computer architecture*** ***Supercomputers*** ***Parallel computation*** ***Distributed computation***
	Operating systems	***Networks*** ***Real-time systems***
Discrete mathematics Numerical methods Mathematical programming	**Numerical and symbolic computation**	***Computational science*** ***Scientific computation***
	Software methodology and engineering	***Software engineering*** ***Data security***
Information retrieval	**Database and information retrieval systems**	***Databases*** ***Data mining***
Heuristic programming Pattern recognition and learning systems	**Artificial Intelligence and robotics**	***Robots*** ***Natural language processing*** ***Vision***
Computer graphics	**Human-computer communication**	***Human-computer-interaction*** ***Graphics*** ***Visualization***
Digital devices and circuits Mathematical logic Information theory and coding Analog and hybrid computers Combinatorics and graph theory		***Management information system*** ***Virtual reality*** ***Decision support systems*** ***E-commerce*** ***Workflow***

Rosenbloom regards computing as the fourth great scientific domain additional to physical sciences (physics, chemistry, astronomy, geology), life sciences (biology, ecology) and social sciences (psychology, economics, history ...).[60] Similar to Informatics Europe he divides computing into pure computing (or core computing) and multidisciplinary computing. Multidisciplinary computing is the result of the overlap with the traditional disciplines. On the one hand, computing has roots in the traditional sciences and on the other side, computing allows representation of processes, data of that domain by computational means. It creates difficulties e.g. in academic circles. Rosenbloom refers to his experiences in artificial intelligence. Psychologists saw him as computer scientist and computer scientists saw him more as psychologist. In his view, computing is a science on its own and 'not only the handmaiden of the other sciences'.

In summary, the patent system has to take into account computing as a science on its own. Nevertheless, it is a driving force for other fields. The specifics of computing should not be squeezed into traditional terminology of the patent system that was created mainly at the time of industrial revolution (end of eighteenth and beginning of nineteenth century). Deeper computational knowledge is necessary for patent professionals.

§2.06 FUNDAMENTAL TERMS OF COMPUTER SCIENCE WITH REFERENCE TO PATENT LAW

[A] Introduction

Even if there is a positive view on the patentability of software-related inventions the answer to apparently simple questions like 'What is software? What is a computer program?' can end up in discussions and/or misunderstandings. An example at the European Patent Office is the Referral to the Enlarged Board of Appeal G3/08.[61] In the referral, it was stated that 'claims for a computer program and a computer implemented method can be seen as having an identical scope'. The Enlarged Board clarified in answering question 2 'that the skilled person understands the word "program" to refer to the sequence of instructions specifying a method rather than the method itself'. This difference had been already emphasized in a few amicus curiae *briefs*.

Legal uncertainty can occur if patent law gives terms a meaning that differs from the meaning in computing.

The specifics of CS and in particular the nature of software compared to traditional technologies like mechanics, chemistry ... are:

60. Rosenbloom, P.S. *On Computing: The Fourth Great Scientific Domain* MIT Press 2012.
61. EPO, G3/0008, Opinion of the Enlarged Board of Appeal, Opinion of 12 May 2010 http://documents.epo.org/projects/babylon/eponet.nsf/0/DC6171F182D8B65AC125772100426656/$File/G3_08_Opinion_12_05_2010_en.pdf (accessed 21 April 2017).

(1) Software can be copied easily; it does not grow old in the traditional sense. It can be developed and produced by a group of people located at different areas of the world.
(2) It is invisible for the human being. This characteristic makes it difficult to classify it in economic systems (is it a product? ...), in the system of sciences, ...
(3) The functionality of one and the same piece of hardware can be modified by different software (e.g. smartphone: radio, text processing, media, phone ...).
(4) Computer systems and in particular software are highly modular.
(5) CS exists in everyday life and in more and more traditional fields of technology as a flexible means for implementing functionality. Thus, the same fundamental principles (e.g. memory allocation) and development characteristics can be applied for solving problems over a huge range of similar tasks.

[B] The Stored Program Computer: Von Neumann Computer

The majority of computers have the same basic universal architecture for nearly seventy years.[62] They work according to the stored program concept or paradigm. The architecture of such computers is very often called **'von Neumann architecture'** named after one of the contributors to the '**stored program concept**'.[63] The components of this computer architecture are:

(1) the Arithmetic/Logic Unit;
(2) the Control Unit;
(3) the Memory Unit;
(4) the Input/Output Devices.[64]

62. Wood, L. *The 8080 Chip at 40: What's Next for the Mighty Microprocessor?* Computerworld from IDG, 8 January 2015 http://www.computerworld.com/article/2865938/the-8080-chip-at-40-whats-next-for-the-mighty-microprocessor.html (accessed 21 April 2017).
63. Bauer, F.L. *Historische Notizen zur Informatik* Springer, 2009, 134; 'John von Neumann did not invent the stored program concept'.
64. Wikipedia *Von Neumann architecture* http://en.wikipedia.org/wiki/Von_Neumann_architecture (accessed 21 April 2017).

Figure 2.2 Basic Components of a Computer System Based on the Von Neumann Model

Stored Program Computer
(von Neumann Computer)

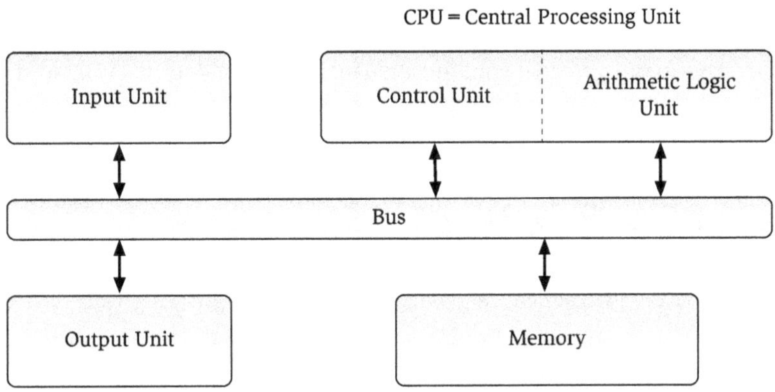

Data and instructions stored in the memory are transferred to the Central Processing Unit (CPU) and executed under the control of the control unit. Afterwards, the result is transmitted to the memory. The program in the memory can usually be changed without change of the hardware. Data/Instructions can be entered over input means. Different kind of output means allow indication of information to the user or other equipment. While the technological implementation (transistor technology, density) changes, the logical structure remains the same.

Specific computer hardware architectures exist for some fields of technology as can be seen in the next section.

[C] Classification of Computers

The first digital computers were room-filling mainframes in the 1960s. With growing miniaturization (microprocessor, storage technology...), better data communication technologies, displays, improved software... various types of computers were brought to market over the years. An overview on the historical development of computers can be found e.g. in the book 'From Mainframe to Smartphone' authored by M. Campbell-Kelly et al.[65] According to Hennessy, five different mainstream computing classes exist nowadays:[66]

- personal mobile devices (including cell phones);
- desktop;
- server;

65. Campbell-Kelly, M. et al. *From Mainframe to Smartphone* Harvard University Press, 2015.
66. Hennessy, J.L. et al. *Computer Architecture: A Quantitative Approach*, 5th ed., Elsevier, 2012.

- cluster/warehouse-scale computer:
- embedded processors.

Each class has specific properties and requirements like restricted energy consumption for mobile devices. It is important to know that embedded processors represent the highest number of computers. Computers, very often largely unnoticed by normal users, control the functionality of devices in different areas of life. Server systems and clusters of computers combined with servers are essential for cloud computing. Due to progress in communication technology and further miniaturization, computers will be more and more connected to each other (e.g. the Internet of Things, cyber-physical systems[67]).

For patent law it means that on the one hand, all computing classes with their specifics and suitability for a range of tasks have to be considered. On the other hand, one has to know that basic principles of data processing remain the same over a broad range of hardware architectures.

[D] Software/Computer Program/Algorithm and Data Structure

Some fundamentals of CS have to be considered for the discussion on protection of software by patents.

The two fundamental terms '**software**' and '**computer program**' are often taken as synonyms. In a general context the term 'software', which was coined in the 1950s, shows the flexible, 'soft' part of a computer in comparison to 'hardware'. Both parts were seen as a unit and were sold together at that time. The history of the software industry with the creation of software products is described e.g. by Campbell-Kelley.[68] It is said that in the beginning of the 1970s the famous IBM 'unbundling decision' triggered the creation of a software industry and the existence of software as a separate product on the market. Software was not always sold together with hardware but as separate product. The general distinction of software in **system software** and **application software** has one root in IBM's decision to price software products (cf. also Figure 2.4 in Chapter 2, §2.06 [E]).

The increased importance of software and its complexity in professional systems lead to improved explanations. ISO IEC 24765:2010 indicates for 'software':

(1) all or part of the programs, procedures, rules, and associated documentation of an information processing system;
(2) computer programs, procedures, and possibly associated documentation and data pertaining to the operation of a computer system;

67. Wikipedia *Cyber-physical system* http://en.wikipedia.org/wiki/Cyber-physical_system (accessed 21 April 2017) 'A **cyber-physical system (CPS)** is a system of collaborating computational elements controlling physical entities. Today, a precursor generation of cyber-physical systems can be found in areas as diverse as aerospace, automotive, chemical processes, civil infrastructure, energy, healthcare, manufacturing, transportation, entertainment, and consumer appliances.'
68. Campbell-Kelly, M. *From Airline Reservations to Sonic the Hedgehog* MIT Press, 2003.

(3) program or set of programs used to run a computer.[69]

Modern software systems are usually complex systems that can be seen from different views. Different parts can or cannot be protected under different IP law. Patent law cannot protect documentation. For this reason, the term 'software patent' can be misleading if the term 'software' includes documentation (e.g. development documentation, user manuals).

CS can be defined as the science of **algorithmic problem solving**. According to SWEBOK®V3.0:[70]

> computer software gives problem solving a flavour that is distinct from general engineering problem solving. To solve a problem using computers, we must answer the following questions.
>
> - How do we figure out what to tell the computer to do?
> - How do we convert the problem statement into an algorithm?
> - How do we convert the algorithm into machine instructions?

Simplified, in a first step the problem to be solved is usually expressed as a method described in human language. This description is normally independent from the computer to be used and a programming language. In a next step, this method should be expressed as an **algorithm** that in the context of CS according to Sedgewick/Wayne allows 'describing a finite, deterministic, and effective problem-solving method suitable for implementation as a computer program'.[71] They describe the difference between original problem statement and an implementation in the programming language Java by **Euclid's algorithm**:[72]

> English-language description
>
> Compute the greatest common divisor of two non-negative integers *p* and *q* as follows: If q is 0, the answer is p. If not, divide *p* by *q* and take the remainder *r*. The answer is the greatest common divisor of *q* and *r*.
>
> Java-language description

```
        Public static int gcd(int p, int q)
        {
if (q = = 0) return p;
int r = p% q;
return gcd(q, r);
        }
```

The basic algorithm is more than 2000 years old and it is directed to the computation of the greatest common divisor of two non-negative numbers. The Java programming language is used as an implementation of the algorithm as a computer

69. International Standard Organisation *ISO/IEC /IEEE 24765:2010 – Systems and software engineering - vocabulary*; http://www.iso.org/iso/home/store/catalogue_tc/catalogue_detail.htm?csnumber=50518 (accessed 21 April 2017).
70. Bourque, P. & Fairley, R.E. (eds). *Guide to the Software Engineering Body of Knowledge, Version 3.0*, IEEE Computer Society, 2014; www.swebok.org. (accessed 21 April 2017).
71. Sedgewick, R. et al. *Algorithms* Addison-Wesley Professional, 2011.
72. Sedgewick, R. et al. *Algorithms Part 1* Addison-Wesley Professional, 4th ed., 2011.

program. A different programming language could be used for the implementation of Euclid's algorithm.

Meanwhile collections of fundamental algorithms exist in books and in program libraries. They can be used in a plethora of application areas. Complex problem statements have to be decomposed into smaller subtasks. The choice of an appropriate algorithm is crucial for an effective computational problem solving (e.g. speed and correctness, use of resources). It has to be seen in connection with **data structures** (cf. Figure 2.1, Chapter 2, §2.05 [C]). With a narrow meaning, they are seen as a specific representation of data used in computer programs. Specific data structures are more suitable for specific algorithms, and therefore, they can highly influence processing speed. Data structures are also important for databases. They can have a broader meaning for the description of groups of bits for digital media.

In the context of patent law it is important to know that the terms **method**, **algorithm**, **data structure** and **computer program** have a specific meaning in CS. Some terms are used in patent law but sometimes they are given a meaning different from the one in CS.

For instance, the claim category 'computer program (product)' can be used under the legal practise of the EPO. Unfortunately, it leads to many interpretations as already described e.g. by Beresford in 2000.[73] The content of the claim is more similar to an algorithm – a component of the computer program. It does not mean that the content of the claim constitutes a computer program as a sequence of instructions in a programming language in the sense of CS. It also does not mean to ignore the exclusion of computer programs as such according to Article 52(2,3) EPC which primarily means that a sequence of instructions (hundreds of lines of code) cannot be subject of a patent claim. Instead of 'computer program' different formulations can be used like 'computer-readable data carrier ...'. The focus of the protection is not on the data carrier (e.g. memory) itself as a physical device without stored information but on the algorithm embedded in the program stored on the data carrier.

Furthermore, *the method underlying a computer program is usually subject of patent law* (taking into account the specific limitations of the respective patent laws and its legal interpretations). Simplified, a computer program as a specific implementation form of the patented method (algorithm) can be protected by patent law. Figure 2.3 shows the possibility to implement one algorithm in Java, C + + or C# programming language. Different programs can be created. The algorithm is the same the programming language differs. Thus, even if an algorithm is implemented in another programming language, patent protection can become effective. This is supposed to be the advantage over protection by copyright. Copyright just provides protection against copying the respective computer program.

73. Cf. e.g., Beresford, K. *Patenting Software under the European Patent Convention* Sweet & Maxwell, 2000.

Figure 2.3 Algorithm Translated into Different Languages

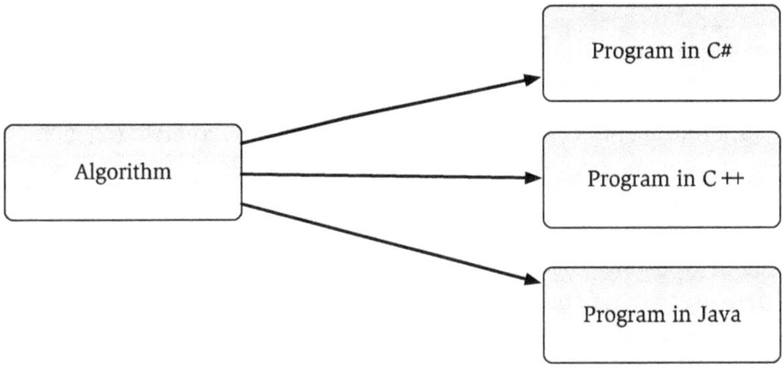

Additionally, it can be seen that in principle inventions can result from the methods underlying a computer program (algorithm) but also from an inventive computational implementation (hardware and/or software) of an e.g. well-known problem solving method.

Documentation is an important part in professional program development. It means comments in the program itself and explanations in human language explaining how the problem was solved, e.g. a structure of the program was created. This is important since the computer program could be looked at later during maintenance of general modifications of a system. Other computer professionals should be able to understand the program without major time investments. User manuals as part of documentation explain how to use the program. Details of the concrete implementation are usually not given.

The term 'algorithm' can be used in a broader or in a narrower sense. Algorithm in a narrower sense means very often the description of smaller but fundamental, general sequences like sorting of data.[74] Specific algorithms are very beneficial for specific data structures. In a broader sense, the term algorithm is used to describe a general sequence of computational steps on a high level of abstraction. The big picture is given. Usually such an algorithm can be subdivided into smaller ones.[75] In some computing literature, no difference is made between algorithm and program. The algorithm is seen as an abstraction of the program. However, patent law and copyright require a distinction.

It is important to know that the content of a claim can be seen as something similar to an algorithm in order to emphasize that the claim is not a computer program but an important element of a computer program. However, patent offices do not evaluate the properties of an algorithm in the sense of CS.[76] (cf. Chapter 12, The Indian

74. Knuth, D. *The Art of Computer Programming, Fundamental Algorithms* Vol. 1, 2nd ed., Addison-Wesley Publishing Company, 1973.
75. Bourque, A.P. & Fairley, R.E. (eds). *Guide to the Software Engineering Body of Knowledge, Version 3.0*, IEEE Computer Society, 2014; 13-4, 7. Algorithms and Complexity, www.swebok.org. (accessed 21 April 2017).
76. Färber, C. *Patentfähigkeit angewandter Algorithmen* Herbert Utz Verlag, 2014, 23–25.

Patent Office excludes algorithms from patent protection. There is no indication that examination includes whether an algorithm is one in the sense of computing.) The skilled person has to recognize that the described method is executable in principle. An inventive improvement/technical effect can be seen if a new algorithm directly leads e.g. to the use of less resources or an enormous increase of processing speed compared to former algorithms.

The differences under the patent law of different countries/regions and the borderlines of patentable subject matter are subject of discussions in the interested circles. A few countries indicate the exclusion of algorithms from patent protection in their laws (e.g. India). How it is interpreted has to be seen.

To sum up, despite some similarities among the terms, patent law should follow the more detailed view of computer professionals:

Method ≠ Algorithm ≠ Computer Program

[E] Coping with Complexity

Modern computers/computer networks are complex systems. In order to cope with this complexity computer designers have developed specific techniques.[77] The most important ones are:

(1) abstraction;
(2) modularity;
(3) layering;
(4) hierarchy.

A computer/computer network can be described on different levels of ***abstraction***. In the easiest case, the computer can be seen as a hierarchical system of different ***layers***.[78] Each layer can be further subdivided into layers that are more detailed. The hardware layer could be seen on the level of printed circuit boards, on the layer of integrated circuits or lower levels of abstraction. As a result, a computer can be seen as the combination of a hardware layer module and a software layer module. The latter is located above the hardware layer. The software layer can be further subdivided into a layer of the **system software** and the higher layer of the **application software**.

77. Saltzer, J.H. et al. *Principles of Computer System Design – An Introduction* Morgan Kaufmann, 2009.
78. Tanenbaum, A.S. *Structured Computer Organization* Pearson Prentice Hall, 2006.

Figure 2.4 Basic Layered Model of a Computer

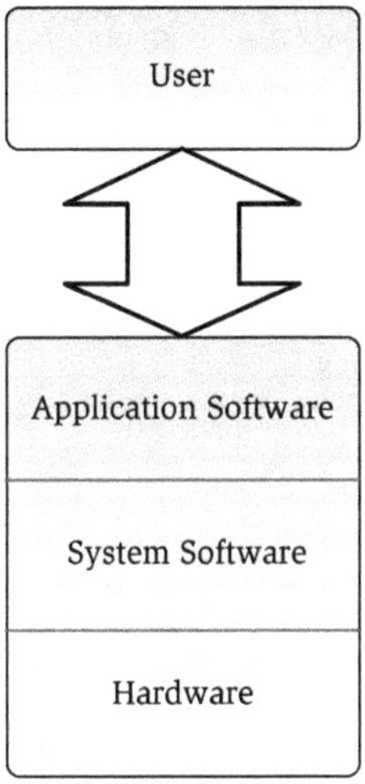

A major part of **system software** is the **operating system**. The hardware and the respective operating system is often called **platform.**[79] The operating system controls the internal work of the computer like memory allocation, task scheduling, input/output. **Utility programs** (e.g. Virus scanner), program translator software (compiler, assembler, interpreter) also belong to system software. **Program libraries** are important parts as well. They provide pre-written code (e.g. graphical user interface) and data as service to other programs. The end-user interacts with the application software. The user is normally not aware of details of lower layers. Each software layer could be further subdivided into more detailed layers. A well-known layered model of a computer network is the ISO-OSI seven layer model. Abstraction and modularization are important principles for hardware and software structures.

79. Merriam Webster *Definition of PLATFORM* '5b: operating system; also: the computer architecture and equipment using a particular operating system' https://www.merriam-webster.com/dictionary/platform (accessed 21 April 2017).

Figure 2.5 Abstraction Layers on a Language Level

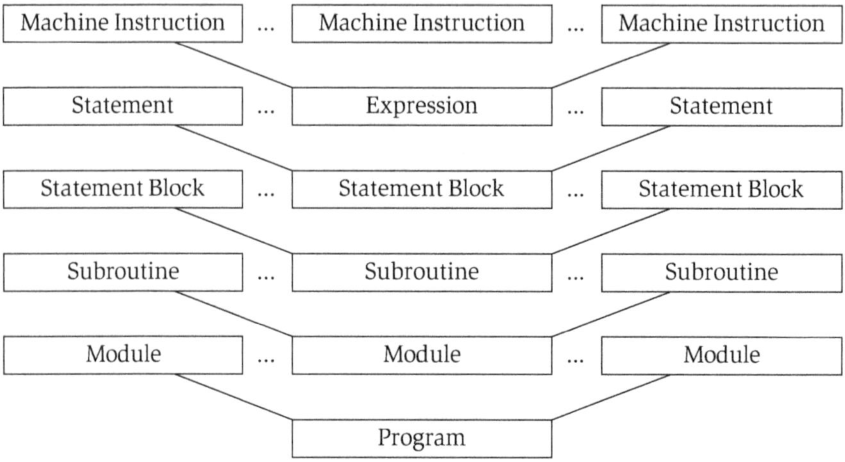

Figure 2.5 indicates a possible subdivision of a computer program into smaller elements (module, subroutine, statement block, statement, expression, machine instruction). Modules/subroutines can stem from libraries. One program can be part of a software package.

There is an enormous amount of possibilities for **application software**. Application software exists for a broad range of tasks like general-purpose office software for private and business tasks, games, software for the control of functionality of embedded systems. Application software can range from a small private program for mathematical calculations to e.g. complex calculations and simulations in chemistry that run on high performance supercomputer.

Figure 2.6 Coarse Abstraction Levels on Network Scale

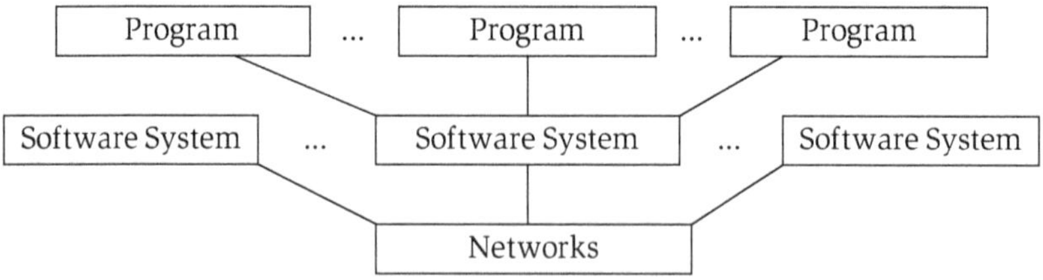

Abstraction layers in a network are shown in Figure 2.6. Several software systems (e.g. operating system) can exist in a network. One software system can consist of several programs that can be located at different entities of the network physically. Agreed interfaces are necessary for the cooperative work in heterogeneous networks.

The idea of ***modularity*** is connected to the layered view and the idea of abstraction. As mentioned earlier, a variety of different applications can run on one platform. As a result, application programs in several areas can be created without knowing the details of the underlying hardware or the operating system.

Even if it sounds banal today, it is astonishing that based on one and the same hardware (basic module) but different software (other modules) a computer can execute completely different functionalities. In other words, the same hardware module (e.g. a supercomputer, a smartphone) can be used for the implementation of a broad range of functionalities that is executable on hardware of a specific processing power. Ensmenger indicated that division of labour was like in other industries one reason for modularity in software: '... a complex program could be neatly broken down into simple, modular components that could be easily understood by any programmer ...'.[80] Code reuse and modular programming are aims in program development. Main advantages are faster software development, easier testing and maintenance of programs. Web services are an example for reusable code in cloud computing.[81]

Baldwin and Clark explain the general principles: 'A module is a unit whose structural elements are powerfully connected among themselves and relatively weekly connected to elements in other units.'[82] Gradations of modularity exist. Interaction between modules needs well-defined interfaces. They underlined that modularity reshaped the computer industry from a vertically integrated industry in the 1960s to a horizontally one in the 1990s. Some companies sell hardware modules (e.g. processors, displays, memories ...) and others only software modules (operating system, business software, games ...). Internals of a module can be changed without the change of other modules, as long as the interface is preserved. This enormous advantage is true for hardware and software. The software developer can rely on interfaces mainly **Application Programming Interfaces (APIs)** for the development of application software. The details of the platform (hardware, operating system) do not have to be known. Hardware and/or software modules can be replaced, modified or tested without rebuilding the whole system. Interoperability will play a major role in cloud computing.

In patent law, it has to be considered that patent applications might describe a computer system on different levels of abstraction. The level of abstraction can be seen in correspondence to the phases of the software development life cycle even if the phases are not executed sequentially in real life. Patent applications can relate

(1) to the complete computer (hardware and software);
(2) to a computer network;
(3) to the software only;
(4) to the computer as part of another system (embedded computing – e.g. lawn mower).

80. Ensmenger, N. *The Computer Boys Take Over – Computers, Programmers and the Politics of Technical Expertise* The MIT Press, 2010, 61.
81. Jamsa, K. *Cloud Computing* Jones & Bartlett Publishers, 2013.
82. Baldwin, C.Y. et al. *Design Rules: The Power of Modularity* MIT Press, 2000.

For example, a high level of abstraction might just indicate functional features of the task to be solved (e.g. a business method), but the claim could also indicate software implementation details. Modularity of CS is visible as well in patent applications/patents and their interpretation. The right level of abstraction (disclosure of the invention) is an ongoing topic under several patent systems. Discussions on overbroad claims play a major role in the US.

If the focus is only on software protection it might make sense from the perspective of computer professionals to omit hardware features in the patent claim. Already in the 1990s the US-patent attorney Stephens argued in the context of object-oriented program development:

> Including superfluous hardware elements often serves as nothing more than needlessly obscuring the underlying invention. Normally, the hardware elements of an object-oriented design are merely incidental and should not be included in the claim. ... Incorporating generic hardware elements into a software object claim rarely differentiates the invention in any way from the prior art. In fact, omitting hardware elements from a software object claim more appropriately points out and distinctly claims the subject matter of the invention[83]

The incorporation of unnecessary computer hardware elements in the claim can lead to needless discussions on inventive step. According to general requirements of the patent law documents have to be provided as evidence for prior art. Here, some limits of the patent system become visible with respect to 'software patents'. In scientific literature of CS software professionals mainly discuss properties of software without mentioning generic hardware features. In Chapter 2, §2.07 [C] Example 1 shows the creation of a company payroll program. In this context no details of computer hardware is indicated. It is assumed that there is a computer with the normal components that allows the run of the payroll program. Scientific literature will not mention that the computer has a processor, a memory and input/output units. Such features will be implicit. People not familiar with the layered and modular structure of modern software systems will require a prior art document for generic hardware features (e.g. processor, input unit ...) in combination with features implemented in software. If such a document cannot be provided, the risk rises for so called 'trivial patents'.

From the perspective of computer scientists (here: programmers) the hardware is usually not interesting in the context of software creation. Ensmenger points out:

> The vast majority of computer specialists, from the earliest day of commercial computing to the present, spend little time interacting with – and probably understand little about – the inner workings of an electronic computer. Their association with the computer is much more tenuous and abstract ..., the computer people are mainly concerned with the application of computers (and computer applications), not the computer itself.[84]

83. Stephens, K. et al. *Software Objects: A New Trend in Programming and Software Patents*, Santa Clara Computer & High Tech. LJ, 1996.
84. Ensmenger, N. *The Computer Boys Take Over – Computers, Programmers and the Politics of Technical Expertise* The MIT Press, 2010, 4–5.

Consequently, adding generic hardware elements to a patent claims is strange and often seen as unnecessary by programmers and software developers if there is a focus on software protection by patents. On the other hand, in some situations it seems to be the only possibility to distinguish the claimed subject matter from mental acts, etc.

To sum up, complexity of computer systems is a growing challenge for the patent system. The right level of abstraction has to be found which satisfies the requirements of disclosure and definition of the invention and which provides a reliable position in litigation. The indication of generic hardware elements in a patent claim is controversial.

§2.07 SOFTWARE DEVELOPMENT/SOFTWARE ENGINEERING

[A] Introduction

A major part of problem solving with the use of computers consists in *enabling* a computer/computer network to do so. This chapter will focus on fundamentals of software development in the area of professional software development. Creation of software by hobby programmers is not dealt with here. Furthermore, the creation of new processor/computer architectures in combination with new programming languages will not be dealt with. Software development can be part of system development, which is also not considered here.

Concurrent design of hardware and software will also not be tackled here. However, it is a growing area in particular due to the ongoing achievements of fields like cyber-physical systems and IoT (Internet of Things). An overview on past and future developments in hardware/software codesign is e.g. given by Teich.[85]

From the perspective of patent law one can see that here the possibility to implement functional requirements as hardware **or** as software is most visible. The borderline between hardware and software is 'blurred'.

In Chapter 2, §2.06 [C] different kinds of computers were described. The very basic steps of program development were explained under Chapter 2, §2.06 [D]. Simplified, program development starts with general human thoughts for problem solving. The aim to solve problems is a driving force for many inventions in all fields. Problem solving in a systematic way can be supported e.g. with the tools of the theory on inventive problem solving (TRIZ).[86] Such tools are mainly applied in the field of traditional technologies. Physical contradictions (e.g. a more powerful engine increases the speed of an airplane but also the weight) can be the starting point. They aim is usually the improvement of classical technical systems. In software development, the whole process ends with a detailed program that is executed on a computer.

85. Teich, J. *Hardware/Software Codesign: The Past, the Present, and Predicting the Future* Proceedings of the IEEE, Vol. 100, 13 May 2012.
86. Altshuller, G. et al. *40 Principles: Keys to Innovation* Technical Innovation Center, Inc., 2002.

Figure 2.7 Levels of Abstraction in Program Development

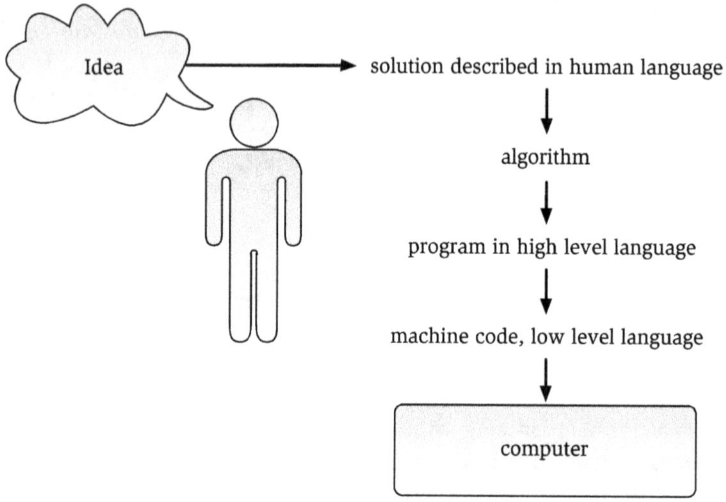

Figure 2.7 illustrates the simplified steps of program development. It starts from human ideas. This idea is usually directed to the solution of a problem. First, the solution has to be expressed in human language. It is the basis for the creation of algorithms as basis for a program in a higher programming language. This program will be transformed into machine code that is executable by the computer. In reality, the steps do not have to be completely sequentially. Due to the different types of computers and their use one can distinguish between program development for a private use (e.g. amateur programmer) and professional software development.[87]

A private computer program is often used only by one amateur user wherever several users in different companies will use a professional software product. Private programs are often small and do not need detailed documentation. Hence, different development characteristics and requirements exist. Professional software development by a team of several people (very often at different locations) is usually done according to principles of software engineering. For very large projects, complexity is reduced by decomposition into several modules that allows independent development of modules by different sub teams. The development of different programs and their interconnection for one system is sometimes designated as 'programming in the large' contrary to 'programming in the small' (term created in the 1970s). The latter is more directed to coding of short programs and software reuse.[88] It became clear that methods suitable for development of small programs are not suitable for large systems. Large projects might require the use of specific software development tools.

87. Sundar, D. *Software Engineering* Laxmi Publications, Ltd., 2010.
88. Roebuck, K. *Functional Programming Languages: High-Impact Strategies – What You Need to Know: Definitions, Adoptions, Impact, Benefits, Maturity, Vendors* Lightning Source, 2012; The concept of 'programming in the large vs. programming in the small' was introduced in 1976 by Frank de Remer and Hans Kron.

The difficulty for the patent system consists of taking into account such differences e.g. when looking at the person skilled in the art. Conclusions of one area might not be easily generalized.

[B] Professional Software Development/Software Engineering

Similar to other fields of technology the question as to what is eligible for patent protection plays a major role for software. It is a general rule under patent law that 'know how' is not patented but the invention on a respective level of abstraction. It follows, in the context of patent law something on a higher level of abstraction is patentable which appears before the final creation and execution of the code. The latter can be seen as not patentable 'know how'. For this reason, it is important to look at professional software development and its levels of abstraction.

Development of software systems can be directed to rather small but also to very large projects. Due to the nature of software (intangible, without constraints in material or natures of law, easy to copy ...) several possibilities exist to develop software. In 1968 the term 'software engineering' was created. It emphasizes the necessity to apply processes known from engineering for software production.[89] The aim was the increase of software quality (an ongoing topic). Teams develop complex software systems. Major requirements are:

(1) production of software taking into account financial and organizational constraints;
(2) good software should satisfy requirements of:
    (a) maintainability;
    (b) dependability and security;
    (c) efficiency;
    (d) acceptability;
(3) support of software development due to creation of a specification, design, test and maintenance normally not necessary for the creation of individual, small programs.

Nowadays, software engineering becomes more and more important since large technical systems are dependent on the correct functioning of software, in particular in systems that require high safety standards.

The difference between 'computer program' and 'software' becomes visible also in this context.[90] Sommerville points out:

> Many people think that software is just another word for computer programs. However, when we are talking about software engineering, software is not just the programs themselves but also all associated documentation and configuration data that is required to make these programs operate correctly. A professionally

89. Sommerville, I. *Software Engineering* Pearson, Internat. ed., 9th ed. 2011.
90. Sommerville, I. *Software Engineering* Pearson, Internat. ed., 9th ed. 2011, 5.

developed software system is often more than a single program. The system usually consists of a number of separate programs and configuration files that are used to set up these programs. It may include system documentation, which describes the structure of the system; user documentation, which explains how to use the system, and websites for users to download recent product information.

Over the years, several models were developed in order to specify software development. Irrespective whether the models describe more sequential and/or parallel phases of development some characteristics are valid for all models. The general principle of 'abstraction' plays also a major role in the different phases of software engineering.

Before a computer program can be executed, several phases are available in professional software development. This is usually a complex process. The whole process of software development is designated as **Software Life Cycle Process**. The process includes testing and maintenance. It can be part of a system development (not only software).

An enormous amount of literature /models exists with respect to software development. Terminology is not harmonized and different models are useful for selected areas. Nevertheless, industry and academic circles continue to bundle and structure the knowledge in software development.

In the last twenty years 'Agile methods' (e.g. Extreme programming, Scrum ...) became more popular contrary to traditional development models (waterfall model, spiral model, ...). They promise more flexibility, shorter development times but seem to be not suitable for complex software intensive systems.

Which concrete method is used and plays a role depends on the type of software application. Sommerville distinguishes the following seven application types:[91]

(1) Stand-alone applications – e.g. PC not connected to a network.
(2) Interactive transaction-based applications – Applications that execute on a remote computer and are accessed by users from their own PCs or terminals. These include web applications such as e-commerce applications.
(3) Embedded control systems – software control systems that control and manage hardware devices. Numerically, there are probably more embedded systems than any other type of system.
(4) Batch processing systems – business systems that are designed to process data in large batches. They process large numbers of individual inputs to create corresponding outputs.
(5) Entertainment systems – systems that are primarily for personal use and which are intended to entertain the user.
(6) Systems for modelling and simulation – systems that are developed by scientists and engineers to model physical processes or situations, which include many, separate, interacting objects.
(7) Data collection systems – systems that collect data from their environment using a set of sensors and send that data to other systems for processing.

91. Sommerville, I. *Software Engineering* Pearson, Internat. ed., 9th ed. 2011, 10.

(8) Systems of systems – systems that are composed of a number of other software systems.

IEEE Computer Society in SWEBOK® Version 3.0 gives a detailed overview on generally accepted methods.[92] Different phases and views of software engineering are explained in detail.

[C] SWEBOK®3.0: Software Engineering Book of Knowledge

From the perspective of software development inventions can appear in different phases. This is similar to traditional product/process development methods. The Guide to the Software Engineering Body of Knowledge, SWEBOK® Version 3.0 (first published in 2004, Version 3.0 in 2014), describes fifteen Knowledge Areas (from requirements engineering over design and modelling to testing and maintenance). They describe in a hierarchical structure elements of software engineering with literature for each area. Standards are indicated in an Appendix. The Guide describes the portion of the body of knowledge that is generally accepted. One aim is 'to promote a consistent view of software engineering worldwide'. Information on SWEBOK is at the SWEBOK-Wiki webpage.[93]

The basic questions of what the computer should do and how to create software that enables the computer to do so can be seen as problem solving using programs. The complex process is expressed in a condensed form by SWEBOK® Version 3.0:

> To the discipline of software engineering, the ultimate objective of problem solving is to transform a problem expressed in natural language into electrons running around a circuit. In general, this transformation can be broken into three phases:
> (1) Development of algorithms from the problem statement.
> (2) Application of algorithms to the problem.
> (3) Transformation of algorithms to programs.

Software development according to principles of software engineering is usually described in software life cycle models. Separate models exist e.g. described in standard ISO/IEC/IEEE Std. 12207 'Software Life Cycle Processes'. According to SWEBOK®3.0 they reach from linear over iterative to agile models.

Different wordings exist for the software development life cycles. In some cases, the cycle is more or less detailed. Phases overlap in real life. Here a condensed version is described based on SWEBOK®3.0. Real software production for complex systems (e.g. airplane) is voluminous and has many aspects. Several specialists (managers, requirements engineers, software engineers, programmers ...) are more or less involved in different phases and very often at different geographical locations.

92. Bourque, P. & Fairley, R.E. (eds). *Guide to the Software Engineering Body of Knowledge, Version 3.0*, IEEE Computer Society, 2014; www.swebok.org. (accessed 21 April 2017).
93. Software Engineering Body of Knowledge – WIKI http://swebokwiki.org/Main_Page (accessed 21 April 2017).

Figure 2.8 The Basics of the Software Development Life Cycle (SDLC)

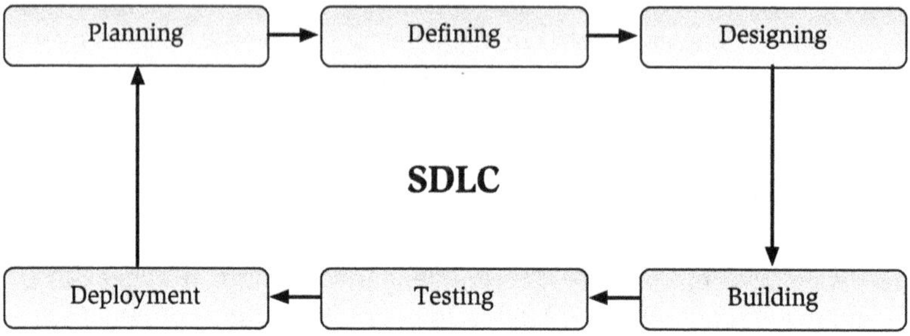

Figure 2.8 shows the very basic phases of software development. During **Planning and Defining** the requirements are determined, which enable the final software system to solve a customer/user defined real-world problem. A document – the software requirements specification (sometimes combined with a systems specification) – is created which is basis for repeated review. Prototypes, models and acceptance tests can be part of the requirements specification. In this phase, basic software architecture can already be created.

During the phase **Designing** the structure of the software is created. Specific design tools provide support. Usually a high-level design describes the organization of software into components and the lower level the behaviour of the components (e.g. design pattern). Irrespective of the specific domain, many fundamental design principles exist such as abstraction, coupling and cohesion, decomposition and modularization and others. Key issues are quality concerns such as performance, security, reliability, usability, etc. The structure of software or its architecture can be observed from different views. Well-known views are the logical view concerning functional requirements, the physical view on the distribution of components (on hardware, on different components of a network ...) and others. Software reuse, use of design patterns can play a role. The inclusion of the software in families of programs or frameworks might be important. User Interface Design is an important part of the software design process. Very often, it needs adaptation to different human languages, cultures and perceptions.

Software **Designing** is followed by **Building**. Both phases are highly interrelated. Similar terms for **Building** are software construction or implementation. Software construction fundamentals include according to SWEBOK® V3.0:

- minimizing complexity
- anticipating change
- constructing for verification
- reuse
- standards in construction.

Several development standards exist for construction. They can be directed to communication methods, programming languages, coding standards (e.g. name conventions), and platforms (e.g. interface standards for operating system calls). Coding activities can include considerations like:

- creating understandable source code (naming conventions, source code layout);
- use of classes, enumerated types, variables ...;
- use of control structures;
- handling of error conditions;
- prevention of code-level security breaches (like buffer overflows);
- resource usage via use of exclusion mechanisms and discipline in accessing serially reusable resources (including threads and database locks);
- source code organization (into statements, routines, classes ...);
- code documentation;
- code tuning.

Patents for inventions on this level of detail are contentious. Several countries (e.g. US, EPO, JPO) grant to a certain degree patents for inventions created in the phase of software construction. Handling of error conditions, resource usage via exclusion mechanisms is normally patentable. Other countries (e.g. India) might see such inventions probably as excluded subject matter. Naming conventions, use of classes, code documentation are probably not patentable.

Testing and maintenance (**Deployment**) are further important phases in order to guarantee the required functionality under changing conditions/environments over a longer time period.

Inventions can result from all phases of SDLC. The probability is high for the first four phases.

[D] Algorithmic Problem Solving: Three Simple Examples

In the following three very simple examples are indicated in order to illustrate software development. They are related to a payroll program, functionality of a petrol pump (an example for embedded systems) and software for an operation system. It should not be forgotten that real life software development is a lot more complex.

[1] Example 1: Company Payroll Program

The following example is based on a problem solving case study indicated by Dale, Weems and Headington.[94]

The problem posed consists in the creation of a company payroll program. The result has to be displayed at an electronic display. In the current case, the basic

94. Dale, N. et al. *Introduction to Java and Software Design* Jones and Bartlett Publishers 2003, 33–40.

sequence is nothing new. Calculation of wages was done for years by hand, by mainframe computers or partly with the aid of pocket calculators.

A basic process (calculating weekly wages for employees) exists already. It is assumed that an accountant gives it to a programmer. There is no need to develop a new method for calculating weekly wages by an accountant.

In the following, some basic activities to be done by the programmer will be indicated in a short form. For the view of the complete example, the book of Dale et al. has to be looked at. Since Java is an object-oriented programming language, the programmer has to determine objects. General objects exist already for some features. Objects are e.g.:

- Input file, datafile.dat, represented by one of the Java file classes
- Outputfile, payfile.dat, represented by another Java file class
- Display window, represented by a Java Frame class
- Window closing event, represented by a Java Event class
- Employee identification number
- Pay rate
- Hours worked
- Wages
- Total wages.

The general sequence for each person is:

(1) Get the data
(2) Compute the results
(3) Output the result.

Step 1 involves three smaller steps:

Read the employee number Read the pay rate. Read the number of hours worked.

According to Dale et al. a main algorithm has to be created. It includes a subalgorithm for calculation of the pay. It is stressed by Dale et al.: 'Notice that the algorithm is simply a very precise description of the same steps you would follow to do this process by hand.'

'Main Algorithm
Prepare to read a list of employee information (open file object datafile.dat)
Prepare to write a list of the employees' wages (open ...)
Set the payroll to zero
While there is more data on file dataFile

Read employee number
Read the pay rate
Read the hours worked
Calculate pay
Add the employee's wages to the payroll
Write the employee's number, ... onto the list (file payFile)
Prepare an empty window (a Frame class object)
Write the total into the window
Show the window on the screen
Respond to the window-closing event by removing the window and stopping the program'

The following block shows the subalgorithm for calculating pay taking into account possible overtime.

'**if** number of hours worked is greater than 40,0 then
wages = (40,0 x pay rate) + (hours worked - 40,0) × 1,5 x pay rate
else
wages = hours worked × pay rate'

The use of a computer requires a step that does not exist for a calculation done by hand.

This step is the display of the result on a window of a display. Hence, the programmer has to think about additional steps resulting from implementation on a computer.

The display of the total wages requires the following basic steps:

'Prepare an empty window
Write the total into the window
Show the window on the screen
Respond to the window-closing event by removing the window and stopping the program'

A test is usually done by hand before the implementation of the program. The final program (source code) in Java programming language is not indicated here but in Dale's book. For such a simple program it has already about 100 lines of code. For the sake of completeness, it has to be mentioned that the Java program is compiled into Bytecode - a standard machine language. The Bytecode is interpreted by the Java Virtual machine (JVM) in order to allow execution. JVM and the interpreter are seen as system software. The payroll program is a typical application program in the business field.

This very simple example was chosen to highlight several topics in the context of patent law:

- It illustrates the difference between algorithm and computer program. The final computer program as Java program or as machine code cannot be indicated in a patent claim.
- It shows that parts of the main algorithm existed already without a computer. This has some implications for patent law. A process claim without any computing feature would be regarded as mental act. A patent claim could be formulated like 'A computer-implemented method for the calculation of weekly wages with the steps …'. It just mentions that a computer can be used for the execution a well-known method. A search for payroll calculation in patent literature or in computing literature could not be sufficient because the algorithm existed already before its implementation as computer program. It was done by hand in the past. The basic algorithm without computer will probably not be found in patent documentation since patent documentation is primarily directed to technological literature.
- The main algorithm has two parts: the basic algorithm (which existed already without a computer) resulting from the application area (here: business) and steps necessary to enable the computer to read, store, process and indicate data when a specific programming language is used.
- The algorithm could be seen as 'business method as such' in countries/regions which exclude business methods as such. The skilled person is the accountant. The known algorithm is just implemented as computer program. The programmer without any inventive activity apparently did this implementation. Otherwise, the applicant would have added some inventive features that were necessary to allow execution of the payroll program. In has to be borne in mind that the current example is a very simple one.
- In Dale's example, the focus is on the development of the computer program. It is assumed that there is *generic computer hardware and software* that allow storing data, processing them and displaying them in a window of a screen. This is how amounts of software are developed. Details of the computer hardware and its functionality are not provided due to the assumed high modularity in computing. Such generic features are assumed to exist. They are only mentioned if a modification is required for the execution of the specific software. It is assumed that a computer program in Java can run on such a computer. When an invention results from modified software (algorithm or implementation) which runs on a normal computer it should not be necessary to indicate such generic features in the claim by the applicant. Accordingly, it should not be necessary for the Patent Office to provide prior art documents for the very basic computer features.

Modern systems become more and more complex and heterogeneous in terms of software and hardware. Many systems are software-intensive systems. They can be characterized by its functionality on a high level of abstraction (e.g. a web shop with customers) but also by the specific architecture of its software. The area in which a user uses the software is often called 'domain' or 'application domain'. A domain expert possesses domain knowledge that characterizes a specific domain. A domain can result from different sciences (physics, chemistry, biology, engineering, economics ...). Large software systems can be developed according to principles of domain-driven design. A full overview is outside the scope of this book.

In countries/regions with a requirement of technicality a claim with features of a business method in combination with features of the software implementation could be seen as 'mixed invention' (e.g. at the EPO). Eligibility to patent law might be seen in different ways in several countries. Different views might exist among patent examiners.

The challenge for the patent system is the determination of subject matter eligible for patent subject matter for such software-intensive systems. Which level of abstraction is really necessary?

[2] Example 2: Petrol Pump (Example for Embedded Systems)

It is said that 99% of all processors become part of an 'embedded system'.[95] It means that the processor is part of a larger physical system (not a computer).

Part of each processor is software that controls functionality of the system. Software development differs from software development for a Personal Computer. The system has very often to react within a certain time limit (real-time processing). The software for an airbag in a car has to decide within milliseconds if the airbag should open or not. Very often the system has restrictions in memory or energy availability. Many systems comprise real-time operating systems. Barr et al e.g. indicate application areas of embedded systems.[96] The list provides just some examples:

'Home Appliances	Dishwasher, washing machine, microwave, Top-set box, security system, ..., garden sprinkler system
Office Automation	Fax, copy machine, ..., scanner, printer
Security	Face recognition, finger recognition, eye recognition,...
Academia	Smart board, smart room, OCR, calculator
Instrumentation	Signal generator, signal processor, power supplier
Telecommunication	Router, hub, cellular phone,..., web camera
Automotive	Fuel injection controller, anti-locking brake system, airbag system,..., cruise control
Entertainment	MP3, video game, Mind Storm, smart toy
Aerospace	Navigation system, automatic landing system,..., space explorer, space robotics

95. Barr, M. et al. *Programming Embedded Systems: With C and GNU Development Tools* 'O'Reilly Media, Inc.' 2007.
96. Qian, K. et al. *Embedded Software Development with C* Springer Science & Business Media, 2009, 4.

Industrial Automation	Assembly line, data collection system, monitoring systems on pressure, voltage, current, temperature, hazard detecting system, industrial robot
Personal	PDA, iPhone, palmtop, data organizer
Medical equipment	CT scanner, MRI, Glucose monitor, blood pressure monitor, medical diagnostic device
Business automation	ATM, smart vendor machine, cash register
Misc.	Elevator, tread mill, smart card, security door.'

In embedded systems real-time behaviour is very often an important requirement for software systems. The software has to provide a correct result within the required response time of the specific system (e.g. car braking system).

The overview on embedded systems gives some impression on where computing is used. Some examples are already outdated (e.g. PDA). New examples exist. Specific devices will be connected to each other in future (e.g. Internet of Things). The normal user is very often not aware of the little computer/microprocessor in the device. In all these application areas functionality of the device/system or parts of it are described in a model that is basis for the respective algorithm and finally the software.

Figure 2.9 State Machine Model of a Petrol (Gas) Pump

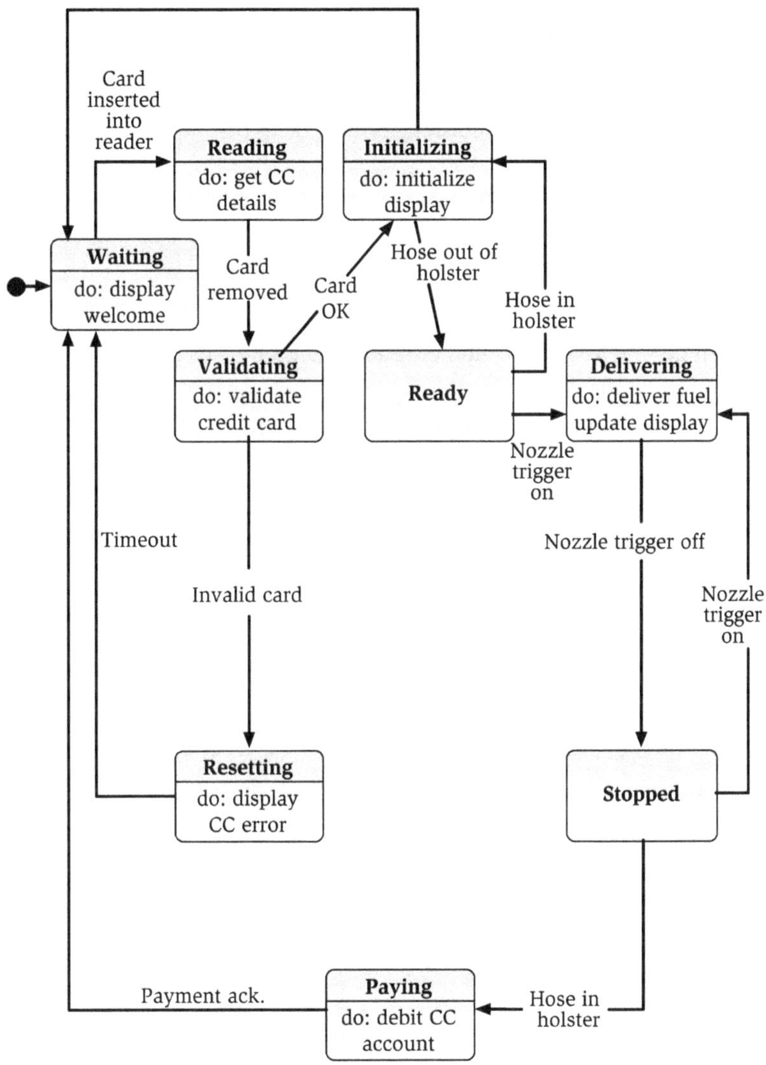

Figure 2.9 shows the state machine model of the gas pump.[97] A state machine is a fundamental means in computing to model a workflow in an event-driven manner. States, activities and transitions are the major elements. The state machine is an abstraction. For this reason, it has limitations for certain workflows. State machines are often used to model real-time systems since it is more visible how a system reacts to a certain input. A transition takes place from one state to another one.

97. Sommerville, I. *Software Engineering* Pearson, Internat. ed., 9th ed. 2011, Chapter 21, 545.

The state machine model does not show a computer. This is an implicit feature. Aspects of the algorithm are shown which have to be created for the implementation as computer program. The petrol pump is normally in a *Waiting* state. A customer has to insert the smartcard that will be read. A transition to state *Validating* occurs after removal of the card. If the card is valid transition to state *Initializing* follows. After initialization the customer can take the hose out of the holster and fuel will be provided. If the hose is back in the holster payment takes place according to the amount of fuel taken. Afterwards, the software will return to the initial state *Waiting*.

In the past patents might have been existed for petrol pumps. Probably they comprised a method claim directed to the different states of the pump during its use by a person. The payment was a separate manual action between human beings. The use of computing in combination with specific input means - here the card - allows the combination of former separated technical and manual processes. An invention could result from an inventive modification of the whole process or parts of it.

[3] Example 3: Real-Time Operating System (Embedded Systems)

Figure 2.10 shows elements of a real-time operating system and the interaction between the elements.[98] Operating systems represent the most essential part of system software.

98. Sommerville, I. *Software Engineering* Pearson, Internat. ed., 9th ed. 2011, Chapter 21, 559.

Figure 2.10 Components of a Real-Time Operating System

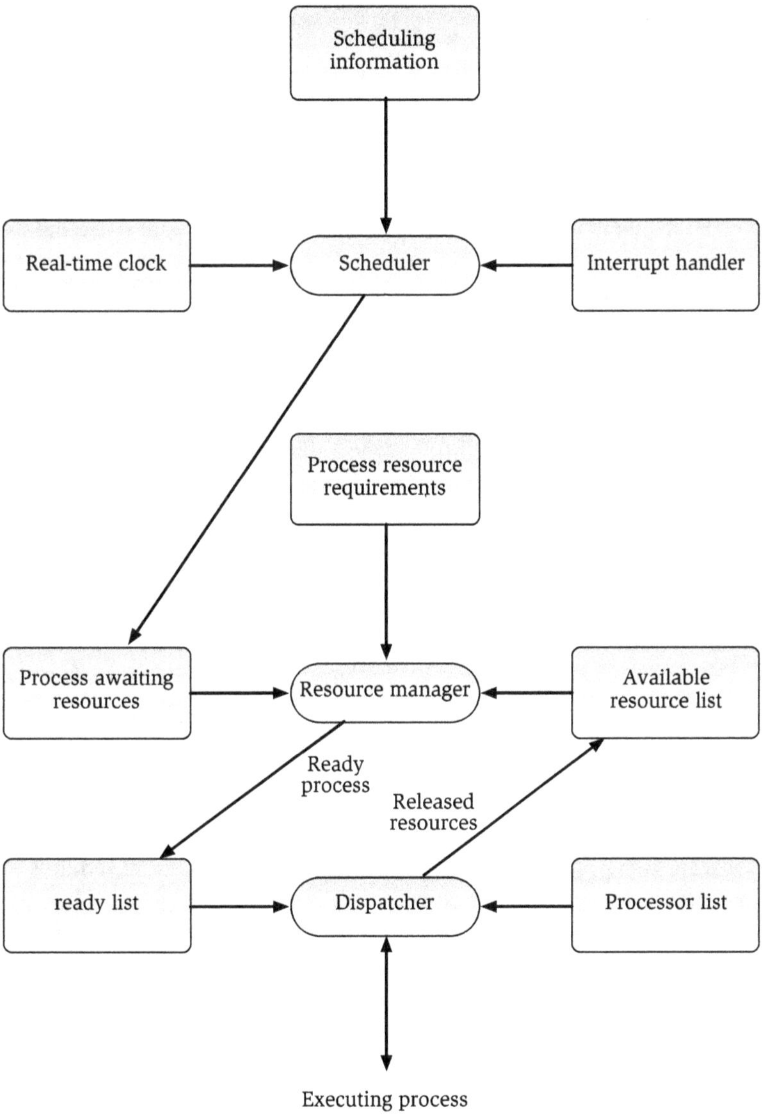

The operating system resulted from the separation of repetitive tasks in the computer itself (e.g. memory allocation) from the tasks to be done by the specific application programs. The application programmer was no longer responsible for tricky features of the computer itself. It could be seen as a major step into the direction of modularity. First operating systems were created in the 1960s for mainframes.[99]

In Figure 2.10 the scheduler decides which program or process among several ones is the next. Interrupt handling is based on priorities of interrupts. E.g. if a signal is received that battery is low some functionality (e.g. bright display on a smart phone) might be no longer allowed. High priority interrupts have to be processed very fast. For the execution of processes specific resources (e.g. amount of memory) are needed.

Patentability disputes exist in the area of operating systems. They are mainly caused by political views and by the interpretation of an invention in the field of technology. Some general proponents of patents for software want to exclude areas of system software. Technicality is not seen e.g. by the functionality of a resource manager in an operating system since no technical process outside of a computer is controlled.

Some open source groups are of the opinion that in particular features of an operating system should not be patented. The LINUX operating system created in a team of programmers and based on ideas of Linus Torvalds was and is a success story.[100] Richard Stallman, creator of the Free Software Foundation in 1985 and fore fighter for open source, has to be mentioned as well.[101] In the view of open source proponents, operating systems as well as e.g. browser represent crucial modules of software that should be protected only under different forms (licences) of copyright.

Meanwhile, there is coexistence between open source and patents. Both are sometimes combined in open source projects. Companies license patents to the members of the project. They will not attack each other by patents in project related topics.[102] One example is Open stack – 'OpenStack is a cloud operating system that controls large pools of compute, storage, and networking resources throughout a datacentre …'.[103] Open Invention Network (OIN) is an example in the area of the LINUX operating system.[104] It 'is a defensive patent pool and community of patent non-aggression which enables freedom of action in Linux'.

General proponents of the patent system argue sometimes that in the area of system software there is hardly ever a 'technical effect' if the law requires such an effect. No physical transformation in the classical sense takes place. A 'physical entity' does not play a role. This is a narrow interpretation. It is caught up in traditional thinking when the term 'technology' is heavily related to 'physical machine'.[105]

Other views start from the fact that a computer/microprocessor is a technical device. Schneider et al. pointed out that:

99. Schneider, G.M. et al. *Invitation to Computer Science* Cengage Learning 6th ed., 2013, 315.
100. Moody, G. *Rebel Code: Linux and the Open Source Revolution* Perseus Publishing, 2001.
101. Moody, G. *Rebel Code: Linux and the Open Source Revolution* Perseus Publishing, 2001, 14–30.
102. Anthes, G. *Open Source Software No Longer Optional*, Comm. of the ACM, Vol. 59, No. 8, August 2016, 15–17.
103. Openstack *Welcome to Open stack* http://docs.openstack.org/ (accessed 21 April 2017).
104. openinventionnetwork® http://www.openinventionnetwork.com/ (accessed 21 April 2017).
105. Willoughby, K.W. *What Can Be patented?* 2014, 165.

system software has the following responsibilities, analogous to those of the automobile dashboard:

- Hides the complex and unimportant (to the user) details of the internal structure of the Von Neumann architecture
- Presents important information to the user in a way that is easy to understand
- ...[106]

For people without a background in computing this internal work might be seen as something mystical and perhaps unconsciously as non-technical. The computer professional is aware of the high importance of system software for the functioning of many computing systems.

As indicated by H.-J. Petsche, fundamental philosophical views of German philosophers on technology are not easy to apply to CS.[107] While the physical processes (flow of electrons in transistors) on the hardware layer during the run of a computer program can be explained, different views on 'technicality' exist if higher levels of abstraction are considered. Not all aspects of the controversial topic of 'technology' in the context of patent law and computing can be dealt with in this book.

To sum up, the three examples indicate that 'software patents' do not only exist in the field of core computing (**real-time operating system**). The example of the **petrol pump** shows that computing means become an essential part of many devices. Such devices are connected over communication links to remote computing systems. The example **payroll calculation** shows that former manual (or mental) processes are transformed into computer programs. A programmer without detailed knowledge of the computer hardware can create such a program.

Simplified, an invention could result from the inventive modification of a known algorithm, the inventive implementation of a known algorithm or from both: algorithm, implementation.

The text in a patent claim is usually more similar to what is called 'algorithm' in CS. In other words, the algorithm for application software can stem from an enormous amount of fields (economy, organizational processes, vehicles, transportation, medical, consumer systems ...). The field (or sometimes domain) of an algorithm may play a role in eligibility to patent law.

Patent claims describing processes similar to algorithms in system software are seen controversial with respect to eligibility to patent law for several reasons. Algorithms can exist without a computer. This can be a problem in the search for prior art. The text of a patent claim similar to an algorithm can be combined with hardware features of the computer or with features of the system (petrol pump) in which the computer is arranged. Furthermore, the text similar to an algorithm can be combined with features necessary to implement the algorithm as computer program.

106. Schneider, G.M. et al. *Invitation to Computer Science* Cengage Learning 6th ed. 2013, 278.
107. Petsche, H.-J. *Technikbegriff und formale Prozessontologie* in Kornwachs, K. *Technik-System-Verantwortung* Lit 2004.

[E] Patent Law and Software Development Life Cycle

Protection of computer programs under patent law results mainly from landmark cases that try to develop general interpretation rules. Despite attempts to generalize interpretation of specific cases there is the risk to disregard general principles of computing. One example is the discussion in the area of business methods and computer-implemented business methods.

Some patent offices created specific Guidelines on the protection of software including some explanations of fundamental computing terms. This helps patent professionals to base argumentations on the right fundamentals, to harmonize legal practise between different areas (e.g. medical, vehicles ...) and to avoid unsubstantiated discussions only based on end-user knowledge. Confusion in the interpretation of terms can be observed regularly with respect to the term 'computer program'. The introduction of the claim form 'computer program [product]' leads to such misconceptions that the content of the claim is a computer program in the sense of computing. A distinction between legal language and language of computing is not made. Furthermore, the difference between the algorithm underlying a program and the different forms of a computer program (code: source code, object code) is not made. Therefore, it is not seen that an invention can result from different phases of software development with the involvement of plenty of specialists (requirements engineer, software engineer, software architect ...).

A major difficulty of the patent law results from the possibilities to create software that incorporates algorithms resulting from traditional non-technical areas. The OECD science and technology classification of 2007 (Frascati manual) is one example for classification of sciences.[108] It comprises:

- Natural sciences (Mathematics, Computer and information sciences, Physics, Chemistry, Biology, ...
- Engineering and Technology (Civil engineering, Electrical engineering, electronic engineering, mechanical engineering, information engineering,
- Medical and Health Sciences
- Agricultural Sciences
- Social Sciences (Psychology, Economics and business, Educational sciences, Law, Media and communications, ...
- Humanities (History and archaeology, languages and literature, Art, philosophy, ...)

It can be seen that 'technology' is nothing static. Furthermore, the patent system that was created at a time of growth of natural sciences and engineering is not really compatible to the interdisciplinary character of computing. The classification of a software system in a specific area can be challenging under the International Patent

108. OECD *Revised Field of Science and Technology (FOS) Classification in the Frascati Manual* 2007 http://www.oecd.org/sti/inno/38235147.pdf (accessed 21 April 2017) regular revisions take place; Annex II comprises a table with the view of 2002 and the revised version.

Classification (IPC) that is structured according to traditional technologies. Additionally, the patent documentation is directed to traditional sciences (physics, chemistry, engineering ...).

It is assumed that eligibility for patent protection depends on the field of an algorithm. If it does not result from traditionally patentable areas it might be seen as outside of the patent system.

No structured documentation exists at patent offices for long existing business methods or other areas of social sciences and humanities. The examiner usually will not find the respective documents in the traditional patent literature during the given amount of time. Modern computer systems allow the creation of systems the functionality of which is based on principles of human interaction. Such interaction is not as predictable as functionality under the principles of natural science. The whole area of e-commerce and social networks are an important example. Several authors illustrate the difficulties of the patent system with Biotechnology and Software in the book 'Biotechnology and Software Patent Law: A comparative Review of New Developments'.[109]

K.W. Willoughby shows the trouble in the understanding of technology in the context of patent law in his book 'What can be patented?'.[110] It is primarily directed to the legal practise of the USPTO and the EPO. The sometimes observable limitation of 'technicity' to 'physicality' is discussed.

Another difficulty of the patent system results from the characteristic of software to be part of a system/apparatus but also to be a completely separate commercial product.

In the formulation of an apparatus claim the hardware elements of the respective device/system is usually indicated and the added functional features implemented as computer program are in this combination accepted.

The formulation of a patent claim only with functional features of the software is more difficult. This is in particular true if the software relates to system software that does not show a possible control of data outside of the computer. The current practise of several patent offices requires at least the indication of generic hardware elements in the patent claim. For many computer professionals the 'computer readable data carrier' is an implicit feature of every computer program based on the knowledge that most computer systems are highly modular in terms of hardware and software.

The discussions on 'software patents' are mainly related to *computer programs*. The patent protection for different kind of *digital data* (on a data carrier) as a separate commercial product is connected to that question. Such data are digital data for media (music, sound, video ...) but also test data, text.... They are not dealt with here.

To summarize, in most patent systems patentability of software-related inventions is no problem if the algorithm underlying the software and described in a similar form in the claim is directed to features of an algorithm that results from a traditional technological area. That is, if the embedded computer directly controls the brake of a

109. Arezzo, E. & Ghidini, G. (eds). *Biotechnology and Software Patent Law: A Comparative Review of New Developments*. Edward Elgar Publishing, 2011.
110. Willoughby, K.W. *What Can Be Patented?* Scholars' Press, 2014.

car, the speed of the computer-controlled lawn mower, the amount of insulin for a patient based on real-time data or a chemical production process e.g. in chemical reactors. The probability to get a patent can decrease under some jurisprudence if the invention results from a specific software implementation of such a (well-known or new) algorithm. The appropriate level of abstraction for avoiding overbroad claim wording but for achieving a reliable scope of protection is difficult to determine. What is indicated in a patent claim is very often more similar to an algorithm in computing then to the real computer program in a programming language. This results from the similarity of algorithm to process, method, sequence of steps, etc. Nevertheless, the term algorithm has to be used cautiously because it includes several requirements in the narrow sense of computing.

§2.08 WHAT MIGHT BE A SOFTWARE PATENT?

One source of misconception results from the interpretation of the term 'software patent'. It is a colloquial term but it can be misleading.

First, as indicated in Chapter 2, §2.06 [D] the term 'software' includes not only computer programs but also user manuals, documentation, test data, non-executable software (music, sound ...), etc.[111]

Second, it is generally accepted that the complete code in a programming language (here identical to computer program) cannot be subject of a patent claim. If a patent law of a country excludes patentability of computer programs (or computer programs as such) it means usually that the computer program in a programming language is forbidden in the patent claim.

In order to cope with terminology patent offices of some countries introduced specific guidelines for software-related patents (e.g. Japan, India, Austria). The term '**Computer-Implemented Invention**' (CII) became popular in Europe. After some modifications it finally means that at least one feature of a claim *is implemented* as computer program.

Here is the explanation of CII at the EPO:

> Inventions involving programs for computers can be protected in different forms of a 'computer-implemented invention', an expression intended to cover claims which involve computers, computer networks or other programmable apparatus whereby prima facie one or more of the features of the claimed invention are realised by means of a program or programs.[112]

It has to be considered that different publications use different interpretations of terms. For example, a study on 'The economic impacts of computer-implemented inventions of the European Patent Office' explains to be conservative. The term CII

---

111. ISO/IEC *SEVOCAB Software and Systems Engineering Vocabulary* www.computer.org/sevocab (accessed 21 April 2017) content of standard ISO/IEC/IEEE 24765:2010 Systems and Software Engineering - Vocabulary.

112. EPO *Guidelines for examination in the EPO*, November 2016, Part G, Chapter II-5, 3.6 Computer programs. http://documents.epo.org/projects/babylon/eponet.nsf/0/0791474853510FFFC125805A004C9571/$File/guidelines_for_examination_part_g_en.pdf (accessed 21 April 2017).

seems to be based on an older interpretation taking into account only new features implemented as computer program. Furthermore, applications/patents are seen as 'software as such' in large areas of core computing (including features of operating systems, fault-tolerance, databases, etc.) in G06F and H04L.[113] Nevertheless, the increased importance of software in industry is emphasized.

Here again the wording is important. The term 'can be implemented as computer program' does not mean 'is identical to a computer program' for a computer professional.

[A] 'Software Patent' and Patent Classification

Different statistics exist depending on what is meant by a 'software patent'. A short look at the history of the IPC is necessary. A real classification for software was never developed within the framework of IPC. This might have been caused by the basic possibility to implement an algorithm in hardware and/or in software.

In the past, the majority of subject matter that belonged obviously to core areas of computing (hardware and software) was part of Section G (Physics). Due to the unclear legal situation for the protection of software by patents in the early years of computing, it is difficult to find out how many software patents were disguised as hardware solutions.

The German computer pioneer Friedrich L. Bauer reported that the German patent application for the stack (DE AS 1 094 019 – filed 30 March 1957) allowed:

> quite functional descriptions of methods, the German application stayed free of drawings for electrical circuits; it was possible to design from it immediately a program with programmed cellar structures, later called stacks' but 'the U.S.-American application contained an abundance of *and* and *or* gates.[114]

The later US patent US 3,047,228 filed on 28 March 1958 was modified in order to avoid the impression of a patent for software.[115]

Applications/patents with digital computing were classified in Class G06F. At the beginning of the 1990s, Class G06F (IPC5) included nearly all inventions relating to fundamentals of computing as well as to 'Design or construction of the computing part, adapted to a specific application' (G06F15/20 and subclasses). In other words, patent applications relating to all kind of *application software* were also mainly classified in G06F. Computing in numerical controlled machines was already classified in G05B.

113. 4ip council *The economic impact of computer-implemented inventions in Europe Overview and highlights* Study on computer-implemented inventions 2015 http://www.4ipcouncil.com/news-events/news/4ip-releases-highlights-new-study-computer-implemented-inventions/executive-summary (accessed 21 April).
114. Bauer F.L. *From the Stack Principle to ALGOL* in *Software Pioneers – Contributions to Software Engineering*, Broy, M. & Denert, E. (eds), Springer, 2002.
115. Bauer F.L. *From the Stack Principle to ALGOL* in *Software Pioneers – Contributions to Software Engineering*, Broy, M. & Denert, E. (eds), Springer, 2002; Friedrich Ludwig Bauer and Klaus Samelson Patent: Automatic Computing Machines and Method of Operation, US 3,047,228 filed March 28, 1958 and granted on July 31, 1962.

The extension of the application related fields and the creation of indexing schemes in IPC6 (1990–1995) indicated the higher interest in patents for inventions related to the use of computer for different functions and/or applications (cf. following list).[116]

G06F 151/00 For invoicing **[6]**
G06F 153/00 For inventory purposes; For order filling **[6]**
G06F 153/02 For seat reservation **[6]**
G06F 155/00 For betting on the outcome of an event, e.g. a race, an election; ... **[6]**
G06F 157/00 For bank or analogous accounting; For calculating earned income **[6]**
G06F 159/00 For medical or biological purposes **[6]**
G06F 161/00 For game playing **[6]**
G06F 163/00 For traffic control **[6]**
G06F 165/00 For guiding a vehicle, missile or the like along a course, ...**[6]**
G06F 167/00 For nuclear physics or engineering, e.g. radiation-hardened **[6]**
G06F 169/00 For meteorology **[6]**
G06F 171/00 For gun laying; For bomb aiming **[6]**

Some exceptions existed. Applications in the area of numerical programme-control (NC machines, numerical control machines) were traditionally classified under G05B 19/00 in IPC4 (1985–1989).

Progress in computing and other technologies (networks, displays ...) lead to proliferation of computing to even more fields of science and technology.

At the end of the 1990s, new classification classes were created like Class G06T for computer graphics and digital image processing, just as one example among others. Furthermore, if a patent application was mainly directed to a process/method of a specific application area and not to the details of its computational implementation such a patent application was usually classified in the specific application area outside of G06F (e.g. A61 for medical science, A63 for games).

A few application related areas like business methods remained in G06F since they did not really exist outside G06F. The major business method related areas of G06F17/60 became G06Q with IPC 2006.1. Due to extension of digitization convergence of formerly separated areas of computing, telecommunication, etc. is in progress. As a result, patent applications relating to distributed systems (in the sense of computing) can be found in G06F and in parts of H04L or related areas.

A generally accepted classification of software in **system software** and **application software** exists outside of the patent system in computing publications and in

116. WIPO, International Patent Classification Version 6 http://web2.wipo.int/classifications/ipc/legacyipcpub6#&version=19950101&symbol=G06F0015000000&viewmode=h&notion=scheme&refresh=page (accessed 7 May 2017).

standards. Based on that distinction one can see that major parts of system software-related patents can be found mainly in G06F and parts of H04L. Application related patents (Computational X, embedded systems) can be spread all over the classification.

A huge amount of 'software patents' exists outside of G06F based on the view of computer professionals. If software is used to automate processes in vehicles, medical systems, agriculture, industrial process control, etc., the respective fields of the classification have to be considered.

In a US-GAO study on patent quality in the US, the following is indicated: 'Software-related patents occur in a variety of technologies containing at least some element of software, and cover things like sending messages or conducting business over the Internet (e.g., e-commerce). According to USPTO officials, USPTO does not have a definition of or collect information on "software-related patents."'[117]

[B] Software Patent: View on Claims and/or Description

In the following, 'software patents' are differentiated based on common claim formulations and the description. The distinction is made according to direct or indirect indication of features implemented by means of a computer program in a claim. Furthermore, a difference is made according to whether those features are in the independent claim(s), in the dependent claims(s) or only in the description:

(1) The *independent claim(s)* and the whole application indicate directly and unambiguously features of core computing with software implementation. Examples are Method and system for providing load balancing for virtualized application workspaces - US9317333 (B2) — 2016-04-19' or 'Method and system for associating resource pools with operating system partitions - EP1480124 (B1) — 2014-04-02'.

(2) The *independent claim(s)* and the whole application indicate directly and unambiguously features of computing with software implementation (e.g. computer-implemented method) in combination with features of a device that includes the computer or with method steps executed outside of the computer. Examples are: 'Apparatus, computer program and method for controlling an agricultural implement - EP2338322 (B1) — 2013-05-29' or 'Heat treatment apparatus, heat treatment method, medium on which heat treatment program is recorded, and steel product - US6891139 (B2) — 2005-05-10'.

(3) There is a *claim* that is worded 'A computer program (product) ...' or with a similar formulation ('A non-transitory computer-readable recording medium ...'). Example: 'File cloning and de-cloning in a data storage system - EP2787439 (B1) — 2016-04-27' or 'Control apparatus and control method for master slave robot, robot, control program for master slave robot, and

117. United States Government Accountability Office *Patent Office Should Define Quality, Reassess Incentives, and Improve Clarity, June 2016* http://www.gao.gov/assets/680/678247.pdf (accessed 21 April 2017).

integrated electronic circuit for control of master slave robot - US9415516 (B2) — 2016-08-16'.

(4) The independent claim(s) indicate a process claim or a system claim with functional features (process steps). *Dependent claims* indicate that a computer, microprocessor, digital programmable unit or a similar unit is used in the embodiments. Example: 'Cuffless blood pressure monitoring appliance - US7539532 (B2) — 2009-05-26' or 'Model airplane - EP1688167 (B1) — 2010-07-07'.

(5) The claims indicate a process claim or a system claim with functional features (process steps). A computer/microprocessor is not indicated in the claims. They indicate a general term like control unit, processing unit, steering unit. The *description* discloses the use of a microprocessor/computer or equivalent device. Example: 'Insulin Pump Based Expert System - US8657779 (B2) — 2014-02-25' or 'Laser scanning apparatus and laser scanning microscope - EP2045640 (B1) — 2011-01-12'.

In summary, it can be concluded that 'software patents' can be found in different fields of technology. They might be directly visible from the formulation of independent or dependent claims or more hidden because a computer, a (micro)-processor or a similar digital programmable device is only indicated in the description. Many applications do not explicitly indicate a computer but e.g. a 'control unit'. The reader will assume that there is a computational device or a computer network a prerequisite for the execution of a claimed method that is implemented as computer program.

§2.09 SUMMARY

Computing is a major driving force for inventions and innovations in plenty fields of society. While the patent system tries to keep pace with that development by allowing a more or less growing range of patentable subject matter it struggles with explaining the boundaries between patentable and non-patentable subject matter and the respective claim construction. One reason seems to be the insufficient knowledge of fundamentals and specifics of CS compared to traditional fields. Chapter 2 tried to give a very basic introduction to the binary system, the classical stored program computer and the different kinds of computers. The basic terms software, computer program, algorithm and data structure were explained. A deeper look into the development of software with different levels of abstraction was provided. The knowledge on the intellectual traditions of computing (logico-mathematical, engineering, science) can avoid one-sided views in the patent system. The extreme degree of modularity (with different levels of abstraction) in computing and in particular in software has to be respected. Legal guidance can be increased by including basic terms of computing in guidelines, examination manuals.

The possibility to implement methods/procedures formerly outside of patentability by means of computer programs could require the extension of prior art documentation and patent classification to non-technical areas. This could also influence education requirements of patent professionals. Modern search tools will probably increase search possibilities in non-patent literature.

An interpretation of the term 'software patent' was briefly given. One was based on a short view at the development of the classification – IPC. The other was based on computer related formulations in the claims and in the description of a patent application.

Increased efforts have to be made in order to keep the patent system attractive for the growing digitization. The future will show if the patent system will adapt to the new technologies or if a 'sui generis' law (discussed already years ago) will be a more appropriate means for the legal protection of software.

CHAPTER 3

Patenting Software: Obstacles and Challenges

Software is special as it differs in various aspects from other 'conventional' fields of technology. Software is an intangible asset. It does not need a specific apparatus, but can be executed on a plurality of physical structures in a distributed manner. It even may be virtualized. It is digital and may be provided via download and copied easily.

What makes software so special for patent law systems all over the world?

First, data processing operations may be implemented in software and/or in hardware (e.g. in a digital circuit, like a Field Programmable Gate Array (FPGA)).[1] According to a major theorem in computer science relating to computability[2] and thus from a technical viewpoint, both of these solutions (software and hardware) are exchangeable and show advantages and disadvantages (relating to costs, runtime, reliability and frequency of use). Thus, hardware and software are logically equivalent.[3] However, from a patent law view point, hardware intuitively will be judged to be technical, whereas for software concerns arise.

In former times roughly 90% of computer based development was done by means of hardware and 10% was implemented in software. Nowadays, the situation has completely changed: 90% is implemented in software and only 10% in hardware.

Therefore, it would be wrong to stipulate software-related inventions in general as being non-technical. But where to draw the line between patentable and not patentable is a major legal challenge.

Secondly, software has a dual character as it may be applied to technical problems (e.g. mechatronic applications) and to non-technical problems (e.g. pure business methods without any technical features).

1. *See* for example: EPO GL, G, 3.6.
2. The Church-Turing Thesis.
3. *See* for example: B. Randell, *Hardware/Software Tradeoffs: A General Design Principle?*, 13(2) ACM SIGARCH Computer Architecture News 19–21 (June 1985).

Some patent laws define the requirement of technicality (as for example in Europe and China). In the USA the distinction between patent eligible and non-eligible is based on the question whether the invention is based on an abstract idea.

In sum, it can be concluded that the more references a computer-implemented or software application shows to conventional fields of technology (e.g. electrical engineering, mechanical engineering, physics) the higher the chance that it will be judged to be patent eligible.

In contrast to other technical developments, where a high rate of technical know-how is necessary to copy the invention, software solutions may be copied easily, which strengthens the need for protection of intellectual property.

Keeping all these aspects in mind, the question is, how to draft claims and descriptions for this kind of intangible asset?

From a practical point of view, if it is necessary to decide on seeking national or international patent protection for a Computer-Implemented Invention (CII), it would be helpful to briefly analyse the challenges for that specific invention in that specific state in order to save money where obstacles are too high.

In the following chapters the major hurdles and challenges are summarized, which should be kept in mind when drafting computer-implemented applications irrespective of the specific jurisdiction or national patent law requirements.

§3.01 FIRST CHALLENGE: IS SOFTWARE PATENT ELIGIBLE? A HEATED DEBATE

The question of the patentability of 'new' technologies, like computer science and software, is a hot topic in patent law systems all over the world. There have been debates relating to patentability of biotechnology (which nowadays are mainly resolved and biotech applications are patent protectable) and now there are discussions worldwide on how to distinguish between patentable software subject matter and software excluded form patent protection.

A fresh wave of discussions has been encouraged after the decision of the US Supreme Court in the case of *Alice Corporation v. CLS Bank International*, which was published in June, 2014.[4] Considering the significant role played by the software industry in contributing to the growth of the economy worldwide, it is necessary to ensure that the patent systems can adapt to and assimilate new, innovative technologies for the growth and development of software industry. On the one hand, patent protection should be available for software-related subject matter as it is for other technologies. On the other hand, patent protection must not be overly broad, to hinder innovation (key phrase: no monopoly on general ideas).

Based on this dichotomy the question arises as to where to draw the delimitation line.

Some national or regional patent laws, like the European Patent Convention and the German Patent Law, have the requirement of 'technicality' or technical character.[5]

4. Available at: https://www.supremecourt.gov/opinions/13pdf/13-298_7lh8.pdf (accessed 18 March 2017).
5. Often also referred to as 'technicity'.

This means that an invention needs to have technical character in order to be patentable. However, this general rule only gives pure guidance as software has a dual character and may be used for non-technical and for technical systems.

In the USA, there is no such technicality requirement. However, abstract ideas are not patentable.[6] While abstract ideas, natural phenomena, and laws of nature are not eligible for patenting in the USA, methods and products employing abstract ideas, natural phenomena, and laws of nature to perform a real-world function may well be. Thus, much discussion still exists as to how to differentiate between an abstract idea, an idea and a technical application of an abstract idea (e.g. in a computer program). In major philosophical schools every 'idea' is judged to be 'abstract' by definition.[7]

In this field in particular, and due to the widespread discussions not only among legal experts, some people mistakenly believe that 'software' patents have little chance of surviving a validity challenge. However, a brief look in the statistical data (here: from the USPTO[8]) reveals another impression. More and more patents are granted for software and are maintained in inter partes review proceedings (which became available in 2013 under the America Invents Act (AIA)).

Figure 3.1 US Patents Granted for Selected Software-Related Technology Classes

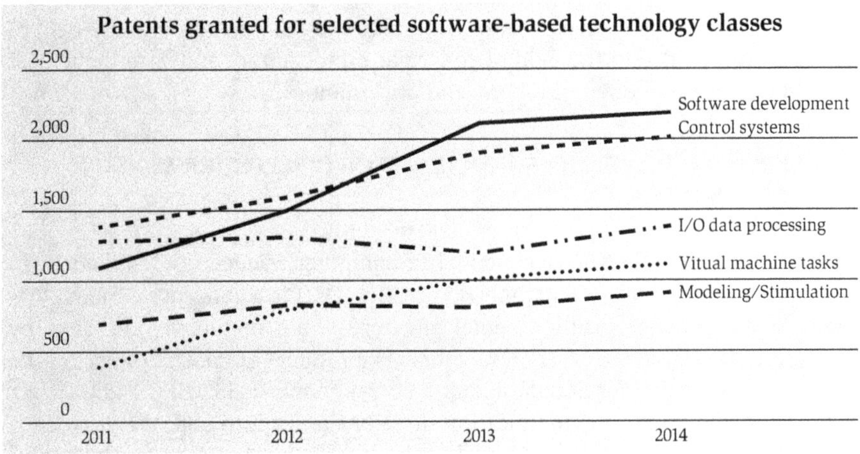

Source: U.S. Patent and Trademark Office, Patent Technology Monitoring Team (2015). Patenting in Technology Classes, Breakout by Geographic Origin (State and Country). Retrieved from http://www.uspto.gov/web/offices/ac/ido/oiep/taf/tecstc/classes_clstc-gd.htm.

---

6. *Diamond v. Diehr*, 450 U.S. 175, 185, 209 USP'Q 1, 7 (1981); accord, e.g. *Chakrabarty*, 447 U.S. at 309, 206 USPQ at 197; *Parker v. Flook*, 437 U.S. 584, 589, 198 USPQ 193, 197 (1978); *Benson*, 409 U.S. at 67–68, 175 USPQ at 675.
7. *See* for example: https://plato.stanford.edu/entries/abstract-objects/. Transferring the suggested definition from objects to ideas, the definition would read: 'An idea is abstract (if and) only if it fails to occupy anything like a determinate region of space (or space-time).'
8. Elliot C. Cook, Brandon S. Bludau & Darren M. Jiron, *U.S. Software Patents: Obtainable, Enforceable, and as Important as Ever*, Managing Intellectual Property (June 2015).

Today's innovations and even our society itself strongly rely on Information and Communication Technology (ICT). ICT permeates many technical areas and our everyday life as well. Without software, a computer cannot operate. So, it is no wonder that intellectual property protection of software is crucial not only for the software industry, but also for other industries and businesses. However, some aspects of the patent system (independent of very specific national law) are not suitable for software-related matter.

In particular, two major views among the stakeholders exist: first, software-related inventions should be protected (only) via copyright protection; and secondly, software-related inventions should be protected by means of patent protection in order to provide protection for the content and for the functionality of the software, independent of its implementation (e.g. in a specific language).

There exist several primary arguments in favour of both viewpoints. Thus, the intellectual property protection of computer software has been and still is highly debated at different national and international levels (e.g. around the turn of the millennium a draft Directive on the Patentability of CIIs was discussed in the European Union (EU) in order to harmonize the interpretation of the national patentability requirements for computer software-related inventions).

Software technology challenges intellectual property law, in particular patent law and copyright law. In this respect, it is worth mentioning that not only in the field of patent protection but also in the field of copyright protection for software there exist major legal problems and open questions and uncertainties.

§3.02 SECOND CHALLENGE: SUFFICIENCY OF DISCLOSURE VERSUS LAYER MODEL

In Chapter 2 the abstraction or layer model in computer science was explained. In particular, the Open Systems Interconnection model (OSI) is a conceptual model that characterizes and standardizes the internal functions of a communication system by partitioning it into abstraction layers. The model is a product of the OSI project at the International Organization for Standardization (ISO), known as ISO/IEC 7498-1.

The OSI model groups communication functions into seven logical layers. Each layer serves the layer above it and is served by the layer below it. For example, a layer that provides error-free communications across a network provides the path needed by applications above it, while it calls the layer below to send and receive packets that make up the contents of that path. Two instances in one layer are connected by a horizontal connection on that layer.

Inventions in computer science may often be described by different layers of abstraction. Patent law, however, urges the applicant to specify as much as possible lower (nearer the hardware) layers in order to show technical character or technicality of the invention.

In Europe and Germany, as well as China, more and more decisions are issued which deal with a lack of disclosure and refuse the patent application or revoke the patent due a breach of Articles 83 and/or 84 EPC or Section 34 (4) German Patentgesetz or with Article 26.3 and 26.4 Chinese Patent Act.[9]

How can this challenge be addressed? This is indeed a big issue, since often even inventors do not know the specifics of the lower layers, because they only apply them in their software product. They usually know about the interfaces but not the technical details of the lower layer modules they use.

Thus, it is advisable to include technical explanations for all or selected claim features in different layers of abstraction in the description. This may serve as a fallback position in the examination proceedings. Usually, this kind of information is not actively provided by the inventor. The drafter is therefore well advised to generate appropriate questions.

§3.03 THIRD CHALLENGE: CLARITY AND CONCISENESS OF THE CLAIMS VERSUS VIRTUAL AND 'RESULT TO BE ACHIEVED' FEATURES

According to a number of expert discussions we have had with many patent professionals in companies and in law firms, drafting many CIIs, our impression is that especially in this field inventors tend to describe their invention using a 'result to be achieved' language.[10] For example, there are often indications in the invention disclosure such as that the provided solution is 'generic', 'efficient', 'easily implementable' or 'platform independent'.

To incorporate those aspects directly and 'as they are' as features in the application and even in the claims opens the door for discussion with the examiner. Therefore, this is not a good idea. These aspects or advantages should be transferred into concrete technical features, which serve to provide a solution to a technical problem. The drafter is well advised to confront the inventor with respective questions in order to get the necessary information.

Moreover, CIIs are often conceptual inventions, which are described on an abstract level in abstract language (e.g. 'providing an encryption/decryption scheme for data transfer' without specifying what kind of concrete encryption algorithm is to be used). Here again, it is the drafter's responsibility to elaborate and prepare relevant questions in order to specify at least one possible concrete technical implementation.

Failure to do so, may at best lead to another office action–reply round. From a technical perspective, this is due to the fact that in computer science, a software routine may most easily be defined by its result (e.g. 'function for providing data compression'). The software developer uses the 'compression toolbox' and in fact may not provide more detailed information about how this toolbox is implemented. In patent

9. *See* 17 W (pat) 52/08 of the German Federal Patent Court, dated 12 January 2012.
10. *See EPO Examination Guidelines* F, IV, 4.10: 'As a general rule, claims which attempt to define the invention by a result to be achieved should not be allowed, in particular if they only amount to claiming the underlying technical problem.'

law, however, the examiner analyses, whether the invention is sufficiently disclosed.[11] If the applicant only mentions the compression module without giving further explanation as to how this module works, the examiner may even refuse the application (of course depending on the requirements of the national patent law).

Another aspect concerns the language used in computer science. Generally, metaphoric language is used (e.g. computer mouse, encryption/decryption keys, browser) which is often not uniquely defined. Therefore, once more, it is necessary to define the terms used within the application, if possible in a top-down manner. This aspect also makes software applications different from applications in other fields of technology. In mechanical engineering, for example, it is not required to explain the structure and function of a 'nail' as 'attachment means'.

Another aspect relates to the functional features.

Typically, software-related inventions encompass several steps, such as receiving data, processing data and providing result data on an interface. Intuitively, a drafter will use functional claim language for these features.

As stated above, software may be applied in different technological areas and in different embodiments. It is neither sufficient to repeat the same functional features of the claims for support in the description, nor is it sufficient to use boilerplate language without specific reference to the actual application.

It is worth the drafter working out and presenting in detail a definition for each functional feature - if possible - on different layers of abstraction.

For example, for the claim feature 'receiving data', a definition may be given:

> receiving data refers to detection of measurement data. The data may refer to measurement data, which are automatically detected by means of sensors, such as ... The receiving may be executed by at least one input interface to the sensors. In another embodiment, the input interface may be a human machine interface. In another embodiment, it is possible that the data are read in from a storage/database. The input interface may be a modem or a network card

As can be seen in the example above, it is helpful to add in the description a passage with at least one relation between each functional feature and a device structure (apparatus feature) which is configured to perform the function.

In this respect, it should be kept in mind that from an international perspective it is not sufficient to describe a specific embodiment and add boilerplate definitions in the description. Instead, the description should provide support for the particular claim features in various implementations.

11. According to EPO: The application has to be drafted in accordance with Article 83 EPC, which requires that the European patent application discloses the invention in a manner sufficiently clear and complete for it to be carried out by a person skilled in the art.

§3.04 FOURTH CHALLENGE: TERRITORIALITY VERSUS DISTRIBUTED CHARACTER OF SOFTWARE OR HOW TO DRAFT CLAIMS IN THE CLOUD?

In network technology and in other areas of computer science software is not usually operated on a stand-alone system, locally, but will be provided for clients via download from a server which may be located anywhere (possibly in a country without patent protection) or operated virtually in a distributed system of computing nodes.

Thus, software has a virtual and distributed character. Whereas, like all IP rights patents are subject to the principle of territoriality and only have effect in the country for which they were granted. This is a general conflict of objectives.

Therefore, in particular for cloud or network based CIIs, questions relating to direct and indirect infringement play an important role.

So, in network technology, functionality is usually distributed over a plurality of co-operating computers and is no longer tied to specific hardware (computers, computer network nodes, servers, etc.). In most of the different fields in computer technology or where the same is going to be applied, we are currently facing a trend towards 'cloudification' and 'virtualization'. Moreover, certain processes and steps for operating a computing platform (e.g. a cloud) may be outsourced to other service providers and need not necessarily be performed on the computing platform itself.

This strongly influences the patent drafting process.

In a distributed scenario, such as a client-server network architecture (or a base station/client station architecture or sender/recipient architecture) or for cloud-based systems, it is necessary to identify which function is to be performed on which physical entity. In former system architectures it was possible to relate particular functions to particular physical nodes. But in a virtual cloud-based system this relationship may change and, thus, claims should not be restricted unnecessarily.

In patent law, this topic has also been discussed under the phrase 'divided infringement'.

Some problematic issues are discussed below with examples in a generalized form. It has to be noted that these examples only address the question of claim drafting and scope of protection. The state of the art and questions of novelty and inventive step or obviousness should not be considered.

A typical example for a divided infringement scenario is a sender/receiver environment:

Sending computer A sends a message to receiving computer B. Computer B processes the messages and provides a result.

There are two concepts for drafting the independent claim in the abovementioned scenario: the unitary and the central approach.[12]

According to the central approach, the overall method or system is claimed involving the steps of the sending computer A and steps of the receiving computer B. This may be drafted as:

---

12. *See* Mark A. Lemley et al., *Divided Infringement Claims*, 33(3) AIPLA Quarterly Journal (2004).

Method for data processing, comprising the steps of:

- sending a message by a sending computer A to receiving computer B;
- processing the message at the receiving computer B;
- providing a result by the receiving computer B.

The central approach has a drawback in that the patentee often has to rely on contributory infringement in case the infringer only executes some of the claimed steps but not all. However, the advantage is that if inventiveness lies within the interaction between computer A and B, it will presumably be important to claim the whole method according to the central approach.

According to the unitary approach, the claim only relates to one unit (in the example above: the receiving computer B) and relates to a single-actor view (only one single-actor, such as computer B, for all steps). For example, a claim according to the unitary approach may be drafted as:

Method for data processing at receiving computer B, comprising the steps of:

- receiving a message;
- processing the message;
- providing a result.

Whether it makes sense to further include another independent claim in the same method category for the other unit, here the sending computer A as well has to be evaluated in each case. In this case, an independent claim for the sending computer A only comprises the step 'sending the message to computer B', which is presumably not worth claiming.

The decision as to which approach should be applied is to be taken in each case. Both approaches show advantages and disadvantages. The unitary approach may be a better basis for claiming direct infringement, whereas the central approach may be more advantageous for arguing inventive step during prosecution, in particular if the inventiveness lies in the interaction between sending computer A and receiving computer B. However, with a claim according to the central approach one would perhaps rely on contributory, induced or indirect infringement, which is significantly more difficult to enforce than direct infringement.[13]

With respect to the distributed character of modern software (swapping deployments in the cloud, virtualization) further aspects need to be considered.

Consider the following example of a process providing a certain technical service XYZ, comprising the steps of:

- receiving input information;
- processing input information for determining a result dataset;
- transmitting a notification message with the determined result dataset.

13. *See* US Supreme Court decision *Limelight Networks, Inc. v. Akamai Technologies, Inc. Supreme Court*, decided 2 June 2014.

According to the unitary approach proposed by Lemley, this method could be claimed as:[14]

> XYZ machine, which is configured to:
> 1. Receive input information;
> 2. Process input information for determining a result dataset;
> 3. Transmit a notification message with the determined result dataset.

A major drawback of this claim type, directed to the XYZ machine, is that it would not be infringed directly if one of the steps mentioned is performed on another machine. For example, if the result dataset is calculated (step 2) on (external) machine W and not on machine XYZ, there is no longer direct infringement. Machine W will then forward its result to machine XYZ providing the result dataset for further processing, i.e. transmitting the notification message. Generally, all the three steps need to be executed on the same entity for direct infringement. As the software may be easily implemented on different machines, it is relatively straightforward to circumvent this type of claim. An accused infringer may easily transfer a single step onto another machine in order to avoid the scope of protection.

A solution is to use a more general claim language for a system rather than the specific machine. In the description it should be explained sufficiently and properly that system XYZ may comprise machine W as well, and in particular for performing the step of processing the information as in the example given above. It would thus be possible to outsource some of the steps to different or other machines within the system. The abovementioned example would be covered with this kind of claim type. A further advantage with this kind of more generalized claim wording is that it might be easier to argue for unity and from a litigation perspective the damage threshold may be raised.

Consider a scenario in which the step of 'transmitting' may be executed by another external machine. Also this scenario should be covered by the claim. Besides the extension of the system, another option is to use a reference for the 'externalizable' step(s) and to only include the steps which might be performed on other machines via a reference. An example would read as:

> An XYZ system, which is configured to:
> - receive input information;
> - process input information for determining a result dataset;
> - cause transmission of a notification message with the determined result dataset.

With the wording 'causing < the externalizable step > ...' the claim also covers the step of transmission being executed on an external machine. The same result may be achieved with a similar wording by only including a reference to the step, such as 'initiating transmission of a notification message with the determined result dataset'. The 'transmission' does not necessarily need to be executed on the same computing

14. *See* Lemley et al., 'Divided Infringement Claims' 2004 (n. 12).

machine that performs the other steps of receiving and processing for direct infringement.

In sum, unlike other technical domains, for drafting high quality CII claims, a few more aspects (other than in different fields of technology) have to be checked and considered.

§3.05 FIFTH CHALLENGE: ENFORCEABILITY FOR CII CLAIMS

A brief look at national statistics reveals that the application figures for software-based technologies continue to expand. Therefore, it becomes more and more important to draft and obtain enforceable software-related patents.

Enforceability is at issue, in particular in virtual systems, where functionality is decoupled from physical machines or apparatuses.

This is the case, for instance, in telecommunications, where a plurality of co-operating entities are distributed over several patent-protected and non-patent-protected countries. Further, some entities are operated by clients and some by competitors or operators. However, enforcement of one's own patent should not be directed to the end user, but to the competitor operating the respective entity (e.g. server).

All these aspects may become critical issues and, therefore, care should be taken when drafting the claims.

The virtual and distributed character of software requires it to evaluate which formats should be used in a respective claim set. Computer program, product and signal claim formats should be taken into consideration, depending on the national requirements.[15]

As explained in §3.04, it is worth elaborating on which apparatus/entity specific steps/functions may be performed. Independent claims should be drafted per entity, for example in a client-server system, a first claim set should be drafted for the server and a second claim set for the client, each only encompassing server-related functions and client-related functions respectively. This has the important advantage that said entity-perspective claims are much easier to enforce than claims including functions or steps from further entities for which direct infringement typically is very hard or even impossible to prove. Typically, a system claim (as 'overall claim' and unitary claim) covering server and client-related steps is advantageous for arguing inventive step, when inventiveness lies in the combination or interaction between client and server.

However, with respect to enforceability, care should be taken when drafting such unitary system claims, including a plurality of modules (or methods including a plurality of steps) that may not be practised by any one party/physical entity. Instead,

15. Signal claims are only allowed before the EPO, according to T 0163/85 (*Colour television signal*) of 14 March 1989, available at: https://www.epo.org/law-practice/case-law-appeals/recent/t850163ex1.html (accessed 19 March 2017). However, care should be taken, whether the signals merely carry information or the signals carry information representing a technical system and bringing the technical effect of that system.

such claims are only directly infringed through the collective activities of multiple parties.

In modern networked technology, cross-border applications are becoming more and more common. Sometimes not all of the limitations of a particular claim are located in the relevant jurisdiction.[16] Lemley refers to this kind of claim construction as 'divided'. Such divided claims make it difficult to prove direct infringement by a single party.[17]

Finally, when assessing enforceability, it should be considered whether or not it is possible to assert infringement of a specific feature, e.g. relating to the internal functioning of the computer. Thus, another helpful approach might be to ask where the software, when being executed on a machine, will show a perceived result. Often, steps related to input and/or output may be an indication. Therefore, it might sometimes be helpful to present in detail the interactions between different computing entities and to formulate features on the entity's interfaces and include the provision of output and/or input to/from other entities.

Another important aspect for evaluation of enforceability is the question of how to protect the downloading process and not the machine on which the software is provided for download. As mentioned earlier, one of the aspects that make software so special is that it is very easy to locate a server machine in a non-patent protected territory. The question now is: what kind of means do we have to attack the operator of the server machine for providing access or do we need to attack the (end) users who download the software in a patent-protected territory?

One means is to focus on a unitary drafting approach. Another advantage is to draft the claims from a functional point of view, as explained earlier.

Finally, an option is to draft independent claims in other formats if these are available in the respective jurisdiction, such as computer signal claims or computer program claims.

§3.06 SUMMARY FOR THE MAJOR APPROACHES OF THE DIFFERENT JURISDICTIONS

The current legal situation all over the world (i.e. in the major patent countries) is very dynamic: New Guidelines are released, new case law is generated. You will find more details to this in the Chapters 4–12 below.

For example in China new Guidelines have been issued. According to these new Guidelines (2017) a much more liberal approach shall be applied. Even business methods may be eligible for patent protection in China if they are directed to a technical problem and meet the requirements of novelty and inventiveness/creativity.

Whereas in the USA in the Post-Alice World, a trend towards a much more stricter regime relating to §101 may be observed. Further, legal certainty is still a critical issue, because there is less guidance for assessing abstractness of features and claims.

---

16. *See NTP, Inc. v. Research in Motion, Ltd.*, 418 F.3d 1282 (Fed. Cir. 2005). In this case, some claim features were proofed not in the USA, but only in Canada.
17. *See* Lemley et al., 'Divided Infringement Claims' 2004 (n. 12), 255.

In Europe and Germany a slight trend to more liberalization may be observed, although there are no significant changes in case law development.

The following table summarizes the essential aspects in the major patent jurisdictions worldwide.

Table 3.1 Overview over Major National Patentability Requirements for CII

Challenge	*EPO*	*DE*	*USA*	*CN*	*KR*	*JP*	*IN*
Application of eligibility criteria	Liberal acc. to G03/08	Liberal, but stricter than EPO	Post-Alice: strict relating to §101	Liberal acc. to 2017 Guidelines	Lenient	Liberal	Strict
Technicality requirement	Yes	Yes	No[18]	Yes	Indirectly yes	Yes	Yes
Relevance of sufficiency of disclosure	Yes	Yes	Lesser	Yes	Yes	Yes	Yes
Admissibility of signal claims	Yes	Yes	No	No	No	No	No
Patentability of business methods	No	No	Strict; relating to §101	Maybe, acc. to 2017 Guidelines	No	No	No

18. Besides so called 'covered Business method patents', which will be considered on a case-by-case basis: whether the claimed subject matter as a whole recites a technological feature that is novel and unobvious over the prior art and solves a technical problem using a technical solution (*see also* Chapter 8, USA; §8.01 [B]).

Chapter 4
Legal Practice on Computer-Implemented Inventions at the EPO

§4.01 FUNDAMENTALS

The European Patent Organisation is an inter-governmental organization. It is not a body of the European Union. The European Patent Convention EPC was signed in 1973. The European Patent Office, one body of the Organization, started working in 1978. The other body, the Administrative Council, monitors it.

The EPC has its roots in the national law of the European Member States with the tradition and role to focus on patents in the fields of technology.[1] The procedures of Western European States influenced the creation of the EPC. This influence came mainly from Germany, the Netherlands, Sweden and Switzerland all of which conducted substantive examination at that time. Their views constituted models. Furthermore, the new PCT influenced the EPC with regard to excluded subject matter. The 'travaux préparatoires' (preparatory works) provide some background information on the creation of the EPC.[2] The material on Article 52 EPC gives some insight into the controversial discussions on the exclusion of computer programs as such. Some saw computer programs as purely mathematical methods, but their importance in industry was already established. They had to be protected to a certain degree. Some flexibility for later interpretation was intended by a more general wording. A major reason for the exclusion of computer programs as such was seen in the inability to do a reasonable search in computer programs. Possible differences between the German term 'Datenverarbeitungsanlagen', the French term 'ordinateur' and the English term 'computer' were discussed. FICPI remarked that the German 'Programme für Datenverarbeitungsanlagen' could be interpreted broadly. This could be dangerous since algorithms, the

1. Waage, E. *Principles of Procedure in European Patent Law* European Patent Office 2002.
2. *EPC 1973 Legal History* http://www.epo.org/law-practice/legal-texts/epc/archive/epc-1973/traveaux/documents.html (accessed 13 March 2017).

structures underlying programs, could be excluded resulting in problems for large industries. In the overall context of patentability, it was decided not to incorporate the requirement of technical progress 'since it is self-evident that an invention contributes to technical knowledge and must therefore constitute technical progress'. Thus, technicality was already an implicit requirement for a patentable invention at that time. The general intention was to leave some flexibility for interpretation so that later technological developments in computing could be taken into account.

Some general challenges for the patent system became known during the creation of the EPC. In 1972, the German Professor Beier underlined the roots of the patent system that had been created at a time when there was a specific scientific, economic and technical situation.[3] The spirit of those times was to promote only technological inventions. In other words, not all inventions in the broader sense are patentable. Mental acts and other topics could not be patented. The 'technical character' became the central criteria even if not defined in law and difficult to define. It was already the practice in many countries to limit patents to some extent to technological inventions. It was seen as important to adapt the concept of the technical invention to new technologies. Professor Beier observed a major discrepancy in the patentability of computer programs between Anglo-Saxon and Central-European countries. The former were in favour, the latter against patentability of computer programs. In the view of some critics, the substantive law of the EPC did not meet the needs of modern technologies.

In 1973, the legal protection of computer programs was also considered by Mr Gert Kolle, later Principal Director of International Legal Affairs and Patent Law at the EPO.[4] He underlined the economic importance of computer programs. Starting with program development, he discussed possible elements of protection. He made a distinction between the general mathematical-logical approach for the solution of a problem using a computer independent from the concrete computer program, and the 'naked' program as such. The scope of protection is a lot larger for a patent on the algorithmic formulation of the solution – the first one- than the protection by copyright for the program as such – the latter. A further distinction was made based on the purpose of the programs. It might be relevant whether a program serves business-organizational purposes like company payroll accounting, or whether it serves scientific-technological purposes like numerically controlled machine tools. Particular significance was given to system programs.

The book 'Patenting Software Under the European Patent Convention' published in 2000, authored by K. Beresford, gives some further historical information on the different views during the creation of the EPC.[5] The general aim of the EPC drafters was according to Beresford 'that inventions representing the technical progress or technological improvement should be patentable but those which were purely abstract should not'. Patentability of computer programs or software was one of many controversial

---

3. Beier, F.-K. *Zukunftsprobleme des Patentrechts* GRUR 1972, H5, 214–225.
4. Kolle, G. *Der Rechtsschutz von Computerprogrammen aus nationaler und internationaler Sicht*, GRUR 1973, H. 12, 611–620.
5. Beresford, K. *Patenting Software Under the European Patent Convention* Sweet & Maxwell 2000.

topics. It resulted in the exclusion of computer programs as such (Article 52(2) and (3) EPC). This was intended to ensure 'that inventions which would be patentable in accordance with normal criteria ... should not be excluded from patentability merely because they utilise or involve computer programs'.

§4.02 EARLY DEVELOPMENTS

In 1978, the EPO began its work, with examiners at the branch in The Hague (Netherlands) performing search only and in Munich (Germany) substantive examination only.[6] The former International Patent Institute (IIB) and its 714 employees were integrated into the EPO. In 1989, the BEST project (Bring Examination and Search Together) was started and gradually extended. This was completed in 2002 when all examiners at all locations (later also the sub-office in Berlin) became entrusted with search and examination. The EPO's three official languages are German, English and French. An Examination Division consists of three members. Before taking a decision one examiner is entrusted with the procedure. Members of the search, examination and opposition Divisions are primarily technically qualified employees as are the members of the Boards of Appeal. If necessary, a Division can be extended by a legal member.

§4.03 SOURCES OF INFORMATION

Legal information on software related patents are contained in the general legal sources (EPC, Guidelines, Official Journal ...). The eighth edition (2016) of the book 'Case Law of the Boards of Appeal of the European Patent Office' is also an important source of information in a condensed form. In recent years, some e-learning tools as well as a small brochure with general information have also been created.[7] There are no specific separate guidelines on software related patents. Respective passages exist in the different parts of the meanwhile voluminous Guidelines for Examination in the EPO. The whole Guidelines are subject to annual updates.

This structure has some disadvantages. In Part G it is not really visible that today most of the topics (business methods, rules of games, presentation of information ...) under Article 52(2) can be implemented as a computer program or in digital form (images, graphical user interfaces ...). Thus, computational basics valid for all these topics (if implemented as a computer program) are not taken into account. Topics not in that list are hardly ever dealt with. Even a reader familiar with the different and complex fields of computing cannot find information straightaway. It follows that, information in the important area of system software, for example operating systems, does not exist or is hard to find. Fundamental computational terms like 'computer program as a list of instructions in a programming language' and 'algorithm' are not

6. EPO, *The history of the EPO* http://www.epo.org/about-us/office/timeline.html#year19781982 (accessed 13 March 2017).
7. EPO, Brochure *Patents for software?* http://documents.epo.org/projects/babylon/eponet.nsf/0/a0be115260b5ff71c125746d004c51a5/$FILE/patens_for_software_en.pdf (accessed 13 March 2017).

explained. This results in ongoing confusions with legal terms (e.g. claim category: computer program (product)) and misinterpretation of the exclusion of computer programs as such under Article 52(2, 3) EPC.

§4.04 AMENDED GUIDELINES 1985

The increase in software related or later Computer-Implemented Inventions (CII) has resulted in an enormous amount of Board of Appeal (BoA) decisions over the years. During the first three decades CII related decisions were concentrated in a few Technical Boards. Due to the growing importance of software CII now appears in many fields of technology with about 200 decisions per year during the last five years.

When the EPO started its work in 1978 there were doubts as to it would be accepted by industry. Such doubts quickly disappeared because of a permanent increase in incoming patent applications. This was particularly the case for software related patents. It was, therefore not surprising that the 1985 amendment of the Guidelines for examination included major passages on computer programs.[8] A major step in the interpretation of the EPC took place.

The following amendments were made:

A disclosure of the invention with a description only in a programming language was not sufficient. Short excerpts from programs written in commonly used programming language could be accepted in the patent description. A similar wording can still be found in GL, Part F, Ch. II-9, 4.12. For complex technical fields including computers, sufficiency of disclosure required not only a description of structure but also of function, unless the function was immediately apparent.

The sections relating to Article 52(1) EPC were revised with respect to computer programs. What was meant by 'invention' was not defined. Article 52(2) EPC was considered to be a non-exhaustive list.

Firstly, it was emphasized that 'the basic test for patentability was whether the invention, as claimed, had a "**technical**" character'.

Secondly, in applying the test the contribution of the claimed subject matter, considered as a whole, to the known art has to be determined. The examiner should concentrate on the real content of the claim. If this contribution was not of a technical character, there was no invention within the meaning of Article 52(1) EPC. As an example for a non-technical contribution to the art, a claim was assumed which describes a known manufactured article having a painted design or certain written information on its surface. Here, the contribution to the art was merely an aesthetic creation or presentation of information. It was excluded as such from patentability. This approach became the so called '**contribution approach**' *for the determination of eligibility for patent protection under the EPC* (abandoned in about 2000). If the examiner could determine technical contribution, patentability should not be denied just because a computer program was involved in the implementation. Examples for

8. EPO Guidelines OJ EPO, 6/1985, 173–179, http://archive.epo.org/epo/pubs/oj1985/p157_186.pdf (accessed 13 March 2017).

patentable inventions were given. Program-controlled machines and program-controlled manufacturing and control processes should be regarded as patentable. The internal work of the computer like the virtual extension of a memory could also result in a technical effect.

Thirdly, a computer program claimed by itself or as a combination of a physical record on a carrier (at that time tape or disc) was unpatentable irrespective of its content. It was still no more than a computer program. It related to excluded subject matter as such. On the other hand, the combination of a known computer and a new program loaded into it could be patentable if the program caused the computer to operate in a new way from a *technical* point of view. Similarly, a method of operating a known computer under the control of a new program could be patentable.

In 1987, Mr Holzwarth, at that time director of the computing directorate in Munich, gave some guidance on the amended Guidelines.[9] He explained that while the term 'technical character' is not explicitly used in the EPC (1973), there are several Rules in the Implementing Regulations to the Convention on the Grant of European Patents relating to it, such as: the invention has to be in a technical field (Rule 27(1)b)); it has to be based on a technical problem (Rule 27(1)d)); it has to be characterized by technical means (Rule 29(1)). The approach for determination of patentability was explained ('contribution approach'). Fruitless general patentability discussions should be stopped and replaced by more fact-based argumentations including prior art documents. He also referred to decision T0208/84[10] that became the landmark decision VICOM. Holzwarth stated that the decision did not primarily refer to a computer program but to a mathematical method underlying the invention. Furthermore, he pointed out that there were usually no applications for computer programs as such. Technical devices or processes were claimed in which a computer program played a role.

In the 1980s, these legal interpretations were seen as revolutionary by those in favour of patent protection because this gave modern computing technologies a chance. Inventions in computing were not only restricted to hardware solutions. Applicants did not have to reformulate or 'hide' software related inventions as hardware applications.

§4.05 THE 1990s: CONTRIBUTION APPROACH, PROBLEM-SOLUTION APPROACH AND OTHER DEVELOPMENTS

A trilateral cooperation between USPTO, JPO and EPO began in 1983.[11] A comparative study in the area of software related patents was part of this cooperation in the 1990s.

9. Holzwarth, A. *Richtlinien für die Prüfung im europäischen Patentamt – Sachprüfung von Patentanmeldungen, die sich auf Programme beziehen* in Kilian, W. et al. *Schutz von Computersoftware- Technische und rechtliche Aspekte* 1987.
10. EPO BoA T0208/84- VICOM http://www.epo.org/law-practice/case-law-appeals/recent/t840208ep1.html#q (accessed 13 March 2017).
11. Trilateral Cooperation EPO, JPO, USPTO http://www.trilateral.net/index.html (accessed 13 March 2017).

The examination approach for two hypothetical patent applications was discussed.[12] The first application related to a 'Curve generating method using tangent vectors' and the second application to an 'Automatic ordering system'. The results of project 24.2 are available on the JPO website.[13] Differences existed in the approaches of the three patent offices.

Discussions both within the EPO and with interested circles continued, primarily with regard to the meaning of 'computer program as such'. Many expressed the opinion that first and foremost the mysterious 'computer program as such' means a list of instructions in a programming language, in other words source code or object code. Mr Betten, a patent attorney, proposed deleting the wording 'computer program as such' from Article 52(2, 3) EPC.[14] The wording apparently lead to the bias that all software related inventions were excluded from patentability.

The so called 'contribution approach' for determining patentability in the field of software- related inventions was seen as more problematic with the official introduction of the 'problem-and-solution-approach' as part of the 1994 Guidelines.[15] The problem-and-solution approach should normally be used for determining *inventive step* at the EPO. It has its roots in the patent system of many European states.[16] Mr G.S.A. Szabo explained the problem-and-solution-approach in an article emphasizing that this approach does not try to reflect the real situation of the inventor (subjective problem) but to find the objective problem in relationship to the closest prior art.[17]

[A] Criticism of the Contribution Approach after Official Introduction of the Problem-Solution Approach: Specifics for Software Related Inventions

In 1996, Mr Paul van den Berg summarized concerns (unnoticed by many) about the contribution approach in an article on software-related inventions.[18] He explained:

> The main objections to the contribution approach seems to be that the system of law as presented in the EPC, requires that the first step in substantive examination should be whether the invention is not excluded under Art. 52(2),(3) EPC before any examination as to whether it satisfies the three requirements [novelty, inventive step, industrial application] summed up in Art. 52(1) EPC.

---

12. Trilateral Cooperation EPO, JPO, USPT, *Computer related inventions* http://www.trilateral.net/projects/Comparative/computer.html (accessed 13 March 2017).
13. JPO, *Report on Comparative Study Carried Out Under Trilateral Project 24.2* http://www.jpo.go.jp/shiryou_e/toushin_e/kenkyukai_e/utp242_m.htm (accessed 13 March 2017).
14. Betten, J. *Patentschutz von Computerprogrammen* GRUR 1995, H.12, 775–789.
15. OJ EPO, 1994, H. 12, 959–967, *Amendment of the Guidelines* http://archive.epo.org/epo/pubs/oj1994/p875_981.pdf (accessed 13 March 2017).
16. WIPO, Standing Committee on the Law of Patent, Study on Inventive Step, 2015 http://www.wipo.int/edocs/mdocs/scp/en/scp_22/scp_22_3.pdf (accessed 13 March 2017).
17. Szabo, G.S.A. (former Chairmen of a BoA, EPO) *Der Ansatz über Aufgabe und Lösung in der Praxis des Europäischen Patentamts* Mit. d. deutsch. Patentanwälte, 1994, H. 9, 225–239.
18. Van den Berg, P. (former Chairman of a BoA of the EPO) *Patentability of Computer-Software-Related Inventions* in *The Law and Practice of the Enlarged Board of Appeal During Its First Ten Years* Carl-Heymanns Verlag 1996, 29–47.

Furthermore he indicated, that based on early decisions of the BoAs, fundamental requirements were also valid for software related inventions. He indicated that 'once certain 'excluded' fields have become computerized; inventions made in those fields may become patentable'. This could lead to a 'mix' claim, a claim with technical and non-technical features. Thus, the borderline between patentable and non-patentable subject matter could be small for a topic usually excluded but computerized. The mix as a whole had to solve a technical problem. The technical character was emphasized. Van den Berg admitted that the definition of a software-related invention 'is difficult to define in the usual 'technical' terms'.

Van den Berg illustrated the difficulties with 'computer programs' as part of Article 52(2) EPC. In his view:

> The exclusions ... generally concern subject matter of an abstract, non-material nature ... Under certain circumstances, programs for computers may constitute an exception to this abstract character. In the list, this terms covers both computer programs which, when used in a computer programmed accordingly, may contribute to a non-excluded field, and computer programs, which when so used, do not so contribute.

Furthermore, for the computer programs that do contribute he makes a distinction between computer programs excluded as such but not excluded 'when so used'. Mr van den Berg points out that 'searches in listings of computer programs instructions written in a programming language' would be difficult as well as the creation of 'a properly classified prior art documentation'. Nevertheless, 'a computer program listing expressed in programming language may constitute prior art' but 'is not considered to constitute sufficient disclosure of an invention'.

An upcoming development was also mentioned by van den Berg: applicant's (mainly US) wish to formulate claims for a computer program on a recording medium. This would allow 'to sue for immediate direct infringement'. A method or an apparatus claim (involving a computer program) allowed only contributory infringement.

This early article indicates the barriers still valid today. J. Pila criticized the difficulties with computer programs that are part of Article (52) EPC about twenty years later.[19]

Without any statistics it can be assumed that in the field of software-related inventions there are more 'mixed claims' (features not excluded combined with features excluded if claimed as such) which makes search and substantive examination more challenging. As will be seen later, this became most visible in the area of computerized business methods (cf. Chapter 4.6.4).

It can also be that the claimed subject matter relates to several fields excluded as such. For example, a computerized business [forecasting] method could be expressed with mathematical formulas, or computerized rules of games could be combined with payment rules (business method). A further challenging field is presentations of information, such as aesthetic features created by a computer program on a display.

19. Pila, J. *Dispute Over the Meaning of 'Invention' in Article 52(2) EPC: The Patentability of Computer-Implemented Inventions in Europe* IIC: International Review of Industrial Property & Copyright Law (2005).

Van den Berg also explained how to deal with a 'mix' claim. His approach was derived from traditional technological fields based on T0603/89 which relates to a keyboard instrument with keys (technical) combined with markers relating to the tones of the key (non-technical). The BoA concluded that the existing technical means were not used for a solution of a technical problem. A technical effect could result from an interaction between technical and non-technical features. The headnote of this early decision is cited in later software-related cases with a mixed claim, but for a computer professional the meaning of interaction (the action or influence of things on one another)[20] between the algorithm of e.g. a business method (non-technical), its implementation as a computer program (technical?) and the computer hardware (technical) is difficult to understand or to transfer to programming.

The question was discussed as to how the subject matter in the claim has to be formulated when it relates to a computer program. If it is a computer program in a programming language then it is excluded as a computer program as such even if that computer program is used in a technical field. As already pointed out by A. Holzwarth, the EPO hardly ever received patent applications with a complete computer program in a programming language in the claim. This is still the case and for this reason, this meaning of the exclusion of computer programs as such is very often forgotten nowadays. Claims are usually formulated based on methods (similar to algorithms cf. Chapter 2) which are the starting point for an implementation of that method as a computer program. It should not be forgotten that such methods could also be implemented by logical circuits in hardware.

[B] T0410/96: General Purpose Computer with Different Computer Programs

During its first twenty years the BoA of the EPO published several decisions relating to different areas of software related applications. They mainly resulted in the statement that some claimed subject matter was not to be seen as a computer program as such excluded under Article 52(2,3) EPC.

In the area of computer programs methods play a major role (similarity of method to algorithm). A general purpose computer is very often used for the execution of the method. The hardware does not have to be changed for the execution of the method (implemented as a computer program). For this reason, the computer with its basic configuration has a different functionality due to the computer program. Thus, the computer can be defined by 'means for' executing method steps. Decision **T0410/96** (25.7.1997) confirmed this view. However, the decision was only indicated in the Case law book of the EPO. It was indicated in the Guidelines only in the reviewed version of November 2016. It relates to the reference of one independent claim to another. A device claim for a computer can refer to the independent method claim. In order to avoid long repetition of method steps in the *long version*, a *short version* is possible. A

20. Dictionary Merriam-Webster *Definition of interaction* http://www.merriam-webster.com/dictionary/interaction (accessed 13 March 2017).

possible claim formulation for the short version is: 'Data processing system comprising means for carrying out the steps of the method according to any one of the claims 1 to X'. After the acceptance of a computer program product claim such a claim can also refer to a method claim (long or short version). Nevertheless, it must be ensured that the invention is sufficiently disclosed in order to enable the skilled person to execute the invention without being inventive.

§4.06 TURN OF THE MILLENNIUM

The end of the 1990s and the beginning of the twenty-first century was a very dynamic period in the field of software related patents at the EPO:

- an enormous increase of incoming software related patent applications in many fields;
- the Conference on the revision of the EPC (EPC 2000) took place including the suggestion to delete 'computer programs' from Article 52(2) EPC;[21]
- the European Union submitted a 'Proposal for a Directive of the European Parliament and of the Council on the patentability of computer-implemented inventions' for discussion in 2002;[22]
- limitations for business methods (pure and computer-implemented) should be diminished following a new US practice;
- claims of the form 'computer program on a carrier' should be allowed as they are in the US.

Towards the end of the 1990s in the area of software related patents the EPO was confronted with:

- An increased criticism on the grant of 'software patents' by open source circles.
- The wish for a more liberal granting policy for software-related business methods.
- The wish to allow claims of the form 'computer program on a carrier'.

The increase of software-related inventions became visible in new IPC classes like G06T for computer graphics.

No final agreement was reached concerning the deletion of 'computer program' in Article 52(2) EPC. However, Article 52(1) was amended in that 'in all fields of technology' was added. This was intended to underline the limitation of patents to technological inventions under the EPC 2000.

21. European Union Law, *Proposal for a Directive of the European Parliament and of the Council on the Patentability of Computer-Implemented Inventions*, 2002 http://eur-lex.europa.eu/legal-content/EN/TXT/?uri=COM:2002:0092:FIN (accessed 13 March 2017).
22. European Union Law, *Proposal for a Directive of the European Parliament and of the Council on the Patentability of Computer-Implemented Inventions Explanatory Memorandum* http://eur-lex.europa.eu/legal-content/EN/TXT/HTML/?uri=OJ:JOC_2002_151_E_0129_01&rid=1 (accessed 13 March 2017).

[A] Draft EU Directive: 'Computer-Implemented Invention' – EPC 2000

As in Biotechnology, there was the intention to create a directive on patentability of computer-implemented inventions. The EPO as a Non- EU institution could have followed such a directive. In 2002, the European Commission submitted a proposal. Harmonization was one aim at the level of the status quo as defined by the practice and jurisprudence of the EPO at that time. However, heavy protests mainly of open-source circles lead to the rejection of the proposal in 2005.

The term 'computer-implemented invention' (CII) already used in a similar form by other patent offices was explained in Article (2) (a) of the proposal:

> **'computer-implemented invention'** means any invention the performance of which involves the use of a computer, computer network or other programmable apparatus and having one or more prima facie novel features which are realised wholly or partly by means of a computer program or computer programs

The term was later taken over by the EPO in a slightly modified form. The criteria that the features implemented as computer program have to be prima facie novel was dropped. It no longer matters whether the at least one feature implemented as computer program is new. The EPO explanation in the Examination Guidelines, Part G (Nov. 2016):

> Inventions involving programs for computers can be protected in different forms of a 'computer-implemented invention', an expression intended to cover claims which involve computers, computer networks or other programmable apparatus whereby prima facie one or more of the features of the claimed invention are realised by means of a program or programs.[23]

The revised version of the EPC 2000 entered into force in 2007.

[B] T1173/97 and T0935/97: Computer Program (Product) Claims

The publication of the decisions **T1173/97 (Computer program product/ IBM) of 1.7.1998** and **T 0935/97 (Computer program product II/IBM) of 4.2.1999** was preceded by several discussions on the allowance of claims directed to a computer program on a record carrier. Such a form of claim known in the US as 'Beauregard – claim' (US5710578) was held to overcome problems in infringement. Someone who lets the program run on a computer can only infringe a method claim. However, this is normally the end user. As pointed out by S. Davies 'the patentee will generally want to enforce its patent against the supplier of the program'.[24] Due to the appearance of the software industry computer programs became a separate product that do not have to be sold with a computer. Method and device claims allow only contributory or indirect infringement that is more complex and more expensive. According to Professor Lee A.

23. EPO, Guidelines EPC, November 2016, Part G – Chapter II-5, 3.6 Programs for computers.
24. Davies, S. *Computer Program Claims – The Final Frontier for Software Inventions* EIPR 1998, 11, 429–433.

Hollar this form of claim could have been avoided in the US by amendment of infringement law e.g. by the sentence 'Distributing a computer program implementing a patented process infringes the patent on a process'.[25]

The two decisions were relevant for several reasons:

- mainly for the allowance of a claim 'computer program on a physical record carrier';
- the introduction of the 'normal' and 'further technical effect' when a computer program runs on a computer; and
- a first hint of abandoning the 'contribution approach'.

The reasons for the introduction of the claim category are not indicated in the decisions since infringement is not a matter for the EPO. Nevertheless, the limitations of the existing infringement law based on the traditional claim categories 'device', 'process' lead to the introduction of the new claim formulation in the area of computing.

[1] Claim Formulation, Claim Category

The original patent application EP0457112 (A2) of T1173/97 indicated two claims formulated as a computer program product: claim 20 indicated 'a computer readable medium'. Claim 21 referred to claim 20. Finally, two independent claims 20 (computer program) and 21 (computer program product) were allowed. Claim 21 included a 'computer readable medium'. Both claims indicated a reference to the method claims (according to T410/96).

The BoA decided that different claim formulations might be possible (T1173/97, reasons 13.): 'It does not make any difference whether a computer program is claimed by itself or as a record on a carrier.'

There are different views on the category of the computer program claims. Some consider them to be a 'normal' product claim since there is always implicitly or explicitly a record carrier. However, a computer program with its underlying algorithm usually represents a sequence. From this perspective, its nature is nearer to a method claim than to a product claim. It is not defined by the criteria (structural features) which define a normal product. The Patent Attorney Beresford gave several possible interpretations of different claim formulations.[26] The proponents of an explicit indication of a carrier want to emphasize the non-abstract or non-mental nature of a computer program. Others see the carrier as an implicit means when talking about computer programs.

The patent application EP0767419 (A2) of T0935/97 had two computer program claims:

25. Hollar, L.A. *Justice Douglas Was Right: The Need for Congressional Action on Software Patents* in American Committee for Interoperable Systems (ACIS) membership committee meeting, 2 February 1996, Santa Clara, CA, US.
26. Beresford, K. *Patenting Software Under the European Patent Convention* Sweet & Maxwell 2000, chapter 'claiming the computer program' 90–93.

7. A computer program comprising computer program means adapted to perform all the steps of claim 1(method) when said program is run on a computer.

8. A computer program as claimed in claim 7 embodied on a computer readable medium.

The description indicated:

that computer programs can be delivered to a computer in many forms; including but not limited to:

- Information permanently stored on a non-writable storage media (e.g. read only memory devices with a computer such as ROM ... or CD-ROM disks ... readable by a computer I/O attachment);
- Information alterably stored on writable storage media (e.g. floppy disks ... and hard drives ...); or
- Information conveyed to a computer through communication media such as network ... and telephone networks via modem

Data storage for the modern computer can be based on different technologies. In the context of 'computer program product' claims the focus of patent protection is usually not directed at the technology of the record carrier but to a computer program stored on the record carrier or transmitted over a wireless carrier. The invention has to result from the method/algorithm underlying the computer program.

In the greater discussion, it should not be forgotten that the claim category is 'computer program' or 'computer program product' but this is just a name for the claim category. The content of the claim is never a complete computer program in a programming language as seen by computer professionals.

[2] Normal and Further Technical Effect

Figure 4.1 shows a possible illustration for the explanation of the **normal technical effect** and the **further technical effect**. It is not an official EPO explanation but based on the known layered model of a computer (Chapter 2, §2.06 [E]) the further technical effect is easier to understand. Computer A is connected to computer B. Both computers interact with a user. Additionally, computer A can get information from sensors 1...n of a technical system. Both computers A and B are shown as layered models. When a program runs on a computer, it will cause the flow of electrical current in the transistor level of the hardware. That is the normal technical effect caused by each computer program when executed on a computer. Depending on the invention, a further technical effect can be created e.g. in computer B on the level of system software. This might be the case when the operating system includes a method for the efficient access to resources. A further technical effect could result from application software in computer A when the application software controls a function of the technical system.

Some critics of patent protection of software disregard the effects inside a computer caused by an operating system as 'technical effect'.

Based on the layered model of a computer with hardware and software layers one can see that the *normal technical effect* of a computer program occurs at the *transistor level.* An application program is supposed to fulfil a required functionality. In a washing machine the program might control several functions (temperature, amount of water ...). Modern airplanes are 'flying computers' which control an enormous amount of functions. In a camcorder image capture, storage and modification is done under the control of computer programs. Modern smartphones are supposed to replace 'normal computers' soon.[27] They might contribute to a remote control of functionality of devices e.g. in the Internet of Things (IoT).

Figure 4.1 Normal and Further Technical Effect Resulting from a Computer Program When Executed

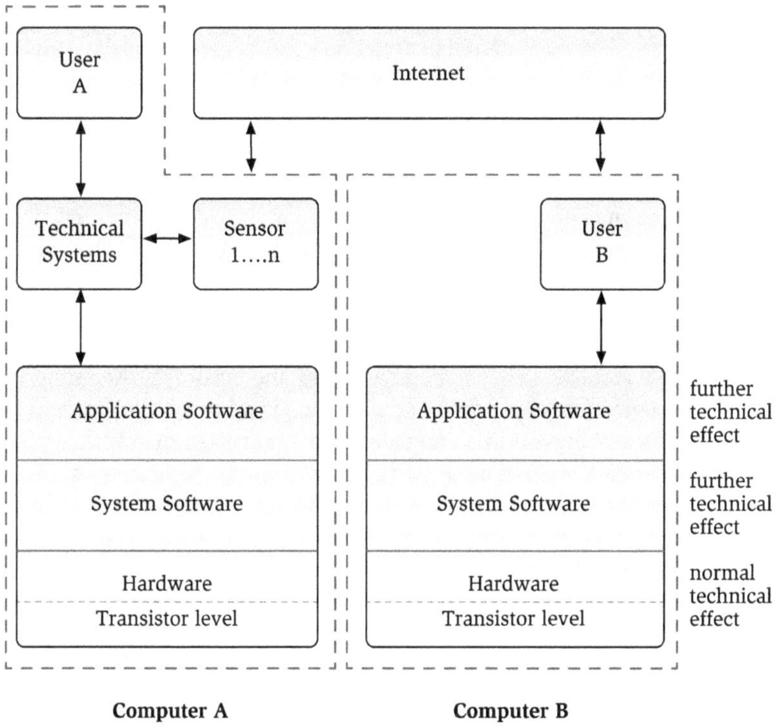

As explained in T1173/97 and T0935/97 the EPC legislators intended neither to exclude all computer programs nor to allow all. The Board was looking for criteria to follow this intention. Therefore, they concluded that 'physical modifications of the hardware (causing, for instance, electrical currents) deriving from the execution of the instructions given by programs for computers cannot per se constitute the technical character required for avoiding the exclusion of those programs'. No program would be excluded if the 'normal technical effect' would constitute the basis for the 'technical

27. Bonnington, C. *In Less Than Two Years, A Smartphone Could Be Your Only Computer* 2015 http://www.wired.com/2015/02/smartphone-only-computer/ (accessed 21 April 2017).

character'. However, it was not the intention of the legislators to provide protection for all computer programs.

[3] Subtle Hint to Abandon the 'Contribution Approach'

Both decisions T1173/97 and T0935/97 comprise a subtle hint (one sentence in reasons, point 8) about possibly abandoning the determination of exclusion from patentability using the 'contribution approach'. The relevance of the passage only became clear later.

Abandoning the 'contribution approach' should not be interpreted as the general abandonment of the 'technical contribution' as required in the determination of an inventive step according to the problem-solution approach. When reading older decisions of the BoA the reader should bear in mind the change in the determination of exclusion from patentability.

[C] T1194/97 Data structure Product Claims

It became apparent that not only computer programs could be recorded on a data carrier but also digital content or digital data. (The term data and data structure can be used with different meanings.).

T 1194/97 (Data structure product/PHILIPS) of 15.3.2000 relates to a picture retrieval system. Claims are directed to the whole system, a read device and a record carrier with coded pictures. The read device and the record carrier may be sold separately. Such claims for separate components of a system are allowed and known, e.g. as 'plug and socket' inventions. The picture data consisted of several consecutive picture lines. Picture data was recorded on a disc-shaped record carrier in a spiral track. Recording had to allow the data to be read later by a reading device. Therefore, the recording on the disc has to be in line with the properties of the reading device and the possible presentation of the pictures later.

The difference between presentation of information and representation of information was explained. Presentation of information means directly bringing information to a human whereas representation means 'to serve as a symbol of'. Presentation of information as such is excluded from patentability under Article 52(2, 3) EPC. Furthermore, a distinction was made between '**cognitive data**' and '**functional data**'. The loss of cognitive content results in a humanly meaningless picture on a television screen. The loss of functional data will disturb the technical operation of the system. In the context of the picture retrieval system functional data includes a data structure defined in terms (here coded picture line synchronizations, line numbers, and addresses) which inherently comprise the technical features of the system (here read device plus record carrier) in which the record carrier is operative.

The meaning of 'data structure' in the narrower sense of computing was not discussed.

[D] Computer-Implemented Business Methods and Pure Business Methods

Business methods if claimed as such are excluded from patentability under Article 52(2,3) EPC. Patentability of business methods is also limited under PCT regulations (cf. Rule 39.1 (iii) and Rules 67.1 (iii)).[28]

The first decade of the new millennium was marked by different views on the patentability of pure and computer-implemented business methods. The area of computer-implemented business methods became the clearest area to show that methods and procedures from areas outside of traditional technological fields can be implemented by computer programs. The majority of applications related to computer-implemented business methods. Features of the computational implementation were often indicated on a high level of abstraction. In other words, details of the computational implementation were not disclosed.

Those in favour of patentability emphasized a higher economic importance of intangible assets. Furthermore, from the perspective of computing a general-purpose computer with a different computer program based on a different algorithm (business method) was seen as a new computer. The boom in Internet and Worldwide Web technologies allowed new business models such as those illustrated by Hammer and Champy in their book 'Reengineering the Corporation: A Manifesto for Business Revolution' (1993).[29] Arguments against patentability were based on a view from a technical perspective emphasizing technicality. If the different business method (similar to an algorithm) of a computer program, programmed based on normal programming features, was the only difference to a general-purpose computer or standard computer network then no solution of a technical problem could be seen.

Discussions on business methods were triggered by a very liberal legal practice in the US resulting mainly from the State Street Bank decision of the Federal Circuit in 1998.[30] The patent US 5,193,056 entitled 'Data Processing System for Hub and Spoke Financial Services Configuration' was granted to the Signature Financial Group. State Street Bank took the view that the patent was invalid because it was directed to excluded subject matter either 'mathematical algorithm' or 'business method'. The Federal Circuit did not follow this view. A flood of business patent methods resulted.

The EPO was 'flooded' with respective patent applications both as European and as PCT applications. Early business method related decisions were T1002/92 (6.7.1994) Petterson and T0769/92 (31.5.1994) Sohei. The first decision did not see a 'business method as such' in a system for determining the queue sequence for serving customers at a plurality of service points. The subject matter of the Sohei decision was directed to a computerized management system directed to inventory and financial

28. WIPO *Regulations under the PCT* http://www.wipo.int/pct/en/texts/rules/rtoc1.htm (accessed 13 March 2017).
29. Hammer, M. et al. *Reengineering the Corporation: A Manifesto for Business Revolution* Harper Business first ed. 1993.
30. US, Federal Circuit, *State Street Bank & Trust Co. v. Signature Financial Group*, 149 F.3d 1368 (Fed. Cir. 23 July 1998) https://www.law.cornell.edu/patent/comments/96_1327.htm (accessed 13 March 2017).

management. The decision was more liberal in that 'technical considerations' were seen as a technical contribution to the art. Opponents found that this criterion was too easy to overcome. It soon became clear that the EPO would not follow this liberal practice. Table 4.1. shows landmark decisions with respect to business methods from the year 2000 onwards. All decisions can be found in the decisions database accessible on the EPO website.[31]

Table 4.1 Landmark Decisions on Business Methods (Pure and Computer-Implemented)

No. of Decision	*Official Journal EPO*	*Claimed Subject-Matter*
T0931/95 (8.9.2000) Pension Benefit	OJ 2001, 441	Computerized management of a pension system
T0641/00 (26.9.2002) COMVIK	OJ 2003, 352	Subscriber identity module with two identities
T0258/03 (27.11.2003) Hitachi	OJ 2004, 575	Auction method
T0388/04 (22.3.2006) Pitney Bowes	OJ 2007, 16	Undeliverable mail; Unspecified technical means
T1242/04 (20.10.2006) MAN	OJ 2007, 421	Provision of product-specific data
T0154/04 (15.11.2006) Duns Licensing	OJ 2008, 46	Estimating sales activities

The decisions not only gave guidance for business methods but also new guidance to determine the exclusion from patentability under Article 52(2, 3) EPC. The 'contribution approach' was no longer relevant. In T0931/95 (Pension Benefit), it was stated that the 'contribution approach' has no basis in the EPC. Referring to T1173/97 and T0935/97 the requirement of a technical character was stressed. A distinction was still made between method and system (apparatus) claim. The method claim was considered not to exhibit technical character despite some technical features in the method claim. The system claim was considered to exhibit technical character. This distinction was later removed so that whenever there was a technical feature in the claim technical character existed. It was no longer necessary to compare the closest prior art to determine the exclusion from patentability.

At the beginning of the first decade of the new millennium/twenty-first century plenty of business method-related patent applications indicated no technical features in the claim other than a business method, some not even in the description. Others included only generic or notorious technical features of computing (e.g. the computer; generic elements of the 'von Neumann' computer: processor, memory, input/output unit; Internet; computer-implemented ...) in combination with a business method in

31. EPO, *Search in the board of appeal decisions database* https://www.epo.org/law-practice/case-law-appeals/advanced-search.html (accessed 13 March 2017).

the claims and in the description. It therefore became clear that no search could be done. Different publications on CII and on business methods are indicated in Table 4.2.

Table 4.2 Publications in the Official Journal of the EPO Concerning Business Methods

Official Journal	*Content*
OJ 10/2001, 482[32]	PCT, EPC, conditions for 'no search'
OJ 1/2002, 52[33]	Limitation of the EPO's competence as a PCT authority for biotechnology and business methods
OJ 3/2002, 175[34]	Practical recommendations on the limitation of competence for business methods
OJ 11/2007, 592[35]	Business methods under PCT and EPC
OJ 11/2007, 594[36]	Examination of computer-implemented inventions at the European Patent Office with particular attention to computer-implemented business methods
OJ 11/2014, A117[37,38]	No more limitations on PCT work

In 2001, the EPO declared that 'pursuant to Rule 39.1(iii) PCT it will not carry out an international search on an application to the extent that its subject-matter relates to no more than a method of doing business, in the absence of any apparent technical effect'.

For European applications the following was state:

> The EPO also wishes to remind applicants that methods of doing business per se are excluded from patentability pursuant to Article 52(2)(c) and (3) EPC. Claims to such methods and their commonplace technological implementation in European patent applications will not be searched because it would not serve any useful purpose to do so. In such cases no search report will be established.

In 2002, the EPO published its limitation of competence as PCT authority for international searches and international preliminary examinations in fields of business methods and biotechnology for any international application filed by a national or

32. EPO OJ, 10/2001 http://archive.epo.org/epo/pubs/oj001/10_01/10_4821.pdf (accessed 13 March 2017).
33. EPO OJ 1/2002 http://archive.epo.org/epo/pubs/oj002/01_02/01_0522.pdf (accessed 13 March 2017).
34. EPO OJ 3/2002 http://archive.epo.org/epo/pubs/oj002/03_02/03_1752.pdf (accessed 13 March 2017).
35. EPO OJ 11/2007 http://archive.epo.org/epo/pubs/oj007/11_07/11_5927.pdf (accessed 13 March 2017).
36. EPO, OJ 11/2007 http://archive.epo.org/epo/pubs/oj007/11_07/11_5947.pdf (accessed 13 March 2017).
37. EPO, OJ 11/2014 http://www.epo.org/law-practice/legal-texts/official-journal/2014/11/a117/2014-a117.pdf (accessed 13 March 2017).
38. EPO, *No more limitations on PCT work* http://documents.epo.org/projects/babylon/eponet.nsf/0/fe9b7f7048bf6529c1257d7900469114/$FILE/No_more_limitations_to_PCT_work_en.pdf (accessed 13 March 2017).

resident of the United States of America with the USPTO or the IB as the receiving office. Respective applications were transmitted to the USPTO as competent ISA and IPEA.

In 2007, the EPO clarified its practice primarily in search on business methods (pure and computer-implemented) for PCT and EPC. Two practices existed and still exist. They are sometimes colloquially known as 'no search' and 'no document search'.

> **'No search'** for pure business methods
> The examiner did not do a search if the whole application was directed to a 'business method as such' and if the examiner could not find an indication to solve a technical problem. In practice, the applicant received the form of the search report but without the indication of any document.
> **'No document search'** for a business method combined with notorious (generic) computer features
> When the claim and the description comprised only generic computing features in combination with methods of doing business, a document for the notorious features was not indicated in the search report nor was it sent to the applicant. The computer was used as a normal means to automate a business method. It seemed that there was no intention to solve a technical problem by technical means. The 'No document search' was seen as a pragmatic approach to cope with the flood of incoming applications. It was based on the well-known high modularity principles of a computer (universal machine) in that, the functionality of the computer can be changed just by changing the computer program. The examiner assumed that the applicant used a normal standard computer or a standard computer network (e.g. client/server system). Otherwise, details of inventive features (hardware, software) would have been indicated by the applicant in the claims and in the description. Since the applicant apparently did not invent a new computer in terms of technological features of a computer it did not make sense to send a document on a standard computer (e.g. with the von Neumann architecture) to hundreds of applicants. Some search reports indicated an 'L' in the document category column. When the guidelines were amended in 2015, this marking was dropped.
> If the examiner is of the opinion that a meaningful search is not possible, the applicant will be informed according to Rule 63 (Incomplete search).
> It could be sometimes observed that applicants were reluctant to indicate the solution of a technical problem in the description e.g. because of the 'prosecution history estoppel'. In their view it might limit the scope of protection in later procedures. However, the applicant ran the risk that a search was not done because the examiner could not see which technical problem would be solved.
> The applicant could try to overcome the argumentation during examination. If the examiner could be convinced that within the context of a business method a technical problem was solved by technical means a respective search would be done.

From 2015 onwards, the EPO's limitation of competence was lifted due to the change of legal practice in the US. Applicants indicated more details of a technical implementation in the application. It should not be forgotten that the EPO notice dated 1 October 2007 concerning search and examination for business methods remains applicable.

Experience has shown that there are still different views on what is regarded as technical in a claim with a combination of computing features and features of a business method. Furthermore, different views also exist on what are notorious features. It is no wonder that there are different views because the field is very dynamic.

The absence of a written document for the prior art was already allowed earlier in T0932/92.[39] Inventive step argumentation could be based on common general knowledge that belongs to the 'mental furniture' of the person skilled in the art. In some cases, a search was not done due to the combination of 'notorious features' and steps of a business method. The Board did not see the necessity to carry out an additional search if the technical features were notoriously well known. Such decisions were: T0688/05 - computer controlled event ticket auctioning system; T1875/07 - predicting traffic on internet sites; T0711/08 - A procurement system which automatically calls for bids on predetermined subjects; T0506/08 – auction system, T1281/10 – BAYESIAN SCORING; T0401/10 – Restricted trading; T0972/07 – Goods collection; T0460/09 – Sensitivity approach; T0541/10 – Sensitive Information and T1755/10 – software structure.

In many other decisions the Board remitted cases back to the first instance and required an additional search since non-technical features were seen as technical, or formerly notorious features were regarded as not notorious. In decision T1242/04 (OJ 2007, 421) Provision of product-specific data/MAN the Board emphasized the role of the search in the patent granting procedure. A search fee has to be paid. The potential relevance of the search for substantive examination should not play a role. Declarations that a meaningful search is not possible should be exceptional, for example only if the whole set of claims clearly has no technical character. On the other hand the Board pointed out that the examining division can raise lack of inventive step without documented prior art 'if the claimed subject matter is already anticipated by the common general knowledge or is obvious from that knowledge in terms of its technical contribution'. The application was remitted to the first instance. An additional search was done. Finally, the application was refused for lack of inventive step (T0946/08) in 2013.

Other decisions required an additional search after a declaration that no meaningful search was possible. In many cases, this was the result of amended claims. Such decisions were T1287/04 – Internetbasierte Datenbank; T0690/06 – Financial records maintenance system; T0279/05 – Predicting availability; T1515/07 – Cost estimate; T1411/08 – Pairing providers with consumers; T2411/10 – Ortungssystem; T0698/11 –

39. EPO OJ 6/1996 http://archive.epo.org/epo/pubs/oj1996/index_e.htm (accessed 13 March 2017).

Packaging specification; T2086/09 – Lean inventory management; T0964/12 – Supply chain fulfilment coordination; T0426/09 – Alert notification.

Discussions on the level of abstraction in claim formulations with a mix of computing features and features of a business method are still ongoing today. Further guidance was given by:

[1] T 1670/07 (Shopping with Mobile Device/NOKIA) of 11.7.2013

Simplified, the application concerned shopping using a mobile device. It was refused for lack of inventive step. Claim 1 of the main request:

> A method of facilitating shopping with a mobile wireless communications device (12) to obtain a plurality of purchased goods and/or services from a group of vendors (14) located at a shopping location (16) comprising:
>
> communicating from the mobile wireless communications device with at least one server (18) a selection of two or more goods and/or services to be purchased by a user of the mobile wireless communications device on or before the user shops at the shopping location;
>
> the at least one server, in response to information stored therein regarding vendors located at the shopping location and the goods and/or services offered by the vendors and the selection of the plurality of goods and/or services to be purchased by the user, causing at least an identification of the vendors from which available ones of the two or more goods and/or services may be purchased and the available ones of the two or more goods and/or services to be transmitted to the mobile wireless communications device; and
>
> the mobile wireless communications device providing to the user an identification of the available ones of the goods and/or services to be purchased and an itinerary (120) of the user setting forth at least a choice of an order in which the user visits the identified vendors to obtain the goods and/or services to be purchased wherein the itinerary is a function of at least one profile of the user.

The BoA explained three misconceptions or 'fallacies'. Applicants very often argue that the combination of steps of a business method with technical implementation details leads directly to a technical problem. It is believed that the intrinsic technical nature of the implementation leaks back into the intrinsically non-technical nature of the problem. This is called the **'technical leakage fallacy'.** Thus, the 'selection of vendors' is not a technical effect and the mere 'interaction' with technical elements is not enough to make the whole process technical as required by the jurisprudence.

The **'broken technical chain fallacy'** following decision T 1741/08 – GUI layout/SAP can often be observed in the area of GUI. It is wrongly assumed that a technical effect might result from the user's reaction to information seen on the display. In T1670/07 the possible final technical effect brought about by the action of a user cannot be used to establish an overall technical effect because it is conditional on the mental activities of the user.

A further argument was that there are non-technical aspects which result in no need to modify a system of the prior art. The Appellant argued that the solution of the closest prior art system was to be used to order several items; it would only return information on a single vendor that could supply all the items. There might be no single vendor capable of doing this, or the vendor might be a long way away from the customer. The invention would be able to find more than one vendor which/who could fulfil the order together. Thus the invention solved the problem of reducing the number of failed attempts to fulfil an order. The skilled person was not motivated to modify the prior art system. Such an argumentation was seen as **'non-technical prejudice fallacy'** by the BoA.

Thus, decisions with a mixture of technical computing features (to a certain degree notorious) in combination with features of a business method (excluded if claimed as such) show the challenges in the area of business method-related applications. While computer hardware features are always considered to be technical, different views exist on technicality for features that represent software.

In general, legal practice with respect to pure and computer-implemented business methods continues to be based on the COMVIK approach and the body of case law which follows this approach.

[E] The COMVIK Approach: Prima Facie Determination of Technical Character

During the first ten years of the new millennium there was a change from the 'contribution approach' to a new approach, later referred to as the 'COMVIK approach' (according to T0641/00 - 26.9.2002),[40] or outside the EPO the 'any hardware approach'.[41] T0641/00 is among the most cited of all BoA decisions. Several decisions gave guidance over time with respect to patent applications with a mix of technical and non-technical features.

In the new approach the primary difference was determining technicality prima facie without comparison to the closest prior art. Furthermore, this approach is important for computer-implemented inventions having claims with a mixture of technical and non-technical features. This occurs usually when the technical computing means are used to implement an algorithm (non-technical) as a computer program.

T0641/00 is based on EP-0579655 (priority 12 April 1991). It was granted with effect from 5 March 1997. The patent was opposed.

Main request:

> 1. Method in a digital mobile telephone system of the GSM type, in which subscriber units (MS) are controlled by a subscriber identity module (SIM), **characterized in** that the subscriber identity module (SIM) is allocated at least two identities (IMSI 1, IMSI 2), information thereon being stored in a home database of the system, said at least two identities being selectively usable, wherein only one identity (IMSI 1 or IMSI 2) can be activated at a time, the user when using a subscriber unit (MS) selectively activating the desired identity in said home

40. EPO BoA, T0641/00 - 26.9.2002 - COMVIK http://www.epo.org/law-practice/case-law-appeals/pdf/t000641ep1.pdf (accessed 13 March 2017).
41. Bently, L. et al. *Intellectual Property Law* 4th ed., Oxford University Press, 2014, 467.

> database from the subscriber unit, wherein the selective activation is used for distributing the costs for service and private calls or among different users

There is one auxiliary request with a replacement of the text after 'wherein' as follows:

> when one identity (IMSI 1 or IMSI 2) is selectively activated, involving a change of identity, the previous identity is deactivated, controlled by the subscriber's home database (HLR), an incoming call being set up against the activated identity controlled by the information in the home database, the selective activation being used by the home database for distributing the costs for service and private calls or among different users.

The appeal was not allowed due to lack of inventive step.

First, the Board made a distinction between inventions within the context of the EPC and inventions which might be seen as inventions in general but not under the EPC (e.g. the non-exhaustive list of topics which is excluded if claimed as such - Article 52(2,3) EPC. Shortly after the revision of the EPC (EPC 2000) the Board followed the amendment of Article 52(1) EPC in that 'patents shall be available for inventions *in all fields of technology*'. It follows that **technical character** is an indispensable and essential (Latin: sine qua non) condition for an invention under the EPC.

In confirmation of T0026/86 (X-ray apparatus/Koch&Sterzel)[42] a claim with a **mixture of technical and non-technical features** was allowed. Claims are not immediately excluded if they comprise a non-technical feature. Even if the majority of the features of a claim are seen as non-technical, the claimed subject matter is not excluded. The restriction to inventions in all fields of technology has implications for several details in search and examination.

It also follows that comparison to the closest state of the art means *closest state of technology* (more visible in the French and German texts of the EPC). This view was later confirmed later by T0172/03 - Order management/RICOH.[43]

Examination of inventive step is based on the *problem-and-solution approach.* The following has to be borne in mind:

- The invention has to lie in a *technical field.*
- The person skilled in the art is a *person skilled in technology, not e.g. an accountant.*
- A *technical problem* has to be solved. If no technical problem can be derived from the application, then there is no invention in the sense of the EPC.
- Assessment of inventive step is only done based on features that contribute to the solution of a technical problem by providing a *technical effect.*

The Board refers to some important conditions for the problem-and-solution approach which regularly create difficulties:

42. EPO, BoA, T 0026/86 (X-ray apparatus) of 21.5.1987 http://www.epo.org/law-practice/case-law-appeals/recent/t860026ep1.html#q (accessed 13 March 2017).
43. EPO, BoA, T 0172/03 (Order management/RICOH) of 27.11.2003 http://www.epo.org/law-practice/case-law-appeals/recent/t030172eu1.html (accessed 13 March 2017).

In some cases, the description includes neither a clear technical problem nor a vague one. The description indicates only general non-technical aims. This might be done in order to avoid a possible limitation of the scope of protection in a later prosecution. However, the examiner might not recognize the attempt to solve a technical problem.

The difference is sometimes underestimated between the *general aim* to be achieved e.g. in a non-technical field (e.g. economic procedures, aesthetic attractiveness ...) and the *technical problem* (e.g. an implementation by specific computer program means) to be solved. This general aim can appear in the framework of the formulation of the technical problem but they are not the same. Finally, in the case of doubt the applicant has to show the solution to a technical problem by the technical means which lead to the wished technical effect.

It is also important that the formulated technical problem should not contain pointers to the solution or partially anticipate it.

Thus, the general mistakes are to show no technical problem, a very general one (not related to the features different from the prior art) or a general non-technical aim only.

In general legal practice the technical problem to be solved is usually the *subjective technical problem*. The final technical problem based on comparison to the closest prior art done by the examiner is the *objective technical problem*.

The concrete examination of inventive step was based on a document representing the closest prior art. It was a Global System for Mobile communication (GSM) network standard which describes a technical implementation of about 1990. A Subscriber Identity Module (SIM) card is part of a mobile station and stores subscriber-related elements. The GSM standard includes technical issues and commercial aspects of network management, among them charging the calling costs to the individual subscriber. Usually each SIM card is allocated an identity. Respective data are stored in a network home database. The differences to the GSM standard consisted in

(i) The SIM is allocated at least two identities;
(ii) Said two identities being selectively usable; and
(iii) The selective activation being used for distributing the costs for service and private calls or among different users.

The Board concluded that cost distribution (features (i) and (iii)) is not a technical function of the system. Cost distribution is a financial concept that does not require technical skills. It does not involve the solution of a technical problem. Furthermore, technical considerations that might be necessary in the technical implementation of feature (iii) derive for the person skilled in GSM technology in a straightforward way. Such considerations do not involve any technical ingenuity.

Thus, claim 1 of the main request has technical character (despite some non-technical features) but there is a lack of inventive step since all technical features are obvious from the GSM standard. The features that distinguish claim 1 from the GSM standard are considered to be non-technical. No technical problem is solved. The same is true for the auxiliary request.

The 'COMVIK' approach is sometimes called **'any hardware' approach** outside the EPO. However, a formalistic view has to be avoided. Thus, a technical character was denied for a claim directed to the simulation of nuclear core loading (T0914/02 – Nuclear core loading), for a system (not related to software) making use of some god energy (T0748/03 – Pyramids) or e.g. the creation of an object-oriented model of a vehicle (T1171/06 – objektorientierte Modellierung/BOSCH) despite the occurrence of some hardware features in the claim. Technical considerations were seen as insufficient for a method which can exclusively be carried out mentally. Technical character may be provided through the technical implementation of the method resulting in the method providing a tangible, technical effect.

On the other hand, in some areas patents are granted with software-related method claims that do not indicate any hardware feature. Very often there is a method claim (without an explicit hardware element) and an apparatus claim. It is also assumed that the whole context of the application makes it clear that the claimed subject matter relates to software that needs hardware for execution. Examples:

- EP 0751459 B1; Object-oriented coding compiler.
- EP 1522028 B1; Encoding/decoding structured elements, especially XML documents.
- EP 2840495 B1; Container-based processing (the term container here is not a hardware element but a term in software development).[44]

Outside the EPO, some have different views.[45] However, the basic approach is the same as later confirmed by the Enlarged Board of appeal with G3/08 in 2010. The separation between method and apparatus claim (T0931/95 – Pension Benefit) was not followed.

In COMVIK and in later decisions the BoAs used the term 'aspect' instead of 'feature' to indicate that both technical and non-technical aspects are meant. Sometimes this raises the question whether there is a difference in meaning between the term 'feature' and 'aspect'. Normally, features should define the claimed subject matter in a claim (Rule 43 Implementing Regulations). A systematic use with a specific meaning cannot be observed but 'aspect' is very often used for mixed claims. In T0619/02 – 22.3.2006 (Odour selection/QUEST INTERNATIONAL)[46] the Board emphasized the technical character that requires that 'the potential of a claimed method to solve a problem of a technical nature should be discernible from the aspects of the method actually claimed'. Furthermore, in headnote IV it was pointed out:

> Neither the fact that the result of a method may be usable in a technical or in an industrial activity, nor the fact that the result may be qualified as being useful,

44. Wepopedia http://www.webopedia.com/TERM/C/container.html In software development terminology, the word container is used to describe any component that can contain other components inside itself. Examples of containers include Java applets, frames and windows. (accessed 13 March 2017).
45. Waelde, C. et al. *Contemporary Intellectual Property: Law and Policy* 4th ed., 2016, 540.
46. EPO, T0619/02, 22 March 2006 BoA http://www.epo.org/law-practice/case-law-appeals/pdf/t020619ep1.pdf (accessed 13 March 2017).

practical or saleable expresses a sufficient condition to establish the technical character of the result of the method or of the method itself.

The term 'aspect' is often used in the area of CII when a non-technical task (one aspect) has to be implemented by technical computing means (technical aspect). Sometimes 'aspect' is used instead of feature and 'aspect' can also relate to specific circumstances, considerations from different perspectives.

When looking at the problem of mixed claims with technical and non-technical features (or sometimes aspects), steps of software development should be taken into account. As is known from the phases of software engineering one can start from a non-technical task (e.g. shopping) which has to be implemented by means of computer programs. One detailed example for an on-line shop is provided with the NetBeans E-commerce Tutorial.[47]

No harmonized view exists among patent professionals as to technicality of software implementation features. Concrete numbers cannot be provided here.

G0001/04 - 16.12.2005 (Diagnostic methods) is very often used for CII. It reads: 'The subject matter of a claim including technical and non-technical features may satisfy the requirements of Article 52(1) EPC if the non-technical features interact with the technical features in order to bring about a technical effect'. Reference is made to T0603/89 (OJ EPO 1992, 230, point 2.5 of the Reasons) mentioned earlier. However, T0603/89 was directed to keys of a keyboard with markings. A technical effect could not be observed. G0001/04 relates to diagnostic methods (exceptions to patentability – Article 53(b) EPC2000, former Article 52(4) EPC1973). Technical means can be used which interact with the human or animal body. It is questionable if this kind of interaction in medical diagnosis is transferable to software development. For instance in the case of an online shop non-technical steps of a business method (e.g. ordering a product) do not interact with technical features. The non-technical step (e.g. ordering, paying) is transformed into a form executable by a computer by means of a programming language. The example shows that legal statements from other areas of technology are difficult to apply to computing.

In summary, the most important outcome of the landmark decision T0641/00 is:

The 'COMVIK approach'
Step 1:
The technical character is determined without comparison to the closest prior art.
Step 2:
If a claim represents a mixture of technical and non-technical features the ones which contribute to the technical character are taken into account for the determination of inventive step.

47. Netbeans Community *The NetBeans E-commerce Tutorial – Introduction* https://netbeans.org/kb/docs/javaee/ecommerce/intro.html (accessed 13 March 2017).

[F] Debate on COMVIK, G0003/08 in 2010

The change in legal practice in the US after 2000 resulted in more appeals and led to several decisions relating mainly to computer-implemented business methods and also pure business methods. For this reason, applications about business methods were sometimes seen as identical to software patents that is not at all true.

The ones relating to business methods and published in OJ EPO were already indicated in Table 4.1. They tackled specific situations or emphasized details in the context of the problem-and-solution approach for the determination of inventive step.

T0767/99 (13.3.2002) – Processing mail/Pitney Bowes resulted in the maintenance in amended form for a patent on mail processing. The opponent had raised the objection that apparatus claim 1 was in fact a method for doing business as such and therefore excluded from patentability. The Board did not agree. The patent was remitted to the first instance with the order to maintain the patent in amended form.

T0172/03 (27.11.2003) – Order management/RICOH has a focus on the meaning of 'state of the art' that means 'state of technology' not state of the art in commerce and business methods.

T0258/03 (21.4.2004) – Auction/Hitachi underlines that a technical problem (here slow data transmission) in an auction system has to be solved by technical means and not by amendment of the auction method itself.

In 2004 the twelfth Symposium of European Patent Judges took place. The topic of computer-implemented inventions played a major role.[48] The EPO was represented by Mr S. Steinbrener, at that time Chairman of the Technical Board 3.5.01. He summarized the amended legal practice by underlining what was said about ten years before by Mr Van den Berg, namely: 'There is no legal basis for "examining for the existence of an invention" on the basis of a contribution made by the claimed subject matter to the state of the Article De facto, such an approach has more to do with examination for inventive step'. Determination of eligibility to patent law (technical character) is a first step followed by the second general step, i.e. the examination of novelty, inventive step and the other requirements. The two steps should not be mixed up. While the hurdle of the first step (technical character) seems to be low, the hurdle of the second step should not be forgotten.

T0388/04 (22.3.2006) – undeliverable mail/Pitney Bowes continued with the earlier argumentation line of COMVIK.

[1] T0154/04 (15.11.2006): Estimating Sales Activities/DUNS LICENSING ASSOCIATES

In several appeals, a referral to the Enlarged Board of Appeal was requested. According to Article 112(1)(a) EPC a referral is possible if a decision is required in order to ensure uniform application of the law or if a real important point of law (not only theoretical)

48. EPO, Special Edition of the Official Journal 2004, *12th European Patent Judges' Symposium Brussels 22 to 24 September 2004*, http://archive.epo.org/epo/pubs/oj005/05_05/05_sup.pdf (accessed 13 March 2017).

arises. During the appeal procedure of T0154/04 the appellant had submitted questions for a referral.[49] However, the request was refused. Nevertheless, the Board explained fundamental requirements on patentability under the EPC in detail. Reference was made to several other decisions as well as to national European jurisprudence. The important points are:

(A) Article 52(1) EPC sets out four requirements to be fulfilled by a patentable invention: there must be an invention, and if there is an invention, it must satisfy the requirements of novelty, inventive step, and industrial applicability.
(B) Having technical character is an implicit requisite of an 'invention' within the meaning of Article 52(1) EPC (requirement of 'technicality').
(C) Article 52(2) EPC does not exclude from patentability any subject matter or activity having technical character, even if it is related to the items listed in this provision since these items are only excluded 'as such' (Article 52(3) EPC).
(D) The four requirements invention, novelty, inventive step, and susceptibility of industrial application are essentially separate and independent criteria of patentability, which may give rise to concurrent objections. Novelty, in particular, is not a requisite of an invention within the meaning of Article 52(1) EPC, but a separate requirement of patentability.
(E) For examining patentability of an invention in respect of a claim, the claim must be construed to determine the technical features of the invention, i.e. the features which contribute to the technical character of the invention.
(F) It is legitimate to have a mix of technical and 'non-technical' features appearing in a claim, in which the non-technical features may even form a dominating part of the claimed subject matter. Novelty and inventive step, however, can be based only on technical features, which thus have to be clearly defined in the claim. Non-technical features, to the extent that they do not interact with the technical subject matter of the claim for solving a technical problem, i.e. non-technical features 'as such', do not provide a technical contribution to the prior art and are thus ignored in assessing novelty and inventive step.
(G) For the purpose of the problem-and-solution approach, the problem must be a technical problem which the skilled person in the particular technical field might be asked to solve at the relevant priority date. The technical problem may be formulated using an aim to be achieved in a non-technical field, and which is thus not part of the technical contribution provided by the invention to the prior art. This may be done in particular to define a constraint that has to be met (even if the aim stems from an a posteriori knowledge of the invention).

The basis of the decision was EP94 912 949.8 (international publication No. WO-A-94/23382 – priority 1993) entitled 'Estimating product distribution'. During the appeal procedure a main request and four auxiliary requests were submitted. Claim 1 of the main request reads:

1. A method for estimating sales activity of a product at sales outlets (U1,U2) comprising:
receiving sales data for said product from a plurality of first sales outlets (S1-S5);

49. EPO, BoA T0154/04 – Estimating sales activity / DUNS LICENSING ASSOCIATES http://www.epo.org/law-practice/case-law-appeals/pdf/t040154ex1.pdf (accessed 13 March 2017).

> providing a database (205) of sales outlets, said database including geographic data and characterizing data from said first sales outlets (S1-S5) and at least one other sales outlet (U1,U2);
> determining the distance d between said other sales outlet (U1,U2) and each of a selected plurality of said first sales outlets (S1-S5) using said geographic data;
> formulating a weighting factor for each of said selected plurality of said first sales outlets and said other sales outlet, said weighting factor being a function of said distance and said characterizing data; and
> estimating the sales of said other sales outlet (U1,U2) using said sales data for said selected first sales outlets (S1-S5) and said weighting factors.

It was decided that claim 1 of the main request is excluded from patentability since it represents a *business method as such* according to Article 52(2)c) and 52(3) EPC. Even the use of some physical parameters or geographical data could not convey technical character to the method. They did not contribute to the solution of a technical problem.

The claims of the auxiliary requests were amended by adding technical features (processor, central station). In this way, they could overcome the so-called first hurdle. The respective claim represented a mixture of technical and non-technical features that is allowed and is typical for many computer-implemented inventions. The claims fulfilled the first absolute requirement in that they had technical character. However, they did not pass the second hurdle – the three relative requirements under Article 52(1) EPC: novelty, inventive step and industrial applicability. It was pointed out that the formulation of a technical problem, as required in the framework of the problem-and-solution approach, is not easy if there is a creative concept outside any technological field. As already indicated in COMVIK the indication of the general non-technical aim (estimating sales activities) is allowed as part of the formulation of the technical problem. This contributes to better intelligibility and results in automatic cut out of non-technical topics of the assessment of inventive step. Items of the general non-technical aim cannot be taken as technical features by mistake. The claimed subject matter was compared to the closest prior art which disclosed a computerized marketing system. The new algorithm for the determination of the sales activities was seen as non-technical and could not be taken into account. The technical problem consisted in the implementation of the algorithm in a computerized marketing system. However, no inventive solution could be identified. Finally, inventive step was denied due to the use of obvious technical means for the implementation of the non-technical business method.

T0306/04 (2.3.2007) Scheduling tasks/HONEYWELL pointed out that a method of scheduling tasks (creation of timetables, planning operations ...) in an industrial process (e.g. in an industrial refinery) is excluded from patentability. Here a technical purpose was not sufficient to overcome exclusion under Article 52(2, 3) EPC). However, one has to know that scheduling, as internal functioning of a computer i.e. of an operating system is generally not excluded. The display of a schedule as dealt with in T0756/06 was seen as a mix of technical and non-technical features. No inventive step existed.

The 'Amazon-one-click' – patent and its grant in several countries created heavy international discussion. The original application with publication number EP0902381 was withdrawn in 2001. However, divisional applications had been submitted. In 2003, the European Patent with publication number EP0927945 was granted followed by an opposition (T1616/08 (11.11.2009) Gift order/AMAZON. Remittal to the first instance took place with the order to continue the prosecution. In 2013, the patent was revoked. One divisional application with publ. no. 1134680 was refused in 2011.

[2] G 0003/08 (Programs for Computers) of 12.5.2010

In 2008 the then President of the EPO, Ms Brimelow, referred a point of law to the Enlarged Board of Appeal (Article 112(1)(b) EPC).[50] This is possible if two Boards have given different decisions on a point of law of fundamental importance. Here it related to the exclusion of computer programs as such. The referral comprised four questions. Question 1 related to the alleged divergence between T1173/97 (computer program product/IBM and T0423/03 (clipboard/MICROSOFT) and the exclusion of a computer program as such in relationship to different claim formulations. The other questions related to claim formulations avoiding exclusion, effects of a computer program and the possible involvement of technical considerations during programming. About a hundred amicus curiae briefs were sent to the EPO in which large companies, associations, open source groups and private persons all expressed their views.[51]

In 2010 the referral was seen as inadmissible under Article 112(1)(b) EPC. The EBoA could not find simultaneous diverging decisions of different Boards. T0423/03 was published about seven years after T1173/97. The opinion provided valuable views on CII. It took into consideration a long list of decisions of the BoA and of international law. Without going into the details some important points will be shown:

A definition of 'technical' was not given but illustrated in that 'a computer-readable data storage medium' and 'a cup' have technical character. A cup with a picture is not excluded from patentability irrespective of the picture.

The abandonment of the so called 'contribution approach' was explained in detail. Comparison to the closest prior art was no longer necessary for the determination of exclusion under Article 52(2,3) EPC. It started with T1173/97 (computer program product/IBM) and went on with plenty of other decisions among them T0641/00- COMVIK and T0154/04 Duns.

Wrong interpretations resulted from confusion between computer program and method. The logical distinction was made between a method carried out by a computer and the sequential list of instructions that specify that method (the computer program). This difference is very important in computing. A program and a method are not synonyms.

50. EPO, Letter of the President to the Chairman of the Enlarged Board of Appeal http://documents.epo.org/projects/babylon/eponet.nsf/0/2B5ECD8AA2D95ECAC12577750042CB3C/$File/G3-08_en.pdf (accessed 13 March 2017).

51. EPO, G3/08:Procedural documents http://www.epo.org/law-practice/case-law-appeals/eba/pending/g3-08.html (accessed 13 March 2017).

For the determination of the technical character all features of a claim have to be taken into consideration. There is no requirement that *one feature* has to cause a technical effect on a physical entity in the real world. There also has to be a technical effect but it is not limited to a physical entity outside the computer in the real world.

In the answer to the last question the EBoA explained that programming includes technical considerations but it is a misconception to believe that any technical considerations are sufficient to confer technical character on claimed subject matter.

§4.07 COMPUTER-IMPLEMENTED INVENTIONS IN SYSTEM SOFTWARE AND APPLICATION SOFTWARE

Based on the general categorization of software in **system software** and in **application software** some examples of different fields will be given. A complete overview cannot be given due to the amount of decisions over the years.

Table 4.3 Decisions of the Board of Appeal 2011–2016 in Core Areas of Computing and Business Methods

Year	*G06F (IPC)*	*G06Q (IPC)*	*G06F17/60 (IPC)*
2011	83	1	11
2012	129	5	26
2013	129	11	26
2014	164	11	15
2015	150	12	12
2016	130	5	4
	785	45	94

Table 4.3 provides an impression of the number of decisions of the Technical Boards of Appeal. The numbers result from an on-line search in the EPO database on decisions of the Board of Appeal.[52] The selection was done based on the International Patent Classification (IPC). G06F is the main area of core computing related to most of the components of a computer and its internal functioning (e.g. task scheduling, parallel processing, memory allocation, storage access, input/output). G06F17/60 is the old classification for business methods and G06Q is the newer one. G06Q was introduced with IPC 2006.01.[53] It relates mainly to computer-implemented business methods (also pure business methods). Thus, older cases can be found under G06F17/60.

52. EPO *Search in the board of appeal decisions database* http://www.epo.org/law-practice/case-law-appeals/advanced-search.html (accessed 13 March 2016).
53. WIPO, International Patent Classification 2006.01 http://web2.wipo.int/classifications/ipc/ipcpub/?notion = scheme&version = 20060101&symbol = none&menulang = en&lang = en&view mode = f&fipcpc = no&showdeleted = yes&indexes = no&headings = yes&notes = yes&direction = o2n&initial = A&cwid = none&tree = no (accessed 13 March 2016).

A minor number of decisions might relate to hardware only. The majority are directed to computer-implemented inventions. Consequently, there is at least one feature in the claim that is implemented by means of a computer program.

The decisions include opposition cases and appeals on refusals at first instance.

It is important to notice that decisions on patent applications/patents directed to the use of a computer for a specific purpose are classified in the respective areas of the IPC outside of G06F. This is true for areas of telecommunication, computer graphics and image processing. Decisions on devices, systems, methods including computers (and the respective software) like cars, toys, industrial applications, agriculture ...) are classified in the respective area of the IPC. Different Technical Boards of Appeal deal with such cases.

All EPO decisions can be found free of charge on the website of the European Patent Office on the webpage 'Search in the board of appeal decisions database'.[54]

Patent applications in the area of CII can be seen from different perspectives. One and the same patent application might relate to a combination of features excluded if claimed as such. They can relate to different software application fields (business, rules of games, medical topics, aesthetic features, mental acts ...). Therefore, it is of utmost importance to indicate the technical problem to be solved by technical means.

The explanations of the cases focus on technicality discussions. Other topics like added subject matter, clarity, etc. which may occur in the case are normally not indicated to reduce complexity.

[A] System Software: Internal Function of the Computer: General

System software deals with the internal work of a computer/processor. Programming tools, test software, networks, etc. belong to this area.

Patents are granted for the functioning of processors, multi-core processors, operating systems, memory access, interrupt processing, communication between software parts at different physical/logical locations, virtualization, multithreading, fault-tolerance, saving energy, security arrangements .... A huge number of patents have been granted since the amendment of the Guidelines in 1985 that indicated that the technical effect can result from the internal work of the computer (e.g. the virtual extension of a memory). Unlike other fields of technology, oppositions are hardly ever filed.

Decisions of the Boards rarely relate to a mixture of technical and non-technical features. The claimed subject matter is usually technical. Appeals are based on the usual objections like clarity, inventive step, etc. A stricter view can be observed in the area of modelling as a prerequisite for programming. Difficulties arise if the claimed subject matter comprises features which if seen as such (Article 52(2, 3) EPC) are non-technical. This is in particular true for interactive graphical user interfaces.

54. EPO, *Search in the board of appeal decisions database* http://www.epo.org/law-practice/case-law-appeals/advanced-search.html (accessed 13 March 2016).

Proximity to scientific theories (e.g. for programming paradigms, programming languages, theories on databases) can result in different views on technicality.

[1] T 0424/03 (Clipboard Formats I/MICROSOFT) of 23.2006

The original application with publication number EP 0717354 dealt with a broader range of clipboard formats. The claimed subject matter primarily allows improved data transfer by a conventional clipboard, by drag-and-drop mechanisms and by OLE (object linking and embedding) data transfer mechanisms. Six divisional applications were filed. Five of the divisional applications have proceeded to the appeal stage before the Board (T0411/03, T0425/03, T0467/03, T0468/03, T0469/03). The Board processed the parent and the five divisional applications in parallel to ensure that the appeal cases were dealt with synoptically.

The Examining Division refused the application for lack of inventive step:

> 1. A method in a computer system (10) having a clipboard for performing data transfer of data in a clipboard format, said method comprising the steps of: providing several clipboard formats including a text clipboard format, a file contents clipboard format and a file group descriptor clipboard format, selecting data that is not a file for a data transfer operation,
>
> > using the file contents clipboard format to hold said data by converting said selected data into converted data of said file contents clipboard format and storing the converted data as a data object, using the file group descriptor clipboard format to hold a file descriptor holding descriptive information about the data that is to be encapsulated into a file during the data transfer operation,
> > completing the data transfer by providing a handle to said data object,
> > using said handle to paste said data of said data object to a data sink,
> > using said descriptive information to enable the computer system to create a file at the data sink and
> > encapsulating the data object into said file.

The application had an independent method claim 1, dependent method claims 2 to 4 and a computer-program product claim 5. Claim 5 was directed to a computer-readable medium having computer-executable instructions adapted to cause the computer system to perform the method of one of claims 1 to 4.

The claimed subject matter was seen as eligible to patent law. A computer system including a memory (clipboard) is a technical means. The method steps solve a technical problem by technical means in that functional data structures (clipboard formats) are used independently of any cognitive content (*see* T 1194/97 - Data structure product/Philips;...) in order to enhance the internal operation of a computer system with a view to facilitating the exchange of data among various application programs.

Independent claim 5 has a technical character since the computer-readable medium is a technical product (cf. T0258/03 - Auction/Hitachi). The computer-executable instructions have the potential to achieve a further technical effect, i.e. the internal operation of the computer is enhanced (cf. T1173/97 - computer program product/IBM).

Furthermore, the Board distinguished the category 'method' from the category 'computer program' that was allowed with T1173/97 (computer program product/IBM). The Board also explained the difference between 'method' with steps and a 'computer program' as a sequence of computer-executable instructions. A method, in particular, a method of operating a computer, may be put into practice with the help of a computer program. Method and computer program are not the same!

Windows 3.1 was seen to represent the closest prior art. The method of claim 1 solves the problem of how to facilitate a data exchange across different data formats, in particular when transferring non-file data. Finally, the claimed subject matter was considered to be inventive. The application was remitted with the order to grant a patent.

The granted patent was opposed and revoked. An appeal was submitted against the revocation.

In 2016 all the patents were revoked for lack of inventive step:

- Parent: T 1789/11.
- Divisional 1: T 1800/11.
- Divisional 2: T 1799/11.
- Divisional 3: T 1797/11.
- Divisional 4: T 1798/11.
- Divisional 5: T 1796/11.

[2] T 2048/07 (Dynamic Data Type Enrichment/SAP) of 24.11.2011

The application was directed to an application program with basic data types which receive metadata during the runtime of the application program in order to increase program robustness. Original claim 1 of EP1403764 (A1):

> 1. A method (400) for dynamic data type enrichment comprising the steps: using (410) at least one basic data type (110) in a predefined application program(210); and adding (420) metadata (150) to the at least one basic data type (110) at runtime when the application program (210) is executed.

The Examining Division refused the application for lack of inventive step. During the appeal procedure, amended claims were submitted. The feature 'computer implemented' was added to claim 1 together with further limiting features. Based on general aspects of programming the Board came to the result that no 'further technical effect' could be found. The Board argued that the program 'contains only features that are necessary to ensure its proper functioning, independent of any technical context in which it should be used. As a consequence, the program lacks a "further technical effect", ...'. With reference to G3/08 (13.5) 'The way in which a formal specification is implemented in a computer program is part of the art of computer programming, which by virtue of Article 52(2) c) and (3) EPC cannot of itself be adduced as an indication of "technical" activity ...'. Finally, the Board argued that 'reading in data is part of the fundamental definition of computing ... reading in data does not go beyond the normal technical effects that would be caused by any program within the computer system on which it runs, i.e. that reading data is not a further technical effect in itself.' Due to the lack of a further technical effect, no technical problem was solved. The appeal was dismissed due to lack of inventive step.

[3] T 1122/08 (Event Structures/COMPUTER ASSOCIATES) 11.9.2012

The application was directed to an event management system for a highly distributed computing system. An event can result e.g. from discrete events, conditions, alarms. Individual events in this context are represented as instances of a predefined data type – referred to as 'event structures' – with multiple fields. During the examination procedure, the applicant had amended the claims by adding features from the description to the claim. No additional search was done. The amended subject matter was seen as obvious for the skilled person. During the appeal procedure, the Board did not agree with the Examining Division's argumentation. However, it raised some clarity objections by observing contradictions between independent claims. The Board remitted the application to the department of first instance for further prosecution, i.e. to deal with the clarity objections and to do an additional search.

[4] T 0318/10 (Load Distribution/CLUB IT) of 2.9.2014

The application was directed to load balancing in a client/server system. A load distribution software for executing the load balancing could be installed on any server in the network. The Examining Division refused the application based on the view that the 'remaining differences refer only to non-technical mathematical formulation of the optimization function'. The Board did not follow this view. The difference between an abstract mathematical method as such and the one used in a concrete technical context was explained. Here a mathematical method (… the optimization function) is used in a technical process (… assigning a server from among a plurality of servers to process a client request), that process is carried out on a physical entity by some technical means implementing the method and provides as its result a certain change in that entity. The optimizations function as defined by claim 1 results in a change in the resource consumption of the server system which is a technical effect. The application was remitted to the department of first instance with the order to grant a patent.

[5] T 0780/11 (Rechenleistungszuteilung/FUJITSU) of 6.8.2015

The title is 'Computer system and method for partitioning and allocating computing power within a computer system'. The computing power is allocated to virtual computing units. Several units could be in a group. A customer may buy certain computing power. Claim 1 only indicates a computer indirectly. Thus, it could be assumed that the method is done by paper and pencil. Assuming that a computer is used the question has to be raised whether the method is just an automation of an existing (manual) method. The allocation of computing power is done based on commercial not on technical purposes. The Board considered that claim 1 of the main request and of the auxiliary request were not inventive. A detailed comparison to a written prior art document was not done. The subject matter of auxiliary requests three and four was not clear. The fifth request was not allowed.

The case underlines the importance of technical implementation details in order to distinguish a method possible with paper and pencil from a computerized one.

[6] T 1512/10 (Digital DNA/LOGIN PEOPLE) of 29.10.2015

The application was directed to a process for securing access to the resources of an Information Handling System (IHS). Before access was made information on the system components (hardware, operating system ...), they were collected and stored with a signature protection. The Board considered *common general knowledge* (Microsoft Windows XP) as the closest prior art instead of a document which indicated the assignment of a trust level to the computer only at boot time by using specific hardware. Windows XP checks a change of hardware components during login only. The distinguishing features solve two problems:

- The validation of the system components (called ‘digital DNA’) before any transaction solves the problem of replacing or adding licence validation by the introduction of access control to a remote server.
- The second problem is the simplification in detecting hardware changes. This is solved by using Application Programming Interface (API) calls for accessing detailed information on hardware components (e.g. manufacturer).

The case was remitted with the order to grant a patent.

Due to the high complexity and growing modularity of software components all kinds of interfaces play an important role in the communication between different computer components. Internal interfaces are such as API which plays a role in the communication between application programs and the operating system. Synchronization of databases was dealt with in T1263/08 (Synchronizing databases I/FUSION ONE), T1266/08 (Synchronizing databases II/FUSION ONE) and (Synchronizing databases III/FUSION ONE) – all decisions made on 28.10.2016. APIs played a role in the evaluation of inventive step. T1894/08 (19.12.20012 – Operating system abstraction/Interdigital) was directed to an application with the title ‘Wireless device operating system (OS) Application Programmer’s Interface API’. The application was refused for lack of clarity of both requests. Sufficiency of disclosure and lack of novelty of the main request lead to the inadmissibility of the appeal. Lack of clarity resulted from the use of terms like ‘software model’, ‘operating environment’ and also ‘porting’ which are often used but have no well-defined technical meaning. The description did not define the meaning of the vague terms in the claimed generality. Different interfaces (API, GUI) played a role in T0651/11 (16.3.2015 – Control pattern/MICROSOFT) which was directed to the provision of information on functionality of user interface element to an application program, e.g. graphical elements of a GUI are provided to an application program. Such a program can transform e.g.

graphical elements of a GUI into sound information resulting in visually impaired people being able to receive this information. The appeal was dismissed due to lack of inventive step.

The following chapter presents a selection of cases primarily on GUI.

[B] System Software: Human Computer Interfaces, in particular Graphical User Interfaces

HCI is a field with different legal practices, in particular in the area of graphical user interfaces. Here, a distinction can be made between a specific presentation of information (the user will not interact directly) and a user interface with immediate interaction (language, gesture, visual…). In the field of GUI the patent claims often only show some visual elements of the screen together with features of how the user will interact with the interface (press a button e.g. mouse, keyboard, gesture, …). The claim does not often include features that show how the features on the screen are created technically (by internal computer programs). Consequently, claims very often represent a mixture of technical and non-technical features. The contribution of non-technical features to the technical character is difficult to determine. Computer-related graphical user interface technology is more and more used in other fields (navigation system, industrial machines, robots, medical devices…) some examining divisions or Boards come to different conclusions with respect to technicality. Furthermore, the formulation of the objective technical problem is a challenge. Specific aims are the 'improvement of usability' or of 'user satisfaction' or increase of 'attractiveness' (e.g. for computer games). The user will be better able to recognize forms, colours, static and dynamic features, dangerous situations …. Whilst these are all legitimate aims, the applicant must ultimately show which technical problem has to be solved to achieve a higher usability.

Over the years, the Boards have developed a practice in which a distinction is made between *technical* and *cognitive features*. In many cases, the claimed subject matter has technical character but fails to fulfil the requirements as to inventive step. The claimed subject- matter is nearly always a mix of technical and non-technical features. Features that can be seen as non-technical relate not only to aesthetic features but also to features relating to business, rules of games, mathematical methods … Hence, claim formulation by the applicant and search and examination at the patent office requires careful balancing of the different aspects. Due to the huge amount of decisions, only a few examples can be given here.

In T1194/97 – (Data structure product/PHILIPS) a distinction was made between data which encode a cognitive content (e.g. image data representing a landscape, …) and technical data which allow the technical functioning when data is recorded and/or displayed. Such functional data (data on picture lines, synchronization …) cannot result in exclusion of the subject matter as presentation of information as such.

In T0643/00 – (Searching image data/CANON) a liberal approach was taken in that the arrangement of menu items on a screen was seen as technical consideration and the task to enable a user to search image data more efficiently was seen as technical task. The involvement of a mental step (selection of images), which per se does not fall within the meaning of 'invention' (Article 52(1) EPC), did not qualify the whole subject matter as non-technical. The following passage of method claim 6 comprises the step performed by the user 'selecting an image from said displayed image data'. In the view of many patent professionals this step could have been reformulated to indicate the method steps performed by the technical system which receives data from the outside world. For example: 'receiving an image selection data from input means':

> 6. A method of searching for an image, the method comprising: inputting image data into an image processing apparatus; storing in storage means hierarchically encoded image data derived from the input image data in an order of registration; decoding encoded image data stored in said storage means; and storing the decoded image data in a video frame memory
>
> > ...
> > displaying said second image data;
> > ***selecting an image from said displayed second image data***;
> > clearing said video frame memory in response to a command to display the selected image

While this 'selecting' step was allowed, it must be noted that a claim formulation differs from a description of how to use a system in a user manual. The steps indicated in the claim should not be formulated as follows: 'The user clicks on button A, a list appears and the user selects one option; as a result window X pops up ...'. It is important that, the technical system has to be described.

T0125/04 – (Assessment system/COMPARATIVE VISUAL ASSESSMENTS) of 10.5.2005 the Board concluded that the task of designing diagrams is non-technical. This is so, even if the diagrams arguably convey information in a way that a viewer may intuitively regard as particularly appealing, lucid or logical.

In **T0049/04** – (Text Processor/WALKER) of 18.10.2005 the Board came to the conclusion that improving text on a display to allow better readability and thus enabling the user to work more efficiently, relates to how cognitive content is conveyed to the reader. The physical arrangement of the text on the display was seen as a contribution to a technical solution to a technical problem. Other Boards did not follow this view with respect to the technical problem.

In T 1357/10 (Selecting a font/MICROSOFT LICENSING) 16.3.2016 a technical problem was solved with a method for selecting a font. The operating system comprises a glyph generation module which selects a suitable font for a printer or a display based on language information (e.g. from keyboard), code (Unicode value) of a glyph (concrete graphical representation of a character) and the content of a mark-up language document. The technical problem to be solved consisted in providing improved font selection to programs in a computer.

The user interface and in particular the graphical user interface plays an important role in all kinds of **computer games**. Scenarios of all kinds of games known from the real world can now be shown on a screen. Additionally, depending on the level of technology (processing speed, properties of a display, input means, network options ...) artificial worlds can be created which allow games not possible in the real world. Instead of creating a stack of real wooden blocks without holes this can be done on the computer (e.g. Tetris). The real world wooden blocks become digital information. Additional former mental, business or organizational steps (rewards, prices for winner, game community, difficulty level, …) can be added, implemented in the game software.

Decision **T 0928/03** (Video game/KONAMI) of 2.6.2006 was about the display of an interactive computer game (football). The rules of the football game were seen as non-technical. They do not contribute to the technical character.

In the prior art a player was marked by a triangle above his head. This was replaced by a ring-shaped guide mark G1, G2 around the foot of the respective player. Thus, the mark was not so easily concealed by nearby players. It allowed a continued user-machine interaction and thus contributed to the technical character. However, the shape of a ring was seen as an aesthetical feature.

A pass guide mark was seen as a feature contributing to inventive step. Due to the small size of the screen the user could not easily see all players and in particular not the one to whom his player could pass the ball. Therefore, a pass guide mark G3 was located near the foot of the teammate. This technical contribution had to be considered for inventive step.

If the player himself was no longer visible parts of the pass guide mark were positioned at the edge of the screen.

Figure 4.2 Computer Game: Football – EP0844580

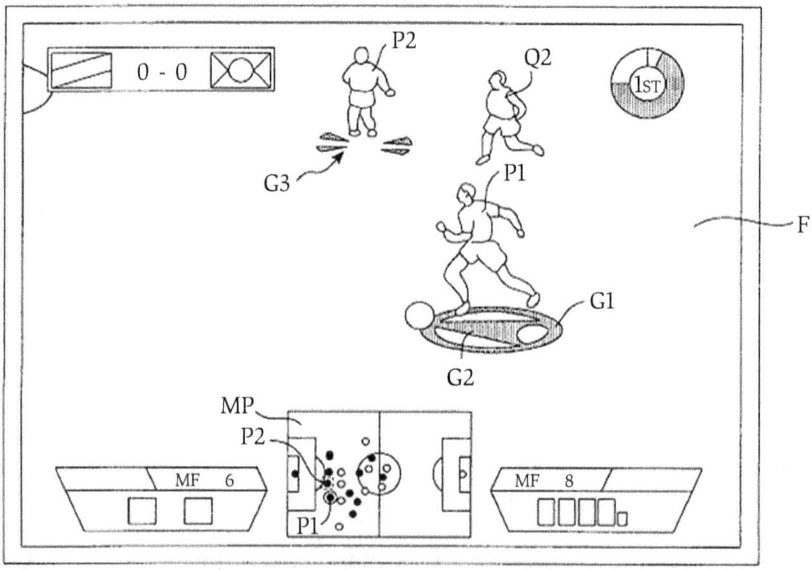

Figure 4.2 (Figure 7 of EP0844580) shows a screenshot with players P1 and P2 of one team and Q2 of the other team. The more visible marks G1 and G2 and pass guide mark G3 are shown. The description indicates flowcharts as a basis for parts of the computer program. The Board underlined the importance of determining inventive

step according to the COMVIK approach. This allows features that may not be seen as technical at first glance to be considered. In the end, a patent was granted.

A similar case was T 1793/07 (guide display/KONAMI) of 2.7.2008. The video game device comprised: a character processing unit for displaying an area mark belonging to one of the main characters and the enemy character and having a specified size, a judging unit for judging whether the other character has continued to be inside the area mark for a predetermined time, and a game result output unit for obtaining the result of the competition when the other character continued to be inside the area mark for the predetermined time. Readability of the display and thereby improved operability of the video game device which enhanced a continued man-machine interaction was seen as a clear technical objective. It was also argued that with reference to T 717/05 (IBM) and T 115/85 (IBM) of 5.9.1988 'the area mark colour change informs the user of an internal state of the machine which again is a technical feature solving a technical problem'.

Unfortunately, here the Board considered colour change caused by specific game rules as indication of a computer's internal state. In EP0052757 (B1) which is the basis for T115/85 the computer is programmed to indicate a text which informs the user on specific deficiencies of basic computer components. At that time the user had to close a diskette door manually. This was often forgotten and the computer could not read the data. Therefore, the system recognized the open door, a message build program was called which finally, with the support of an index table, allowed access to prestored words like 'Close Diskette Door'. Such words were displayed to the user. In contrast to EP1052000 underlying T1793/97, the independent method claim of EP0052757 (B1) (T115/85) indicates in detail the interaction between hardware (memory, ...) and software means (message build program, pointer, index table, ...).

Further decisions relating to cognitive content in the context of games are:

T 1023/06 (game process/IGT) of 7.12.2006 a method of operating a video poker game which displays poker hands with playing cards. A higher reading quality was seen as contributing to the technical character. However, the solution was not inventive. T 0336/07 (multiplay poker/IGT) of 11.10.2007 also relates to a poker game. The Board emphasized the question as to how the per se excluded subject matter (e.g. a game or business method) is implemented. Furthermore, the Board differentiated between the rules of the game and the method and means for playing it:

> A set of game rules defines a regulatory framework agreed between players and concerning conduct, conventions and conditions that are meaningful only in a gaming context. It is perceived as such by the involved players and as serving the explicit purpose of playing a game. As such an agreed framework is a purely abstract, mental construct, but the method and means for carrying out game play in accordance with such a set of rules may well be technical in nature.

The person skilled in the art is a gaming software engineer who is given the gaming rules and who implements them on the game machine. The implementation of the game by electronic means allows the display of 'shared hands' and makes the game 'easier' for the player compared to the traditional playing of poker with 'shared hands'.

Here the Board concluded that no inventive step existed since the improved readability was achieved by a 'straightforward visual format'.

Different evaluations as to graphical marks can be seen in decisions T1121/02 (24.11.2003) Electric Fencing element and T1749/06. T1121/02 does not relate to computing but to an electric fence. Claim 1:

> An elongate electric fencing element (T) characterised in that said fencing element has along its surface contrasting markings (D,L) which are a deterrent to an animal, said contrasting markings being such as to resemble the warning patterning of another animal and being selected from the group consisting of:
>
> (i) a repetitive linear array of transverse stripes;
> (ii) a repetitive linear array of diagonal markings; and
> (iii) regular or irregular shapes on a contrasting background.

The Board decided that the markings represent non-technical features which cannot be taken into consideration for inventive step. The contrasting markings are seen as presentation of information. There is no technical effect. Animals simply work out that they should avoid fences with such markings.

In T1749/06 (24.2.2010) 3Dicon/NOKIA the application is directed to the creation of 3D-icons (Figure 4.3) on a low resolution screen for example a mobile phone. Small prefabricated digital images (e.g. in bitmap format) are stored in a memory. The Board argued that a test like 'happens in the brain of the viewer' is not valid as many inventions like the cinematograph are based on human perception. That is the projection of a rapid succession of still images on a screen which creates the illusion of fluent motion.

Original claim 1:

> 1. A computer-readable medium encoded with a data structure for use in providing a graphical icon for display on a display of a portable communications device, characterized in that said data structure is encoded as digital data indicative of said graphical icon defined by alternating light and dark stripes, that selected stripes of said light and dark stripes change from light to dark and back to light to indicate a shadow adjacent an edge of said icon and from dark to light and back to dark to indicate a highlight adjacent another edge of said icon, and that altogether said light and dark stripes with shadows and highlights provide said icon with a three-dimensional appearance.

Figure 4.3 Icons with a Three-Dimensional Effect: EP1209651

Figure 4.4 The Flowchart of a Possible Computer Program Producing the Display of an Icon: EP1209651

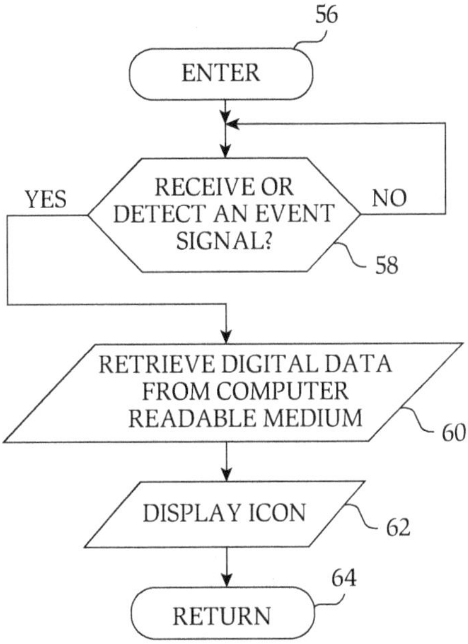

The decision is an example of the attempt to patent a certain appearance on the display contrary to the means for generating it. As can be seen in the flow diagram of Figure 4.4 (Figure 4 of EP 1209651) the image of the icon is simply loaded from a memory when an event is detected. Former patent applications on cinematographic equipment were intended to patent the technical means for creating the illusion not the illusion itself. An icon is just a little digital image. The creation of icons for Personal Computers and later for smart phones can be achieved by using painting programs or special icon-creating programs.[55]

[1] T 1741/08 (GUI Layout/SAP) of 2.8.2012

The Board took a stricter view and decided that' lowering the cognitive burden of the user' is not in itself a technical effect. T 01143/06 was followed but not T 0049/04. In the Board's view the layout of the menu on the screen was achieved by conventional software means. No inventive step could be seen.

Claim 1 of the main request:

(1) A method of entering of data in a data processing system comprising:

55. King, J.R. *Geeks On Call Windows® XP Five Minute Fixes* John Wiley & Sons 2006.

(a) displaying a first horizontally aligned linear sequence (402; 702) of top-level icons (i);
(b) displaying a second horizontally aligned linear sequence (420; 902; 1320) of second-level icons for a selected one of the top-level icons, the position of the leading icon of the second linear sequence being vertically aligned with the selected one of the top-level icons of the first linear sequence;
(c) displaying at least one data entry field (422; 922; 1022; 1122; 1322; 1422; 1522) for a selected one of the second-level icons for entering the data, wherein the at least one data entry field (422; 922; 1022; 1122; 1322; 1422; 1522) is displayed spatially separated from the first and second linear sequence while the first and second linear sequence is displayed;
(d) entering the data into the at least one data entry field;
(e) going back to step (c) for a consecutive one of the second-level icons until all data entry steps of the second linear sequence have been completed;
(f) going back to step (b) for a consecutive one of the top-level icons.

[2] T 0307/09 (API-Based Operator Interface for Automotive in-Dash Accessory/Microsoft) of 6.2.2014

The case illustrates the difficulties evaluating basic computing topics applied to fields outside of core computing (interdisciplinary character). The original International Patent Application had a US-priority dated 1998. The application with the publication number EP1044118 is entitled 'Graphical interface components for in-dash automotive accessories'. It was classified in B60R 16/02 but not in an area of general graphical user interfaces. The International Search was done in B60R and G09B but apparently not in general fields of graphical user interfaces. Claim 1 of the granted patent EP1044118 (B1-9.11.2005:

> 1. A computer-readable storage medium (91,92) having instructions for implementing an operator interface in an automotive accessory, the instructions being executable to perform steps comprising:
> scrolling a plurality of application icons (102) in response to user scroll commands, wherein the application icons (102) correspond to different applications in the automotive accessory;
> focusing on any application icon that is scrolled to a fixed focus position;
> activating the application corresponding to the focused application icon (104) in response to a user selection command.

The patent was opposed and revoked by the Opposition Division. An appeal was filed by the Patent Proprietor. During the appeal procedure amended claims with further limiting features were submitted. The original application mentioned the use of graphical interfaces for desktop computers. However, no prior art which might have indicated the start of applications by clicking on respective application icons (e.g. NEXTSTEP user environment) was taken into account.

[3] T 1834/10 (Image Selection/EBAY) of 25.2.2015

The application concerned the automatic selection of images to be included in a webpage (e.g. of an online shop). It allows a flexible adaption to new conditions. The Board considered the web designer's task to allow selection of attractive images and reducing the cognitive burden as a non-technical aim. The technical implementation of the image selection was taken into account to determine inventive step. The claims of all requests represented a mix of technical and non-technical features. The few general technical features of the claim such as 'instruction identifying a utility program that dynamically selects an image for insertion into the document' were well known from the prior art. Finally, lack of inventive step was determined.

[4] T0366/14 (Presentation of Operating Instructions/GAMBRO) of 2.9.2015

Patent EP1668556 (B1) was granted with the title 'A user interface for an extracorporeal blood treatment'. The user interface was a touch screen. An opposition was filed resulting in maintenance of the patent in amended form. An appeal was filed. Based on the discussion of many former decisions the Board concluded a stricter approach with a higher focus on

Claim 1 of the main request:

> A user interface for an extracorporeal blood treatment machine, which user interface comprises at least one touch screen, at least one memory containing at least two images, and at least a controller programmed for displaying on a screen (16) of the touch screen at least one display; at least two distinct areas (161) and (162) being included in the at least one display, a first area (161) of the two distinct areas exhibiting at least two touch keys (17), wherein the controller is further programmed for:
>
> - detecting activation of the at least two touch keys (17);
> - displaying in a second area (162) of the at least two areas of the at least one display, a first of the at least two images, when a first of the at least two touch keys is activated;
> - displaying in the second area (162) of the at least two areas of the at least one display, a second of the at least two images, when a second of the at least two touch keys is activated;
>
> characterized in that:
>
> - the memory comprises a plurality of data relating to the machine and the controller is programmed to display the data on the first area (161) of the at least one display, each item of the data being displayed in a visually associated position to a touch key of the at least two touch keys (17);
> - the plurality of data comprises operating instructions for readying the machine for use;
> - the at least two images are pictographs which represent configurations of the machine correlated to the operating instructions.

The claim represents a mix of technical and non-technical features. Operating instructions and pictograms are seen as cognitive data and not functional data. In the

Board's view they directly address the user of the blood treatment machine and are consequently meaningful only to a human mind. The use of an electronic screen for conveying information on how to operate a device does not make the claimed subject matter more technical than a paper manual. The information on the screen is not related to an internal system state. Such effects like better comprehensibility of steps or minimizing errors in using the device were not seen as technical effects by the Board. The information on the screen addressed the human mental process of an average user of the machine. No technical effect was caused. The patent was revoked due to lack of inventive step.

The Board came to the conclusion:

> In the assessment of inventive step of a claim which comprises technical and non-technical features ('mixed invention') and in which the non-technical features relate to cognitive content presented to the user of a graphical user interface (GUI), i.e. relate to 'what' is presented rather than 'how' something is presented, it has to be analysed whether the GUI together with the content presented credibly assists the user in performing a technical task (related to 'why' that content is presented) by means of a continued and/or guided human-machine interaction process.

In summary, it can be seen that the field of HCI remains a controversial field. There is a tendency for GUI to claim what is visible on the screen and how this look changes according to events (caused by the user or caused by conditions of the program) of the respective application area (game, business, medical ...). Main arguments are often better conditions for the user (readability, recognizing dangerous situations, minimize errors, high ease of use due to less input steps, ...). Furthermore, it is argued that the ease of use for the user results in general technical effects like higher machine speed, processing power or use of less memory. However, many decisions do not consider such general technical effects to *directly* result from a technical feature. If the user does not act as supposed, the technical effect will not result. How something is programmed or implemented plays a minor role. The technical features of implementation very often remain at a high level of abstraction (processor, display, memory, user input means). The claimed subject matter is often defined with broad functional terms like 'software code module', 'drawing module' (e.g. T0983/10 – Customizable ornamental appearance/APPLE). Thus, there is a high risk that generic technical features are well known for the skilled person.

[C] System Software: Databases/Information Retrieval

This field is very often a grey zone of patentability since it is close to scientific theories such as database structures, non-technical linguistic principles, and mathematical methods. The use of databases can be related to non-technical application areas like business data. GUI can be a neighbouring field if the subject matter concerns the presentation of information retrieved. An attractive or more convenient display of data on the screen is usually non-technical (e.g. T1214/09 image data).

In T1755/13 a method of maintaining a history of queries and results was seen as technical but finally as not inventive. In T2348/09 the Board considered the claim determining a characteristic function of a matrix using a predetermined scheme as obvious. The matrix is an arrangement of data records. Such a method could be used e.g. in the financial area for the determination of risks. The Board considered the subject matter as a mix of technical computer features and non-technical mathematical data. No limitation to a technical purpose was given. The description indicated the use of the method for non-technical business data only.

In T0328/09 the Board evaluated the storing of unmodified and modified portions of text-data and the use of attributes to retrieve the unmodified and the modified portions as being directed to the solution of a non-technical problem. The technical problem did not go beyond setting up a database for text-data and its subsequent revisions. The text-data considered in the application was directed texts of legislation and its permanent revisions. Thus, the claimed subject matter was directed to particular requirements of the end user who may wish to retrieve a particular version of just a portion of text.

[1] T 0598/14 (Enhanced Retrieval/BRITISH TELECOMMUNICATIONS) 6.11.2014

The application was directed to an information retrieval apparatus for enhanced retrieval of documents based on semantic similarity of search terms. In particular, it was a method for generating, from an input set of documents, a word replaceability matrix defining semantic similarity between words occurring in the input document set. The word replaceability matrix could be used for determining document similarity and to enhance search queries for retrieval of information from the document set. It was refused for lack of inventive step:

> An information retrieval apparatus for use in retrieving information from a set of one or more documents, comprising:
> an input for receiving a search query;
> generating means for generating a set of probabilities indicative of the semantic similarity of words selected from said set of one or more documents;
> query enhancement means for modifying a received search query with reference, in use, to said generated set of probabilities; and
> information retrieval means for searching said set of one or more documents for relevant information using a received search query modified by said query enhancement means,
> wherein said generating means are arranged, in use:
>
> (i) for each word selected from said set of one or more documents:
>   (a) to identify, in documents of said set of one or more documents, word sequences comprising the word and a predetermined number of other words;
>   (b) to calculate a relative frequency of occurrence for each distinct word sequence among word sequences containing the word; and
>   (c) to generate a fuzzy set comprising, for groups of word sequences containing the word, corresponding fuzzy membership values calculated from the relative frequencies determined at step (b); and
>
> (ii) to calculate, for each pair of words of said plurality of words, using respective fuzzy sets generated at step (i), a probability that the first word of

> the pair is semantically suitable as a replacement for the second word of the pair.

Based on a prior art document on information retrieval the Board concluded that the distinguishing features relate to some linguistic specifics on semantic similarity of text. Such non-technical aspects cannot be taken into consideration for inventive step. The applicant argued that these specifics are not purely linguistic because they are transformed into a mathematical model that allows automation by means of computing. The Board agreed that there could be some implicit general technical considerations. However, they were considered to be not sufficient to provide technical character. Finally, claim 1 lacked inventive step (Article 56 EPC).

[2] T 1724/10 (Document Indexing/DASSAULT) of 27.1.2015

The patent was opposed and then revocated by the Opposition Division. The patent proprietor appealed the decision. Claim 1 of the patent:

> 1.A computer-implemented process for searching among a collection of Internet or HTML documents (30, 32, 34, 36, 38, 40, 42), the collection comprising referencing documents and referenced documents referenced in the referencing documents by use of links such as Universal Resource Locators, wherein said referencing and referenced documents contain index terms, the process comprising:
>
> - for a referencing document of the collection:
> - recognising documents referenced in said referencing document; and
> - aggregating (70) said referencing document (32) with documents (34) it references to form an aggregate document, said aggregate document formed being a single logical document associated with the documents forming said aggregate document;
> - indexing said aggregate document, based on index terms contained in the referencing and referenced documents forming said aggregate document, to form an index, wherein an entry in the index table is associated with the referencing and referenced documents forming the aggregate document;
> - searching (74) among aggregate documents by operating on said index; and
> - providing (74), as a result, an aggregate document.

Contrary to the opinion of the Opposition Division the Board decided that a technical problem to be solved could be formulated. Discussions took place on which document represented the closest prior art. Finally, based on comparison to the closest prior art the subject matter of claim 1 was considered as inventive. The patent was remitted for maintenance as granted.

[3] T 1003/09 (Virtual Index Changes/GOOGLE) of 29.4. 2015

The appeal against the refusal of the application for lack of inventive step was successful. The application comprised a set of claims – method, apparatus and computer program.

Claim 1 of the main request:

> 1. A computer-implemented method for viewing changes to an original optimization plan for a query to a database (212), the database (212) having an original table (308) with data stored therein, and the query including a reference to the original table (308),
> characterized by the method comprising:
> defining (402) a virtual table (312) that is a copy of the original table (308) but which excludes data stored in the rows of the original table (308), wherein defining (402) a virtual table (312) includes copying the original table statistics to the virtual table (312), wherein the original table statistics include column statistics, histograms and segment storage;
> defining (404) a virtual index, the virtual index being an index associated with the virtual table;
> replacing (406), in the query, the reference to the original table (308) with a reference to the virtual table (312);
> determining (408) a new optimization plan (324) for the query;
> replacing (410), in the new optimization plan, a reference to the virtual table (312) with a reference to the original table; and
> displaying (412) the new optimization plan (324).

In the Board's view the concept of a 'virtual table', as a copy of the original table which excludes data stored in the original table but includes the original table statistics, is not disclosed in any of the available prior art. Therefore, the whole claimed subject matter was inventive.

[4] T 2413/10 (Database Synchronization/NOKIA) 23.5.2016

The invention relates to synchronizing databases storing application data on two devices, for example a portable client terminal and a network server, based on the SyncML ('Synchronized Markup Language') synchronization protocol. The Examining Division had refused the application for lack of clarity (Article 84 EPC) and extended subject matter (Article 123(2) EPC).

The applicant submitted amended claims and could overcome the objections raised in the refusal. Based on the comparison to the closest prior art, a version of the SyncML synchronization protocol, the Board regarded the claimed subject matter as inventive.

The set of claims comprised six independent claims:

> Claim 1: 'A method of arranging synchronization of databases ...'
> Claim 6: 'A synchronization system ...'
> Claim 7: 'A telecommunications device comprising means for establishing a logical data transmission connection to at least one other device for synchronizing databases ...'
> Claim 8: 'A synchronization device comprising means for establishing a logical data transmission connection to at least one other device for synchronizing database ...'
> Claim 9: 'A computer program product loadable into the memory of a telecommunications device and comprising a code which is executable in the telecommunications device ...'

> Claim 10: 'A computer program product loadable into the memory of a computer functioning as a synchronization device and comprising a code which is executable in the synchronization device ...'

The application was remitted to the first instance with the order to grant a patent.

The case indicates very well the importance of several independent claims for CII in network systems.

[5] T 0779/11 (Case Law Database/THOMSON REUTERS GLOBAL RESOURCES) 23.6.2016

Simplified, the application relates to the access to several databases that comprise legal and other information. This should be possible with one query. During the PCT phase the EPO as ISA issued a declaration under Article 17(2)(a) PCT to the effect that no international search report was established because no meaningful search was possible. The search examiner referred to the publication in OJ 2007 explaining that the technical means (e.g. client/server network) were known to the public at the priority day. The data stored by the client or the server was non-technical (legal information). No additional search was done during the European phase and the application was refused for lack of inventive step based on notorious knowledge.

Claim 1of the main request:

> A system (100) comprising: a server (120) for an online legal-research provider, the server coupled to one or more databases (110), including:
>
> a subscriber database (123) containing authentication credentials for a plurality of subscribers to an online legal research service;
>
> a case law database (111) containing a plurality of judicial decision documents; and
>
> a database (112, 113, 114) containing a plurality of litigation documents associated with at least one judicial decision; and
>
> means associated with the server (120) for returning search results to a client access device (130) in response to a submitted legal-research query, wherein the search results identify one or more of the judicial decision documents and at least one user-interface element (1382) operable to enable a user of the access device to request information regarding litigation documents related one [sic] or more of the identified judicial decision documents.

Independent claim 9 of the main request:

> A computer-implemented method comprising: receiving a query for judicial decision documents; responding to the query with a listing of one or more judicial decision documents, wherein one or more of the listed judicial decision documents includes a link for accessing at least one litigation document associated with the judicial decision.

An appeal was filed. The appellant argued that a search is always necessary. Reference was made to T 1242/04 (OJ EPO 2007, 421) which in the appellant's view stated that not doing a search should be exceptional. The Board did not agree with the appellant's arguments. The Examining Division was right in refusing an application for lack of inventive step where the objection was based on knowledge that was 'notorious' or indisputably formed part of the common general knowledge. This approach has been followed in a number of other decisions. Thus, it is not true that there might be 'secret' prior art.

The Board started with examination of inventive step for the very broad method claim 9. It agreed with the Examining Division's arguments that web-based search engines were notorious at the priority date of the application, i.e. on 31 December 2003. The subject matter of claim 9 differed from this notorious prior art only in that the query results were 'judicial documents' and that the link included in one or more of these documents pointed to a 'litigation document associated with the judicial decision'. These features related only to the non-technical cognitive content of the documents and therefore do not contribute to inventive step. Claim 9 lacks inventive step (Article 56 EPC). Lack of inventive step was also decided for independent claim 1.

Additional features limited the claims of the auxiliary requests. Since a search had not been done the case was remitted to the first instance for further prosecution.

The Board confirmed it was appropriate not to search claims with generic features of a computer/computer network in combination with non-technical features where it is not evident that a technical problem has been solved by technical means.

[D] System Software: Simulation

Computers made it possible to program and execute computer simulations.[56] Progressive and conservative views exist on simulations which can be seen as a third way of doing science somewhere between theory and experiment.[57] Simulations can be done for traditional scientific fields (physics, chemistry, biology ...) but also in the area of social sciences. Simulations replace experiments with a real physical system like an airplane. Simulation cannot be done without a model of the topic to be simulated. Models can be created by different means. Mathematical models will be transformed into computational algorithms. Modelling requires understanding the nature (important parameters, relationship between parameters ...) of the topic to be modelled.

Due to the position of simulation /modelling between theory and the real world, it is no wonder that different views exist in legal practice. Furthermore, its proximity to mathematics can result in difficulties in determining if it is an excluded mathematical method as such (Article 52(2, 3) EPC). In general, some reluctance can be observed towards patent computerized models or simulation methods. Furthermore, different interpretations exist as to the meaning of 'simulation'. Sometimes, 'virtual worlds' or 'virtual systems' are designated as simulated systems.

Different criteria play a role in simulation/modelling:

- Is the simulation computer-implemented or can it be seen as a mental process or something done with paper and pencil?

56. Winsberg, E. *Science in the Age of Computer Simulation* University of Chicago Press 2010.
57. Gruner, S. *Book Review – Eric Winsberg: Science in the Age of Computer Simulation* Mind & Machines 2013, 251.

The claim has to show that the simulation method is not a mental act. In T306/04 a method of scheduling tasks in an industrial process was seen as non-technical. The same was true in T0930/05 that was directed to the modelling of a process network. In T0914/02 a method for designing a core loading arrangement for loading nuclear reactor fuel bundles into a reactor core to optimize several process parameters was considered as a mental act. Only after adding 'using a suitably programmed computer' to claim 1 was the method considered as having technical character. A similar approach was taken in T0471/05. The general design of an optical system had no technical character. The design with the support of a computer changed the situation. The whole method was considered to solve a technical problem.

- What is simulated – a technical or a non-technical system/process?
  In T0953/94 a computerized method of generating a data analysis of the cyclical behaviour of a curve (mathematical expressions) was considered as non-technical when the curve was generated for abstract data and business data, but allowable if the method was limited to physical data. The landmark decision T0208/84VICOM was followed.

A technical effect was rejected for simulating an efficient schedule for telephone call centre agents – T1265/09. No technical problem was solved.

A simulation of a security checkpoint e.g. at an airport was seen as technical but not inventive since the use of a computer for simulating a non-technical process is obvious – T0531/09. The same was true for marketing simulations – T0953/04.

Simulation of technical systems as part of general industrial control is patentable according to several cases such as: T0118/10 – method for continuously casting a metal strand; T0756/09 and T2440/12 – fluid simulation or T1106/01 – simulation of the look of textile material.

Simulation of an integrated circuit expressed by a complex mathematical formula was considered as technical due to the clear technical purpose and the concrete technical use for producing integrated circuits. The mere amount of mathematics in the claim did not render the claim unpatentable as a mathematical method as such.

[E] System Software: Software Development/Modelling/Programming

Modelling as part of software development is seen as restrictive. In many cases the claimed subject matter is prima facie technical but lacks an inventive step due to the obvious use of technical computing means for the implementation of non-technical activities. A claim often represents a mix of technical computer features and non-technical data or process models (e.g. T1073/06, T0354/07, T1359/08, T0042/09, T1370/11). In T1171/06 the object-oriented modelling of a mechatronic system in a vehicle was considered to have no technical character at all. It was excluded under Article 52(2, 3) EPC. A technical problem was not solved. A claim directed to a method but to an apparatus with features of the former method claim was considered to be not inventive. The use of a computer for the modelling was regarded as obvious. T2247/10 was directed to a descriptive data structure in the context of a secure data structure.

The granted patent was revoked by the Opposition Division. The Board came to the same conclusion. Technicality was not discussed since the context of security and digital rights management assigned technicality to the claimed subject-matter.

[1] T0049/99 (Information Modelling/INTERNATIONAL) 5.3.2002

Creating a model of a physical system in the sense of object-oriented programming was seen as non-technical:

> 1. A method for modelling a physical system in a computer that executes an object-oriented information model based on the physical system, comprising the steps of:
>
> (a) identifying physical elements in the system and their characteristics;
> (b) deriving abstract objects and their attributes from the physical elements and their characteristics;
> (c) defining relationships between objects;
> (d) defining instances of the objects by assigning instance characteristics to the attributes; and
> (e) creating an object type hierarchy within the objects, the objects lower in the hierarchy being subtypes of the objects higher in the hierarchy and inheriting attributes from the higher-level objects;
> characterized in that
> (f) a sub-set of the object types within said hierarchy are designated as base types;
> (g) all objects, their attributes and the relationships between the objects are stored in tables with relational database technology, said tables including an [corrected by the Board, originally reading 'and'] object table and a plurality of type-specific tables, each type-specific table corresponding to a particular base type;
> (h) said object table stores entries for objects of a plurality of different object types, each entry including attributes that are not specific to any particular object type; and
> (i) said type-specific tables store attributes specific to their respective base types.

The Board considered information modelling as a formalized process carried out by a system engineer or a similar skilled person in the first stage of software development. A sort of real world model of the system is created on paper. They pointed out that 'although information modelling embodies useful concepts and methods in developing complex software systems, it is as such an intellectual activity having all traits typical for non-technical branches of knowledge and thus being closely analogous to the non-inventions listed under Article 52(2)(a) and (c) EPC'. The broad meaning of 'physical system' led to the interpretation that the modelling according to claim 1 was seen as an abstract non-technical activity using abstract constructs like objects, types, attributes, and relationships. This part was not taken into account for the determination of inventiveness based on the problem-solution approach. The Board would have allowed a limitation to a concrete technical system but this was not wished by the applicant. Part 2 of claim 1 was seen as technical since it related to the technical implementation of the abstract model on a computer system. The technical person responsible for this task, i.e. the person skilled in the art, is the programmer. He is given the complete program description including the abstract data structures making up the information model. Finally, no inventive step could be seen.

[2] T 1399/10 (Computer Game Software Build/MICROSOFT) 16.4.2015

Three auxiliary requests were submitted. Claim 1 of the second auxiliary request indicated that the multimedia software is game software. Claim 1 of the main request:

> 1. A method for enabling a software build for content of an interactive multimedia software application comprising:
>
> creating at least one file according to a standardized file format (70 - 74,86 - 100) containing metadata related to said content, wherein said content is provided in form of various binary content files and wherein said metadata is that which is necessary to perform a software build of said content for a plurality of different interactive multimedia software applications that use the same said content.

Claim 1 of the main request was not new and that of the first auxiliary request was not inventive. The second request was not admitted and the third request lacked clarity.

[F] Application Software: Telecommunication

This field is traditionally seen as technical. In industry, one can see a growing convergence with computing fields. Topics of computing like GUI databases appear in telecommunications. The current trend is to combine all kind of 'things' with a network connection – IoT – The Internet of things. As a result more and more products of traditional industrial and/or consumer fields (e.g. toothbrush, heating device, and vehicle) are combined with network features. An example is T2241/11 that is directed to windfarm networks. In this case, wind turbines were connected by means of LAN (local area network). No inventive step could be found. Different views exist with respect to inventive step if 'normal' network features are applied to formerly unconnected devices. More oppositions are filed here compared with core computing fields. The reason is seen in standardization that is important in telecommunication. It is said that 'the typical notebook computer embodies more than 250 different standards. Some smartphones incorporate as many as 250,000 patents'.[58] There were 'Patent wars' between Apple and Samsung in several countries. A major debate on patentability created the use of granted patent EP 1 215 867 B1. This patent with a priority of 2000 was granted in 2008 on an 'Emoticon input method for a mobile terminal'. Patentability as well as inventiveness was discussed amongst the public. The completely contentious topic of standardization and patents in particular in computing and telecommunications cannot be dealt with here.

Here follow some Boards of Appeal decisions.

58. Schneiderman, R. *Modern Standardization* Publication of Standards Information Network IEEE Press 2015.

[1] T 2334/13 (Erweitertes Nutzerprofil/VODAFONE) of 10.2.2016

The application was directed to a method for creating user profiles and a method for providing information on objects. It was refused by the Examining Division for lack of novelty. The user profile was created based on transmitted images of objects like real estate. Such user profiles could be used for the evaluation of customer creditworthiness. Time information determines whether a user is more active at night or at other times. The Board concluded that the very general technical implementation details were obvious for the person skilled in computer networks or image processing. The refusal was confirmed based on lack of inventive step.

[2] T 1588/12 (Automatic Network Configuration/INTEL) of 26.2.2016

The application had the title System and Method for dynamically configuring and transitioning wired and wireless networks. The appeal against the refusal for lack of inventive step was not successful due to added subject matter (Article 123(2) EPC) and lack of clarity (Article 84 EPC). The features 'creating a virtual map of the network in volatile memory based on the referenced list of network components' and 'selecting appropriate resources to support the transition' and 'selecting a network component...to effect the transition' were not clear. Neither the claim nor the description gave a clear indication on the functionality.

[3] T 1890/13 (Generation of Security Keys/ERICSSON) of 21.6.2016

The patent was directed to a security solution in an Evolved Packet System EPS. The patent was opposed but maintained as granted. The opponent filed an appeal. The patent comprised two independent method claims and two respective apparatus claims.

The broadest independent claim 7:

> 7. A method in a User Equipment (11), UE, of an Evolved Packet System, EPS, of establishing a security key, K_eNB, for protecting RRC/UP traffic exchanged with a serving eNodeB (12), the method comprising the following steps:
>
> - Sending (31, 51) a [sic] NAS Service Request to a Mobility Management Entity, MME, the request indicating a [sic] NAS uplink sequence number, NAS_U_SEQ;
> - Deriving (35, 56) the K_eNB from at least said NAS_U_SEQ and from a stored Access Security Management Entity-key, K_ASME, shared with said MME.

The technical problem to be solved, as indicated in the description, was to prevent replay attacks without using complex sequence number estimation and synchronization, or requiring explicit downlink NAS service accept messages from Mobility Management Entity (MME) to UE. In comparison to the closest prior art the Board concluded that the claimed subject matter was inventive. The patent was maintained.

[G] Application Software: Medical/Biological

Computing technology is a major trigger in the medical area. An increase of applications can be observed. Technological solutions in that area are usually patentable. Exceptions to patentability relate to surgical, therapeutical and diagnostic methods practised on the human or animal body (Article 53(c) EPC). Furthermore, proximity to excluded subject matter under Article 52(2, 3) EPC can result in mixed claims. Determination of technicality can be a challenge for the application of GUIs to the medical area e.g. for simulation of medical operations, for indication of user (nurse, physician) instructions e.g. to set-up a medical device.

Due to the growing amount of decisions in that area only some examples can be given. Early decisions concerning the use of computing in the medical area were T0026/86 Koch& Sterzel (X-ray apparatus) and T0537/93 Pacemaker/VITATRON.

Many patents can be found in the area of medical image processing. Supporting a doctor by improved images (T0542/06 – Vizualization/Brainlab) is usually patentable while the indication of steps of how to use a device or how to work it is not (T0635/07- Step-by-step guidance to dentists/VANNOYE; cf. under GUI – T0366/14- Presentation of operating instructions/GAMBRO). In T1827/07 the claimed subject matter was related to a method for segmentation and identification of a non-stationary time series. In fact, the method could be used for the analysis of medical data like EEG data. However, the original claims did not relate to concrete data. The final decision was lack of clarity. T1587/10 describes a computer-implemented system for tracking and controlling infections. The applicant submitted amended claims that overcame lack of clarity (Article 84 EPC). The case was remitted to the first instance for further prosecution.

If the claimed method in the areas of medicine or biology fulfils all the EPC requirements then its implementation as a computer program is usually accepted.

[1] T 0310/99 (Down Syndrome/MACRI) of 1.4.2003

The patent proprietor (appellant I) and the opponent (appellant II) both lodged appeals against the Opposition Division's interlocutory decision, which had maintained the patent on the basis of the second auxiliary request.

Appellant I submitted eight independent claims during the appeal procedure. Independent claims 11, 13, 14 and 17 indicated a computer for calculating specific data of the method in claims 1 to 9. Only claim 13 of the main request is given as an example here:

> 13. Use of an apparatus for the method of any of claims 1 to 9, said apparatus comprising: means adapted for receiving the data of measurement of the pregnant woman's maternal blood level of free beta (hCG), means adapted for receiving the data of measurement of the pregnant woman's maternal blood level of alpha fetoprotein, and computer means for calculating a set of normative data from a set of reference data containing reference values of the level of free beta (hCG) and the level of alpha fetoprotein at various gestational ages in: (1) pregnant women carrying Down syndrome fetuses and (2) pregnant women carrying normal

> fetuses, and for incorporating said data of measurements of said levels of said free beta (hCG) and alpha fetoprotein, and said pregnant woman's gestational age into a probability density function, thereby comparing said levels and said pregnant woman's gestational age to the set of normative data to determine said pregnant woman's risk of carrying a fetus with Down syndrome.

The final decision was to remit the patent with the order to maintain the it based on the first auxiliary request (with amended claims 4, 9 and 10).

[2] T 1171/01 (Detecting Malignancy-Associated Changes/MONOGENE) of 27.9.2006

The invention was directed to a method of detecting malignancy-associated changes (MACs) in a cell sample. An appeal was filed against the Examining Division's refusal.

Claim 1 (with corrections) and a further claim formulation:

> 1. A method of detecting malignancy-associated changes in a cell sample, comprising the steps of:
>
> obtaining a cell sample; staining the sample to identify cell nuclei within the sample;
>
> obtaining an image of the cell sample with a digital microscope of the type that includes a digital CCD camera and a programmable slide stage; recording the image in a computer system; focusing the image;
>
> identifying objects in the image; calculating a set of feature values for each object; and
>
> analyzing the feature values to determine whether each object is a cell nucleus; and computing a set of feature values for each nucleus found in the sample and from the feature values determining whether the nucleus exhibits malignancy-associated change, and characterized in that
>
> the determination is made by a classifier constructed from a first database comprising feature values obtained from apparently normal cells of a healthy patient and a second database comprising feature values obtained from apparently normal cells of an abnormal patient.
>
> A classifier for detecting the presence of malignancy associated changes (MAC) in a cell nucleus, wherein the classifier is constructed using a first database comprising feature values obtained from apparently normal cells which were known to come from healthy patients and a second database comprising feature values obtained from apparently normal cells which were known to come from cancer patients, wherein data from said databases is used to develop a discriminant function that can discriminate between MAC-positive nuclei and MAC-negative nuclei.

Claim 1 comprises steps implemented by means of a computer program – the classifier. A separate claim was submitted just for the classifier. Both claims were considered as technical but not as inventive.

[3] G 0001/07 (Treatment by Surgery/MEDI-PHYSICS) of 15.2.2010

With G1/07 decided on 15 February 2010 the EBoA answered three questions posed in the interlocutory decision T0992/03 – Chirurgische Behandlung/MEDI-PHYSICS

(20.10.2006). The questions were related to an MRI imaging method comprising surgical steps possibly excluded under Article 53(c) EPC. No computer or software is mentioned but those skilled in the art will know that functionality of MRI imaging results from software. A critical step was seen in an injection of polarized **(129)Xe into the heart, as envisaged in the description. This step was encompassed by the wording of claims 1, 11 and 17. Such an injection could be regarded as a method for surgical treatment of the human or animal body within the meaning of Article 52(4) EPC 1973:

> 1. A method for MRI imaging the pulmonary and/or cardiac vasculature using dissolved-phase polarized **(129)Xe, comprising the steps of:
> positioning a patient in an MRI apparatus having a magnetic field associated therewith;
> delivering polarized **(129)Xe gas to a predetermined region of the patient's body, the polarized gas having a dissolved imaging phase associated therewith;
> exciting a predetermined region of the patient's body, having a portion of the dissolved phase polarized gas therein with at least one large flip angle RF excitation pulse; and
> acquiring at least one MR image associated with the dissolved phase polarized gas after said exciting step.
>
> 11. A method for deriving a spectroscopic signal representative of a blood volume or a blood flow rate of a patient, comprising the steps of:
> positioning a subject in an MR spectroscopy system capable of detecting spectroscopic signals in a subject having a pulmonary vasculature;
> delivering gaseous polarized **(129)Xe to the subject;
> dissolving a portion of the gaseous polarized **(129)Xe into the pulmonary vasculature having an associated blood flow path;
> exciting the dissolved portion of the **(129)Xe with an MR spectroscopy RF excitation pulse; and
> deriving a spectroscopic signal associated with the dissolved phase **(129)Xe representing a blood volume or blood flow rate.
>
> 17. A cardiac imaging method, comprising the steps of:
> positioning a subject having a cardiac blood flow path in an MRI system;
> delivering polarized **(129)Xe to the subject;
> dissolving at least a portion of the polarized **(129)Xe into the subject's cardiac blood flow path;
> exciting dissolved polarized **(129)Xe in a target region along the blood flow path with at least one large angle RF excitation pulse; and
> generating an MR image associated with the excited dissolved polarized **(129)Xe.

The EBoA did not consider the claimed subject matter as an excluded diagnostic method. Based on a detailed evaluation of former case law and the interpretation of the term 'treatment by surgery' the EBoA gave the following answers:

1. A claimed imaging method, in which, when carried out, maintaining the life and health of the subject is important and which comprises or encompasses an invasive step representing a substantial physical intervention on the body which requires professional medical expertise to be carried out and which entails a substantial health risk even when carried out with the required professional care and expertise, is excluded from patentability as a method for

treatment of the human or animal body by surgery pursuant to Article 53(c) EPC.

2a. A claim which comprises a step encompassing an embodiment which is a 'method for treatment of the human or animal body by surgery' within the meaning of Article 53(c) EPC cannot be left to encompass that embodiment.

2b. The exclusion from patentability under Article 53(c) EPC can be avoided by disclaiming the embodiment, it being understood that in order to be patentable the claim including the disclaimer must fulfil all the requirements of the EPC and, where applicable, the requirements for a disclaimer to be allowable as defined in decisions G 1/03 and G 2/03 of the Enlarged Board of Appeal.

2c. Whether or not the wording of the claim can be amended so as to omit the surgical step without offending against the EPC must be assessed on the basis of the overall circumstances of the individual case under consideration.

3. A claimed imaging method is not to be considered as being a 'treatment of the human or animal body by surgery' within the meaning of Article 53(c) EPC merely because during a surgical intervention the data obtained by the use of the method immediately allow a surgeon to decide on the course of action to be taken during a surgical intervention.

In T1695/07 exceptions to patentability played a role in a blood measurement method in haemodialysis shunts. However, a claim directed to an apparatus was finally allowed.

[4] T 0821/12 (Dilution Apparatus and Computer Program) of 31.3.2016

The invention was directed to a dilution apparatus and the respective computer program. An opposition was filed and the Opposition Division rejected the opposition. The opponent filed an appeal.

Claims 1 and 10 of the patent as granted:

> 1. Apparatus for determining a patient's circulatory filling status, adapted to provide a dilution curve and to derive the ratio between the patient's global end-diastolic volume (GEDV) and the patient's intrathoracic thermal volume (ITTV) from the dilution curve by means of the degree of asymmetry of the shape of the dilution curve.
>
> 10. Computer program for determining a patient's circulatory filling status, having instructions adapted to carry out the steps:
> generating a dilution curve on basis of provided measurement data of dilution versus time,
>
> - determining the patient's circulatory filling status on basis of the ratio between the patient's global end-diastolic volume (GEDV) and the patient's intrathoracic thermal volume (ITTV),
> - determining the degree of asymmetry of the shape of the dilution curve, and
> - determining the ratio between the patient's global end-diastolic volume (GEDV) and the patient's intrathoracic thermal volume (ITTV) by means of the degree of asymmetry of the shape of the dilution curve when run on a computer.

In the Opponent's view, the claim was a combination of technical/non-technical features. The claimed formation of a ratio between Global End-Diastolic Volume (GEDV) and Intrathoracic Thermal Volume (ITTV) was considered to be an abstract method or a mathematical transformation without any technical effect. However, as indicated in the description, the technical effect underlying the distinguishing features is that, by means of the degree of asymmetry of the shape of the dilution curve, the ratio between GEDV and ITTV is less affected by temperature drift and blood recirculation. The objective technical problem, as indicated in the patent, is to provide an apparatus allowing a more accurate determination of the patient's circulatory fill status. The BoA did not see a mixed claim. The patent was maintained.

[5] T 0690/11 (Dialysis System) of 1.3.2016

The granted patent was opposed on the ground of lack of inventive step. The Opposition Division rejected the opposition. The decision was appealed. Claim 1 of the granted patent.

> 1. A dialysis system (10,100) comprising:
> a display device (40); and
> a web browser (602) and web server(604) embedded in the dialysis system, characterized in that the browser and the server operate with the display device to:
> display a plurality of dialysis therapy set-up procedure screens that require an operator input, and
> display a plurality of dialysis treatment screens that graphically illustrate the progress of at least one step in the dialysis therapy in at least substantially real time.

The technical character of the claimed subject matter was discussed. The display of set-up procedure screens was seen as non-technical by the Opponent. The BoA did not agree with this argument and saw the objective technical problem in how to provide a more user-friendly and safer dialysis system. Surprisingly, the technical effect was seen in that the operator is forced to go through the whole set-up procedure of the dialysis system and can readily obtain system state information during operation, under the control of a suitable software platform. The patent was maintained.

The argumentation in T0336/14 differs from T0690/11 (Presentation of operating instructions for a blood treatment machine/GAMBRO – cf. in Chapter GUI).

[6] T1286/10 (Detection and Correction of False Descriptions in IUB Code Input Data for Linkage Disequilibrium Analysis) of 14.4.2015

The application was refused for lack of inventive step by the Examining Division. Claim 1 of the main request:

> 1. A data input support system for inspecting genotype data input into a program for linkage disequilibrium analysis, wherein the genotype data is described in the IUB code description format, wherein the system comprises:
> a storage section for retaining error types for genotype data corresponding to the program for linkage disequilibrium analysis, said error types corresponding to false descriptions of genotype data, an error detection section checking the input genotype data for the error types and detecting errors;

> means for displaying the report of the detected errors as well as a proposal what the correction to the input data could be; and
> error correction means which accepts a user input confirming to correct the reported error in the input genotype data according to the proposed correction and corrects the genotype data according to the proposed correction,
> wherein one of said error types is the occurrence of three or more alleles at a locus,
> and wherein the error detection section checks for one or more of the following conditions:(i) missing data is accidentally described as a one-byte blank character or tab,(ii) a heterozygous genotype is accidentally described as two alleles separated by a one-byte blank character,(iii) a heterozygous genotype is falsely described at each locus.

Claim 1 of the main request did not fulfil the requirements of inventive step because it was seen as obvious for a software engineer to apply rules for detecting typographical errors in text to IUB code description format.

Claim 1 according to a first auxiliary request had the following additional features:

> wherein one of said error types is the occurrence of three or more alleles at a locus, and wherein the error detection section checks for one or more of the following conditions:(i) missing data is accidentally described as a one-byte blank character or tab,(ii) a heterozygous genotype is accidentally described as two alleles separated by a one-byte blank character,(iii) a heterozygous genotype is falsely described at each locus.

The technical effect was seen in correcting description data. The specified error type rules according to the additional features were regarded as technical means in that functional data structures of the error correction means were thereby defined (*see* T 1194/97 - Data structure product/Philips; OJ EPO 2000, 525). This resulted in the enhanced correction of input data by allowing the repair of a genotype data set that contains correct biological measurement content but description errors. Those functional data structures each contributed to the technical character of the claimed invention. The application was remitted with the order to grant a patent based on the first auxiliary request.

[H] Application Software: Vehicles

The control of technical parameters of a vehicle by means of a computer program is usually technical. Like in other application areas difficulties arise for user interfaces in a vehicle, in particular for GUI (e.g. navigation systems, indication of user manuals for a car driver). No decisions relating to user interfaces are indicated here.

As in other areas devices and products are connected to the Internet. In T 1725/08 (Wireless communication system/CELLPORT SYSTEMS) of 16.10.2012 inventiveness was seen in information transmission involving one or more remote computing stations and a vehicle. In T1928/07 a claim directed to a processor unit for executing event processes in response to occurrences of a plurality of predetermined events for controlling an engine in a vehicle lacked clarity (Article 84 EPC). The case indicated the risks of using 'computing jargon' which can have different meanings.

In T1171/06 the object-oriented modelling of a mechatronic system in a vehicle was considered to have no technical character at (cf. chapter software development/ modelling/programming).

[1] T 1253/10 () of 6.11.2013

The patent was directed to a method, arrangement and computer program for controlling a hill hold brake. It was revoked in an opposition procedure:

> 1. A method of controlling a hill hold brake in a vehicle, comprising the steps that:
> - sensing vehicle speed, rpm of output axle of vehicle gear box, vehicle braking pressure, and vehicle accelerator pedal position,
> activating the hill hold brake in response to that the speed is equal to a predetermined speed, that the rpm is equal to a predetermined rpm, that the braking pressure is equal to a predetermined braking pressure, and that the accelerator pedal is inactive, characterized by activating the hill hold brake after a predetermined delay.

The BoA concluded that claim 1 lacked an inventive step. The appeal of the Patent Proprietor was dismissed.

[I] Application Software: Games

Computer games and in particular video games represent an enormous amount of application software. From the perspective of computer professionals, different aspects exist. The basic architecture of a computer game is indicated by Smed. It has three components following the MVC model (model-view-controller).[59] The Model part comprises the software for most of the game rules and their evaluation. The View part mainly comprises the computer programs that create the view indicated on the display (e.g. synthetic players, virtual worlds, play cards, game boards ...) but also the software that creates sound or sensory feedback. The creation of the software usually involves a graphic designer e.g. if a 'realistic' world has to be created by means of computer graphics.

The Controller part receives input signals from the human player and sends information to the Model part to trigger the respective reaction on the output device. Modern computer video games allow several players to participate at different locations. Thus, the software is connected over a network. The computer programs have to deal with typical algorithmic problems like creation of random numbers to achieve indeterminism.

Therefore it is not surprising that patentability of inventions in the area of computer games struggle with several topics excluded if claimed as such (Article 52 (2, 3)EPC). Rules for playing games, presentation of information and methods for doing

59. Smed, J.et al. *Algorithms and Networking for Computer Games* John Wiley & Sons 2006.

business as such are excluded from patentability. Many claims represent a mixture of technical computing features with non-technical features of excluded subject matter. The majority of cases relate to claims that overcome the first hurdle of technicality (usually due to notorious computing features like computer, processor and memory) but fail to overcome the second hurdle of inventive step. Non-technical features are implemented in an obvious, non-inventive way.

An invention was seen in the following cases:

T1769/10 – A specific technical communication between a server for maintaining the player database with a plurality of game outcome servers was inventive. Based on comparison to the closest prior art the objective technical problem was seen in improving the player's access to games while maintaining confidentiality of the player's data in the player database.

T1225/10 – a computer game in which a player character is moved on a display through a field of background objects, and in which collisions with certain objects elicit a game response that depends on collision direction. Under certain conditions, the field indicated on the display is rotated. The specific rotation of the display field was seen as technical and not as a game rule. Two objective technical problems were stated: how to efficiently realize a rotated display field and how to determine collision direction in a gaming system such as that of a Gameboy Advance playing 'Super Ghouls 'n Ghosts'. Image rotation was done by normal rotation means and thus obvious. However, avoiding collision detection based on points on the player character was neither known nor obvious.

T0683/11 relates to a gambling method that comprises inventive features to increase the game's security. Such features were the combination of information of a random number generator, log data collected during offline gambling and user selections.

T2172/13 – describes an inventive technical solution that enables videos to be streamed over a home network to a game console whilst ensuring that sufficient bandwidth exists between the game console and an HD tuner.

T2127/09 – relates to a case where the Search Division did not provide written prior art. The claimed subject matter was seen as a combination of notorious hardware for the implementation of game rules. The closest prior art was seen in the game 'Tetris'. The substantive amendment of the claims during the appeal procedure resulted in claims which in addition specified the control of the sequence bar in accordance with a counter when a predetermined count value is reached. The case was remitted to the first instance for an additional search.

The consistent use of the 'COMVIK' approach to claims with a mixture of technical and non-technical features (i.e. game rules) results in decisions where the subject matter is technical but not inventive. Such cases are T0336/07, T1543/06, T1782/09, T0042/10, T1938/10, T1385/12, T2321/12, T0414/12, T2184/12, T1884/13 and T2172/13.

[1] T 0414/12 () of 10.4.2013

The application was directed to a system and method for mapping results from sporting events to game inputs. The Examining Division refused the application for lack of inventive step. Claim 1 of the main request:

> 1. Electronic gaming apparatus, comprising: memory means (52) operable to store a set of game rules for defining an electronic game which includes a simulated randomising device, said simulated randomising device being simulated dice, simulated playing cards, simulated slot machine reels, a simulated roulette wheel, a simulated money wheel or simulated numbered balls; and processor means (50) operable:
>
> (i) to receive a bet relating to said game,
> (ii) to determine at least one substantially unpredictable input value to the game, said input value being a value defined by said simulated randomising device when the game is played, and
> (iii) to determine the result of the bet based at least in part on said determined input value and said game rules;
>
> characterized in that said processor means (50) is operable:
>
> (a) in response to receiving the bet, to execute one or more algorithms to select, on the basis of received sporting event information, a sporting event from a plurality of sporting events,
> (b) to assign the bet to the selected sporting event,
> (c) to receive one or more event results of the selected sporting event, and
> (d) to determine said at least one input value at least in part on the basis of said received event results so that the result of the bet is based at least in part on the received event results of the selected sporting event; and further characterized in that:
> (e) the memory means (52) is operable for storing a plurality of sets of input value determining rules for the game, and
> (f) the processor means (50) is operable for determining said one or more input values by selecting a set of input value determining rules from said plurality and utilising the selected set of rules to the [sic] determine the input values.

The general aim of the invention was to increase player interest with new playing experiences. Instead of using a normal random generator used in games, the outcome of sports events was combined with the game.

The BoA analysed claim 1 and decided that a gaming apparatus with a processor and memory operable to play a betting game using a random number generator was notorious means. Additionally, the use of a memory and a processor to implement different game rules was seen as obvious for the skilled person (software engineer). The Appellant argued that the new betting system would be less susceptible to tampering than games with a normal random number generator. In the view of the BoA the rules of the game were changed instead of finding a new technical solution. Thus, a technical solution was circumvented. Thus, no inventive step resulting from a technical solution could be found.

[J] Application Software: Mathematical Methods

Mathematical methods as such are excluded from patentability according to Article 52(2) a) and 52(3) EPC. It could be concluded that they are considered as non-technical and therefore, they are disregarded in the evaluation of inventive step like business methods. However, an important difference exists. Mathematics is a well-known means to express and describe relationships between objects of natural science and engineering.

From the historical perspective computer science has major roots in mathematics. Mathematics is still a fundamental component of computer science but according to contemporary views computer science is not a branch of mathematics but a science in its own right. From a strict scientific perspective, many computer professionals argue that a computer program is mathematics and patents should not be granted.[60] However, this view does not take into account software as a growing part of real systems. Fundamental views on mathematics as part of computer science are indicated in Chapter 2, §2.05 [C]. They are not discussed here.

The general provisions on the presentation of the patent application documents allow (Rule 49(9) IR) that the description, the claims and the abstract may contain chemical or mathematical formulae.

A long existing legal practice exists in that the nature of the data represented in a mathematical formula plays an important role as well as the purpose of the claimed invention.

In the landmark decision T0208/84-VICOM a method for processing digital images in the form of a two-dimensional data array was not considered as a mathematical method as such and not as a computer program as such. The method was not an abstract method dealing with numbers without any special meaning and without any relationship to a technical system but to an image processing system. The mathematical method represented a digital filter that influenced the properties of digital images. The image signal was seen as a physical entity of the real world. The BoA confirmed that an invention can exist in a mathematical method provided that this method is part of a technical process. However, the mathematical expressions have to fulfil the requirements of clarity (Article 84 EPC) and sufficiency of disclosure (Article 83 EPC). Decision T0026/86-Koch& Sterzel confirmed this view for image processing in the context of an X-ray apparatus. T0059/93 – A method for interactive rotation of displayed graphic objects was not a mathematical method as such, not a computer program as such, not a mental act as such, not a business method as such and not presentation of information as such. However, in T0790/92 the presentation of a numerical chart, in particular chart for business purposes was seen as a solution without a technical effect. No technical problem was solved.

The legal practice shows that in areas like cryptography, security, data compression (e.g. sound, images, video), data transmission in networks and computer graphics plenty of inventions result from advantageous mathematical modifications.

60. Klemens, B. *MatH You Can't Use – Patents, Copyright and Software* Brookings Institution Press 2006.

Several decisions indicated that the data to be processed according to the mathematical method and the purpose were decisive, not the amount of formulas in the claim. The use of a computer or a computer-implemented mathematical method for calculations in financial or business areas is usually technical (due to features like computer, Internet), but is without inventive step if no technical problem is solved by technical means.

In T0953/04 (15.7.1996) the patent with the title 'A method of functional analysis' was opposed. According to the old contribution approach, the BoA evaluated the method as a mathematical method as such. Thus, claim 1 as granted was not patentable despite the feature 'computer' in the claim. The method of claim 1 of the main request was directed to 'a method of generating with a digital computer a data analysis of the cyclical behaviour of a curve represented by a plurality of plots relating two parameters to one another, ...'. The parameters as indicated in the claim had no specific technical meaning. The BoA did not agree to a limitation to 'financial' or 'industrial' parameters. A limitation to 'physical' parameters was finally allowed.

An enormous amount of mathematical formulas in a claim does not mean automatically that the claimed subject matter is an excluded mathematical method as such. This became evident with T1227/05-Infineon I and T0421/06-Infineon II. The cases were directed to the simulation of an integrated circuit, in particular to a computer-implemented method with mathematical steps for simulating the performance of a circuit subject to 1/f noise. The *technical purpose* provided the technical character to the method. Here, simulation was seen as a normal step in the production of integrated circuits.

In T0042/09 a method of designing products using CAD (computer-aided-design) and of manufacturing products using CAM (computer-aided-manufacturing) based on a general product data-model did not solve a technical problem. No reference to any concrete physical representation of the product data-model was indicated. A contribution of the data-model to a concrete solution of a technical problem could not be seen.

Processors or digital circuits as parts of a digital computer for executing specific mathematical operations are patentable. T1093/05 dealt primarily with the correction of a granted patent. Technicality and inventive step were not disputed for a method for a multiplication circuit using Booth's method and the respective multiplication circuit.

[1] T 0556/14 (Masking a Private Key/CERTICOM) of 28.7. 2016

The BoA considered the set of claims as technical. A technical problem was seen in the protection of a cryptographic computation against power analysis attacks if, and only if, the computation is actually carried out on hardware and thus open to such attacks:

1. A method of masking a private key used in a cryptographic operation of multiplying a point, P, on an elliptic curve with the private key, the method comprising the steps of
   (a) dividing said private key into a plurality of parts b1, b2 and storing the parts on a smart card;
   (b) generating a random number pi;

(c) deriving new parts b1 = b1 + pi mod n and b2 = b2 - pi mod n, where n is the number of points on said elliptic curve, such that the new parts when added are equivalent to the original private key;
(d) storing the new parts on the smart card; and
(e) utilizing each of the new parts instead of the private key in said cryptographic operation by evaluating b1P + b2P.

2. A computer-readable medium comprising computer readable program code embodied thereon for causing a cryptographic processor to perform the method of claim 1.

The patent was maintained.

As already indicated in the paragraph about simulation, no completely harmonized legal practice exists in the area of simulation/modelling.

[K] Application Software: Mental Act

A few decisions exist on features considered to represent a non-technical mental act as such.

In T0497/11 the BoA considered a method for an aviation system to temporally manage the flow of a plurality of aircraft with respect to a specified system resource as a non-inventive automation of a mental act by generic computer means.

In T2374/11 instruction emulation ('static binary translation' of legacy processor object code to host processor object code) was evaluated as a mental act which did not contribute to the technical character. The final decision was that no inventive step existed.

T1073/13 considered the presentation of a specific sequence of buttons to avoid an inadvertent configuration of a flow measuring device as presenting cognitive content which merely addresses the user's mental process such that the 'user is not required to memorise or know the particular button sequence' prior to the configuration action.

[L] Application Software: Business Methods

The historical development and the current state are indicated in §4.05 [D].

[M] Application Software: Industrial Applications, Others

Patentability is usually without problems if the method that will be implemented as a computer program represents a clear technical method. In many applications, 'a controller' for the execution of a method is indicated in the claims. Sometimes it can only be seen from the description that the controller is a computer or microprocessor. Details of an implementation as computer program are hardly ever disclosed.

There follows a few examples form different areas.

[1] T 1682/07 (On-line Control of a Chemical Process Plant/EXXONMOBIL) of 9.6.2010

The granted patent was opposed. An appeal was filed against the decision of the Opposition Division by the Patentee. Claim 1 according to the main request:

1. A method for online control of a process that has a plurality of steps and that produces a finished product with a property P having a desired value D, whereby a spectrum for a test sample at an intermediate step in said process is measured and used to control said product property P, comprising:
   (a) obtaining a set of measured spectra having measurement errors for a set of calibration samples representative of at least one intermediate step in said process;
   (b) producing a set of correction spectra that simulate data that arise from the measurement process itself and are not due to components in the calibration samples;
   (c) correcting said measured spectra for said measurement errors by orthogonalizing said set of measured spectra with respect to the set of correction spectra to produce a set of corrected spectra for said set of calibration samples;
   (d) determining a set of weights from the set of corrected calibration sample spectra relating said corrected spectrum of each of said calibration samples to a set of orthonormal basis functions;
   (e) obtaining a value of said property P of the product that corresponds to each calibration sample of said set of calibration samples;
   (f) determining a predictive model relating said value for said property P of said product to said set of weights;
   (g) measuring a spectrum for a test sample at said at least one intermediate step in said process;
   (h) obtaining a corrected spectrum for said test sample at said at least one intermediate step in said process by orthogonalizing said measured spectrum for said test sample with respect to the set of correction spectra;
   (i) determining an estimated value E for said property P of the predicted product corresponding to said test sample from said predictive model and said corrected spectrum of said test sample; and
   (j) controlling said process using a calculated difference between said estimated value E of said predicted product and said desired value D, wherein said process is a polymerisation process.

Independent claim 28 relates to a corresponding process plant.

The feature 'online control' could be interpreted as the involvement of a computer. The description indicates the use of a computer for executing the online control. In the end, the case was remitted to the department of first instance with the order to maintain the patent in amended form.

T 1743/09 of 7.2.2012 was directed to a patent on a **process and systems for the epoxidation of an olefin**. This is a normal technical process. The patent was opposed. During the appeal procedure, different requests were submitted by the Appellant. Claim 1 of the main request:

1. A process for the epoxidation of ethylene, which process comprises reacting a feed comprising ethylene, oxygen and a reaction modifier in the presence of a

highly selective silver-based catalyst at a reaction temperature T, and with the reaction modifier being present in a relative quantity Q which is the ratio of an effective molar quantity of active species of the reaction modifier present in the feed to an effective molar quantity of hydrocarbons present in the feed, and which process comprises the steps of:

operating at a first operating phase wherein the value of T is T1 and the value of Q is Q1, and

subsequently operating at a second operating phase at a reaction temperature which is different from the reaction temperature employed in the first operating phase, such that the value of T is T2 and the value of Q is Q2, whereby Q2 is determined by calculation and Q2 is defined by the formula

$Q2 = Q1 + B (T2 - T1)$

wherein B denotes a constant factor which is greater than 0 and wherein the reaction modifier comprises an organic chloride.

The main request included further independent claims. Independent claim 15 of the main request was directed to a method for making a 1,2-diol or a 1,2-diol ether comprising the step of converting ethylene oxide obtained by a process of claim 1 into 1,2-diol or a 1,2-diol ether. Independent claims 16, 17 and 19 referred to a reaction system suitable for performing the claimed process, a computer program product suitable for instructing a data processing system of a computer system to execute the calculations for the claimed process and a computer system configured to receive instruction from the computer program product.

Finally, the BoA dismissed the patent proprietor's appeal due to lack of disclosure for all requests. Lack of disclosure was based on details of the chemical process itself.

[2] T 1036/08 of 12.6.2012 Solder System

The Examining Division refused the application for lack of inventive step. Based on amended claims inventiveness was seen by the BoA:

1. A solder material test method including:
   a first detecting step of detecting a first intensity at a particular wave number of infrared ray reflected from a test-sample solder material by illuminating light to the test-sample solder material;
   a second detecting step of detecting a second intensity at the particular wave number of infrared ray reflected from a comparative-sample solder material by illuminating light to the comparative-sample solder material; and
   a test step of testing a deterioration degree of the test-sample solder material relatively to the comparative-sample solder material, depending upon the first and second intensities detected, wherein the solder material is a solder paste.

18. A solder material test apparatus comprising:
   a light source that illuminates light to a test-sample solder material and a comparative-sample solder material;
   intensity detecting means that detects a first intensity at a particular wave number of infrared ray reflected from the test—sample solder material due to illumination of the light, and a second intensity at the particular wave number of infrared ray reflected from the comparative-sample solder material due to illumination of the light; and

control means that outputs a deterioration parameter indicative of a comparative deterioration degree of the test—sample solder material relatively to the comparative-sample solder material, depending upon the first and second intensities detected, wherein the solder material is a solder paste.

19. A control program for a solder material test apparatus, wherein function in the control means according to claim 18 is realized by a computer.

20. A computer-readable recording medium recording the control program according to claim 19.

Agriculture is also a field where computers automation is growing. Several cases relate to robots for milking animals.

[3] T 2180/10 of 11.9.2014

The claim was considered as inventive. A computer is indicated in the claim:

1. i) A construction including an implement for milking animals, such as cows,
   ii) whereby the implement is provided with adjusting means with the aid of which the milking duration, i.e. the period of time in which the animal is milked, is adjustable,
   iii) the adjusting means comprising a computer, characterized in that
   iv) the computer is suitable to compare the actual milk yield with the optimal milk yield and that, when the actual milk yield has achieved the optimal milk yield, milking is ended
   v) such that the milking machine is only used during that period of time in which the cow gives her milk at the highest rate.

In T2421/09 the patent was directed to a seed drill comprising adjusters which allowed the working depth of the tools to be adjusted by a control unit using stored data about the soil type, wetness, temperature, type of seed being sown and weather conditions. It is assumed that the control unit is a computer. In the end, the patent was revoked based on a lack of inventive step.

Typical control functions executed by a computer e.g. for cutting and engraving are patentable according to T 2126/10 of 16.7.2014 or T2203/12 of 12.7.2016.

In T2531/10 of 12.12.2014 the patent was directed to a method for producing a metal. In addition to the method claim, there was a claim on calculation means (computer) for controlling and modelling a cooling line and a claim on a plant for producing a metal. The cooling line model comprised a temperature model. In the end, the patent was revoked based on lack of inventive step.

§4.08 CLAIM FORMATS

The reviewed Guidelines for Examination in the EPO dated November 2016 include in Part F, Chapter IV - Claims (Article 84 and formal requirements) a new section on claim formulation for CII:[61]

61. EPO, Guidelines for Examination in the EPO, Part F, Chapter IV, 3.9, November 2016, http://documents.epo.org/projects/babylon/eponet.nsf/0/0791474853510FFFC125805A004C9571/$File/guidelines_for_examination _part_f_en.pdf (accessed 13 March 2017).

3.9 Claims directed to computer-implemented inventions
3.9.1 Cases where all method steps can be fully implemented by generic data processing means
3.9.2 Cases where method steps require specific data processing means and/or require additional technical devices as essential features

The definition for CII is repeated. This is also indicated in Part G, Chapter II, '3.6 Programs for computers'.

The following non-exhaustive list of allowable claim formulations is indicated under paragraph 3.9.1.:

(i) Method claim (claim 1)
  - A computer-implemented method comprising steps A, B, ...
  - A method carried out by a computer comprising steps A, B, ...

(ii) Apparatus/device/system claim (claim 2)
  - A data processing apparatus/device/system comprising means for carrying out [the steps of] the method of claim 1.
  - A data processing apparatus/device/system comprising means for carrying out step A, means for carrying out step B, ...
  - A data processing apparatus/device/system comprising a processor adapted to/configured to perform [the steps of] the method of claim 1.

(iii) Computer program [product] claim (claim 3)
  - A computer program [product] comprising instructions which, when the program is executed by a computer, cause the computer to carry out [the steps of] the method of claim 1.
  - A computer program [product] comprising instructions which, when the program is executed by a computer, cause the computer to carry out steps A, B, ...

(iv) Computer-readable [storage] medium/data carrier claim (claim 4)
  - A computer-readable [storage] medium comprising instructions which, when executed by a computer, cause the computer to carry out [the steps of] the method of claim 1.
  - A computer-readable [storage] medium comprising instructions which, when executed by a computer, cause the computer to carry out steps A, B, ...
  - A computer-readable data carrier having stored thereon the computer program [product] of claim 3.

For interrelated products of a computer network more independent claims might be necessary.

Claims to data structures or a data carrier having stored thereon a data structure are also possible but they are less used. The term 'data structure' is primarily used as an equivalent for data format, e.g. as a sequence of bits or groups of bits which have a specific meaning. Examples can be found in the area of media transmission and processing where e.g. a specific video format or audio format is claimed. The term 'data stream' is also allowable in such areas. A data structure claim is usually not allowed without indication of the method for creating this structure.

'Data structure' can have a specific meaning in the area of databases and information retrieval. The description of the technical effect might be difficult due to the proximity to abstract non-technical methods. A few explanations are given in the Guidelines for Examination, November 2016, Part G, Chapter II, '3.7.2 Data retrieval, formats and structures'.

'Data structure' in the sense of data types in programming languages are probably less patentable due to the lack of a technical effect.[62]

The EPO also allows claims starting with 'signal' in combination with computer programs or other digital data. However, such claim formulations are very rare. It is assumed that more restrictive formulations in the US could be the reason.

Passage 3.9.2. relates mainly to formulations which cover what many computer professionals often call 'embedded system'. The following example is indicated:

Example

1. A method of determining oxygen saturation in blood in a pulse oximeter, comprising:
   - receiving in an electromagnetic detector first and second electromagnetic radiation signals from a blood-perfused tissue portion corresponding to two different wavelengths of light;
   - normalising said electromagnetic signals according to steps A, B and C to provide normalised electromagnetic signals;
   - determining oxygen saturation based on said normalised electromagnetic signals according to steps D and E.
2. A pulse oximeter having an electromagnetic detector and means adapted to execute the steps of the method of claim 1.
3. A computer program [product] comprising instructions to cause the device of claim 2 to execute the steps of the method of claim 1.
4. A computer-readable medium having stored thereon the computer program of claim 3.

Claims 1 and 2 do not indicate a computer or a similar term. Implementation of steps by means of a computer program can be identified from claims 3 or 4 only.

A claim can be formulated on a specific level of abstraction in the claim and/or in the description.

Depending on the area of the computer program and the intended scope of protection the claim can be a combination of different modules. The following non-exhaustive list indicates examples of possible combinations:

- only the method (or functional features in an apparatus claim); the implementation of the method as computer program is indicated in dependent claims, in the description or as a computer program claim;
- functional features (method steps) in combination with computer hardware features (processor, storage means, input/output means ...) and/or generic functional computing features like reading data, transmitting data, storing data, ...;
- the method, computer hardware features and features of the system in which the computer is incorporated (e.g. measuring device, ATM, industrial control equipment, consumer product...);
- a non-technical method with software implementation details;
- a computer-readable record medium with instructions for executing a method;

62. EPO, BoA T 2048/07 (Dynamic data type enrichment/SAP) of 24.11.2011 http://www.epo.org/law-practice/case-law-appeals/recent/t072048eu1.html#q (accessed 13 March 2017).

- Data stream for the transmission of ...;
- Data structure in a protocol of a computer network ...;
- ....

If the method is **clearly technical** (chemistry, mechanics, ...) then it is very common that the implementation by means of a computer program is indicated in the description or only in the dependent claims. Furthermore, the claim might comprise features of the general technical system without the computer (e.g. airplane, steel production, lawn mower, chemical analysis ...).

Figure 4.5 indicates a flowchart that is a well-known means of expressing computer algorithms.[63] The flowchart is not the computer program with implementation details in a programming language in the narrower sense of computer science. The flowchart describes some functionality of a hot water supplying system of EP2423617-B1 having an US priority of 21.4.2009; classified in F24H1/18 (IPC). Water from different outlets is mixed in order to get the desired water temperature. The temperature of the water from different outlets is measured and compared. Water from one of two outlets is finally selected.

The granted patent has four independent claims:

1. A storage hot water supplying **apparatus** ....
9. An operation control apparatus for controlling the storage hot water supplying **apparatus** ....
10. An operation control **method** ....
11. A **program** for carrying out an operation control method of claim 10 ... causing a computer ....

Claim 10 is a method claim indicating method steps. This method is more like an algorithm in computer science. One does not know if method and algorithm are identical here because the requirements as to a computing algorithm (cf. Chapter 2, §2.06 [D]) are not checked by the patent office. Claim 11 reads 'A program ... causing a computer to execute ...'. However, in fact steps of method claim 10 are indicated which again indicate more the algorithm then the real computer program in a programming language. The program claim is a mental construction in order to include all possible computer programs in any programming language being an implementation of the claimed method steps.

63. Wikipedia, *Algorithm* https://en.wikipedia.org/wiki/Algorithm#Computer_algorithms (accessed 13 March 2017).

Figure 4.5 Flowchart in EP2423617 for One Embodiment

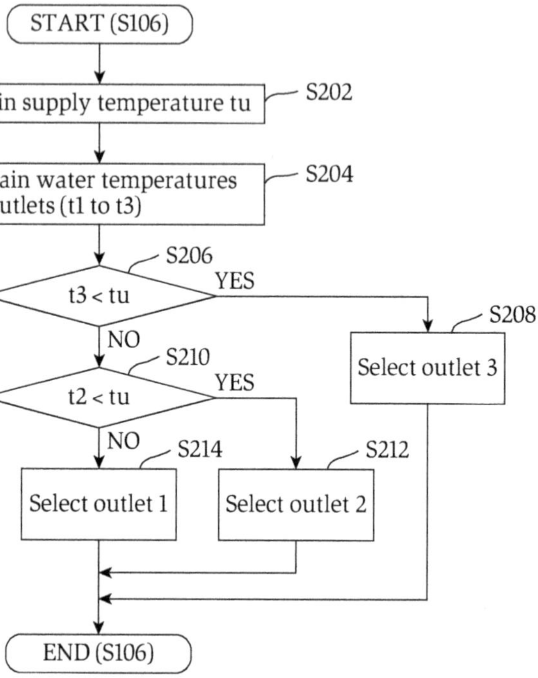

If the algorithm stems from a field excluded as such (Article 52(2,3) EPC) the claim has to show inventive features of a technical implementation. In computing a mixed claim is very often a claim comprising technical computing features in combination with non-technical features which are excluded from patentability if claimed as such (e.g. playing rules of a computer game) but implemented as a computer program.

The two traditional claim categories are apparatus and method.

§4.09 SUMMARY

The exclusion of computer programs as such has two basic interpretations according to legal practice at the EPO (cf. also Table 4.4) below:

- A computer program in a programming language cannot be the subject of a patent claim.
- From all computer programs only those which, when executed, provide a further technical effect inside or outside of the computer are patentable. The real computer program is not known. Based on the method implemented as computer program the effect of an assumed program is examined.

Over the years claimed subject matter is hardly ever refused as 'computer program as such'. The subject of a patent claim is very often a method which is the basis for an implementation as a computer program.

Table 4.4 Difference Between the Legal Term 'Computer Program' and Its Meaning in Computer Science

'Computer Program' as ***Legal Term*** *in Legal Practice under the EPC*	*'Computer Program' in* ***Computer Science***
Very often the term 'computer program' is used instead of method or algorithm; the concrete program is not known; parts of a computer program can be indicated in the description but not in the claim	**In computer science method, algorithm and computer programs are usually not synonyms!** A computer program in machine language code:[64] '00000000101000010000000000001100 00000000100011100001100000100001 10001100011000100000000000000000 10001100111100100000000000000100 ...'
The term 'computer program' designates a **claim category** (T1173/97, T0424/03); other formulations are possible like 'computer readable record carrier comprising instructions ...'	Computer program in the narrow sense of computing: Example for a piece of a program listing in a higher programming language, here an order confirmation program for a webshop:[65] '<eshop:insertOrder var = "orderID" customer = ${customer}"/> <c:choose> <c:when test = "${orderID > 0}"> <p class = "info"> Thank you for your purchase. Your Order Number is: <c:out value = "$ = "${orderID > 0}"/> </p> </c:when> <c:otherwise> <p class = "error"> Unexpected error processing the order! </p> </c:otherwise> </c:choose>'

Legal practice at the EPO for CII has for the last twenty years followed the basic two steps according to the COMVIK (T0641/00) approach:

(i) Eligibility to patent law is checked prima facie without a prior art document. If there is a technical character, then the claimed subject matter is not excluded from patentability.

64. Goel, A. *Computer Fundamentals* Pearson Education India 2010, 121.
65. Zambon, G. *Beginning JSP, JSF and Tomcat: Java Web Development* Apress 2012, 305.

(ii) If there is a technical character then examination of other requirements like novelty, inventive step will be done. A claim can be formulated as a mixture of technical and non-technical features. Determination of the inventive step according to the problem-and-solution approach will be done based on the features which contribute to the solution of a technical problem by technical means and lead to a technical effect.

In the context of computer science and software development the creation of an algorithm is important. An algorithm has to satisfy special requirements in computing. Such an algorithm can be the basis for a patent claim. Method, algorithm and computer program are not synonyms in computing. This distinction is also important because of the different means of intellectual property protection. The 'computer program' is protected by copyright. The method or algorithm is protected by patent law provided it fulfils the EPC requirements as to technicality. Methods of some sciences (e.g. business, social sciences, aesthetics) are not patentable under the EPC if claimed as such.

To sum up, different levels of abstraction exist for formulating patent claims related to computing and in particular of software. Only the most common examples are described here.

There is a low probability for the grant of a patent if features of areas excluded as such (e.g. business, rules of games, mental acts) are just combined with generic computer features (e.g. processor, input means, output means, storage; client/server). In other words, the whole application indicates nothing more than the use of a computer or computer network to automate a known or new non-technical method or algorithm. Mathematical expressions as a representation of a technical system are allowed. The whole context of the claimed subject matter has to be taken into account.

In the area of system software, internal processes of the functioning of the computer itself are claimed. Here, the formulation of the claim at a very high level of abstraction or at a very theoretical level could risk of being seen as too close to mathematical rules as such, and could risk being excluded from patentability.

The computer (microcomputer) and the respective software are becoming more and more part of devices and complex systems in both private and public life. Devices and systems are increasingly connected by all kind of networks. In such cases, patent claims usually describe the technical and/or non-technical functionality of the respective technical system (cf. Chapter 2, example gas pump with payment function). Functionality might include non-technical methods (e.g. financial transactions). In such cases the 'mixed invention' must show that a technical problem is solved by a technical means of the computer itself or of the system in which the computer is included. Claim formulation is a challenge in the area of user interfaces and in particular of graphical user interfaces. This is a result of the mixture of patentable and non-patentable features (e.g. aesthetic features, mental acts).

The future will show how patent law can be adapted to the requirements of modern information and communication technologies.

CHAPTER 5
Germany

§5.01 LEGAL ASPECTS ACCORDING TO GERMAN PATENT LAW

In Germany there is a long tradition of critical discussion of patentability issues with respect to Computer-Implemented Invention (CIIs).

On the one hand, arguments have been used in favour of patenting CIIs as a new type of technology and that patent law must adapt to new technologies.

On the other hand, some politicians voiced concerns because software may also be used for non-technological matters (as pure business methods or mental acts without any technical implementation) and therefore patents for CIIs should be refused.

At the beginning of the twenty-first century, the European Commission tried to codify and 'harmonize' the different European Union (EU) national patent laws and cement the practice of the European Patent Office of granting patents for CIIs provided they meet certain criteria. A directive was initiated and with this a heated debate started between supporters and opponents.[1] It was intended to have a different approach, as in the USA, and to exclude 'business methods' from patentability. Supporters of the proposed directive included Microsoft, IBM, Hewlett-Packard and the European Patent Office. Opponents included the FFII foundation and others, voicing concerns that an overbroad patent protection would suppress innovation and dampen competition. Finally, the directive was rejected.

Around the turn of the millennium the debate was not only discussed in expert circles, but to a large extent also at a political level with a major impact on public perception. The latter, unfortunately, is routinely without deeper understanding of the patent law system and sometimes may argue based on half-knowledge which then makes discussion difficult. For example, an argument often used is that software

1. Accessible at http://eur-lex.europa.eu/legal-content/EN/ALL/?uri=CELEX:52002PC0092 (accessed 13 March 2017).

patents would impede technical software development and that software developers would – if patents on software would be granted – be confronted with patent infringement law suits. Moreover, a warning message was given that Germany would soon be confronted with the same disadvantageous system as in the USA, where – it was argued – patents are possible for purely mental acts, such as raising a hand in school. Thus, the discussion sometimes tended to be very emotional.

Now, looking back, it can be seen that the software industry continues to develop, although patents are granted, and that infringement law suits for software companies are the exception.

However, software is challenging patent law due to a number of reasons as already mentioned in Chapter 3. It is therefore necessary to separate non-technical software applications (e.g. mental acts with software support) from technical software applications.

With technical understanding of computer science it is clear that it would be wrong to say that software is 'technical' in any case from a patent law perspective and also it would be wrong to say that software is 'non-technical' in any case. But, how to differentiate technical from non-technical applications?

§5.02 LEGAL REQUIREMENTS

Section 1 of the German Patent Act (Patentgesetz, PatG) is almost identical to the text of the European Patent Convention (EPC), Article 52(1)–(3) EPC.

Section 1 PatG reads:

> (1) Patents shall be granted for any *inventions, in all fields of technology,* provided that they are new, involve an inventive step and are susceptible of industrial application.
> (2) ...
> (3) The following in particular shall *not be regarded as inventions* within the meaning of paragraph 1:
> 1. discoveries, scientific theories and mathematical methods;
> 2. aesthetic creations;
> 3. schemes, rules and methods for performing mental acts, playing games or doing business, and *programs for computers;*
> 4. *presentations of information.*
>
> (4) Paragraph 3 shall exclude the patentability of the subject-matter or activities referred to therein only to the extent to which a patent application or patent relates to such subject-matter or activities *as such.*

The added emphasis refers to important aspects for CIIs.

Inventive step is coded in Section 4 PatG, which reads:

> An invention shall be considered as involving an inventive step if, having regard to the state of the art, it is not obvious to a person skilled in the art. If the state of the art also includes documents within the meaning of Section 3 item 2, these

> documents shall not be considered in deciding whether there has been an inventive step.

Section 34(4) PatG specifies:

> The description shall disclose the invention in a manner sufficiently clear and complete for the invention to be carried out by a person skilled in the art.

Under Section 14 PatG the content of the claims determines the extent of protection of a patent. An area of the invention that is merely presented in the description and not sufficiently clearly integrated into a patent claim is not protected (BGH, GRUR 1987, p. 626, Rundfunkübertragungssystem). The inventive idea should be described in such an abstract manner that it comprises all conceivable embodiments. Limits are set, however, by the original disclosure and the state of the art.

The German Patent Act generally excludes programs for data processing systems (software) from patent protection only if they are claimed *as such*. How to apply this general regulation in daily examination is explained in the Examination Guidelines.[2]

Section 4.3.1 of the Examination Guidelines (Richtlinie für die Prüfung von Patentanmeldungen) states:

> Inventions involving a computer program, an arithmetical or organisational rule, other software characteristics or a program-related process are in principle eligible for patent protection provided they contain a technical teaching. A technical teaching is a systematic teaching using controllable natural forces to achieve a result with clear cause and effect (BGH, last stated in BlPMZ 2000, p. 276, p. 278, Sprachanalyseeinrichtung).[3]

Section 4.3.2 of the Examination Guidelines explains that programs and rules are excluded from patent protection in so far as they are claimed *as such*. In this context it is stated:

> The subject-matter mentioned in the German Patent Act Section 1(3) is, by act of law, not regarded as inventions; however, patentability is excluded *only* to the extent to which protection is sought for the subject-matter *as such* (Section 1(3) PatG) i.e. it is excluded from patent protection only insofar as it is claimed in isolation from a specific function. But when used to solve a specific technical problem it is – in that context – in principle patentable (BGH, Mitt. 2001, p. 553, p. 555, Suche fehlerhafter Zeichenketten). [Emphasis added.]

Consequently, this exclusion does not apply to program-related inventions, such as for technical instructions contained in programs or technical instructions drafted as a process or apparatus. Insofar as technical processes or apparatus are claimed in connection with subject-matter mentioned in Section 1(2) and (3) PatG, they are in principle patentable. This is true, above all, for programs performing procedural steps

2. An English version of the Examination Guidelines (2004) is available at https://www.dpma.de/docs/service/formulare_eng/patent_eng/4/p2796_1.pdf (accessed 14 March 2017).
3. https://www.dpma.de/docs/service/formulare_eng/patent_eng/4/p2796_1.pdf (accessed 14 March 2017).

in conventional technical fields (cf. BGH, Mitt. 2001, p. 553, p. 555, Suche fehlerhafter Zeichenketten).

Section 4.3.4 of the Examination Guidelines states:

> Program-related inventions may have a technical character even if the technical means used for the solution, e.g. data processing units or computer, circuit or control elements are already known. It is not detrimental if each of the individual elements *separately* operates in a known way. The technical character of a process carried out by means of a program cannot be challenged on the ground that an ordinary data processing unit is used for the intended purpose.[4]

'The assessment of patentability of a claim is to be made independent of the claim category', according to the Examination Guidelines. In other words, a software program will not simply be patentable merely because it is claimed as a computer-readable medium or as an apparatus.[5]

Due to the technical character requirement, this is different to the patent system of the United States of America. Without any technical reference, computer programs are considered as having no technical effect. However, this does not mean that software or CIIs are generally excluded from patentability. On the contrary, a look at the Patent Register reveals that there exists a huge number of granted CII patents. The point is how to draft the claims in order to overcome the official objections.

§5.03 PROCEDURAL AND FORMAL ASPECTS

General information referring to the patent procedure may be found on the website of the German Patent and Trademark Office and will be presented below.[6]

[A] Application Procedure and Request for Examination

In order to actually obtain a patent, an applicant must file a request for examination and pay the examination fee (EUR 350). Only then will the Office carry out the substantive examination of the application required for granting a patent.

The examination request must be filed within seven years of the filing date. From the third year after filing, annual fees must be paid to maintain an application in force.

A separate search request concerning the application can be filed before filing a request for substantive examination. In that case, the Office will indicate which documents might be of relevance for assessing the patentability of the invention.

When a request for examination of the application has been filed, a patent examiner will determine the state of the art relevant for the invention and examine whether a patent can be granted against this background. If the invention does not

4. https://www.dpma.de/docs/service/formulare_eng/patent_eng/4/p2796_1.pdf (accessed 14 March 2017).
5. https://www.dpma.de/docs/service/formulare_eng/patent_eng/4/p2796_1.pdf (accessed 14 March 2017).
6. https://www.dpma.de/english/patent/procedures/index.html (accessed 14 March 2017).

meet the requirements or if the application has other defects, the patent examiner will send an official communication informing of any deficiencies (office actions).

The applicant has the opportunity to respond and to remedy deficiencies within in the time limit fixed in the communication. In contrast to US practice it is important to note that in Germany amendments may not go beyond the scope of the original disclosure, meaning that a complete description of the invention should be submitted on the date of filing.

[B] Opposition Proceedings

Anybody can oppose the grant of a patent within nine months from the publication of the patent specification. If no opposition is filed, the patent becomes legally valid upon expiry of the opposition period. The patent will then become valid retroactively from the date of filing for a period of up to twenty years.

The notice of opposition allows the opponent to state the reasons why he considers the patent to be unlawful. Within the scope of the fee-based opposition procedure, a panel of members of a patent division of the German Patent and Trademark Office re-examines whether the patent meets requirements for grant or maintenance. The patent will be either revoked or maintained as granted or in an amended form of more limited scope.

[C] Appeal Procedure

Appeals against a decision of the patent examiner to refuse the application or against decisions in opposition procedures can be lodged at the Federal Patent Court (Bundespatentgericht), which is located in Munich.

[D] Nullity Procedure

Even after expiry of the opposition period, a patent in force can be challenged by an action for the declaration of nullity brought before the Federal Patent Court.

[E] Means of Redress

Patents are granted only by the German Patent and Trademark Office, located in Munich.

If an application is rejected by an examiner at the Office, the applicant may file an appeal with the German Federal Patent Court. If a negative decision is received from the Federal Patent Court the only redress is to apply to the German Supreme Court, providing that the appeal is allowed by the Federal Patent Court. In most cases, a complaint (appeal to the German Supreme Court) is only available if the lower court has granted leave to complain. The Federal Patent Court will, however, only grant leave to complain in exceptional cases, *inter alia* if a point of law of fundamental importance arises.

The Supreme Court is the highest court in Germany and decides on patent matters in the following situations:

(1) ex-parte proceedings: in appeal proceedings of an applicant whose application has been rejected (by the German Patent and Trademark Office and by the Federal Court as well);
(2) inter-partes proceedings: in appeal proceedings of an opposition case against a patent in dispute (previous instance is the Federal Court); and
(3) inter-partes proceedings: in appeal proceedings of a party in nullity proceedings before the Federal Court.

§5.04 CLAIM FORMATS

In effect (and from a dogmatic point of view), only two categories of claims exist: method and apparatus.

However, for CIIs other claim formats may be used, namely:

- method;
- apparatus;
- system;
- computer program (*see* decision of Federal Court **19 W (pat) 61/03**);[7]
- computer program product (*see* decision of the Federal Court **19 W (pat) 4/09**);[8]
- network;
- computer-readable medium;
- signal;
- protocol.

§5.05 GUIDELINES OR PUBLISHED OFFICIAL INFORMATION

There are no specific guidelines for CIIs.

However, on the homepage of the German Patent and Trademark Office certain information is listed, which is summarized below.[9]

7. http://juris.bundespatentgericht.de/cgi-bin/rechtsprechung/document.py?Gericht = bpatg&Art = en&sid = 5a216307662e2a0238f37dce7980efe9&nr = 18515&pos = 0&anz = 1&Blank = 1.pdf (accessed 14 March 2017).
8. http://juris.bundespatentgericht.de/cgi-bin/rechtsprechung/document.py?Gericht = bpatg&Art = en&sid = 5ed3dc96f9eaa676959983709b3f5cb8&nr = 15857&pos = 0&anz = 1&Blank = 1.pdf (accessed 14 March 2017).
9. https://www.dpma.de/patent/patentschutz/schutzvoncomputerprogrammen/index.html; the information on this website is only available in German (accessed 13 March 2017).

Generally, a technical character of a CII is required.

Technical character will be affirmed if the invention is based on natural forces ('Naturkräfte') or technical means are used, e.g. hydraulic forces, electric currents in circuits or control units or signals in data processing devices.

In order to determine whether the invention has a technical character, the subject matter must be considered in its entirety. It is not admissible to consider an individual feature of a claim isolated from the other claim features. Non-technical features shall also be included. For example, programmed software that controls brakes cannot be patented on its own. As a whole, however, the combination of brakes and control software is patentable (*see* the key decision of the Supreme Court **Antiblockiersystem, X ZB 19/78,** which will be discussed in more detail in §5.06.

For assessment of the technical character of a device, it is also not important whether a (further) technical effect is achieved (unlike for the EPO), whether technology is enriched by it or whether it makes a contribution to the state of the art.

In the case of software for data processing systems, the question arises as to whether the invention is patentable only if the software requires a new and inventive design of the data processing system.

Case law has established that CIIs can have a technical character even if the technical means used (e.g. data processing systems, or computer switching or control elements) are not new. Here, too, the invention is to be considered as a whole. For example, in the decision **Seitenpuffer, X ZB 13/88** (*see* §5.06), the Supreme Court has made it clear that a CII is technical when it concerns the functionality of a data processing system as such and allows the direct interaction of its elements.

The German Patent and Trademark Office has published the following main idea:

> In the examination procedure, it is sufficient if the applicant makes the technical character of the invention credible. If there is clear evidence that the invention is technical, the Office will, in case of doubt, recognize the technical character of the invention.

However, from a practical point of view, our impression is different. In case of doubt, examiners tend to deny the technical character of an invention, because for this kind of rejection the reasoning is easy; it is not necessary to deal with prior art documents and to specifically examine claim features in these documents. Therefore, the applicant is well advised to incorporate as many technical features and technical implementations as possible in the original disclosure. Thus, any possible doubts of the examiner may be dispelled from the beginning.

And another impression is that this assessment differs from examiner to examiner, which does not seem a good basis for legal certainty and transparency.

Regarding the drafting of the claims, the Office notes that in addition to, or instead of, structural features (circuitry details), function and function-related features are also permissible.

For the drawings, the Office suggests using a data flow plan and also a program flowchart.

Finally, it is noted that short extracts from a computer program in a common, well-defined programming language can be allowed in the description.

§5.06 HISTORICAL OVERVIEW

The adoption of patent law to new technical areas, such as computer science, is a recurrent issue in Germany. This was true for several technical areas, such as biotechnology, and is now so for computer science. However, as computer science is present in nearly all classic fields of technology (mechanical engineering, mechatronics, medical technology, automotive technology, etc.), the question of how to deal with this technology from a patent law perspective is hugely important.

In Germany, the starting point for decisions dealing with the patentability criteria for 'new' technical fields is the **Rote Taube** decision of the Supreme Court in 1969, dealing with a method for rearing pigeons.[10]

The Court tried to find a general formula as a delimitation criterion for non-patentable subject matter on the one hand and patentable subject matter on the other hand.

The Court defined the following aspects as playing an essential role in this evaluation:

(1) systematic teaching;
(2) the use of controllable forces of nature; and
(3) reaching a causally foreseeable result.

Even today, some decisions still refer to this central Supreme Court decision.

In the 1980s and 1990s, German courts mainly denied patentability for software-related inventions.

A major change was made 1980 with the key decision of the Supreme Court **Antiblockiersystem, BGH, X ZB 19/78**, dated 13 May 1980, in which the Court held that software which was embedded in a technical system, such as a car's braking system, may very well be technical and patentable.[11] The claim related to an automotive braking system, which was a major cornerstone in legal practice.

Further, the Court stated in this decision that the subject matter as defined in the claims had to be evaluated as a whole.

It is worth mentioning that in this early decision, the Supreme Court already held that for assessment of the technical character of an invention (and thus for evaluating patentability) it is not important whether the technical claim features are known in the prior art.

About ten years later, in 1991, there was further liberalization with the decision **Seitenpuffer, BGH, X ZB 13/88.**[12] The invention related to a multi-step storage system of a computer. The Court held that if the subject matter relates to the functioning of a computing system it has to be judged to be technical in nature.

10. **Rote Taube, BGH, Beschl.** dated 27 March 1969, Az.: X ZB 15/67.
11. http://web.archive.org/web/20040126135012/www.uni-leipzig.de/urheberrecht/ressrc/material/vorles/grur/grur80-849.pdf (in German, accessed 14 March 2017).
12. http://www.jurpc.de/jurpc/show?id=1991_10_30000&type=pdf (in German, accessed 14 March 2017).

A similar argumentation was given 1992 in the judgment **Tauchcomputer, BGH, X ZB 43/91**, where software for a diving computer (due to the processing of technical measurement signals deemed a technical apparatus) was judged to be technical in nature.[13]

At the end of the 1990s, two further critical decisions were issued, **Logikverifikation, BGH, X ZB 11/98** dated 13 December 1999 and **Sprachanalyseeinrichtung, BGH, X ZB 15/98**, dated 11 May 2000. The Supreme Court was also able to maintain the liberalizing trend. Specifically, the Senate judged that even if the user of an invention is involved in the CII process by way of user interaction, this fact does not mean that the subject matter is excluded from patentability (as was held in an earlier decision).

According to the Supreme Court decision **Suche fehlerhafter Zeichenketten, BGH, X ZB 16/00,** dated 17 October 2001, the so-called 'concrete technical problem solution formula' was developed for the first time.

This approach is actually still applied and, therefore, is of major importance in practical everyday work. This approach concerns dividing patentable from non-patentable inventions with the question:

> 'Does the invention provide a solution for a concrete technical problem, which is solved with technical means?'

If so, it will be evaluated as technical; otherwise it will not.

This question is still fundamental in daily practice. Therefore, it is helpful to draft applications in the field of computer science and software in a manner of a technical problem (e.g.: reduction of resources for storage or bandwidth capacity, or faster computation) and to elaborate concrete technical means for solving said problem.

In the decision **Dynamische Dokumentengenerierung, BGH, Xa ZB 20/08**, dated 22 April 2010, the Supreme Court held that the interaction between a client and a server system is technical in nature. However, relating to the question of patentability, the Court held that it is necessary that a technical problem is solved by technical means.

According to established case law, an application generally has to be evaluated as a whole (*see* for example the Supreme Court decision **Steuerungseinrichtung für Untersuchungsmodalitäten, BGH, X ZB 22/07**, decision dated 20 January 2009). All claim features must be considered when assessing patentability issues. A claim may consist of technical and non-technical features, but it is not admissible to split the claim into its features. However, in practice, examiners often tend to do exactly this.

In the judgment **Wiedergabe topografischer Informationen, BGH, X ZR 47/07**, the Supreme Court held that an examination for the existence of an exclusion (for patent protection) only serves as a kind of coarse assessment for filtering those cases in

13. https://www.jurion.de/urteile/bgh/1992-02-04/x-zr-43_91/ (in German, accessed 14 March 2017).

which the patent claim contains no technical instruction at all that can reasonably be taken as the basis for the examination of inventive step.

Thus, in Germany, it is also possible that an application encompassing technical and non-technical features in a claim will be granted. In accordance with EPO practice, for an application consisting of a mixture of technical and non-technical features, only those instructions are to be considered for assessment of the inventive step which contribute to or at least influence the technical solution by technical means (**Wiedergabe topografischer Informationen, BGH, X ZR 47/07** decision dated 26 October 2010 and **Routenplanung, BGH, X ZR 3/12** decision dated 18 December 2012). In contrast, other aspects that do not contribute to a solution of the technical problem are not taken into account for the assessment of inventive step.

In sum, a trend may be indicated of a very restrictive practice that denies patentability of CIIs taking a liberal view, in which software may very well be patentable if it solves a technical problem and further complies with the other requirements of novelty and inventive step. This picture is represented in the following table, which captures major Supreme Court Decisions in timely sequence, in which the right side represents decisions taking a more liberal approach and on the left side, decisions taking a more restrictive approach. The pendulum movement may be perceived easily.

Table 5.01: Overview over major Supreme Court Decisions in Germany in the last fifty years

Liberal View		**Restrictive View**
X ZB 15/67, Rote Taube	1969	
	1976	X ZB 23/74, Dispositionsprogramm P-
X ZB 19/78, Antiblockiersystem, T+	1980	
X ZB 13/88, Seitenpuffer	1991	
X ZR 43/91, Tauchcomputer, T+	1992	
X ZB 11/98, Logikverifikation, T+	1999	
X ZB 15/98, Sprachanalyseeinrichtung, T+	2000	
	2001	X ZB 16/00, Suche fehlerhafter Zeichenketten, P-
	2004	X ZB 34/03, Rentabilitätsermittlung, P-
	2004	X ZB 33/03, Anbieten interaktiver Hilfe, P-
X ZB 22/07, Steuerungseinrichtung für Untersuchungsmodalitäten, T+P+	2009	
X ZB 9/09, Bildunterstützung bei Katheternavigation, T+, P+	2010	
Xa ZB 20/08, Dynamische Dokumentengenerierung T+, P+	2010	

Liberal View		Restrictive View
	2010	X ZR 47/07, Wiedergabe topografischer Informationen, T+, E-
	2011	X ZR 121/09, Webseitenanzeige, T+, P-
	2012	X ZR 3/12, Routenplanung
X ZB 1/15, Flugzeugzustand	2015	
X ZR 37/13 Bildstrom	2015	
X ZR 64/14, Datengenerator	2016	

§5.07 ACTUAL EXAMINATION PRACTICE AND BEST PRACTICE

As noted above, an essential requirement for patentability is assessment of the technical character, pursuant to Section 1(1) PatG.

In contrast to the EPO approach, examination of CIIs in Germany entails a three-step approach:

(1) In the first step, it is examined whether the claimed subject matter is a technical invention within the meaning of Section 1(1) PatG, and thus fulfils the so-called technicality requirement. This is affirmed, if the claimed teaching uses a technical device.[14]

(2) In the second step, it is examined whether the claimed subject matter is not excluded from patentability according to Section 1(3), (4) PatG. According to case law of the Supreme Court (**Elektronischer Zahlungsverkehr, X ZB 20/03**, dated 24 May 2004) this requirement is deemed to be fulfilled if the subject matter contains instructions for solving a concrete technical problem using technical means.

(3) In the third step, the relative requirements are examined, i.e. in relation to state of the art. In particular, novelty and inventive step are assessed.[15] For the assessment of inventive step, the same approach is used in Germany as taken by the EPO: only the technical features are considered when evaluating inventive step.

Compared to the approach taken by the EPO, where a two-step approach is applied, the German practice may be interpreted as being slightly more restrictive.

According to the practice of the German Patent and Trademark Office and of the courts, the main issue is the evaluation of inventive step, which is the most common ground for rejection of an application (e.g. **17 W (pat) 9/14**, dated 19 April 2016).

14. Supreme Court, Flugzeugzustand, X ZB 1/15, dated 30 June 2015.
15. *See also* Claudia Schwarz & Sabine Kruspig, *Computerimplementierte Erfindungen – Patentschutz von Software*, Recital 877 (only available in German).

Best Practice

It is good practice to identify the technical differences with respect to the state of the art and disclose them in the application.

From a practical point of view, examiners tend to refuse an application in the field of computing if some claims features may be evaluated as being non-technical. In particular, if the technicality of these claim features is not explained in the description, examiners tend to construe the claim features in a very broad sense, which may render them non-technical. It might then be argued that the subject matter lacks inventive step. For this reason applicants are well advised to refer to specific technical embodiments and implementations, which need to be described in the description.

In this respect, it is important to mention that it is necessary to incorporate as many concrete technical details which distinguish the application from the prior art as possible into the description, which will be very useful in examination proceedings and may serve as a fallback position.

In particular, it has been established that it is helpful to define and explain the claim features and the terms used in the claims. Defining passages should be incorporated in the description. These definitions should specifically relate to the subject matter claimed. It is not necessary to include well known definitions if they are used in the standard sense (computer, signal processing, etc.). If a specific claim feature should be construed specifically and not according to the 'usual' technical understanding, this is allowed, but the specific meaning should be defined. An application may serve as its own dictionary, according to the Supreme Court in **Spannschraube, BGH, X ZR85/96**, dated 2 March 1999. However, in this case, a specific definition in relation to the subject matter needs to be included into the description. For this reason, it is a good advice to identify and elaborate on concrete technical implementations in order to avoid an objection relating to non-compliance with the sufficiency of clear disclosure requirement (Section 34(4) PatG), *see* for example a rejection of an application in appeal proceedings in case **19 W (pat) 46/06**, dated 19 July 2010.[16]

16. Another Senate of the Federal Patent Court, however, evaluated the question of whether the German Patent Act provides the possibility to refuse a patent application due to a lack of clarity. In the decision **15 W (pat) 33/08**, the fifteenth Senate took the view that a lack of clarity could be no basis for a rejection of an application.

    This legal position is confirmed by a decision of the Supreme Court in **Fugenband, BGH, X ZR 11/13** (dated 27 October 2015). Generally, the claims have to be clear and concise. With respect to the requirement of clarity of the claims, it should be pointed out that an examination of already granted claims for clarity is not provided for either in the European Patent Convention or in the German Patent Act. The patent holder has been granted a legal position with the granted patent or the patent amended in the opposition proceedings, which can be fully or partially recognized only in the cases provided for by law, i.e. if there is an objection or grounds for objection. The European Patent Convention, like national law, regulates conclusively the grounds of objection or invalidity, which do not refer to the lack of clarity (Article 100, 138 EPC, Sections 21, 22 PatG). It follows that an examination for clarity is in any event not at issue insofar as the alleged ambiguity was already contained in the granted claims (*see* EPA, decision of 24 March 2015 – **G 3/14**).

§5.08 SUMMARY

In Germany, before the turn of the millennium, decisions dealing with subject matter involving computer science or in relation to software were often denied patentability according to Section 1(3), (4) PatG. Courts tended to be very restrictive in this field. From a global perspective, in the past, German courts tended to follow a more restrictive approach compared to the EPO.

Nowadays, the situation has changed. Usually, eligibility for patent protection due to absolute grounds and the (non-)existence of an invention in the sense of Section 1 PatG is critically discussed only very rarely.

Today, the main issue is inventive step. Most decisions denying patentability are based on non-compliance with the inventive step requirement. As with the EPO, technical character (Technicality) is a core issue and prerequisite for patentability.

In sum, the following requirements are of particular importance for CIIs, and have to be met:

- technicality requirement - Section 1(1) PatG;
- no exclusion form patentability - Section 1(3), (4) PatG;
- novelty - Sections 1, 3 PatG;
- inventive step - Sections 1, 4 PatG;
- industrial applicability - Sections 1, 5 PatG;
- sufficiency of disclosure - Section 34(4) PatG.

Any amendments, for example made during the examination proceedings for delimiting the subject matter against the prior art and limiting the claim features that are to be added to the application, have to be proven as originally disclosed. It is not admissible to add claim features that are not part of the original disclosure.[17]

§5.09 CASE LAW IN GERMANY

According to the recent annual reports of the German Patent and Trademark Office about 10% of patents relate to software-related or CII applications.[18] This figure is increasing annually. However, as there is no specific class for CIIs, many are associated with and examined under different classes.

The German Patent and Trademark Office examines whether the invention has a technical character, whether the invention as a whole or some of its characteristic features are excluded from patent protection, and the other requirements of novelty and inventive step. Just because software is included in an application it cannot simply be refused. Generally, it is examined whether the claimed subject matter solves a technical problem with technical means. If so, patent protection should be available (provided that the other conditions are also fulfilled).

17. *See* Section 38 PatG.
18. See the sum of the respective figures in Annual Report 2015, German Patent and Trademark Office; an English version is available at: https://www.dpma.de/docs/service/veroeffentlichungen/jahresberichte_en/annualreport2015.pdf (accessed 14 March 2017).

However, an analysis of case law reveals that different argumentation is used within the decisions in the different fields of technology where software and computing may be applied, although from a technical point of view there should be no differences. An example is control software for controlling a piston-cylinder arrangement as opposed to control software for controlling a simulation process, wherein the control software is based on the same aspects.

Therefore, the following sections provide an overview over mainly Supreme Court and some Federal Patent Court decisions in the different fields of computer science.

All the decisions are available for download at the respective publicly available databases:

- Supreme Court decisions: http://juris.bundesgerichtshof.de/cgi-bin/rechtsprechung/list.py?Gericht = bgh&Art = en&Datum = Aktuell&Sort = 12288.
- Federal Patent Court decisions: http://juris.bundesgerichtshof.de/cgi-bin/rechtsprechung/list.py?Gericht = bgh&Art = en&Datum = Aktuell&Sort = 12288.

[A] System Software: Storage, Human Computer Interfaces/GUI, Security Software

Overview

If it was possible to sufficiently describe the technical involvement of the computer program-related aspects in this field, generally eligibility (technical character and no exclusion) are affirmed and patent protection should be possible if novelty and inventive step are present.

[1] Datengenerator

In the Supreme Court decision **Datengenerator, BGH, X ZR 64/14,** dated 13 September 2016, the subject matter refers to apparatus for protecting computer programs against unauthorized access and thus lies within the field of security software. The claim relates to an external data generator which communicates with the program to be protected and analyses this communication for failures. In specific states, an abnormal communication is detected which may indicate a missing user authorization. The Supreme Court judged that feature group 4 (referring to different logical states and the output of data depending on one of these states) has a technical character and overruled the argumentation of the Federal Court in the preceding instance. With regard to technical character and patentability (exclusion as a program as such) the Court affirmed both, but revoked the patent in dispute over lack of novelty.

[2] *Entsperrbild*

The subject matter in the decision of the Supreme Court, **Entsperrbild, BGH, X ZR 110/13**, dated 25 August 2015 relates to a computer-implemented method for unlocking a screen on a mobile phone.

Claim 1 reads:

> 1. A computer-implemented method of controlling a portable electronic device (400, 1000) comprising a touch-sensitive display (408, 1014), comprising:
> detecting (308, 908) contact with the touch-sensitive display (408, 1014) while the device is in a user-interface lock state;
> transitioning (314, 914) the device (400, 1000) to a user-interface unlock state if the detected contact corresponds to a predefined gesture; and maintaining (312,912) the device (400, 1000) in the user-interface lock state if the detected contact does not correspond to the predefined gesture;
> characterized by
> moving an unlock image (402, 1002, 1008) along a predefined displayed path on the touch sensitive display (408, 1014) in accordance with the contact, wherein the unlock image (402, 1002, 1008) is a graphical, interactive user-interface object with which a user interacts in order to unlock the device (400, 1000).

Further claims relate to a portable electronic device and a computer program product.

The Supreme Court held that information-related features are to be evaluated, whether or not they are an embodiment of a technical feature. If they are, the information-related feature has technical character and is to be considered when assessing inventive step.

The Supreme Court affirmed the decision of the Federal Court and denied inventive step.

[3] *Wiedergabe topografischer Informationen*

Another nullity appeal proceeding is the case **Wiedergabe topografischer Informationen, BGH, X ZR 47/07**, dated 26 October 2010. Claim 1 states:

> A method for the perspective display of a part of a topographic map by selecting, in dependence of a position (c) of a vehicle, topographic information from a data structure, where under the influence of a coordinate transformation the display takes place according to a viewing position (k) which moves together with the position (c) of the vehicle and with a solid angle (g) that takes into account the instantaneous motion of the vehicle,
> characterized in that for
> an earthbound vehicle the viewing position is above the earth and the solid angle (g) contains an actual simulated position of the vehicle itself.

Claim 17 refers to a device in form of an apparatus claim.

The Federal Court revoked the patent in suit because the subject matter does not lie within a field of technology as required in Article 52 EPC and was therefore found to be not patentable.

The subject matter refers to a car navigation system and the problem is to display the topographic card information in a more user friendly way. The Federal Court argued that this is a pure ergonomic problem and not a technical one, whereas the Supreme Court disagreed with this statement and judged that the invention is within a field of technology and is not excluded form patentability. However, in view of state of the art, inventive step was denied.

The Court held in its headnote:

> The selection of a manner of visualization of position-related topographical information (here: central perspective) which is appropriate for the navigation of a vehicle is not considered as a technical instruction for the person skilled in the art in the examination of inventive step for a method for reproducing topographic information.

[4] Windows-Dateiverwaltung

The decision of the Supreme Court, **Windows-Dateiverwaltung, BGH, X ZR 27/07,** dated 20 April 2010 refers to the field of operating systems and concerns a file allocation table. The patent in dispute was issued by the EPO, number 0 618 540, with effect for the Federal Republic of Germany. In nullity proceedings before the German Federal Court the patent was revoked due to lack of inventive step. In this respect, the rock ridge protocol, known in the prior art, was referred to.

Claim 1 reads:

> 1. A method of operating a data processing system (10) comprising memory (16) holding an operating system (17), and a processor (12) for running the operating system (18), the method comprising:
>
> a) storing (58, 59) in the memory (16) a first directory entry (18) holding a short filename for a file;
> b) storing (58, 59) in the memory (16) a second directory entry (20) being associated with the first directory entry (18) and holding a long filename for the file, said long filename having more characters than said short filename, said second directory entry (20) further holding information (42) indicating the said second directory entry (20) holds said long filename; and
> c) in case that the operating system (17) permits only short filenames and said information (42) is set to make said second directory entry (20) invisible to the operating system (17), locating the file by accessing said first directory entry (18) or, in case that the operating system (17) permits long filenames and said information (42) is set to make said second directory entry (20) visible to the operating system (17), locating the file accessing said second directory entry (20).

A data processing system and a computer-readable medium is claimed in further independent claims.

The Supreme Court overruled the negative decision of the Federal Court and found that the question of how to store data in a data processing system for access by different operating systems is a technical problem. The invention solves this technical problem with technical means by suggesting a special storage arrangement. In the end, novelty and inventive step were affirmed.

[5] Anbieten Interaktiver Hilfe

In an earlier decision **Anbieten interaktiver Hilfe, BGH, X ZB 33/03**, dated 19 October 2004 the subject matter refers to the purchase and ordering of products via the internet, where a user uses a client which is in data communication with a server system. The invention wants to support the user in his purchase actions. The Supreme Court held that providing information on a user interface in form of an interactive help is not eligible for patent protection. However, the Court also pointed out in the headnote of its decision that to conform with the concrete technical problem solution formula it is sufficient if at least a part of the problem has a technical character. So, in general, there may exist parts of the problem which are non-technical (having for example economic or organizational character), but if at least one part of the problem is technical, then the invention might be patentable.

[B] System Software: Modelling, Simulation, Software Development

Overview

Few decisions exist in this field and, in general, patentability tends to be denied. Only one Supreme Court decision exists. Therefore, in the following, various Federal Court decisions are listed, too.

[1] X ZR 90/14

In the decision of the Supreme Court, **X ZR 90/14**, dated 29 November 2017, the subject matter relates to the field of orthodontics and in particular to producing a digital dataset based on a tooth model and simulating teeth movement.

The claim 1 reads:

> A method for producing a digital data set representing a final tooth arrangement, said method comprising:
> providing an initial digital data set representing an initial tooth arrangement of a patient's teeth;
> presenting a visual image based on the initial data set,
> wherein the step of providing a digital data set representing an initial tooth arrangement of a patient's teeth comprises scanning a three-dimensional model of the patient's teeth or scanning the patient's teeth;
> manipulating the visual image to reposition individual teeth in the visual image,

> wherein the manipulating step comprises:
> defining boundaries about at least some of the individual teeth; and
> moving at least some of the tooth boundaries relative to the other teeth in an image based on the digital data set; and
> producing a final digital data set representing the final tooth arrangement of the patient's teeth with repositioned teeth as observed in the image.

The Federal Court has revoked the patent in dispute due to a lack on inventive step. The Supreme Court held that the subject matter of claim 1 lies in a technical field and the existence of a technical teaching was affirmed (step 1 of the 3-step approach, *see* Chapter §5.07 above) and does not fall under an exclusion of patentability (step 2 of the 3-step approach).

In general, the Supreme Court confirms the opinion of the Federal Court that inventive step is to be denied. However, the Supreme Court applied a more liberal view and judged that all claim features of claim 1 have to be taken into account for assessing inventive step, in particular also features 2.2–2.5 are technical in nature and have to be considered.

Therefore, this decision may be interpreted as a trend for more liberalization in the field of modelling and simulation, because the key argument the Supreme Court used is that if a structure of a model is defined, this contributes to a technical problem solving (*see* recital 30 of the decision).

[2] 17 W (pat) 54/13

In the decision of the Federal Court, **17 W (pat) 54/13**, dated 21 April 2016, the subject matter refers to a CAD system by using a model for products to be manufactured. Claim 1 is drafted on an abstract level and starts 'Electronic data processing system for automatically or half-automatically constructing a technical product…'. In a storage system, different models for different products are provided and rules are applied in order to select an appropriate model for the product to be constructed. The Court denied inventive step and left aside the question of whether or not the subject matter is to be excluded from patentability or if some of the claim features should be regarded as non-technical.

This decision is an example of the general approach of the seventeenth Senate of the Federal Court to dismiss appeals for applications which are drafted on an abstract level. The introduction of a feature 'simulation of a process' with no further details does not generally render the subject matter patentable.

[3] 23 W (pat) 11/13

In the context of a simulation of surgical interventions, the decision of the Federal Court, **23 W (pat) 11/13**, dated 30 June 2015 should be mentioned.

The claim 1 relates to:

> A simulation system for surgical interventions in human and veterinary medicine comprising an anatomically simulated real training and test phantom by producing an anatomical model with real tissue properties.

The claim consists of further features, including 'the system is furthermore formed in such a way that the risk structures are detectable and are electrically conductive structures' and the system comprises 'an electronic control, measuring and evaluation unit for determination of the degree of injury'.

An electric circuit is used for measuring the degree of injury.

In the decision, the Court did not differentiate between technical and non-technical features. The application was granted. It seems that the introduction of technical features (here, the electric circuit) may be helpful although the subject matter lies within the field of simulation, which, in general, is judged more restrictively.

[4] 7 W (pat) 25/11

The decision of the Federal Court, **7 W (pat) 25/11**, dated 14 November 2012 refers to a computer processing system for integration of two frameworks. The claim comprises *inter alia* the features 'providing a generic container for ... providing communication functionality in relation to the frameworks', 'providing an adapter component for connecting one of the frameworks with other instances' among other things. The German Patent and Trademark Office did not carry out a search and rejected the application due to ineligibility for patent protection. The Federal Court remitted the case for examination to the first instance.

[C] Application Software: Telecommunications, Data Transfer, Image Processing

Overview

Generally, applications in the field of telecommunication and video processing are judged to have technical character and are not excluded from patent protection.

Several decisions deal with subject matter involving video technology and processing/display of video signals. Usually, technicality and exclusion form patentability are not critically discussed and eligibility for patent protection on absolute grounds is generally affirmed. In this respect we refer to the decisions **X ZR 29/11**, dated 18 December 2014, **X ZR 101/11**, dated 17 June 2014, **X ZR 102/11**, dated 17 June 2014, **Bildanzeigegerät, X ZR 41/11**, dated 15 October 2013.

[1] X ZR 68/15

A decision in this field is **X ZR 68/15**, dated 25 October 2016. The nullity proceeding is directed against the patent EP 1206881 granted by the EPO with effect for the Federal Republic of Germany, relating to compressed coding and decoding of a video sequence.

Independent claim 17 reads:

A method of decoding encoded information representative of a video sequence, which has been encoded according to the method of claim 1, said video sequence comprising a plurality of video frames, the decoding method being characterized by:

- receiving encoded information representative of a segment of a current frame of said video sequence;
- identifying a coding mode of the encoded information, the coding mode being one of at least a first coding mode and a second coding mode;
- if the identified coding mode is said first coding mode, reconstructing the segment of the current frame of said video sequence using a first motion field model derived using motion compensated prediction with respect to a previously-encoded frame of the video sequence;
- if the identified coding mode is said second coding mode, reconstructing the segment of the current frame of said video sequence using a second motion field model based on a motion field model determined for an adjacent previously-encoded segment of the current frame.

The Federal Court revoked the patent in part due to a lack of inventive step. This decision was overruled by the Supreme Court. It is interesting to read that no claim feature was critically discussed with respect to technicality, although at least parts of the claims clearly refer to a computerized model and the use of statistical methods.

[2] X ZR 100/13

In this field of technology, applications also are filed that consist of a mixture of technical and non-technical features. By way of example, we refer to the decision of the Supreme Court **BGH, X ZR 100/13**, dated 7 July 2015. The subject matter in this decision refers to an internet commerce system for offering and/or purchasing goods and services by means of telecommunications equipment. Claim 1 was originally drafted as:

1. Alternatively, mobile telecommunications system to an electronic ordering and service support, automated telecommunications system to achieve the cordless telecommunications terminals (CTT) for local use, with at least one base station over a local area network LAN communicate, in which at least one base station on a telecommunications line with a telecommunications provider is connected to the Internet services, where the respective cordless telecommunications terminal equipment (CTT) before the communication with the base station, where for a not in the local area network (LAN) registered user of an electronic purchase order settled when the foreign users with its cordless telecommunications terminal equipment (CTT) in the local area network (LAN), a provider access and a two-way communication channel gets in the local area network (LAN) for foreign users open and he gets a digital access, in which the user with its telecommunications terminal equipment (CTT) a product or service ordered and the price to be paid by one on the local area network (LAN) led Depending user account can be debited paid or where the goods or Service then either a machine or personal services or delivered or issued, wherein users of the Internet is a sign or signal to

> send to the Internet service provider or any other telecommunications provider in which he requested one or more Telephone numbers or any other identifiers indicating, with which he wishes to be connected continue to automatically or manually its accessibility and size of the provider the desired connection either packet-switched VoIP or circuit-switched and the participants carry out the links, forward calls.

Improvement of a communication between different electronic devices for e-commerce was mentioned as the technical problem to be solved. The Court held that the priority claim was not valid. The Court confirmed the decision of the preceding instance which revoked the patent in nullity proceedings due to lack of inventive step.

In this respect it should be mentioned that all claims features were judged to be technical in nature and therefore had been taken into account for assessment of inventive step. This decision shows that non-technical aspects (e-commerce) may also be patentable if they are claimed in the context of a technical system.

[3] Druckdatenübertragungsverfahren

The decision of the Supreme Court, **Druckdatenübertragungsverfahren (printing data transfer method), BGH, X ZR 73/12**, dated 13 August 2013, refers to data transfer and communication technology.

Claim 1 reads:

> 1. Method for transmitting data in networks over data lines, characterized in that before and/or during the transmission of data, bandwidth of the data line is subdivided into at least two portions,
> whereby the bandwidth of the at least two portions for data transmission is manually or automatically predefined,
> whereby the subdivision of the bandwidth is manually carried out by a user controlling the data transmission, at least one bandwidth portion is allocated to the data to be transmitted and the remaining bandwidth is provided to the user for the parallel transmission of different data.

As stated in the description, multimedia data and print data are usually sent over an appropriate data line in a constant stream of relatively small packets. With the method according this invention, relatively large packets are used that can optionally be compressed. The speed of transmission is thus additionally improved. With this method, communication with the end device occurs under use of the end device's buffer, whereas data transmission occurs in packets which are calibrated for the end device's buffer. The transmission process is interrupted if the end device's buffer is full. The process restarts once the buffer is again receptive.

The technical problem was seen to be providing a user with the option during data transmission to use the bandwidth of the data channel for other communication processes.

The Court revoked the patent in dispute, because it was obvious for a person skilled in the art and lacked inventive step. For inventive step analysis all claim features have been taken into account.

[4] X ZR 117/13

In the nullity judgment **BGH, X ZR 117/13**, dated 20 October 2015, the subject matter refers to transmission of back channel data in a connection on level 7 of the ISO-OSI reference model between a client device and a server in a packet-switched network.

Claim 1 reads (some minor claim features are omitted):

> 1. Method for transmitting return channel data in a layer 7 (L7) link between a terminal and a sender of a packet-switching network, at least on a section of the return channel optionally with narrow bandwidth via the packet switching network and POTS/ISDN lines or with wide bandwidth via a wideband return channel,
>
> comprising the following steps:
>
> a) setting up an L7 connection between the terminal (1) and the server (4) via the packet-switching network (3),
> b) narrow-band transmission of return-channel data from the server (4) to the terminal (1), wherein data from the server to the switch are transferred...
> c) repeated checking at the switch (5) which is part of the packet-switching network (3) or has access to it, whether a control signal triggered by the user of the terminal (1) or a network manager for adding a return-channel data transmission via wideband return channel is present,
> d) adding a wideband return channel during the existing L7 connection when a corresponding control signal is present, return channel data first being transmitted in wideband width from the server (4) to a wideband access switch (5) and then being applied to the wideband return channel by the wideband access switch (5),
> e) changing back to transmitting the return channel only with narrow bandwidth as long as a corresponding further control signal of the user or of the network manager is present,
> f) wherein an L7 connection between the terminal (1) and the server (4) is generated always by using the switch (5), in particular for transmitting data from terminal to server and from server to the terminal by using the switch,
> g) wherein only the switch (5) checks, whether a control signal is present, which is initiated by a network management for change to a return channel transmission via wideband return channel and
> h) wherein the packet switching network is the internet.

None of the features was discussed with respect to technicality and thus, all features were judged to technical in nature.

The Court ruled that the patent in dispute does not lack inventive step as the Nullity Senate of the Federal Court originally stated. This decision is also interesting because the Court maintained the patent in dispute even though the parallel European Patent was revoked by the EPO in opposition proceedings.

[5] Prepaid Telephone Calls

The subject matter in the judgment **X ZR 2/10**, dated 21 February 2012, relates to the processing of prepaid telephone calls.

Claim 1 reads:

> 1. A method of processing prepaid telephone calls, particularly for use in connection with public telephones, comprising the steps of -
>
> (a) programming the respective Public Automatic Branch exchange (PABX) to become toll-free accessible for incoming calls through dialing any one out of a series of predetermined numbers stored in a data-bank of the PABX;
> (b) enabling the calling party to complete the connection with the called party;
> (c) cutting-off the said connection after a prefixed time/counter pulses interval;
> (d) erasing from the data-bank any number that had once be dialed;
> (e) marking the said series of numbers, each on a vendible carrier member in an invisible - however readily exposable - manner; and
> (f) offering the vendible carrier members for sale to the general public, so that purchasers of the carrier members, after exposing the respective number, are enabled to place a call for the duration of the said interval.

The discussion of inventive step assessment in this decision is very interesting, because features d), e) and f) actually do comprise business method aspects. In particular, in the proceedings before the Federal Court, feature d) (erasing a number) was discussed as a differentiating feature with respect to the prior art. However, neither this feature nor any other claim feature was judged to be non-technical. Finally, the Court revoked the patent due to lack of inventive step.

This decision exemplifies that the field of technology seems to have an impact on the evaluation of technical and non-technical features. In the light of many decisions, one may get the impression that in classic fields of technology (mechanical engineering, automotive, image processing, etc.) panels tend to be less critical with respect to the assessment of features as being non-technical than in other fields.

[6] X ZR 102/11

Another example of a decision in the field of video processing is **X ZR 102/11**, dated 17 June 2014. This decision, however, reveals no interesting aspects with respect to CII and is therefore not discussed further. It was decided that the subject matter of claim 1 in the granted version contains added subject matter in relation to the parent application and therefore is not valid.

[7] X ZR 84/12

The judgment in **X ZR 84/12**, dated 25 February 2014 also concerns video processing.

Claim 1 states:

> Video display device of the multi-frequency type, said video display device being apt to be attached to a wide variety of video adaptor cards of computer systems and having a screen and means for adjusting video display controls, characterized by an on-screen generation means capable of generating visual representations of adjusted video display controls of said video display device wherein the size of said displayed visual representations is controlled across different frequency

> modes of said video display device and the size of said visual representations is kept substantially the same across said different frequency modes, wherein said display device comprises an on -screen display block (16) including a character size control block (36) for controlling the size of said displayed visual representations across different frequency modes of said multi-frequency video display.

Technicality was no issue in this decision, although the subject matter relates to visual representations of information (here, controls). The Supreme Court confirmed the revocation of the patent in suit due to lack of inventive step according to Article 56 EPC (the nullity suit refers to a German part of a European Patent).

[D] Application Software: Medical Technology

Overview

In recent years several decisions came up in this field of technology.

Similar to Article 52(4) EPC, the German Patent Act also excludes methods for treatment of the human or animal body by surgery or therapy and diagnostic methods pursuant to Section 2a(1) 2 PatG. With this statutory regulation, the legislator intended that a doctor may freely choose the method of treatment of the patient by surgery or therapy without being inhibited by patents. This situation is different from that in the USA.

Several decisions deal with the question of what makes a method a diagnostic method, *see* for example BGH, X ZR 88/09 and X ZB 9/09, which will be discussed below with respect to CII aspects. **21 W (pat) 45/05** and **21 W (pat) 38/05** of the Federal Court are also interesting decisions on diagnostic methods.

[1] Bildstrom

An important decision of the Supreme Court is **Bildstrom, BGH, X ZR 37/13**, dated 26 February 2015.[19]

The nullity proceedings refer to the EP 1 474 927 granted by the EPO with effect for the Federal Republic of Germany, which refers to displaying medical data collected by a capsule travelling through the human body and capturing images. The decision addresses very interesting questions for CII matters.

Independent claims 1 and 7 of the disputed patent are drafted as method and system claim and state:

> 1. A method for displaying an image stream, the method comprising:
> receiving images acquired by a swallowable capsule (40), the images forming an original image stream; and displaying simultaneously on a monitor (300) at least two subset image streams, each subset image stream including a separate subset of images from the original image stream.

19. See EPO decision T 1948/13, dated 24.2.2016, referring to a very similar subject matter, where inventive step was affirmed.

> 7. A system for displaying an image stream, the system comprising: an image storage means (21) for accepting an original image stream; and an image display means (300) for displaying at least two subset image streams, each subset image stream including a separate subset of images from the original image stream, characterized that the at least two subset image streams can be displayed on the image display means (300) simultaneously.

This wording makes it clear that several interesting questions arise from this case. First, the question of a possible exclusion due to 'presentation of information'. Secondly, a possible exclusion as a 'diagnostic method' and thirdly, the evaluation of features with respect to their technicality.

In the nullity proceedings, the Federal Court denied inventive step. Relating to the question of whether this subject matter should be evaluated as a 'diagnostic method', the Federal Court took the view that even if the method is predestined as diagnostic method, claim 1 contains no indications or explanations relating to a diagnostic method. Therefore, the Court affirmed eligibility for patent protection and denied an exclusion according to Article 53c EPC.

This view was confirmed by the Supreme Court.

In the reasoning of its decision the Supreme Court held (*see* recital 26) that the technical problem is to process and to display images on a monitor, which are taken by an endoscopic capsule such as a user may perceive them most efficiently in order to evaluate them.

The Court approved eligibility for patent protection and technicality and existence of inventive step and non-exclusion from patentability as a diagnostic method.

This argumentation is very interesting because an efficient manner for displaying information on a display was regarded as a technical problem. Therefore, this decision is interpreted as a major further liberalization of patent practice, which may also be important for user interfaces.

[2] Elektronenstrahl-Therapiesystem

In the decision **Elektronenstrahl-Therapiesystem, BGH, X ZR 88/09**, dated 24 January 2012, the nullity proceeding was directed against EP 0700578 granted by the EPO with effect for the Federal Republic of Germany.

Claim 1 as originally filed reads:

> A mobile electron beam therapy system including: a housing (18); an electron generating means (12) disposed within said housing for generating an electron beam; a linear accelerator (14, 16) positioned in the housing relative to the electron generating means (12) so that the generated electron beam exits said linear accelerator collinearly in the direction electrons travel within said accelerator; and applicator means (19) disposed at the electron beam exit region of the housing (18) for defining the treatment field size; characterised in that the electron beam generated by the electron generating means (12) follows a straight-line path to said applicator means (19); and in that means (50) is provided for positioning the housing (18) so that the applicator means (19) directs the electron beam to a predetermined location in patient treatment.

The Court addressed the question as to whether to evaluate the feature 'system adapted for electron beam therapy' as an apparatus claim - as opposed to such a feature being a method claim - as being a feature related to a particular purpose, which generally does not restrict the scope of protection. But, as the Court stated, although such a feature does not restrict the apparatus claim it is not completely irrelevant. It may contribute to differentiating it from the prior art.

The Federal Court revoked the patent in suit due to lack of inventive step. The Supreme Court modified this ruling of the preceding instance and pointed out that the system according to claim 1 shows an inventive step.

It based its argumentation on the fact that the feature relating to the particular purpose (for an application of the system during surgery, i.e. intraoperatively) makes it necessary that the apparatus/system has a specific construction. Namely, for applying such a system intraoperatively it has to surgically engage with anatomical areas of the patient. This is, however, not possible with state of the art systems. Therefore, this purpose-related feature contributes to a difference over the prior art.

[3] Bildunterstützung bei Katheternavigation

The decision **Bildunterstützung bei Katheternavigation, BGH, X ZB 9/09**, dated 31 August 2010 deals *inter alia* with evaluating a method as a method for treatment of the patient by surgery (and thus as excluded subject matter).

Claim 1 of the parallel US application reads:

> A method for supporting imaging for navigation of a medical instrument inserted into a hollow organ of a human or animal body to a pathological site in the hollow organ, comprising: recording a first image of at least a part of the hollow organ by a medical non-invasive image recording device; locating the pathological site using the first image; displaying a merged image including the first image and a second image continuously recorded angiographically during navigation, the second image including at least a further part of the hollow organ in which a tip of the medical instrument is currently present, the tip visualized in the second image; and indicating the pathological site in the first image.

The Court referred to the EPO decision in G1/07 and pointed out that the purpose-related feature 'for navigation of the instrument in a hollow organ' is to be construed as additional information. The Court did not confirm the statement of the preceding instance, according to which this feature was deemed to contribute to its exclusion from patentability. The Court held that the claimed method is only an intermediate process and is not excluded from patentability.

[4] Steuerungseinrichtung für Untersuchungsmodalitäten

The decision in **Steuerungseinrichtung für Untersuchungsmodalitäten, BGH, X ZB 22/07**, dated 20 January 2009 is an important milestone in the development of case law. It was discussed as further development of the liberalization of case law for CIIs in Germany at the time.

The subject matter refers to the selection of an appropriate examination device dependent on examination data and measurement protocols.

Claim 1 reads:

1. A method for processing medically relevant information for examining a patient, comprising the steps of:
   (a) storing a program, including a data-bank containing stored data selected from the group consisting of symptom-based data and diagnosis-based data, in a data processor;
   (b) entering patient-specific information, selected from the group consisting of symptom-specific information and diagnosis-specific information, into said data processor;
   (c) executing said program in said data processor to select at least one examination modality for examining said patient dependent on said stored data and said patient-specific information; and
   (d) making output information relating to the selected modality available from said data processor,
   wherein step (c) includes generating a protocol, selected from the group consisting of examination protocols and measurement protocols, for conducting the selected modality, and wherein step (d) comprises including said protocol in said output information and examining said patient with said selected examination modality and thereby obtaining examination information, and entering said examination information into said data processor to augment said patient-specific information, and repeating step (c) to select a further examination modality for a further examination of said patient, and
   wherein step (d) comprising making output information relating to the selecting further modality available from said data processor.

The seventeenth Senate of the Federal Court was of the opinion that the subject matter was not an invention in a field of technology in the meaning of Section 1 PatG.

The appeal against this decision was successful. The Supreme Court affirmed technicality and eligibility for patent protection. It referred the case back for further examination to the Federal Court in order to afford the Federal Court the opportunity to deal with the question of inventive step and novelty on the basis of the new legal evaluation created by the Supreme Court (i.e. eligibility of patent protection).

The Federal Court re-examined the case for the second time and came to the conclusion that the application was to be refused due to a lack of inventive step (*see* decision **17 W (pat) 6/04**, dated 29 April 2010).

[E] Application Software: Automotive/Vehicles

Overview

In this area, many decisions concern subject matter relating to the control of automotive modules and which are drafted at a lower level with respect to the ISO-OSI layer. As an example, we refer to the Supreme Court decision **Kommunikationskanal, BGH, X ZR 107/12**, dated 11 February 2014, to the nullity case of the Federal Court in **4 Ni 34/06 (EU)** and **23 W (pat) 14/08**. In this field, eligibility for patent protection and technicality are generally affirmed. Therefore, these decisions do not reveal any valuable information for CII and are not discussed further.

Several decisions deal with subject matter relating to navigation systems. Even where the subject matter in fact is pure software, if it is claimed with interaction of the automotive system, problematic issues do generally not arise. Mainly, eligibility for patent protection and technicality are affirmed. By way of example, *see* **17 W (pat) 302/06** and **17 W (pat) 65/05**.

Subject matter that comprises pure software features and features relating to mechanical, constructive aspects, will in general, be found to be technical in character and eligible for patent protection (*see* e.g. **17 W (pat) 11/16**, dated 24 November 2016).

[1] Fahrzeugnavigationssystem

In the decision **Fahrzeugnavigationssystem, BGH X ZR 27/12**, dated 23 April 2013, the Supreme Court ruled on a navigation system for vehicles. The patent in dispute was EP 973 011 with effect for the Federal Republic of Germany.

Claim 1 states:

A vehicle navigation system for use in a vehicle, the system comprising:

- sensing means for generating data for use by the vehicle navigation system for navigation;
- a user interface for communicating with a user of the vehicle navigation system, and
- a central processing unit which is operable to:
- generate a route from a first position to a destination in response to the selection of the destination by the user, the route including a plurality of manoeuvres;
- generate a plurality of manoeuvre instructions corresponding to said plurality of manoeuvres, selected ones of said manoeuvre instructions being associated with a street name having alphanumeric characters and an indication of a distance to the corresponding manoeuvre;
- present an audio representation of each of the manoeuvre instructions to the user prior to the execution of a corresponding one of the manoeuvres, wherein the audio representation of the selected manoeuvre instructions includes the associated street name and the distance indication;
- include, in response to a request received from a user to repeat a most recently presented manoeuvre instruction that includes a street name and a distance indication, an adjusted distance indication of the distance to the manoeuvre that corresponds to said previously presented manoeuvre instruction;
- generate a repeat manoeuvre instruction comprising said previously presented manoeuvre instruction, said previously presented street name and said adjusted distance indication, and
- present an audio representation of said repeat manoeuvre instruction to said user.

Another independent claim relates to a method.

The Federal Court revoked the patent in dispute, and *inter alia* judged that claim 1 lacks inventive step. The feature relating to the 'audio representation of a manoeuvre instruction also comprising street names' could not be regarded as different to the prior art.

The Supreme Court confirmed this judgment. The technical means which represents the difference to the prior art relates to an improvement in navigation in that user information is now provided audibly and not (only) visually, which may distract the driver's attention.

The Court held that the audio representation of the navigation information (with synthesized language instructions) merely relates to the content of the information or data and cannot be judged to be technical in nature. The patent was revoked due lack of inventive step.

[2] X ZR 121/11

In the decision **X ZR 121/11**, dated 18 December 2012, the Supreme Court ruled on a navigation system for vehicles. The patent in dispute was EP 0945 707 with effect for the Federal Republic of Germany.

Claim 1 states:

> A method for use in selecting a destination in a vehicle navigation system (400), the system having a user interface (436, 440) and a map database (154, 426) associated therewith, in which the method includes the steps of providing a plurality of options for designating the destination in the user interface, a first option (502) employing at least one street name to designate the destination, providing (552) a city list for display (504) in the user interface, in response to the selection of the first option, the city list including a first plurality of cities for which no street names are available for display, and selecting as the destination (510) a first location associated with the first one of the first plurality of cities in the map database in response to the selection of a first one of the first plurality of cities from the city list.

Claim 7 relates to a vehicle navigation system.

The last feature 'selecting as the destination (510) a first location associated with the first one of the first plurality of cities in the map database in response to the selection of a first one of the first plurality of cities from the city list' was discussed in detail with respect to technicality. This feature relieves the user from having to confirm the destination in a particular user interaction. The Supreme Court interpreted this feature as non-technical, because it only relates to ease of use and operating comfort and does not provide any solution to a technical problem. This feature, therefore, cannot contribute to differentiation over the prior art. However, this feature was the only feature that differed from the state of the art. Therefore, the patent in suit was revoked.

[3] *Routenplanung*

The case **Routenplanung, BGH X ZR 3/12**, dated 18 December 2012 also relates – as the title suggests – to a navigation system. The patent in suit was EP 1147375 granted by the EPO with effect for the Federal Republic of Germany. The patent was filed by Bosch.

Claim 1:

> Method for guiding a driver of a vehicle, particularly of a motor vehicle, aircraft or ship, from at least one starting point to at least one destination, where a route of travel from the at least one starting point to the at least one destination is determined,
>
> characterized
>
> in that following the stipulation of a particular characteristic the vehicle driver is presented, as part of the route planning, with those road sections on the route of travel which have the prescribed characteristic for the purpose of individual selection or rejection, and in that rejected road sections are removed from the route planning.

In the patent in dispute it is pointed out that a disadvantage in state of the art navigation systems is that it is only possible to allocate or assign particular (negative) route properties, like tolls and road charges to the route as a whole. A drawback in the prior art that the application overcomes is that it is not possible to assign these properties only to particular road sections. These particular road sections are to be considered individually when computing the route as a whole.

In the preceding judgment (4 Ni 64/09 (EU)), the fourth nullity Senate of the Federal Court decided that the patent fulfils the requirements of novelty and inventive step. In particular, the feature 'following the stipulation of a particular characteristic the vehicle driver is presented, as part of the route planning, with those road sections on the route of travel which have the prescribed characteristic for the purpose of individual selection or rejection' was judged to be technical.

This judgment, however, did not stand up to the legal analysis of the Supreme Court. The Court took the view that this feature merely refers to a selection of data with no technical considerations and refers to presentation of information with no technical indications.

The appellant argued that the feature actually has the technical effect that the number of processing steps may be reduced. For this reason, this feature is to be regarded as a technical feature.

However, the Supreme Court countered that it is immaterial whether an instruction which serves to reduce the processing steps may be judged to solve a technical problem with technical means or at least to contribute to the solving of a technical problem. The Court evaluates this feature as non-technical. This feature was the only difference to state of the art systems. Due to the lack of technicality of this feature, it cannot be considered for the evaluation of inventive step. Therefore, the patent was revoked based on lack of inventive step.

This decision, with the technicality argument mentioned above, was hotly debated in the professional community, because reducing processing resources (in particular reducing processing steps) was usually regarded as a clear technical problem previously. The Supreme Court seems to turn away from this former standpoint and also from a technical understanding of the viewpoint of computer science.

[4] Antiblockiersystem

A very early decision is **Antiblockiersystem, BGH, X ZB 19/78**, dated 13 May 1980. This was a milestone in the development in case law, as at that time a very 'modern' liberal approach was used to evaluate patentability. The Court affirmed eligibility of patent protection and technicality.

[F] Mathematical Methods, Business Methods, Games

Overview

Mathematical methods, pure business methods and games are excluded from patentability as Section 1 PatG suggests. However, a look at the German Patent Register reveals that a vast number of granted patents in all these fields exist.

This is due to the fact that mathematical methods and methods for playing games and doing business are only excluded 'as such' according to Section 1(3) and (4) PatG. Thus, it is up to case law to define the limitation between patentable and non-patentable subject matter.

As a rule of thumb one might say that if a mathematical or business method is claimed in a technical context, eligibility for patent protection is possible, provided that the other requirements are fulfilled.

For games, the patent situation is somewhat clearer: generally, gaming machines might be subject to patent protection, whereas gaming software is usually judged to be non-technical and is excluded from patent protection.

The subject matter of the Federal Court's decisions relates to particular use of statistical methods for operating an internal combustion engine (**5 Ni 14/13**, dated 6 March 2015) or for medical image processing (**17 W(pat) 9/10**, dated 27 May 2014). In these cases, the patent was maintained and granted respectively.

The majority of the decisions of the seventeenth Senate of the Federal Court in the field of mathematic methods, however, deny eligibility for patent protection or technicality, such as the decisions **17 W (pat) 6/06**, **17 W (pat) 16/04**.

In the field of business methods, refer to the decision **Prepaid telephone calls, BGH, X ZR 2/10**, dated 21 February 2012, which was discussed above in section [C] [5].

In Germany, only few decisions exist in the field of games. To our knowledge, the Supreme Court has never judged on a patent (application) in the field of games. Some Federal Court decisions deal with gaming machines, which are mostly evaluated as technical and eligible for patent protection. As far as gaming concepts are concerned, these will mostly be judged to be not eligible for patent protection (*see* for example **17 W (pat) 32/05** or **Jackpotzuwachs, 20 W (pat) 10/03**).

[1] Flugzeugzustand

The subject matter of the decision **Flugzeugzustand, X ZB 1/15, BGH**, dated 30 June 2015, concerns a mathematical method for calculating the position, velocity and status of an aircraft.

Claim 1 relates to a method for calculation of an airplane state, in particular its position, its velocity and its condition. Claim 1 cites features relating to detecting measurement values of an inertial system in an m-dimensional space. These measurement values are then processed by mathematical operations, such as the application of a Kalman Filter.

According to the Supreme Court's judgment, an important feature is to be seen in the selection and processing of data, which are forwarded to the Kalman filter. A Kalman filter is a method for providing reliable values for measurements that are unsecure. The method according to the invention allows for forwarding fewer input values to the Kalman filter, which in turn implies higher processing speed.

In its reasoning, the Supreme Court interestingly points out that, generally, subject matter is eligible for patent protection if it requires the operation of a technical device. The main argument of the Supreme Court is:

> The operation of technical devices (which turns subject matter patent eligible) is given, if a Kalman filter is used, *because* the use of a Kalman filter requires a computer.

Further, the Court states, software is excluded from patentability if it is claimed with no concrete technical implementation. The same holds for mathematical methods.

The Court then states:

> A mathematical method may only then be judged to be non-technical, if – when taken in combination with the claimed subject matter – it has no relation at all to the systematic use of natural forces.
> The use of mathematical methods aiming at a particular technical purpose are to be evaluated as lying in the field of technology.

This is a very important message and seems to be a deviation from former rulings (such as in **BGH, Routenplanung**, discussed in [E] [3]).

With respect to the question of whether the assessment of eligibility for patent protection should be connected to the question of whether the subject matter shows an advantage over known systems, the Supreme Court made a very remarkable statement:

> The eligibility for patent protection is independent of the question of whether the subject matter involves a technical advancement or progress.

Finally, the Court affirmed technical character and eligibility of the subject matter and remitted the case to the Federal Court in order to examine inventive step.

[2] X ZB 4/12

In the field of business related matter, we refer to the decision **BGH, X ZB 4/12**, dated 13 November 2012, which relates to automatic processing of data in documents.

The method involves automatically detecting data in a document based on specified formulations, terms and definitions. The data is evaluated and corrected with respect to errors, inaccuracies and checking relevant characteristic by an automatic, pre-programmed plausibility process. Facilities are automatically selected to correct claims based on remuneration/material cost of the facilities after optimizing specific criteria.

Claim 1 relates to:

> A method for the preparation, analysis and evaluation of data contained in documents through their collection and subsequent analysis and evaluation by means of calculation and plausibility processes, characterized in that
>
> a) the identification and recording of data contained in the documents on the basis of established formulations, terms and/or terms of the procedures carried out automatically,
> b) the evaluation and correction of the data collected for errors, inaccuracies, misstatements and examination-relevant characteristics using an automatic, preprogrammed expert processing plausibility procedure is performed, and
> c) the automatic selection of specialist workshops to address cases of damage by means of a calculation method based on the stored real wage and material costs of the available repair shops within a predetermined radius from the claimant to the optimization of the criteria & resulting costs & distance to the claimant and quality characteristics (association membership, certification) is carried out.

The Federal Court has decided that the invention is excluded form patentability according to Section 1(3), (4) PatG. This decision was confirmed. The Supreme Court held that although technical character has to be affirmed, there is no solution for a technical problem with technical means and thus the subject matter is to be excluded from patentability. Therefore, this decision is an example of the German three-step approach, where technical character is affirmed even though the matter is excluded from patentability.

[3] Elektronischer Zahlungsverkehr

A key decision is **Elektronischer Zahlungsverkehr, BGH, X ZB 20/03**, dated 24 May 2004. The claim relates to a secured execution of an electronic financial transaction via the internet, wherein key information is processed between a client and the electronic banking server. The claim also includes business related features. The Supreme Court held that the subject matter shows technicality and overruled the previous decision. The main argument of the Supreme Court for affirmation of technicality is that security methods are used which should be regarded as technical. In particular, the Supreme

Court pointed out, even the seventeenth Senate of the Federal Court seems to affirm technicality for security based features.

[G] Industrial Applications and Others

Overview

A detailed look at a plurality of decisions reveals that for software applications in classic fields of technology (e.g. mechanical engineering, network technology, automotive) the eligibility and technicality issues tend to be discussed less critically than in computing technology and electronics.

In general, software-based methods for controlling a technical system (electronic devices, automotive modules or manufacturing processes, etc.) are judged to have technical character. For example the decision **X ZR 61/10**, dated 21 March 2013 (selecting an operating modus for a consumer electronic device), and **Sensoranordnung, BGH, X ZR 109/08**, dated 29 September 2011 and **BGH, X ZR 30/08**, dated 22 February 2011, both relating to the control of a restraint system in a vehicle. Technicality or eligibility for patent protection are not critically discussed.

[1] Frästeil

The decision **Frästeil – X ZR 69/11**, dated 7 May 2013 relates to computer aided manufacturing of milled parts. The appeal against the litigation proceedings relates to patent EP 1034865 granted by the EPO with effect for the Federal Republic of Germany.

Claim 1:

> Milling method for producing a desired finished part (2) from a desired blank (1) by means of a milling cutter characterized in that the milling tool along a continuous track (7, 7') of the outer contour of the blank (1) to the contour (2') of the panel (2) is guided and with continuous removal of material a continuous change in shape from the blank (1) to the finished part (2) is achieved.

This claim is an example of no computer or software feature being present in the claims, even though the method relates to computer control. The core of the invention is to calculate a spiral shaped guide path for the raw part to the finished parts. Due to the field of mechanical engineering, technicality was not discussed in this case.

Further subjects of this decision are questions relating to contributory infringement, which will not be discussed further, because they do not relate to CII matter.

[2] X ZR 58/09

The following decision deals with a software based control of a medical system, in particular a hemofiltration system: **X ZR 58/09**, dated 20 March 2012.

Claims 1 reads:

> A continuous hemofiltration system (10) for removal of fluid from the blood of a patient, comprising hemofiltration means (24), means (16) for pumping blood from a patient through the hemofiltration means (24) and back to the patient, a first reservoir (50) for maintaining a supply of infusate (52), first pumping means (60) for pumping the infusate (52) from the first reservoir (50), a second reservoir (74) for receiving drained fluid (76) from the hemofiltration means (24), second pumping means (66) for pumping the drained fluid (76) from the hemofiltration means (24) to the second reservoir (74), first weighing means (54) and second weighing means (78) for monitoring the weight of the infusate (52) and drained fluid (76) and generating weight data signals correlated thereto, and control means(12) operably connected to the blood pumping means (16) and to each of the first and second pumping means (60, 66) and the first and second weighing means (54, 78), the control means (12) comprising a computer for operating the first and second pumping means (60,66), wherein the control means (12) receives the weight data signals generated by the weighing means (54, 78) and determines from the weight data signals the weight of infusate and drained fluid in the first and second reservoirs (50, 74) respectively and wherein the blood pumping means (16) is responsive to control signals generated by the control means to vary the flow rate of the blood through the hemofiltration means (24), characterized in that the first pumping means (60) is for pumping the infusate (52) from the first reservoir (50) to the hemofiltration means; in that the control means computer is programmed to operate the first and second pumping means (60, 66) only when the blood pumping means (16) is operating, in that the control means (12) determines the weight of the infusate and the drained fluid in the first and second reservoirs (50, 74) at regular intervals, compares those determined weights to corresponding predetermined computed weights, and, in response to said comparison, generates control signals to adjust automatically as necessary on an ongoing basis during hemofiltration the rates of pumping of the infusate and drained fluid whereby a preselected amount of fluid is removed from the blood over a preselected time period.

As can be seen in the claim quoted above, the claim contains several mechanical and technical features (reservoirs, pumping means, etc.) and control technology features. The pumping means are controlled by a computer. The solution relates to the computerized control means with a certain functionality.

The Federal Court revoked the patent due to lack of inventive step. This judgment was confirmed by the Supreme Court. The Supreme Court explicitly stated that it could not agree with the view that was taken by the Opposition Division of the EPO and the Technical Board of Appeal relating to the same patent in dispute (which affirmed inventive step).

In recital 38 in the reasoning for this decision, the Court held that defining parameter values for a control which are to be defined according to medical evaluation on the part of a physician cannot contribute to inventive step.

[3] Glasflaschenanalysesystem

An example relating to a software control of a technical system is the decision **Glasflaschenanalysesystem, BGH, Xa ZR 4/07**, dated 4 February 2010.

Claim 1 states:

> An analytical system (1) for analyzing, monitoring, diagnosing and/or controlling a process for manufacturing packaging glass products (4) said analytical system (1) being provided with an infrared-sensitive sensor system (24) and a digital processor (30) connected therewith, said infrared-sensitive sensor system (24) detecting infrared radiation emitted by warm products in the section directly after the glass-shaping process, and said digital processor (30) determining the energy distribution in the material of the shaped product and energy differences between different parts of the shaped product by means of information from the products obtained with said infrared-sensitive sensor system wherein said energy distribution and/or energy differences are compared with criteria, obtained by means of a mathematical reference model, for determining deviations in glass distributions and causes leading to thermal stresses in the product.

As can be seen, the subject matter relates to a software algorithm for controlling a glass product packaging system.

In view of sufficiency of disclosure, the feature 'mathematical reference model' was evaluated in light of the definitions given in the description. The Court decided that the subject matter has without doubt technical character.

The Federal Court dismissed the case. This decision was in general confirmed by the Supreme Court so that the patent in dispute was maintained.

[4] Roboterarm zur Nachbehandlung von Zitzen beim Melken

A further example relating to a software control of a technical system is the decision **Roboterarm zur Nachbehandlung von Zitzen beim Melken, BGH, X ZR 86/07**, dated 7 October 2008.

Claim 1 relates to an apparatus for the automatic milking of cows using a milking robot with a robotic arm. The claim comprises further features relating to processing steps for post-processing the udder by means of the robotic arm.

Technicality was not at issue here. However, the patent in dispute was revoked due to lack of inventive step.

CHAPTER 6

United Kingdom

§6.01 LEGAL REQUIREMENTS

Patents can be obtained directly at the UK Intellectual Property Office (UK IPO) or at the European Patent Office (EPO). In future, it will be possible to get a unitary patent. The United Kingdom has expressed its intention to proceed with the ratification process of the Unified Patent Court agreement. The EPO grants a bundle of national patents based on the European Patent Convention (EPC). The patent granted at the EPO is treated like a patent UK IPO patent if the European patent indicates Great Britain as a designated state. The United Kingdom was among the first seven Member States of the European Patent Organization. Since the EPC represents an intergovernmental treaty outside the European Union, 'Brexit' should not influence membership under the EPC.

The Patents Act 1977 represents the fundamental law relating to patents in the United Kingdom. Detailed procedures are indicated in the Patent Rules 2007.[1] In order to harmonize European patent law The Patent Act 1977 was, like many other European patent laws, based on the EPC. However differences in legal practice remain due to the common law system (judges have an active role in developing rules) compared to civil law systems (based on fixed rules and statutes).[2] Patentability including exclusion from patent law is indicated in the Patent Act 1977 as follows:

> Patentable inventions
> 1.-(1) A patent may be granted only for an invention in respect of which the following conditions are satisfied, that is to say -
> (a) the invention is new;
> (b) it involves an inventive step;

1. United Kingdom, *The Patents Rules 2007 and Patents (Fees) Rules 2007* https://www.gov.uk/government/publications/the-patents-rules-2007-and-patents-fees-rules-2007 (accessed 27 March 2017).
2. *What is the difference between common and civil law?* The Economist, The Economist Newspaper Limited, 16 July 2013.

> (c) it is capable of industrial application;
> (d) the grant of a patent for it is not excluded by subsections (2) and (3) or section 4A below;
>
> and references in this Act to a patentable invention shall be construed accordingly.
>
> (2) It is hereby declared that the following (among other things) are not inventions for the purposes of this Act, that is to say, anything which consists of -
> (a) a discovery, scientific theory or mathematical method;
> (b) a literary, dramatic, musical or artistic work or any other aesthetic creation whatsoever;
> (c) a scheme, rule or method for performing a mental act, playing a game or doing business, or a program for a computer;
> (d) the presentation of information;
>
> but the foregoing provision shall prevent anything from being treated as an invention for the purposes of this Act only to the extent that a patent or application for a patent relates to that thing as such.

Detailed information is provided in the 'Guidance, Patents: Manual of Patent Practice' (MoPP), (First published: 1 July 2014, Last updated: 30 December 2016).[3] The guidance also covers the Copyright, Designs and Patents Act 1988 where it relates to patents.

Technicality is a guiding principle in the legal practice. This is in line with the EPC. Terms like technical character, technical problem, technical feature, technical effect and technical contribution play a fundamental role in the evaluation of inventions. However, the steps for determining patentability differ from the legal practice of the EPO (cf. Chapter 4).

§6.02 PROCEDURAL AND FORMAL ASPECTS

Some legal harmonization exists with reference to the EPC. It is pointed out: '1.09 ... decisions of the EPO Boards of Appeal are of persuasive value; furthermore where the EPO Boards of Appeal have formed a settled view of European patent law, this will generally be followed by the UK courts ...'. Nevertheless, as indicated in the MoPP the following general principle exists in the context of patentable inventions:

> *Using past decisions*
>
> 1.11 The Office is bound to follow the decisions of the UK courts, per the English common law doctrine of binding precedent, which states that courts and tribunals must abide by the decisions of higher courts. Therefore, the Office must follow the interpretation of the Act and the practice set out in such judgments, and apply the legal principles arrived at by the judges in those cases.

3. UK IPO *Guidance, Patents: Manual on Patent Practise* (July 2014, updated December 2016) https://www.gov.uk/government/publications/patents-manual-of-patent-practice (accessed 27 March 2017).

The 'Patents Formalities Manual' or 'Guidance on the procedures the IPO follows when examining the formalities of patent applications' (published July 2014, updated 23 September 2014) provides information on general formal aspects.[4]

Chapter 4 of the 'Patents Formalities Manual' sections 4.13–4.16 relates to computer programs as part of the specification. The patent examiner can decide if computer programs are printed. Lengthy programs will usually not be printed, in particular if they are indicated in an appendix (cf. 'Patents Formalities Manual', Chapter 8, 8.04). The applicant will be informed accordingly.

Chapter 15 provides additional help to applicants who do not have the support of a patent attorney or an agent – so called private applicants. A special unit will check applications according to a specific list indicated under section 15.22. The following is relevant in the context of computer programs.

'5.22 PAU [Private Applicant Unit] Examiners using their experience and knowledge will carefully considering the merits of each application to ascertain whether the application falls into specific categories, in particular if the application describes 'the operation of a computer or describes itself as being "software"' or 'a method for doing business'. Where shortcomings are found the applicant will be informed about options for continuing with the procedure.

§6.03 CLAIM FORMATS FOR INVENTIONS RELATING TO COMPUTER PROGRAMS

MoPP Part I, section 2.11–2.17 indicates the general claim constructions. The following general formulations are possible based on specific decisions:

- apparatus, device;
- material or composition;
- method;
- computer program product, data carrier comprising a program.

There is no information on 'signal claims' or 'data structure claims'. The claims must be drafted in terms of the technical features of the invention. They have to be clear and concise.

In the context of computing, claims are allowed such as 'method performed by running a suitably programmed computer or to a computer programmed to carry out the method. Furthermore, claims to a computer program or a program on a carrier are allowable where corresponding method and apparatus claims are/would be allowable.

Several computer related claim interpretations are explained in the MoPP, Part I-New Domestic Law under Patentability, 1. Patentable Inventions and as part of three specific manuals for biotechnological, medical and chemical inventions.

4. UK IPO *Guidance on the procedures the IPO follows when examining the formalities of patent applications* 2014 https://www.gov.uk/government/publications/patents-formalities-manual (accessed 27 March 2017).

The general rule of interpretation is substance over form. No specific form of claim can get around an exclusion from patentability.

§6.04 GUIDELINES FOR COMPUTER-IMPLEMENTED INVENTIONS

No special guidelines exist for software-related inventions. Detailed information can be found in the MoPP. Part I: New Domestic Law, Patentability, section 1: Patentable Inventions' comprises condensed guidance on section 1(2) (EXCLUDED SUBJECT MATTER) of the Patent Act. Other parts of the MoPP include the following specific guidelines:[5]

- Examining patent applications for biotechnological inventions.
- Examining patent applications for medical inventions.
- Examining patent applications for chemical inventions.

Computing and in particular computer programs play an important role in all the fields. Normally, if software plays an important role for the claimed subject matter the MoPP has to be followed. Specific information on software-related inventions can be found for biotechnological and medical inventions. Detailed information in the general context of computer-implemented inventions can be found later in this chapter.

§6.05 HISTORICAL OVERVIEW

Determination of exclusion from patentability was and is a difficult procedure particularly in the context of computer programs.

The most important cases set out in the MoPP are briefly indicated below. The full text of the decisions can be found via the links in the MoPP.

[A] 1989 to End of 1990s

Merrill Lynch's Application (1989) was directed to a method of doing business and in particular to an automated securities trading system. A known computer system was used controlled by a program coded in any known programming language. Patentability was denied. It was argued that an unpatentable computer program cannot be made patentable by indicating it as a part of a computer system. A technical contribution is necessary (e.g. substantial increase of processing speed like in the Vicom case of the EPO).

Gale's Application (1991) related to a new method of calculating square roots. The method was implemented as a computer program. The patent claim was formulated as an 'Electronic circuitry, in the form known as "ROM"' (Read Only Memory). The program did not solve a technical problem. The application was refused as a

5. UK IPO *Intellectual Property Law and Practise* https://www.gov.uk/topic/intellectual-property/law-practice (accessed 27 March 2017).

computer program as such. It could have been refused as a mathematical method as such since the mathematical method was not used to solve a practical problem.

Fujitsu Limited's Application (1997) was directed to modelling a synthetic crystal structure for designing inorganic materials. Modelling was done with the aid of a computer program. An operator could select elements of the crystal structure. The computer created images of the structure on a display. The set of claims comprised a method for processing images, a computer apparatus for creating a computer image of a synthetic crystal structure and a method of manufacturing a structure. The Patent Office considered the claimed subject matter to be a mental act as such or a computer program as such. The final decision was to reject the application as a computer program as such.

[B] Beginning 2000 to Aerotel/Macrossan 2006

CFPH LLC (2005) was directed to two patent applications relating to 'networked interactive wagering on the outcomes of events, with particular emphasis on reducing processing delays to a minimum so that in circumstances where prices are changing continuously, a client is provided with the most up-to-date information before placing a bet'. The court took the opportunity to discuss several fundamental patent law questions such as 'What is an invention?' and the interpretation of 'excluded subject matter. EPO case law was compared to UK case law. As in many other patent applications an overlap between 'computer program' and 'business methods' was seen in the two patent applications. This results in 'mixed inventions'. The mere fact that a claimed artefact includes a computer program, or that a claimed process uses a computer program, does not establish, in and of itself, that the patent would foreclose the use of a computer program. The court argued that claimed subject matter cannot be excluded just because a computer program is used. The reasoning was: 'There are many artefacts that operate under computer control (e.g. the automatic pilot of an aircraft) and there are many industrial processes that operate under computer control (e.g. making canned soup). A better way of doing those things ought, in principle, to be patentable'. Finally, the subject matter of the two applications was considered to be excluded subject matter.

Halliburton Energy Services Inc. v. Smith International (North Sea) Ltd. (2006) related to the infringement of two European patents (EP1117894 and EP1112433). The patents were directed to roller cone drill bits for down-hole drilling, and particularly to the optimization of drill bit parameters.

EP1112433 (B1) - Claim 1:

> 1. A method of designing a roller cone drill bit comprising a plurality of arms, rotatable cutting structures mounted on respective ones of said arms and a plurality of teeth on each of said cutting structures, the method comprising the steps of:
>
> (a) calculating the volume of formation cut by each tooth on each cutting structure (16) of the roller cone drill bit (10);

(b) calculating the volume of formation cut by each cutting structure per revolution of the drill bit;
(c) comparing the volume of formation cut by each of said cutting structures with the volume of formation cut by all others of said cutting structures of the bit;
(d) adjusting at least one geometric parameter on the design of at least one of the cutting structures; and
(e) repeating steps (a) through (d) until substantially the same volume of formation is cut by each of said cutting structures of said bit (10) when the drill bit is drilling into a formation.

The patents indicate that the design methods can be used for simulations using computer programs. Details of a computational implementation are not provided either in the claim or in the description. During the infringement procedure it became evident that the design can be done with an existing CAD-program (computer aided design — program). The claimed subject matter was seen 'as directed purely to the intellectual content of a design process'. It was held to be a mental act as such which is excluded from patentability. Later, the interpretation was seen as being too wide. In **Halliburton Energy Services Inc.'s Applications** (2012) the claimed subject-matter was no longer seen as a mental act as such because the design method was restricted to a computer-implemented method.

Shopalotto.com Ltd.'s Application (2006) related to a lottery game played over the Internet. The independent claim included general computer and Internet features in combination with game features (excluded if claimed as such). A search for the notorious technical features was seen as not necessary. Common sense and experience are sufficient. Furthermore, it was argued 'Merely to program a computer so that it operates in a new way is not a solution to any technical problem, although the result may be considered to be a new machine'.

Research in Motion UK Ltd. v. Inpro Licensing SARL (2006) was directed to the downloading of webpages from an Internet server. A proxy-server was arranged between the Internet server and a field computer to transpose the data to match the specific size and resolution of the display of the field computer. The field computer can be a handheld computer or a personal digital assistant. It was discussed, whether the invention which could be seen as a collection of computer programs, was excluded from patentability. This was held not to be the case, because a technical effect was seen: 'computers running faster and transmitting information more efficiently, albeit ultimately for the purpose of displaying part of that information'. However, in the end the patent was held to be invalid for lack of novelty or inventive step.

Aerotel Ltd. v. Telco Holdings Ltd & Ors Rev 1 (Aerotel/Macrossan) (2006) related to two appeals. The 'Aerotel appeal' concerned the patent GB2171877 that described a telephone system with specific payment options. The 'Macrossan appeal' concerned a patent application GB0314464.9 of Mr Macrossan, the applicant. The application disclosed a computerized method and system for assisting in the creation of a corporate entity. A person has to sit in front of a computer and communicate with a remote server to answer necessary questions for the incorporation of a company. An application program on the remote server generates the questions.

In both cases, the main topic was the application of Article 52(2) and 52(3) EPC, or in other words the determination whether subject matter is excluded from patentability. The provision was implemented in UK law by section 1(2) of the Patents Act 1977 with a similar wording. After careful consideration of national and international law the court came to the conclusion that decisions of the EPO BoA were mutually contradicting. The following three approaches were identified (versions of the 'any hardware approach' are not indicated):

(1) The contribution approach
Ask whether the inventive step resides only in the contribution of excluded matter - if yes, Art. 52(2) applies.
This approach was supported by Falconer J in Merrill Lynch but expressly rejected by this Court.

(2) The technical effect approach
Ask whether the invention as defined in the claim makes a technical contribution to the known art - if no, Art. 52(2) applies. A possible clarification (at least by way of exclusion) of this approach is to add the rider that novel or inventive purely excluded matter does not count as a 'technical contribution'.
This is the approach (with the rider) adopted by this Court in Merrill Lynch. It has been followed in the subsequent decisions of this Court, Gale and Fujitsu. The approach (without the rider as an express caution) was that first adopted by the EPO Boards of Appeal, *see* Vicom, IBM/Text processing and IBM/Data processor network.

(3) The 'any hardware' approach
Ask whether the claim involves the use of or is to a piece of physical hardware, however mundane (whether a computer or a pencil and paper). If yes, Art. 52(2) does not apply. This approach was adopted in three cases, Pension Benefits, Hitachi and Microsoft/Data transfer (the 'trio'). It was specifically rejected by this Court in Gale.

A conflict was seen between the older EPO decision Vicom and the newer EPO decision Hitachi. The reason for the change was not clear. The determination of exclusion from patentability was important for computer programs. The court explained: 'There are, in principle, two views about what is meant by 'computer program' in Article 52. A narrow view is that it means just the set of instructions as an abstract thing albeit they could be written down on a piece of paper. A wider view is that the term covers also the instructions on some form of media (floppy disk, CD or hard drive for instance) which causes a computer to execute the program — a program which works.' It was emphasized that the framers of the EPC had apparently the intention to exclude 'real computer programs, not just an abstract series of instructions'.

The four steps of the UK approach were pointed out:

(1) properly construe the claim;
(2) identify the actual contribution;
(3) ask whether it falls solely within the excluded subject matter;
(4) check whether the actual or alleged contribution is actually technical in nature.

This was applied to the Aerotel appeal and to the Macrossan appeal.

Aerotel case:

A new physical combination of hardware was seen as the contribution. This contribution was more than a business method. Hence, it was a technical contribution. The patent indicated a technical nature. Method and system claim were not excluded from patentability.

According to another opinion the new telephone system could have been implemented by known components.

Macrossan case:

At first, three options for exclusions were discussed. Mental act, business method and computer program, all 'as such'. The mental act discussion was abandoned due to the higher importance of the other two criteria. New hardware was not invented in the view of the inventor but 'an interactive system which will do the job which otherwise would have been done by a solicitor or company formation agent'. This is a business method without a technical contribution 'beyond the mere fact of the running of a computer program'.

The court found it easy to answer not only step 1 but also the other steps:

> Step 2 – what is the contribution? – is again straightforward. It is to provide a computer program (in practice probably an interactive website) which can be used to carry out the method. The hardware used is standard and is not part of the contribution. Step 3 – is the contribution solely of excluded matter? – is again easy. The contribution is just the devised program up and running. Step 4 – is that contribution technical? – is again easy. No. So the exclusion applies.

The appendix indicated a detailed discussion of cases.

The approach indicated in the decision was confirmed by later UK decisions since the referral to the Enlarged Board of Appeal G3/08 was inadmissible. No divergent opinions between two decisions taken at the same time were seen. There were seven years between the different opinions. That was evaluated as a normal legal development.

[C] After Aerotel/Macrossan 2006

Astron Clinica Ltd. & Ors v. The Comptroller General of Patents, Designs and Trade Marks (2008) followed the international trend to allow claims of the form computer program on a data carrier when method and apparatus are allowable. Reference was made to the former Gale decision. A claim for a ROM (data carrier) with a program to calculate a square root would not have been patentable since a technical effect was not created.

Symbian Ltd.'s Application (2009) dealt with claimed subject matter in the area of system software. The application related to dynamic link libraries (DLL) that are part of operating systems. DLLs store important information for several application programs. Information for several application programs only have to be stored once in a library which is dynamically linked to the application program when executed. The invention sought to overcome problems when new functions were added to a DLL. This was primarily achieved by splitting the DLL into two parts. The claimed subject matter was excluded as a computer program as such by the patent office since no new effect was seen outside of the computer. This opinion was not followed by the court due to the following application of steps 2–4 in Aerotel/Macrossen:

> Stage 2 Identify the contribution: A program which makes a computer operate on other programs faster than prior art operating programs enabled it to do by virtue of the claimed features.
>
> Stage 3 Is that solely excluded matter? No, because it has the knock-on effect of the computer working better as a matter of practical reality.
>
> Stage 4 Is it technical? Yes, on any view as to the meaning of the word 'technical'.

AT&T Knowledge Ventures/Cvon Innovations v. Comptroller General of Patents (2009) relates to two appeals against the UKIPO decision that their claimed inventions were not patentable. The AT&T application relates to 'a content broker hosting service system'. The invention is supposed to solve incompatibilities between digital content (e.g. music) supplied and the actual properties of a device representing the content properly. The problem is solved by storing specific information from the users' devices which is then supplied to the content provider. The Cvon Innovations application relates to 'a mobile telecommunications network messaging system and method, in which group membership of a subscriber is authenticated (or not), and then used as a basis for modifying messages sent between users' terminals, at least one of whom is a subscriber'.

Since a definition of 'technical effect' is too difficult, the following signposts help to determine a technical effect:

> i) whether the claimed technical effect has a technical effect on a process which is carried on outside the computer;
>
> ii) whether the claimed technical effect operates at the level of the architecture of the computer; that is to say whether the effect is produced irrespective of the data being processed or the applications being run;
>
> iii) whether the claimed technical effect results in the computer being made to operate in a new way;
>
> iv) whether there is an increase in the speed or reliability of the computer;
>
> v) whether the perceived problem is overcome by the claimed invention as opposed to merely being circumvented.

The *AT&T application* was refused. It was a mixed invention with a combination of business features and computer features. It was concluded:

> iii) All computers are in a sense technical so that although the mere computerization of a method of doing business is technical, it is not a relevant technical contribution;

> iv) If there is more than a mere computerization of a method of doing business, (e.g. a teaching of how to computerize it) then the mode of computerization adds to the sum of human knowledge and is a relevant technical effect;
>
> v) One way of testing this is to postulate the patent being read by a businessman and a technical person. If only the businessman learns something new, then the patent teaches a method of doing business which is not patentable. But if the technical person (e.g. a software engineer) learns something new then there is a relevant technical effect.

The *Cvon Innovations application* was refused as well. It was evaluated as a business method as such. A major reason was that 'The claimed invention does not provide a technical solution to any alleged incompatibility of formats. It avoids the problem by changing the direction of flow of information'.

Lantana v. Comptroller General of Patents (2013) related to an application entitled 'Methods, Systems, and Computer program products for retrieving a file or machine readable data'. The priority date is 22 February 2008. A user at a 'local station' (i.e. a computer) wishes to access a file stored in a 'remote data storage device', i.e. another computer. A packet-switched network connects the computers. The method is described in a lengthy claim, simplified it reads as follows: 'When required, the local computer creates an e-mail message containing machine-readable retrieval criteria and sends it to the remote computer. The remote computer receives the e-mail, works out if the e-mail contains any machine-readable instruction and, if so, executes that instruction, retrieves the data and sends back an e-mail containing the requested data'.

The examiner refused the claimed subject matter as excluded subject matter, i.e. as computer program as such.

The Aerotel test and the AT&T signposts were followed during the appeal procedure. The invention was seen as 'entirely of software running on a conventional computing arrangement'. Sending e-mails between computers was evaluated as a normal process. The inventors did not invent it. The computers in the claim are not operating in a new way. A problem in the prior art was seen in the need for a continuous connection between computers. The invention tried to avoid this by e-mail communication. However, this was not seen as a technical contribution but as a solution which circumvents a solution of the technical problem. Finally, the computers did not work more reliably or more efficiently.

The Patent Office's decision was confirmed. The subject matter was a computer program as such, excluded from patentability.

HTC v. Apple (2013) related to two European patents EP2098948 and EP1964022. Both patents were directed to a computing device which allows user interaction with the device by a touchscreen. They were found to be unpatentable because they represented a computer program as such.

EP2098948

This patent related to a user-interface that allowed multiple simultaneous touches (e.g. with a human finger) on a touchscreen. This was achieved by dividing the screen into multiple areas (views). Flags (multi-touch or exclusive) are set when the screen receives an input signal (touch event) from a specific area. A general effect of this solution is that application programmers do not have to program functionality for multi-touch screens as part of the application program since the functionality is already part of the system software (operating system).

Claim 1 (with reference numerals added by the judge) reads as follows:

(i) A method for handling touch events at a multi-touch device, comprising:
(ii) displaying one or more views;
(iii) executing one or more software elements, each software element being associated with a particular view;
(iv) associating a multi-touch flag or an exclusive touch flag with each view, said multi-touch flag indicating whether a particular view is allowed to receive multiple simultaneous touches and said exclusive touch flag indicating whether a particular view allows other views to receive touch events while the particular view is receiving a touch event;
(v) receiving one or more touches at the one or more views; and
(vi) selectively sending one or more touch events, each touch event describing a received touch, to one or more of the software elements associated with the one or more views at which a touch was received based on the values of the multi-touch and exclusive touch flags.

Claim 2 adds the following feature:

> if a multi-touch flag is associated with a particular view, allowing other touch events contemporaneous with a touch event received at the particular view to be sent to the software element associated with the other views.

The decision elaborated on the different approaches for determinating eligibility to patent law at the EPO (Duns approach) and in the UK (Aerotel/Macrossan). Nevertheless, the result is the same irrespective of the route taken.

The court went on to discuss the existence of a technical contribution to the art in order to determine if the claimed subject matter is excluded as a computer program as such from patentability.

The court followed the four steps of the Aerotel test. It was pointed out that 'novel and inventive purely excluded subject matter does not count as a technical contribution'. Analysis is based on the 'substance over form' principle. The combination of a computer program with a data carrier or with a computer does not alter the fact that it is a computer program. Furthermore, if the real contribution of a program lies in an excluded area then it is not patentable.

The signposts indicated in AT&T (cf. earlier in this section) were taken as a basis for a more detailed analysis. The division of the screen into multiple views in combination with the assignment of flags to the views relates to the computer's internal operation. The computer operates in a new and improved way. Thus, 'the problem and its solution is essentially technical in nature and ... not excluded from patentability. A technical contribution is made to the art.

The solution for claim 1 was considered to be obvious in the light of common general knowledge. The use of flags to filter events by type was well-known to the person skilled in the art. Such solutions were known from single mouse or single touch environments.

Finally, claim 2 (combination of touch events of different views at the same time) was neither a computer program as such nor obvious.

EP1964022

This patent had the title 'Unlocking a device by performing gestures on an unlock image' (priority 23 December 2005). The patent has independent claims one (method), six (device) and eighteen (computer program product). The general aim of the invention consisted in the creation of 'more efficient user-friendly procedures for unlocking touch screen devices and their screens and applications'. This was achieved by a 'method of unlocking a screen which involves contacting the screen with a finger or an object such as a stylus and moving an unlock image along a predefined displayed path across the screen in accordance with a predefined gesture. Thus the unlock image and predefined display path along which the unlock image must be moved are both displayed to the user and the user is provided with feedback as to the progress of the unlock action.

Claim 1 (with reference numerals added by the judge) reads as follows:

(i) A computer implemented method of controlling a portable electronic device
(ii) comprising a touch-sensitive display,
(iii) comprising detecting contact with the touch-sensitive display while the device is in a user-interface lock state;
(iv) transitioning the device to a user-interface unlock state if the detected contact corresponds to a predefined gesture;
(v) and maintaining the device in a user-interface lock state if the detected contact does not correspond to the predefined gesture;
(vi) characterized by moving an unlock image along a predefined displayed path on the touch sensitive display in accordance with the contact,
(vii) wherein the unlock image is a graphical, interactive user-interface object with which a user interacts in order to unlock the device.

Technicality was not discussed because the claimed subject matter was obvious from prior art (a mobile phone Neonode available with similar features before the priority day; two videos).

§6.06 EXAMINATION PRACTICE

UK legal practice, in line with the common law system, is based largely on UK case law together with EPO case law. In general, the aim is to harmonize legal practice by considering the EPO's practice. However, a major difference remains in determining eligibility for patent protection. The UK uses the 'Aerotel test' which is similar to the earlier 'contribution approach' of the EPO. Nevertheless, both routes very often come to the same result.

One implication of the different approaches is the more frequent tendency to refuse subject matter as excluded subject matter and in particular as a computer program as such. The reason for this can be seen in the EPO's approach. As soon as there is a technical element in the claim (hardware or specific software), the application is not excluded from patentability. The majority of claims have at least one technical feature in the claim. As a result, a technical character exists. In rare cases claims are rejected as a business method as such, as a rule of playing games as such etc. but hardly ever as a computer program as such. However, non-technical features are usually disregarded in evaluating novelty and inventive step at the EPO. Refusals result from an obvious implementation of non-technical features.

In order to determine the technical contribution (**Aerotel test**) of a computer program, the **five signposts** are used as indicated in the decision in AT&T Knowledge Ventures/Cvon *Innovations v. Comptroller General of Patents* (2009).

Furthermore, irrespective of the fundamental approach it seems that the term 'computer program' is interpreted in a broad sense. The reason for this apparently lies in the 'substance over form' principle. No difference is made between the algorithm as a basis for a computer program and the final computer program in a programming language. Even if the claim and the specification only show the method (or algorithm) steps without any details of an implementation as a computer program (e.g. of a programming language or a data structure), the claimed subject matter is interpreted as a computer program. Depending on the kind of method it can also be regarded as a mathematical method as such, a business method as such etc. This evaluation is maintained even if the excluded method is combined with notorious computer features. The examiner does not need to search for such notorious features if the claim is a mixture of notorious computer features in combination with excluded subject matter. As a result, a stricter interpretation of 'computer program' can be expected.

A difference is made between technical effects resulting from the internal work of a computer and the effect of a computer (including software) on something outside of the computer. Thus, since Symbian, inventions are no longer excluded as computer programs as such because there is no technical effect outside of the computer. The technical effect has to operate at the level of the architecture of the computer. Architecture can mean the interaction between elements like the processor, cache memory, or other internal elements of a computer. It follows that methods can be protected when they are implemented as a computer program in the area of system software by a patent, provided that the computer works in a new and non-obvious way.

It is not enough for a program to run faster or use less processing power or make more efficient use of hardware. The whole system in which the computer program runs has to operate in an improved way.

Case law shows that the evaluation of exclusion from patentability for computer programs indicates the difficulties faced by all patent offices in this area. Specific areas of computing like modelling, simulation, and presentation of information with graphical user-interfaces are difficult to evaluate because they seem to be closer to non-technical areas.

Over the years, one can observe the development of less restrictive legal practice in the area of computer programs in general.

CHAPTER 7
France

§7.01 LEGAL REQUIREMENTS

A general overview of the French legal system is given on the European Justice website.[1] The basic requirements on intellectual property are indicated in two parts of the intellectual property code (2006). The first part is about the legislative and the second is about the regulations.

- 'Code de la propriété intellectulle (partie legislative)'.
- 'Code de la propriété intellectulle (partie réglementaire)'.[2]

An English translation is available.[3] The legislative part is subdivided into three parts: Copyright, Industrial Property and, Application to the Overseas Territories and the Territorial Entity of Mayotte. The complete legislative part comprises eight books ('livres').

The National Institute of Industrial Property ('Institut National de la Propriété Industrielle - INPI') manages the fundamental tasks concerning industrial property under the authority of the Minister for Industry.

BOOK VI of the legislative part relates to, Protection of Inventions and Technical Knowledge' with Articles L611-1 to L623-35. The relevant article concerning patentability and excluded subject matter is Article L611-10:

1. Inventions which are susceptible of industrial application, which are new and which involve an inventive step shall be patentable.
2. The following in particular shall not be regarded as inventions within the meaning of the first paragraph of this Article:

1. At https://e-justice.europa.eu/content_member_state_law-6-fr-en.do?member = 1 (accessed 3 April 2017).
2. At https://www. legifrance.gouv.fr (accessed 3 April 2017).
3. At https://www.legifrance.gouv.fr/Traductions/en-English/Legifrance-translations (accessed 3 April 2017).

a) discoveries, scientific theories and mathematical methods;
b) aesthetic creations;
c) schemes, rules and methods for performing mental acts, playing games or doing business, and programs for computers;
d) presentations of information.

3. The provisions of (2) of this Article shall exclude patentability of the items referred to in these provisions only to the extent to which the patent application or the patent relates to such subject matter or activities as such.

The formulation corresponds to Article 52 (1) and 52(2) of the EPC. However, the 'technical fields' are not indicated in the first Article.

The regulatory part comprises more details on the patent application:

> Article R612-3 (inserted by Decree No. 95-385 of 10 April 1995 Official Journal of 13 April 1995)
>
> The patent application shall comprise a request for grant of a patent of which the form shall be laid down by decision of the Director General of the National Institute of Industrial Property and to which shall be attached:
>
> 1°. A description of the invention, accompanied where appropriate by drawings;
>
> 2°. One or more claims;
>
> 3°. An abstract of the technical content of the invention;
>
> 4°. Where appropriate, a copy of any earlier filings of which elements are reproduced as set out in Article L. 612-3; the elements that are reproduced shall be highlighted therein.

The formulation of the claims reads as follows:

> Article R612-16 (inserted by Decree No. 95-385 of 10 April 1995 Official Journal of 13 April 1995)
>
> The claims shall define the matter for which protection is sought in terms of the technical features of the invention.
>
> The claim may not, except where absolutely necessary, rely in respect of the technical features of the invention on simple references to the description or drawings.

Description and claims should comprise technical content and technical features. According to Article R612-13 the description can comprise, at the end:

> Short extracts from computer programs presented in the form of lists written in current programming languages, where necessary for the understanding of the invention'. Furthermore: 'Schematic representations of stages in a process, diagrams and short extracts from computer programs submitted in the form of organigrams required for the understanding of the invention shall be considered to be drawings.

§7.02 PROCEDURAL AND FORMAL ASPECTS

Bouche describes details of the patent procedure in his book 'Intellectual Property Law in France'.[4] To obtain a patent in France, a patent application can be filed at the INPI or at the European Patent Office (EPO) (with France as the designated state). The EPO does the search for the INPI. As a result, the same criteria are applied in principle for French National applications as for European Applications. The search report is accompanied by a written opinion. The search report is published together with the patent application. Third parties can submit objections within three months of publication. When the patent is granted a final search report is created. Any person can request information about the relevance of documents in the search report after the grant (Article L612-23). Third parties can appeal the grant of a patent if the grant causes them damage.

§7.03 CLAIM FORMATS FOR COMPUTER IMPLEMENTED INVENTION (CII)

The usual formats such as method and apparatus/device are allowed. Furthermore, different claim forms are allowed for a claim which directly mentions a computer program. It can be claimed in the form 'computer program', 'computer program product' and also in the form 'data carrier comprising a computer program ...' or similar forms. No information is available on claims about a data structure.

Signal claims are allowed for a colour television signal in the context of presentation of information. It is accepted when the technical features of the signal depend on those of the system that produces the signal. It is not clear if this can be interpreted as a general admissibility of signal claims in the sense of signals for the transmission of computer programs and digital data. Since the legal practice follows that of the EPO it can be assumed that respective claim forms will be allowed.

It should be considered that, while the claim starts with the word 'computer program', the content of the claim does not represent the normal computer program as understood by a computer professional. As in other countries, program listings are part of the patent description (inside or as an annex).

§7.04 COMPUTER-IMPLEMENTED INVENTIONS: OVERVIEW

Patentability of software has been a controversial issue in France since the early years of the computer. Some historical facts on the views in France and in other countries can be found in A. Mancini's book 'International Patent Law is Obsolete'.[5] This book is also about the difficulties the patent system has in adapting to new technology. Patent protection for software was denied primarily due to the lack of materiality of its object.

4. Bouche, N. *Intellectual Property Law in France* Kluwer Law International, 2011.
5. Mancini, A. *International Patent Law is Obsolete* Buenos Books America Llc, 2006.

There are no specific guidelines for computer-implemented inventions in France. Guidance is provided as part of general explanations on the examination procedure.

§7.05 DETAILS ON EXCLUDED SUBJECT MATTER

Some additional (non-binding) information on excluded subject matter is available from a document ('Directives Brevets') entitled 'La délivrance des brevets et des certificats d'utitilité' which can be found on the website of the INPI.[6] The brochure (in French) was last modified in March 2017. The passages concerning excluded subject matter (Chapitre VII BREVETABILITÉ) were last modified in June 2011. The explanations on excluded subject matter indicated in §7.05 result from a translation by the author.

First, the basic legal requirements as to excluded subject matter are repeated. With Article It is explained that with respect to L611-10-2 an invention must have a technical character. The invention should indicate the solution of a technical problem by technical means. There have to be technical features:

> L'invention doit avoir un caractère technique, elle doit apporter une solution présentant des caractéristiques techniques à un problème technique, elle doit donc posséder des caractéristiques techniques.

The requirement of a 'technical character' might be decisive for the determination whether an application is eligible to patent law. This statement is in line with legal practice at the EPO.

Examples are provided for patentable and non-patentable subject matter for the respective excluded topics. In general, it is important whether the excluded topic is claimed as such or whether it is part of a technical solution of a technical problem performed by technical means.

The following examples are examples in extract. The examples are provided for all excluded subject matter with a high probability of implementation as a computer program (e.g. discoveries are not usually in the context of computer programs). A complete translation is outside the scope of this book.

[A] Mathematical Methods

Purely abstract and theoretical methods are not patentable. Whereas a fast division method is not patentable, a calculating machine working according to that method is patentable. A mathematical method for an electrical filter is not patentable but a filter obtained by that method could result in a product claim if there is a technical character. The latter seems to be similar to the Vicom decision at the EPO in the 1980s.

A mathematical method based on iterative interpolation is not patentable even if some general means of an apparatus are indicated. A material structure is missing.

6. INPI *La délivrance des brevets et des certificats d'utitilité* https://www.inpi.fr/sites/default/files/directives_brevets_mars2017.pdf (accessed 3 April 2017).

Integrated circuits are patentable when they represent an implementation of a calculation method.

[B] Aesthetic Creations

A pure aesthetic creation (e.g. painting, sculpture) does not have a functional or practical use. Law outside of patents protects such creations. Aesthetic creations can be patentable in combination with technical features. No examples are provided in the computing field.

A method for producing an aesthetic object might be patentable. A diamond might look beautiful due to a particular form (not patentable). The production method might be patentable as well as the product obtained.

[C] Plans, Principles and Methods

Mental Acts

Pure intellectual methods without any technical implementation are not patentable (e.g. learning languages, solving crossword puzzles). A teaching method, which purports to teach by a sequence of pictures of a technical object, is not patentable.

Rules of Games

Pure rules of games are not patentable. The same is true if means are indicated which are only defined by the rules of playing a game. A patent will not be granted for a two-part claim if the precharacterizing part of a claim indicates the material features of the game but the characterizing part indicates only the rules of playing the game. When the material elements of a game indicate technical features independent from the rules of playing the game a patent might be granted.

Business Methods

Pure Business methods are not patentable even if they are implemented by computing means and in particular by software. Reference was made to three appeal procedures at Courts of Appeal (Cours d'Appel – CA).

'**Arrêt CA Paris Sagem du 24 janvier 2003**': The patent application filed by the Sagem society was refused by the INPI. The patent concerned a method of ordering products near a shopping centre electronically. No technical effect was seen, just an economic transaction that is not patentable. The Court of Appeal pointed out, that the use of technical means for non-technical purposes and for the treatment of non-technical information does not necessarily assign a technical character to each step of the method or to the whole method.

'**Arrêt CA Paris Cotranex du 15 mars 2006**': The French patent application filed by the insurance company Contranex was refused by the INPI. It was entitled

'Procedure for reparation of damage by insurers, uses matching of identity data and item requested from supplier to authorize supplier to issue item to assured'. Generic technical means (e.g. server) were used for processing non-technical data. A technical character was not assigned to the claimed subject matter. The Court of Appeal confirmed the INPI's decision.

'Arrêt CA Rennes Antionietti du 7 octobre 2003': The patent application was about a computing system, which allocates an offer to the best of several customers. The application was regarded as a method of doing business.

The uses of a material object like a piece of paper, which might be characterized by different texts or data on management methods or book keeping, does not make the claimed subject matter patentable.

[D] Computer Programs

Computer programs and software are protected by copyright ('droit d'auteur'). They are not patentable if claimed as such. They are patentable in the context of claimed subject matter that has a technical character.

A patent might relate to

- a computer controlled by a program with a claim directed to the technical features of the machine;
- industrial processes including steps implemented as a computer program with the achievement of a technical effect and an industrial usability.

If the computer program when run on a computer, creates a further technical effect, which is more than the normal technical effect between a computer and a program, it is not excluded from patentability. Such a technical effect can result from the control of an industrial process, or from the processing of data representing physical entities or from the internal function of the computer. It can relate to security aspects, to the management of resources or to the solution of a technical problem for improving the speed of data transmission in a communication system.

The claims have to define all features directed to the patentability of the process implemented as computer program. The necessary features have to be indicated under the assumption that the program runs on a computer. Pure program listings cannot be subject to patent claims. If necessary, they can be indicated in the annex of the description.

The following formulations are acceptable:

- computer program comprising pieces/ means/ code with instructions, which when executed on a computer, cause the computer to execute the steps of a method according to claim (X);
- computer program product comprising pieces/ means/ code with instructions stored on a carrier usable by a computer, comprising:
  (i) computer readable program means for the execution of step A;
  (ii) computer readable program means for the execution of step B;

(iii) computer readable program means for the execution of step C.

when said program runs on a computer.

[E] Presentations of Information

Any presentation of information characterized only by the content of the information is not patentable. Presentation of information as such is not patentable. A carrier solely characterized by the information written or stored on it is not patentable. Examples are discs characterized by the piece of music stored on the disc or books characterized by their content. Methods and devices only characterized by the presentation of information indicated or stored are not patentable.

Technical features might define the way in which information is presented (independent from the content of the information). In such a case, a patent might be possible. Some examples are:

- a communication system which uses a specific code for representing letters (e.g. pulse code modulation);
- a disc for storing sound characterized by a special mode to store stereo sound;
- a data carrier comprising a computer program (under the assumption that the patentability requirements are fulfilled);
- a colour television signal with technical features depending on the system for producing the signal.

In summary, the INPI can refuse patent applications for inventions or parts of inventions which claim unpatentable subject matter in the sense of Articles L. 611-16 to L. 611-19.

§7.06 *ORANGE V. FREE*

In France there are hardly ever infringement cases in the field of computer-implemented inventions. One exception which received public attention is the case *Orange v. Free*, two telecom firms. Orange claimed infringement of the European patent EP204497 entitled 'Switching of multimedia sessions of a mobile terminal to an equipment of a local home network'. The patent was revoked on 18 June 2015 by the 'Tribunal Grande Instance de Paris' because some claims lacked novelty and other claims were directed to a computer program and to a storage medium. Claims 12–15 were considered to be 'computer programs as such' and excluded from patentability:[7]

> Prononce la nullité des revendications 12, 13, 14 et 15 de la partie française du brevet européen n°2 044 797, qui concernent un programme d'ordinateur considéré en tant que tel pour défaut de brevetabilité.

7. Legalis Jurisprudence Logiciel *Tribunal de grande instance de Paris, 3ème chambre 1ère section, jugement du 18 juin 2015* https://www.legalis.net/jurisprudences/tribunal-de-grande-instance-de-paris-3eme-chambre-1ere-section-jugement-du-18-juin-2015/ (accessed 4 April 2017).

This view contradicts the long-standing legal practice of the EPO to allow such claims. They were based on decisions T1173/97 and T0935/97 of the Board of Appeal of the EPO. French opponents of software patents welcomed the decision.

The further procedure is visible from the blog 'Patent my French' of Renaud Fulconis, European patent attorney and Conseil en propriété industrielle.[8] A limitation request was submitted to the INPI. The claims on computer programs were deleted.

§7.07 SUMMARY

Legal practice concerning computer-implemented inventions is generally in line with the EPO's legal practice. Nevertheless, discussions on the protection of intellectual property continue because new technological developments continue to challenge existing legal systems. Views of several experts can be found in the document 'La Propriété Intellectual & la transformation numérique de l'économie' on the INPI's website.[9] Several articles discuss the implications of the 'digital economy' for the intellectual property system. Among them is one article on the protection of algorithms ('Quelle protection juridique pour l'algorithme?' authored by Marc Schuler and Benjamin Znaty). It indicates the difficulties of the intellectual property system, which allows protection of computer programs by copyright (but algorithms as basis of a computer program are not protected by copyright), and a partial or indirect protection of algorithms (implemented in hardware and/or software), when they are part of a patentable invention. This is in particular true when the algorithm results from a traditional area of technology. The Internet of Things and intellectual property are discussed in 'L'Internet des objets et la propriété intellectuelle'.[10]

8. Blog Patent my French, *Orange on a new track* posted 29 November 2016 http://patentmyfrench.com/?s=orange+on+a+new+track (accessed 4 April 2017).
9. INPI *La propriété intellectuelle et la transformation numérique de l'économie* https://www.inpi.fr/fr/services-et-prestations/etude-pi-et-economie-numerique (accessed 3 April 2017).
10. INPI *L'Internet des objets et la propriété intellectuelle* https://www.inpi.fr/fr/l-internet-des-objets-et-la-propriete-intellectuelle (accessed 3 April 2017).

CHAPTER 8
United States of America

§8.01 LEGAL BASICS

A short introduction is given here. The legal system is based on common law (case law) in contrast to the civil law systems of Continental Europe. In such systems, judicial precedent has a higher relevance and is seen as important guidance for legal practice.

The specifics of US patent law are summarized by A. Nemeth in his book.[1] It provides European Patent Professionals with a comparison of the US patent law system and the European Patent Offices (EPO's) legal practice. Guidance can also be found on the website of the United States Patent and Trademark Office (USPTO). The webpage 'How to Find Laws and Regulations' explains the meaning of United States Code (USC) and Citations of Code of Federal Regulations (CFR). CFR explains the implementing regulations in more detail.[2]

35 USC §123(a)
 35 = Title 35
 USC = United States Code 'the law'
 § = a symbol meaning 'section'
 123 = The section number within this particular Title
 (a) = a paragraph within a section

15 CFR §123(a)

15 = Title 15, Federal Regulations are divided into various Titles
 CFR = Code of Federal Regulations 'how to implement the law'
 § = a symbol meaning 'section'123 = The section number within this particular Title
 (a) = a paragraph within a section, labelled '(a)'

1. Nemeth, A. *US Patent Law for European Patent Professionals* Wolters Kluwer 2015.
2. USPTO, *How to Find Laws and Regulations*, https://www.uspto.gov/patent/laws-and-regulations/how-find-laws-and-regulations (accessed 4 March 2017).

The US patent system has its direct roots in the Constitution of the United States. Title 35 USC relates to patents. Part II relates to patentability of inventions.[3] §100 starts with definitions. It should be noted that contrary to other nations the word invention includes inventions and discoveries. §101 reads:

> Whoever invents or discovers any new and useful **process, machine, manufacture, or composition of matter**, or any new and useful improvement thereof, may obtain a patent therefor, subject to the conditions and requirements of this title.

Major changes took place in the US patent system following the implementation of the Leahy-Smith America Invents Act (AIA). It was signed by President Obama in 2011. The key amendments contributed to a more harmonized international patent system.[4] The first-to-file principle replaced the first-to-invent principle. The definition of prior art 'includes non-printed disclosures, including oral disclosures, made available to the public anywhere in the world'. Post-Grant and Inter Partes Review (IPR) Procedures or Post-Grant Review (PGR) of Business Method Patents (Covered Business Method (CBM)) were introduced. The PGR of Business Methods is a transitional action. It is supposed to expire in 2020. The USPTO's webpage explains major differences between IPR, PGR and CBM.[5] Third-party observations from other patent offices, will be accepted in order to help examiners in finding prior art.

37 CFR comprises the implementing regulations to 35 USC. It has five chapters. Chapter 1 has the title 'UNITED STATES PATENT AND TRADEMARK OFFICE, DEPARTMENT OF COMMERCE' and includes rules concerning patents.

The use of the Cooperative Patent Classification (CPC) – in cooperation with the EPO (agreed in 2010) is an important aspect not directly related to AIA.[6]

§8.02 PROCEDURAL AND FORMAL ASPECTS

The revision of patent law with AIA has resulted in far-reaching amendments as already mentioned in §8.01. Nevertheless, the fundamentals of patentability remain. Patentable subject matter is directed to process, machine, manufacture, or composition of matter. However, interpretation in the area of modern technologies like biotech, computing including software (in particular business methods implemented by means of a computer program) has changed over time,. This will be explained later. There is no direct technicality requirement in the law such as that in the European Patent Convention (EPC).

3. US Government Publishing Office *PART II – PATENTABILITY OF INVENTIONS AND GRANT OF PATENTS* https://www.gpo.gov/fdsys/pkg/USCODE-2015-title35/pdf/USCODE-2015-title35-partII-chap10.pdf (accessed 4 March 2017).
4. USPTO *Global Impacts of the AIA* https://www.uspto.gov/patent/laws-and-regulations/america-invents-act-aia/global-impacts-aia (accessed 4 March 2017).
5. USPTO *Major Differences between IPR, PGR, and CBM* www.uspto.gov/sites/default/files/ip/boards/bpai/aia_trial_comparison_chart.pptx (accessed 12 March 2017).
6. *CPC* http://www.cooperativepatentclassification.org/about.html (accessed 4 March 2017).

An important procedural principle refers to procedural estoppel. During the prosecution of an application amendments in claim formulation, which are to the contrary of what was claimed in an earlier phase of prosecution, are not usually allowed. Thus, an embodiment claimed in an independent claim of an early phase cannot be reintroduced at a later phase. There are exceptions, i.e. new prior art documents might cause returning to an earlier version. The relationship between prosecution history estoppel and the doctrine of equivalents was a major topic in the case of *FESTO CORPORATION, PETITIONER v. SHOKETSU KINZOKU KOGYO KABUSHIKI CO., ET AL.* in the Supreme Court in 2002.[7] Prosecution history estoppel contributes to the straightforward procedure at the patent office. The applicant should know what was invented. Infringement usually means literal infringement. However, under the doctrine of equivalents, the patent holder can claim that the protection is greater than what is indicated in the claims. Equivalent elements can be covered but the court will analyse whether such equivalent elements were given up during the examination phase. In Festo the Supreme Court decided that narrowing the claims during prosecution does not bar the doctrine of equivalence. The patent holder has the opportunity to overcome the presumption by demonstrating that the amended claim did not mean giving up a specific equivalent. The court suggested that 'Festo may make such a showing, for example, by demonstrating that the allegedly equivalent elements are later-developed technologies that were not known to persons of ordinary skill in the art and were therefore not surrendered through the claim amendments.'

An overview of US intellectual property law with copyright, patent and trademark is given by Halpern, S.W. et al.[8]

§8.03 CLAIM FORMATS FOR COMPUTER IMPLEMENTED INVENTIONS (CIIs)

According to §101 there are four fundamental claim categories. For computer-implemented inventions the first three forms are usually relevant:

1. Process.
2. Machine.
3. Manufacture.
4. Composition of Matter.

The USPTO amended parts of Manual of Patent Examination Procedure (MPEP) as a result of the latest decisions of the Supreme Court. Major revisions were done in 2015.

7. US, *FESTO CORPORATION, PETITIONER v. SHOKETSU KINZOKU KOGYO KABUSHIKI CO.*, ET AL. No. 00-1543 https://www.uspto.gov/web/offices/com/sol/ambriefs/Festo.pdf (accessed 13 March 2017).
8. Halpern S.W. et al. Fundamentals of US Intellectual Property Law. Copyright, Patent and Trademark – Fifth Edition 2015 Wolters & Kluwer.

They can be found on the USPTO's website.[9] The revision process is ongoing. Thus, further amendments can be expected.

Important information on claim formulation can be found in MPEP (November 2015) Chapter 2100 Patentability.[10]

'Process' describes a series of steps in order to achieve a result. Business methods are described by a process. As will be seen later they are the subject of specific requirements. Nowadays processes can be implemented by computing means and by software. Basic mathematical processes executed by a generic computer are not patentable. Mental processes executed only by a human without any machine are not patentable.

Well-known claim forms are '**machine**' and 'apparatus. A machine is a concrete thing, consisting of parts, or of certain devices and combinations of devices.

Manufacture – an article produced from raw or prepared materials by giving these materials new forms, qualities, properties, or combinations, whether by hand laboratory or by machinery.

Composition of matter – all compositions of two or more substances and all composite articles, whether they be the result of chemical union, or of mechanical mixture, or whether they be gases, fluids, powders or solids, for example.

MPEP, Chapter 2100 indicates 'Non-limiting examples of claims that are not directed to one of the statutory categories:

i. transitory forms of signal transmission (e.g. a propagating electrical or electromagnetic signal per se), In re Nuijten, 500 F.3d 1346, 1357, 84 USPQ2d 1495, 1503 (Fed. Cir. 2007);
ii. a human per se, The Leahy-Smith AIA, Public Law 112-29, sections 33, 125 Stat. 284 (16 September 2011);
iii. a legal contractual agreement between two parties, *see* In re Ferguson, 558 F.3d 1359, 1364, 90 USPQ2d 1035, 1039-40 (Fed. Cir. 2009) (cert.denied);
iv. a computer program per se, *Gottschalk v. Benson*, 409 U.S. at 72, 175 USPQ at 676–677;
v. a company, Ferguson, 558 F.3d at 1366, 90 USPQ at 1040;
vi. a mere arrangement of printed matter, In re Miller, 418 F.2d 1392, 1396, 164 USPQ 46, 49 (CCPA 1969); and
vii. data per se, *Digitech Image Tech., LLC v. Electronics for Imaging*, Inc., 758 F.3d 1344, 1350, 111 USPQ2d 1717, 1720 (Fed. Cir. 2014).'

Not patentable claims from the perspective of CII are: transitory forms of signal transmission, a computer program per se and data per se. Several requirements have to be taken into account in claim formulation. Here the most important ones for CII are indicated only.

9. USPTO Manual of Patent Examining Procedure (MPEP), Ninth Edition, Revision 07.2015, Last Revised November 2015, https://www.uspto.gov/web/offices/pac/mpep/index.html (accessed 9 March 2017).
10. USPTO *MPEP Chapter 2100 Patentability* https://www.uspto.gov/web/offices/pac/mpep/mpep-2100.pdf (accessed 9 March 2017).

Claims concerning **machine-readable media** should not include signals or waves. Tangible forms of machine readable media are allowed e.g. compact disks. When a machine readable media relates to some programming, a functional relationship has to exist between the programming and the intended computer system MPEP Chapter 2100, subchapter 2111.05 Functional and Non-functional Descriptive Material). When the programming performs some function with respect to the computer with which it is associated, a functional relationship exists. No functional relationship exists if the medium just serves as a support for information or data. The same is true if the claim as a whole provides a meaning to a human reader which is independent of the computer system. A claim to a memory stick with tables of batting averages or tracks of recorded music does not indicate a functional relationship. If the instructions stored on the computer readable media relate to an abstract idea, they are not eligible for patenting under 35 USC 101.

MPEP, chapter 2100, subchapter '2114 Apparatus and Article Claims – Functional Language' indicates that an apparatus or article claim can be described by a certain structure but also in functional language. Thus, computer-implemented functional claim limitation is allowed. Such claims can be broad. The term 'computer' is commonly understood by one of ordinary skill in the art to describe a variety of devices with varying degrees of complexity and capabilities.

Functional language means that 'A claim term is functional when it recites a feature "by what it does rather than by what it is" (MPEP Chapter 2100, 2173.05(g) Functional Limitations). The **means-plus-function language** can be used in order to formulate an apparatus claim in computing. The claim language will be interpreted to give the claim the 'broadest reasonable interpretation, in light of and consistent with the written description of the invention in the application'. Hence, claim language has to be seen together with the specification (35 USC 112). Chapter 2100 points out: 'If the means- (or step-) plus-function limitation is computer-implemented, and the specification does not provide a disclosure of the computer and algorithm in sufficient detail to demonstrate to one of ordinary skill in the art that the inventor possessed the invention, including how to program the disclosed computer to perform the claimed function, a rejection under 35 U.S.C. 112(a) or pre-AIA 35 U.S.C. 112, first paragraph, for lack of written description' can be expected.

Functional claiming in the context of software is discussed by M. A. Lemley.[11] After a historical overview Lemley describes the difficulties of functional claiming in the area of software and the possible negative implications of very broad claims based on means-plus-function claiming. One reason is seen in the lack of a standard language in computing compared to chemistry or biotechnology. The other reason is seen in the separation of the structure (hardware) and function (software). This function is also worded on a high level of abstraction. There are several possible ways of implementing the function in software. Lemley points out: 'The process steps implemented in the

11. Lemley, M. A. *Software Patents and the Return of Functional Claiming (Draft)* 2012 https://www.researchgate.net/profile/Mark_Lemley/publication/256028624_Software_Patents_and_the_Return_of_Functional_Claiming/links/56c4fdf108aea564e304da8f.pdf (accessed 9 March 2017).

generally claimed computer are also claimed in broad functional terms. That is, the patentee claims the end it accomplishes, not the means of getting there'. The result is that 'these "capability claims" assert ownership of any device that is capable of implementing that idea, whether or not the device actually does so.' This uncertainty in scope and definition results in a high probability of invalidity of such patents. A negative effect results from so called 'patent trolls' which buy weak patents to sue others. According to Lemley's Section 112 (f) (content of the specification) should be taken seriously. In other words, the specification should provide limitations for broad functional wording. Different solutions are discussed.

Claim limitation for a computer-implemented function must include the algorithm needed to transform the general purpose computer or microprocessor disclosed in the specification. Hence, care has to be taken to describe the claim at the respective level of abstraction. To claim a means for performing a specific computer-implemented function and then to disclose only a general purpose computer as the structure designed to perform that function amounts to pure functional claiming. It is not allowed.

Claim wording has to be clear and should normally be based on accepted terminology. However new terminology can be used if the term is explained in the specification. This may play a significant role in computing with all its metaphors and 'invented' words.

According to MPEP chapter 2100, subchapter 2111.04 'examples of claim language, although not exhaustive, which may raise a question as to the limiting effect of the language in a claim are:

(A) "adapted to" or "adapted for" clauses;
(B) "wherein" clauses; and
(C) "whereby" clauses.

The determination of whether each of these clauses is a limitation in a claim depends on the specific facts of the case.'

Claim formulation and evaluation in the area of CII remains a challenge.

§8.04 GUIDELINES FOR CIIs

Rules for dealing with computer programming cases are usually indicated in MPEP. MPEP is regularly updated. Computer programming rules are explicitly indicated in chapter 2100 and patentability in subchapter 2106. The most recent version of chapter 2100 Patentability dates from November 2015.[12] Older versions can be found on the Internet.[13] In 1995, guidelines on computer-implemented inventions were released.[14]

12. USPTO MPEP Chapter 2100 Patentability, November 2015.
13. USPTO *MPEP 1948–2015* https://www.uspto.gov/web/offices/pac/mpep/old/index.htm (accessed 4 March 2017).
14. Department of Commerce, Patent and Trademark Office, (Docket No. 950531144-5304-02), RIN 0651-XX02 *Guidelines for computer-related inventions*, 1995, https://www.uspto.gov/web/offices/com/sol/og/con/files/cons093.htm (accessed 4 March 2017).

This was an attempt to bundle important information together in one document. This practice was not continued. Major changes have taken place in legal practice since the end of the 1990s. Amendments result from AIA and recent Supreme Court landmark decisions:

- 2012: *Mayo Collab. Serv. v. Prometheus Labs.*[15]
- 2013: *Ass. For Molecular Pathology v. Myriad Genetics.*[16]
- 2014: *Alice Corp. Pty.Ltd. v. CLS Bank Int'l.*[17]

The USPTO created Interim Guidance on Subject Matter Eligibility in 2014. More detailed documents are created stepwise in cooperation with external circles (industry, expert, academics ...).[18]

§8.05 HISTORICAL OVERVIEW

As indicated earlier 35 USC §101 provides a positive and broad definition of patentable subject-matter. There is no limitation to fields of technology. Naturally occurring organisms are not patentable. There is nothing on exclusion of computer programs or other items as in Europe. General requirements are novelty, usefulness and improvement of the invention.

The patentability of computer-related inventions and in particular of computer programs is closely related to the development of the modern digital computer that as in other countries started in the 1940s in the U.S. The US patent system was and is an important part in the economy. Thus, it was not surprising that the patent system was extended to modern digital computers. Over the years, the US patent system has tried to treat computer-related inventions like other inventions, but has struggled with basic terminology (hardware, computer program, algorithm), the enormous and growing range of computer applications and software and the specific nature of software. Furthermore, being able to describe a computer program on different levels of abstraction was and is a challenge in the drafting of patent applications. The patentability of hardware followed the well-known rules whereas patentability of software was seen as more negative. Some reasons were:

- Computer programs were seen as a kind of mathematical algorithm or abstract item.
- Computer programs were sold together with hardware which was expensive.
- Computer programs seen as a list of instructions in a programming language were supposed to be protected by copyright as literary work.

15. US Supreme Court *Mayo v. Prometheus*, 2012 https://www.supremecourt.gov/opinions/11pdf/10-1150.pdf (accessed 4 March 2017).
16. US Supreme Court *Molecular Pathology v. Myriad*, 2013 https://www.supremecourt.gov/opinions/12pdf/12-398_1b7d.pdf (accessed 4 March 2017).
17. US Supreme Court *Alice v. CLS*, 2014 https://www.supremecourt.gov/opinions/13pdf/13-298_7lh8.pdf (accessed 4 March 2017).
18. USPTO *Subject-matter eligibility* https://www.uspto.gov/patent/laws-and-regulations/examination-policy/subject-matter-eligibility (accessed 9 March 2017).

Some scientists were in favour of software patents because an algorithm can usually be implemented in hardware or in software. The USPTO was against patents for software in the 1960s. One reason was the difficulty of doing a search for computer programs (understood as a program listing). Some people interested in patents disguised software as hardware by describing block diagrams in connection with a functional language. The whole application avoided any relationship to software. The value of such patents is not known. Some well-known landmark decisions follow:

[A] Overview 1970s to 1980s

In the beginning of the 1970s the microprocessor and later the personal computer were invented. A software industry started to grow. Word processing, databases and spreadsheets allowed different applications of the computer. Mainframes and personal computers could be increasingly connected by networks (local and wide area networks). Different communication protocols resulted in the Internet infrastructure. Basic ideas of interactive computing (mouse, windows on a display, improved graphics screen ...) were put into practice.[19] The interest in software patents grew.

[1] Gottschalk v. Benson

Gottschalk v. Benson was a 1972 Supreme Court decision. It related to the conversion of binary coded decimal (BCD) numbers into binary numbers. Both method claims (one with and one without hardware — a computer) were held as ineligible for patent protection. The reasoning was based on earlier decisions which concluded that 'phenomena of nature, abstract intellectual concepts, mental processes, and algorithms are not patentable because they are basic tools of scientific and technological work'.[20] In the course of the whole procedure the claim without the computer was seen as an unpatentable mental process. There was no transformation of matter from one physical state to another as in chemical processes. Finally, even if the computer implementation could be seen as positive the grant of a patent would 'preempt all uses of that algorithm'.[21]

[2] Parker v. Flook

Parker v. Flook (1978) was a Supreme Court decision directed to a process for updating an alarm limit on a catalytic conversion of hydrocarbons. The process was also ineligible for patent protection because the algorithm was already part of the prior art. It was not new.

19. Smith D.K. et al. Fumbling the Future: How Xerox Invented, then Ignored, the first Personal Computer, to Excel, 1999.
20. Gemignani, M.C. *Legal Protection of Software: A Survey* Advances in Computers, Vol. 22, Academic Press, 1983.
21. Samuelson, P. *Should Program Algorithms be Patented?* Communications of the ACM, August 1990, Vol. 33, no. 8, 23–27.

[3] Diamond v. Chakrabarty

Diamond v. Chakrabarty (1980) did not relate to computing but to microorganisms.[22] The decision became famous for the liberal view that 'anything under the sun that is made by man' constitutes statutory subject matter.

[4] Diamond v. Diehr

Diamond v. Diehr (1981) related to a process for moulding raw uncured synthetic rubber into cured rubber under the control of a computer.[23] The computer was programmed according to an algorithm based on the so called Arrhenius equation. In this case, the subject matter was not excluded from patentability because a transformation from one state to another took place. The process could not be seen as something abstract because it was directed to an industrial process that was usually subject to patent protection. Furthermore, a patent claim for a process should not be rejected because it includes mathematics or a computer program.

As a result of the lack of clear guidance for evaluating eligibility to patent law, the lower courts developed the so-called **Freeman-Walter-Abele test**. Simplified, the first step was to find out whether there is an algorithm. The second step determined if there was subject matter in the claim additional to the algorithm. If the remaining part related to something tangible then eligibility was given. The test was later dropped because it failed to be predictable.

Patentability of algorithms was discussed in academic circles. Two articles received a lot of attention at that time. In 1986 the patent specialist Donald Chisum argued against the Supreme Court's negative view towards patents for algorithms in *Gottschalk v. Benson*.[24] The computer scientist Allen Newell responded to Chisum's article.[25] Both articles are primarily directed to the nature of algorithms. According to Chisum and Newell a distinction of algorithms into mathematical and nonmathematical ones does not make sense. Such a distinction was made by the appellate court for a period. Newell was of the opinion that the basic conceptual models on algorithms are wrong and lead to confusion. He explained the similarities of thinking (mental steps) and algorithms. Furthermore, in his view there is no real difference between algorithm and computer program. The first is just a description of a program on a very high level of abstraction. A distinction between algorithm on the one hand and method and process on the other hand seems to be contra productive. The general definition of an algorithm as a sequence of steps might not involve all kinds of algorithms. Programming languages exist which enable the creation of algorithms which do not look like a sequence of steps.

22. US Supreme Court *Diamond v. Chakrabarty*, 1980 http://caselaw.findlaw.com/us-supreme-court/447/303.html (accessed 4 March 2017).
23. US Supreme Court *Diamond v. Diehr*, 450 U.S. 175 (1981) https://supreme.justia.com/cases/federal/us/450/175/case.html (accessed 17 March 2017).
24. Chisum, D. *The Patentability of Algorithms* Univ. of Pittsburgh Law Rev. 1986, 47, 959.
25. Newell, A. *Response: The models are broken, the models are broken* Univ. of Pittsburgh Law Rev. 1986, 47, 1023.

At the end of 1989, two appeal court cases – **Iwahashi** and **Grams** – indicated the different views on patents for algorithms. Further cases exist but are not dealt with here.

[5] In re Iwahashi

In re Iwahashi related to an auto-correlation unit for providing auto-correlation coefficients for use as feature parameters in pattern recognition.[26] Such pattern recognition could be used for voice recognition. The Patent Office refused the application as non-statutory subject matter under 35 USC §101 because it was seen as a mathematical method. The appellate court reversed the decision. It did not focus on the mathematical description of the auto-correlation function but on the indication of 'unit' in the claim and the references to a read-only-memory (ROM). Thus, the claim was seen as patentable hardware.

[6] In re Grams

In re Grams related to method of testing a complex system to determine whether the system condition is normal or abnormal.[27] If it is abnormal, the cause of the abnormality has to be determined. The method was partly implemented as a computer program. The invention was applicable to a broad range of areas that is to say to any complex system, whether it be electrical, mechanical, chemical, biological, or combinations thereof. The USPTO refused the application because it was non-statutory subject matter under 35 USC §101. It was seen as either a mathematical algorithm or a method of doing business. The appellate court took a broader view on algorithms as unpatentable subject matter. The USPTO's decision was confirmed. As there was already one ground for refusal the question of whether the claimed subject matter was a business method was not discussed.

Sometimes companies did not apply for software patents because there was a lack of clear guidance by the patent system, or because they feared being involved in lawsuits. They kept their inventions secret. One example is Xerox: 'the Star development team proposed twelve patents having to do with the user interface. The ... patent committee rejected all but two on hardware — one on BitBlt, the other on the Star architecture. At the time ... it was a good decision. Patenting required full disclosure and no precedents then existed for winning software patents suits'.[28] This hesitant behaviour later became a problem in the search for prior. It became clear that plenty of basic inventions in the software were not protected by patents. Thus, such inventions could not be found in patent documentation that is usually the basis for prior art search at patent offices.

26. United States Court of Appeals, Federal Circuit. 888 F.2d 1370 (Fed. Cir. 1989) *In re Iwahashi* https://casetext.com/case/in-re-iwahashi#! (accessed 5 March 2017).
27. United States Court of Appeals, Federal Circuit. 888 F.2d 835 (Fed. Cir. 1989) *In re Grams* https://casetext.com/case/grams-in-re (accessed 5 March 2017).
28. Perry, T.A et al Of mice and menus: designing the user-friendly interface IEEE Spectrum, September 1989, 46.

During the 1980s, software protection by copyright became popular. The pros and cons compared to patents and trade secrets became apparent. Copyright was easy to achieve but protection was only possible if the program was copied. Thus, different options existed for legal software protection.[29]

[B] Overview 1990s

The 1990s were characterized by new possibilities due to the World Wide Web in connection with Hypertext Mark-up Language (HTML) which allowed the digital communication between companies/academic institutions and between private users and companies. Object-oriented programming languages and in particular the development of Java contributed to new computer services. First webportals and social networks appeared. Protecting software with patents was opposed by different proponents of free, libre and open source software (FLOSS) with R. Stallman the prominent representative. The operating system LINUX version 1.0, developed mainly by Linus Torvalds in cooperation with other software specialists, was released in 1994.[30] LINUX became one of the most important open source projects.

[1] In re Lowry

With **In re Lowry** (1994) the US Court of Appeals for the Federal Circuit allowed eligibility of data structures.[31] The beginning of claim 1 reads:

> 1. A memory for storing data for access by an application program being executed on a data processing system, comprising:
>
> a data structure stored in said memory, said data structure including information resident in a database used by said application program and including: ....

The claim was rejected based on the printed matter doctrine. Thus, the data structure was seen in analogy to printed matter. In a former decision **In re Gulack** it was stated that: 'Where the printed matter is not functionally related to the substrate, the printed matter will not distinguish the invention from the prior art in terms of patentability'. The appellate court did not follow this view.

The case is seen as the beginning of a more liberal legal practice towards software patents. As a result, the number of applications increased enormously.

[2] In re Beauregard

In re Beauregard is not a real decision since the appeal was dismissed. The case related to an invention in computer graphics (Computer program product for utilizing fast

29. Task Force on Legal Aspects of Computer-Based Technology *Protection of Computer Ideawork – Today and Tomorrow* IEEE Software, 1984, 74.
30. Torvalds, L. et al. Just for Fun: The Story of an Accidental Revolutionary HarperCollins, 2001.
31. U.S. Court of Appeals Federal Circuit 26 August 1994 *In re Lowry*, 32 F.3d 1579, 32 USPQ2d 1031 http://digital-law-online.info/cases/32PQ2D1031.htm (accessed 5 March 2017).

polygon fill routines in a graphics display system) and it included a computer program product claim.[32] In other words, the claim was directed to a memory device storing a computer program. The following wording was used:

> Claim 1:
>
> '1. An article of manufacture comprising:
>
> A computer usable medium having computer readable program code means embodied therein for causing a polygon having a boundary ...'
>
> Claim 2:
>
> 'A computer program product for use with a graphics display device, said computer program product comprising:
>
> a computer usable medium having computer readable program code means embodied in said medium for causing a polygon having a boundary ...'
>
> Claim 10:
>
> 'A program storage device readable by a machine, tangibly embodying a program of instructions executable by the machine to perform method steps for filling a polygon having a boundary ... the method steps comprising ...'
>
> The claim wording was rejected by the examiner. The description discloses two algorithms for polygon filling in the programming language C. In the end the case was not discussed at the court because the Commissioner of patents stated 'that computer programs embodied in a tangible medium, such as floppy diskettes, are patentable subject matter under 35 U.S.C. §101 and must be examined under 35 U.S.C. §§102 and 103'. Thus, there was no discussion on the interpretation of 'computer program product'.

The reasons for the introduction of this form of claim were limitations of infringement law. As pointed out by Lee A. Hollar, professor of computer science:

> If the invention is claimed as a method, the claim is infringed only when the method is actually used. If the invention is claimed as a machine running the program, again the claim is infringed only when the program is actually loaded into the computer. In both cases, it is the end user of the program who is the actual infringer.
>
> But the true infringer of the patent on the software-based invention is the competitor who included the patented method in their software and sold it to the end users.[33]

Thus, the new claim form made it possible to sue distributers of software comprising a patented method for direct infringement. Software could be distributed and sold as a separate product without a computer. It was usual to sell the software on a tangible data carrier. It seems that distribution by download over a network (Internet) was not considered. According to Professor Hollar the claim form could have been avoided by amending the infringement law, however, this did not occur.

32. United States Court of Appeals, Federal Circuit. 53 F.3d 1583 (Fed. Cir. 1995) *In re Beauregard* https://casetext.com/case/in-re-beauregard (accessed 5 March 2017).
33. Hollaar, L.A. *Justice Douglas was Right: The Need for Congressional Action on Software Patent* in American Committee for Interoperable systems (ACIS) membership meeting, February 2, Santa Clara, CA, US, 1996.

[3] State Street Bank v. Signature Financial Group

The decision **in *State Street Bank v. Signature Financial Group*** (1998) related to a computer-implemented business method. Signature is the patent owner of a patent with claim 1 starting: 'A data processing system for managing a financial services configuration of a portfolio established as a partnership ....'[34] State Street Bank negotiated a licence to use the patent but the negotiations were unsuccessful. State Street filed a motion for summary judgment of patent invalidity at a district court. Signature appealed but the motion was granted.

The Federal Circuit explained that unpatentable subject matter is 'laws of nature, natural phenomena, and abstract ideas'. This was identified by the Supreme Court in ***Diamond v. Diehr***. However, if an abstract idea is reduced to something practical and a 'useful, concrete and tangible result' is produced then the subject matter is patentable. The claimed subject matter was not an unpatentable mathematical algorithm, in other words an abstract idea. Here, the mathematical algorithm was performed by a machine to produce a useful result. The claimed subject matter is statutory even if the result is expressed in numbers, such as price, profit, percentage, cost, or loss. The claim for the machine comprises features written as means-plus-function elements. The written description disclosed the respective structures.

The subject matter was also not an unpatentable business method. A business method exception was never applied. Furthermore, since the 1952 Patent Act, business methods should be subject to the same legal requirements for patentability as applied to any other process or method. The District Court argued that the patent claim was broad. Thus, any other software implementation of the business method by another financial institution could fall under the scope of the claim. The Federal Circuit responded that the breadth of the claim does not fall within §101.

Implementating functional features as a computer program did not play a role in the decision.

The Federal Circuit criticized the use of the Freeman-Walter-Abele test which was created for the identification of unpatentable mathematical algorithms. The test could result in wrong results because a process, machine, manufacture, or composition of matter employing a law of nature, natural phenomenon, or abstract idea could be patentable subject matter. This holds true even if a law of nature, natural phenomenon, or abstract idea itself would be unpatentable.

Finally, the Federal Circuit concluded that the claimed data processing system for managing financial products fulfilled the requirements of §101. A mathematical algorithm was applied to something practical. A useful, concrete and tangible result was produced by the data processing system.

The Supreme Court denied a petition for a writ of certiorari in 1999. Thus, the Federal Circuit's decision opened the door for business method patents.

---

34. *State Street Bank & Trust Co. v. Signature Financial Group Inc.* U.S. Court of Appeals Federal Circuit; 23 July 1998; 149 F.3d 1368, 47 USPQ2d 1596; http://digital-law-online.info/cases/47 PQ2D1596.htm (accessed 5 March 2017).

The decision and the topic of business methods became subject to particular controversy as a result. The so called Amazon one-click patent US5960411 (Method and system for placing a purchase order via a communications network) was granted in the US in 1999. In the US Amazon sued the bookseller Barnes and Noble for allegedly infringing the patent. Finally, the dispute resulted in settlement.[35]

Proponents of the State Street decision argued that patents in the area of computer-implemented business methods are important because of the growing economic relevance of e-commerce. Some economists underlined the fact that the new economy would rely on intangible assets (including software). Such assets should be the subject of patent protection. Opponents criticized the breadth of many business method patents. Furthermore, they argued that the difficulties in finding the relevant prior art documents for business methods resulted in so called 'trivial patents'.

[4] AT&T Corp. v. EXCEL Communications Inc.

AT&T Corp. v. EXCEL Communications Inc. (1999) was a further infringement case dealing with a mathematical method.[36] AT&T's patent relates to long-distance telephone calls with adaptation of subscriber billing. The district court held the claimed subject matter invalid because it was implicitly directed to a mathematical method. The method included generating message record for an interexchange call. This message record comprised a primary interexchange carrier (PIC) indicator. The Federal Court referred to the State Street decision where the exceptions on mathematical algorithms and business methods were discarded. Generating the PIC indicator based on mathematical calculations was seen as a useful result. The set of claims comprised method claims and apparatus claims. The wording of the claim — machine or process — does not affect the determination of eligibility under §101.

The Federal Court did not agree with the argument that there has to be a physical transformation from one state to another when the mathematical algorithm is executed (as in Diehr: uncured to cured rubber). Furthermore, a physical limitation was seen as unnecessary. This was part of the Fremann-Walter-Abele test that was no longer applicable.

The decision indicated a further step in the adaptation of patent law to modern computing technologies. The request to consider the case at a higher instance was rejected by the Supreme Court.

[C] Overview 2000–2010

The more liberal decisions at the end of the 1990s resulted in an increase of software and/or business method related patents. This development was not seen in a totally

35. *Amazon.com and Barnes & Noble.com settle 1-Click patent lawsuit* Outlaw.com https://www.out-law.com/page-2424 (accessed 5 March 2017).
36. 172 F. 3d 1352 – *At&t Corp v. Excel Communications* Inc http://openjurist.org/172/f3d/1352/att-corp-v-excel-communications-inc (accessed 5 March 2017).

positive light. Several critical topics are indicated e.g. by M. Campbell-Kelly in a historical view on software patents.[37]

Major objections against software patents were raised by open source circles. Objections relate to political views on property in society, to the purpose of patents as motivation for software inventions, and to the specifics of software as a cumulative technology with sequential innovation. Patent protection lasts too long. Patents block the sharing of knowledge in the software development process. Patent thickets (several patents for details of one topic) are created which cannot be monitored by SMEs or by larger companies. Prior art is difficult to find.

Objections were raised both in academic and economic circles and by stakeholders. The creation of patent thickets was criticized e.g. by Bessen.[38] The USPTO was repeatedly criticized on the quality of searches. It had to cope with challenges in finding prior art for business methods and for software.[39] One representative, Coggins, explained in 2002:

> It can be extremely difficult to identify business methods that may have been common practice or common knowledge in an industry, but have not been documented properly, nor dated, nor disclosed in a form that is easily accessible by patent examiners.

The USPTO could no longer rely only on searches in patent documentation. Non-patent literature had to be included. Different forms of electronic publications like video and webpages had to be taken into account as prior art. Cooperation with companies started. New ideas for finding prior art developed. One project was Open Source as Prior Art (OSAPA) started in cooperation with the LINUX foundation.[40] Another project was the 'Peer to patent' project which was a reaction to criticism on insufficient searches for prior art in software.[41] Prior art for software was and is created outside of the patent system since plenty of companies have reservations above applying for patents. External persons, companies (third parties) could contribute to the search for prior art especially in the area of software.

Another phenomenon appeared in the patent system – so called 'patent trolls'. R.P. Mergers describes the trouble with trolls.[42] He defines a patent troll 'as a participant ... that does not contribute to the social goal the patent system was meant

37. Campbell-Kelly, M. *Not All Bad: An Historical Perspective on Software Patents* 11 Mich. Telecomm. & Tech.L. Ref. 191, 2005.
38. Bessen, James E., *Patent Thickets: Strategic Patenting of Complex Technologies* (March 2003). Available at SSRN: https://ssrn.com/abstract=327760 or http://dx.doi.org/10.2139/ssrn.327760.
39. Coggins, W.W. Prior Art in the Field of Business Method Patents – When is an Electronic Document a Printed Publication for Prior Art Purposes? Presented at AIPLA Fall 2002, https://www.uspto.gov/patents-getting-started/patent-basics/types-patent-applications/utility-patent/business-methods-17 (accessed 5 March 2017).
40. *OSAPA* https://www.sdxcentral.com/projects/open-source-as-prior-art-osapa/ (accessed 6 March 2017).
41. *Peertopatent* http://www.peertopatent.org/ (accessed 6 March 2017).
42. Merges, R.P. *The Trouble with Trolls: Innovation, Rent-Seeking, and Patent Law Reform,* 24 Berkeley Tech. L.J. 1583 (2009), Available at: http://scholarship.law.berkeley.edu/facpubs/537.

to serve: technological innovation'. Companies or law firms buy weak, outdated or irrelevant patents in order to attack others for infringement, the aim being to secure large awards of damages. Mergers remarked that not all who buy and sell patents can be called a troll. This is for example true for universities – so called non-practising entities. The case ***eBay, Inc. v. MercExchange***, L.L.C. (2006) related to a business method patent. It was an example of how injunctions can be used as a threat to get unjustified damages.[43] The US Supreme Court required the application of the four-factor test for determining if a permanent injunction is warranted. The four-factor test had been used in the past and it was seen as a well-established means of obtaining an injunction. Since the injunction is a powerful tool for patent trolls, the courts were reminded of the need to be very careful when granting injunctions.

[1] In re Nuijten

In re Nuijten (2007) dealt with the question whether or not a signal is patentable subject matter.[44] Watermarks in a signal could cause distortions in that signal. The signal could be modified so as to compensate distortion. The claim on appeal reads:

> A signal with embedded supplemental data, the signal being encoded in accordance with a given encoding process and selected samples of the signal representing the supplemental data, and at least one of the samples preceding the selected samples is different from the sample corresponding to the given encoding process.

The embedded data is the watermark. The signal can be an audio or video signal. The claim language did not represent the usual steps of a method claim. It also could not be seen as an apparatus claim.

The claim was considered to include physical but transitory forms of signal transmission. Such a transitory, propagating signal does not fall under the patentable subject matter of 'process, machine, manufacture, or composition of matter' under 35 U.S.C. §101. The signal cannot be patentable subject matter.

[2] In re Comiskey

In re Comiskey related to the process for ensuring that disputes relating to legal documents are resolved through arbitration.[45] The Federal Circuit considered some of the claims as mental acts. Thus, they were unpatentable. Other claims indicated a combination of a computer with the mental steps. The remaining claims were patentable in the sense of §101 due to the indication of a computer. The claims were remanded to the USPTO. The first instance had to determine whether the addition of

43. US Supreme Court *EBAY INC. ET AL. v. MERCEXCHANGE, L. L. C.* 2006 https://www.supremecourt.gov/opinions/05pdf/05-130.pdf (accessed 6 March 2017).
44. United States Court of Appeals, Federal Circuit. 500 F.3d 1346 (Fed. Cir. 2007) *In re Nuijten* https://casetext.com/case/in-re-nuijten#p1356 (accessed 6 March 2017).
45. United States Court of Appeals for the Federal Circuit 2006-1286 (Serial No. 09/461,742) *IN RE COMISKEY* http://www.bitlaw.com/source/cases/patent/Comiskey.html (accessed 7 March 2017).

modern computers and communication devices was been obvious. If yes, the applicant would have the opportunity to amend the claims.

[3] In re Bilski

In re Bilski (2008) related to a business method.[46] It was directed to a method of hedging in the field of commodities trading. The application was rejected by the examiner on the grounds that the claimed subject matter represented an abstract idea, solved a mathematical problem and that there was no limitation to any apparatus. Thus, it was not statutory subject matter in the sense of 35 USC §101. Furthermore, it was not an invention directed to technological arts.

The Federal Circuit no longer relied on the test used in **State Street** as 'useful, concrete and tangible result' test. The court referred to **In re Nuijten** in order to discuss the term 'process'. The meaning of 'process' in the context of §101 is narrower than the broad meaning in from Webster's Dictionary. A process is not eligible for patent protection if it claims 'laws of nature, natural phenomena or abstract ideas'. Such fundamental truths should remain free. They are basic tools of scientific and technological work. The question is what is claimed – a fundamental principle (e.g. abstract idea) or a mental process. Furthermore, which test can be used to determine eligibility for patent protection?

The Federal Circuit did not follow the test of State Street that if a 'useful, concrete and tangible result' is achieved the claimed subject matter is eligible for patent protection. The Freeman-Walter-Abele test was also not followed. It was used before State Street. The requirement for eligibility of the process claim is: '(1) it is tied to a particular machine or apparatus, or (2) it transforms a particular article into a different state or thing'. This is the only test – the machine or transformation test.

As indicated by the applicant, the claims were not limited to a specific machine. The transformation is important for a process claim. However, a transformation of physical objects or of a substance did not exist. An electronic signal representing a physical object or a substance was not transformed into another state. The claim could be seen as a kind of 'exchange of only options, which are simply legal rights'. The Federal circuit emphasized, that the machine or transformation test cannot be seen as a 'technological arts' test. Nevertheless, the Federal Circuit concluded 'Applicants here seek to claim a non-transformative process that encompasses a purely mental process of performing requisite mathematical calculations without the aid of a computer or any other device, mentally identifying those transactions that the calculations have revealed would hedge each other's risks, and performing the post-solution step of consummating those transactions'. The result was that the claimed subject matter failed to pass the machine or transformation test. The case went to the Supreme Court.

46. United States Court of Appeals, Federal Circuit. 545 F.3d 943 (Fed. Cir. 2008) *In re Bilski* https://casetext.com/case/in-re-bilski#p959 (accessed 6 March 2017).

[4] Bilski v. Kappos

In ***Bilski v. Kappos*** (2010) the Supreme Court turned to the question of whether a business method claimed as a process claim represents patentable subject matter. The invention was directed to a method that explains how commodity buyers and sellers in the energy market can protect or hedge, against the risk of price changes. Claims 1 and 4 were the most important claims. Claim 1 reads:

> 1. A method for managing the consumption risk costs of a commodity sold by a commodity provider at a fixed price comprising the steps of:
>
> (a) initiating a series of transactions between said commodity provider and consumers of said commodity wherein said consumers purchase said commodity at a fixed rate based upon historical averages, said fixed rate corresponding to a risk position of said consumers;
> (b) identifying market participants for said commodity having a counter-risk position to said consumers; and
> (c) initiating a series of transactions between said commodity provider and said market participants at a second fixed rate such that said series of market participant transactions balances the risk position of said series of consumer transactions.

Claim 4 just indicates a mathematical formula for determining a fixed price.

The Supreme Court started its argumentation with a closer look at the fundamental requirements. The four independent categories of Section 101 were indicated. Inventions and discoveries are eligible for patent protection that fall under processes, machines, manufactures and compositions of matter. This §101 enquiry is a threshold test. Even if an alleged invention falls under one of the categories, they must also satisfy the requirements of novelty (§102), nonobviousness (§103) and full and particular description (§112). The law does not indicate exceptions under §101 but there are exceptions that have developed in legal practice over a very long time. These exceptions are 'laws of nature, physical phenomena, and abstract idea'. §100(b) provides some more information on 'process'. It reads: 'process, art or method, and includes a new use of a known process, machine, manufacture, composition of matter, or material'.

The court discussed the applicability of the machine or transformation test. It concluded that the test is an important tool but it cannot be the only test. This opinion was apparently influenced by views given in briefs that worried about negative implication in software protection. The court pointed out that it is unaware of any requirement to tie a process to a machine or to a transformation of an article. Other tests might be developed by the lower instances.

On the one hand, there is no clear exclusion of business methods from patentability, but on the other hand, there is no suggestion for a broad patentability of business methods.

Finally, the Supreme Court came to the conclusion that the claimed subject matter represents an abstract idea just like the algorithms of Benson (conversion of BCD coded to binary numbers) and Flook (update of an alarm limit). Reference was made to the cases Benson, Flook and Diehr. Thus, the decisions of the lower instances were confirmed but without complete confirmation of the argumentation applied by them. The topic of software patentability was not directly taken into account.

[D] 2010 Onwards

As already indicated the signing of the AIA in 2011 resulted in major patent reform. The discussion on the patentability of pure and computer-implemented business methods and of software continued.

In 2013 the USPTO started a software partnership initiative in cooperation with the software community (e.g. companies, academic institutions) in order to continue to deal with specific challenges in the field of computing and in particular of software.[47] One initiative was the Glossary initiative that has since ended. This was an attempt to clearly define the meaning of terms in the specification. This is useful because computing, unlike chemistry for example, does not always have clear terminology. Very often metaphors are used like cloud, container, liquid software, shopping cart.[48,49] The same term can be given a different meaning by different companies. The initiative ended but patent quality is a topic which deals with claim clarity. The other initiative was directed to prior art search which seems to be an ongoing topic.

Patentability of topics in the area of new technologies like Biotechnologies and IT —Information Technology was influenced by three landmark decisions of the Supreme Court.

[1] Mayo v. Prometheus

In 2011, the Supreme Court decided in ***Mayo v. Prometheus*** that a process for optimizing the efficacy in the treatment of autoimmune diseases is not eligible for patent protection.[50] The claims indicated a special relationship between concentrations of metabolites in the blood and the likelihood that a thiopurine drug dosage will prove ineffective or cause harm. This relationship was seen as unpatentable because it represents a law of nature. Further steps of the claim did not relate to a law of nature but to well-known organizational, routine steps, e.g. the 'determining' step' tells a doctor to measure patients' metabolite level. Such steps describe 'well-understood, routine, conventional activity previously engaged in by scientists in the field. The additional steps were 'not sufficient to transform an unpatentable law of nature into a patent eligible application of such a law.'

47. USPTO *Software Partnership* https://www.uspto.gov/patent/initiatives/software-partnership (accessed 17 March 2017).
48. Colburn, T.R. et al. *Metaphor in Computer Science* Journal of Applied Logic 6 (2008) 526–533.
49. Zambonelli, F. et al. *A survey on nature-inspired metaphors for pervasive service ecosystems* International Journal of Pervasive Computing and Communications Vol. 7 No. 3, 2011 pp. 186–204.
50. US Supreme Court, 2011, *MAYO COLLABORATIVE SERVICES, DBA MAYO MEDICAL LABORATORIES, ET AL. v. PROMETHEUS LABORATORIES INC.* https://www.supremecourt.gov/opinions/11pdf/10-1150.pdf (accessed 7 March 2017).

[2] Molecular Pathology v. Myriad Genetics

In 2012 the Supreme Court considered genetics in ***Molecular Pathology v. Myriad Genetics***.[51] The claimed subject matter was directed to the discovery of genes which indicate a risk of breast and ovarian cancer. Specific medical tests could be developed. Furthermore, it is possible to synthesize specific strands of nucleotides known as complementary DNA (cDNA). The court held that 'A naturally occurring DNA segment is a product of nature and not patent eligible merely because it has been isolated, but cDNA is patent eligible because it is not naturally occurring'. The claims did not include method claims; indicating for example new applications for specific genes or an alteration of the order of naturally occurring nucleotides.

[3] Alice v. CLS Bank

In 2014 the Supreme Court decided on the patentability of a computer-implemented business method in ***Alice v. CLS Bank***.[52] The patents were directed to a scheme for mitigating 'settlement risk' i.e. the risk that only one party to an agreed-upon financial exchange will satisfy its obligation. A computer system was used as a third-party intermediary. Three claim types were used:

(1) a method for exchanging financial obligations;
(2) a computer system configured to carry out the method for exchanging obligations; and
(3) a computer-readable medium containing program code for performing the method of exchanging obligations.

The court followed its line in **Myriad and Mayo** and repeated that there are implicit exceptions from patentability, i.e. 'laws of nature, natural phenomena, and abstract ideas'. The exceptions result in that the court 'must distinguish patents that claim the "buildin[g] block[s]" of human ingenuity, which are ineligible for patent protection, from those that integrate the building blocks into something more, *see Mayo Collaborative Services v. Prometheus* Laboratories, ..., thereby "transform[ing]" them into a patent-eligible invention, ...'.

The court continued with two steps which had already been already developed in **Mayo**:

1. Is the subject matter directed to a patent-ineligible concept?

---

51. US Supreme Court, 2012, *ASSOCIATION FOR MOLECULAR PATHOLOGY ET AL. v. MYRIAD GENETICS, INC.*, https://www.supremecourt.gov/opinions/12pdf/12-398_1b7d.pdf (accessed 7 March 2017).
52. US Supreme Court, 2014, *ALICE CORPORATION PTY. LTD. v. CLS BANK INTERNATIONAL ET AL.* https://www.uspto.gov/sites/default/files/patents/announce/alice_v_cls_sct.pdf (accessed 7 March 2017).

2. If so, do the claim's elements, considered both individually and 'as an ordered combination,' 'transform the nature of the claim' into a patent-eligible application?

Step one: The intermediated settlement was seen as an abstract idea that is not eligible for patent protection. With reference to the risk hedging in **Bilski**, the court concluded that 'the concept of intermediated settlement is 'a fundamental economic practice long prevalent in our system of commerce,' '*ibid.*, and the use of a third-party intermediary (or "clearing house") is a building block of the modern economy.

Step two: Do the additional elements of the claim transform the abstract concept into a patent - eligible application?

The additional elements indicated a computer implementation. The court came to the conclusion that: ' "Simply appending conventional steps, specified at a high level of generality," to a method already "well known in the art" is not "enough" to supply the "inventive concept" needed to make this transformation'. A transformation of the abstract idea did not result from adding the words 'apply it with a computer'.

The *method claim* just instructed a practitioner to implement the abstract idea on a generic computer. The separate functional steps of the computer are conventional steps. The ordered combination of the steps does not add something special. The method claims simply repeat the concept of intermediated settlement as performed by a generic computer. They do not improve the functioning of the computer itself. In addition they do not improve any other technology or a technical field. As a result, there is no transformation of the abstract idea into a patent-eligible invention.

System and media claims add nothing of substance to the abstract idea. They are ineligible under §101. As in the method claims, the system claims refer to some generic computer components configured to implement the abstract idea.

The difference between patent eligible subject matter and non-eligible subject matter was described in more detail with reference to earlier cases. The court expressed the view that patentability should be excluded for an idea itself or, in other words, a fundamental truth, an original clause, a motive. No exclusive right should be given to such fundamentals. Basic economic concepts belong to such fundamental truths. Risk hedging indicated in **Bilsk**i and intermediated settlements belong to a fundamental practice well known in the system of commerce. Hedging is a longstanding commercial practice. It is not a truth about the natural world that has always existed but a method of organizing human activity. The fact that hedging was reduced to a mathematical formula in one claim did not play a major role. It did not change the basic opinion on the abstract idea.

An example of a patent eligible process was seen in **Diehr**. It related to curing rubber. The claim included both a well-known mathematical equation and a computer. The reason why it was seen as eligible for patent protection was not the indication of a computer but the use of that equation in a process in order to solve a technological problem in conventional industry practice. A thermocouple constantly recorded temperature measurements inside the rubber mould. At that time this was not usually possible in industry. The data was sent to a computer which calculated the remaining cure time based on the equation. Thus, an existing technological process was improved. Therefore, eligibility to patent law was given. The existing process was not only combined with a generic computer.

The existence of the computer in the physical and not in the pure conceptual world did not change the basic evaluation. The computer is a tangible system. As a result it is a machine in the sense of §101. However, the court refused the idea that the indication of a computer for implementing a concept would make any physical or social sciences principle eligible for patent protection.

The method claims, the system claims and the claim for a computer-readable medium do not comprise additional elements that result in subject matter eligible for patent protection. Hardware elements like 'data processing system', 'communications controller' and 'data storage unit' are purely functional and generic. These elements can be found in nearly every computer. They are necessary to perform basic calculation, storage and transmission functions required by the method claims. In substance, no difference was seen between method and system claims. Finally, the court explained that it has long '"warn[ed] ... against" interpreting §101 "in ways that make patent eligibility 'depend simply on the draftsman's art."'

§8.06 LEGAL PRACTICE AFTER ALICE: TWO STEP TEST

After a period of very liberal legal practice with respect to computer-implemented inventions Mayo, Myriad and Alice resulted in a stricter approach in eligibility to patent law. The decisions try to provide more concrete boundaries for patentable subject-matter. Principles of human ingenuity should remain free. The Alice case was mainly directed to a business method implemented only by a generic computer. In other words, the claims were worded on a very high level of abstraction from a computer professional's perspective. They mainly expressed the use of a computer to automate an existing business method. No details were discussed concerning software patentability in different fields of system or application software. Hence, there is no 'end of software patents'. Nevertheless, it is not easy to answer the question as to what might be an abstract idea in computing and in particular in the area of software.

The USPTO is in the process of creating documents as guidance for examiners and applicants. They are available on the USPTO webpage.[53] There is no final version. Cooperation with external circles is ongoing.

In 2014 the two-step test was published as a flowchart in a Federal Register Notice.[54] Before starting with step 1 the claim has to be read giving it the broadest reasonable interpretation. According to US practice this means to read the claim with reference to all interpretations given in the specification. In Step 1 it has to be determined if the claim is directed to one of the four fundamental categories of patentability in the sense of §101. If this question is answered by 'yes' Step 2A (Part 1

53. USPTO, *Subject matter eligibility* https://www.uspto.gov/patent/laws-and-regulations/examination-policy/subject-matter-eligibility (accessed 10 March 2017).
54. USPTO, 37 CFR Part 1, 2014, *Interim Guidance on Patent Subject Matter Eligibility* https://www.gpo.gov/fdsys/pkg/FR-2014-12-16/pdf/2014-29414.pdf (accessed 7 March 2017).

of Mayo test) follows. The question: 'Is the claim directed to a law of nature, a natural phenomenon or an abstract idea (judicially accepted exceptions)?' In case of 'no', the claimed subject matter is eligible for patent protection. In case of 'yes' Step 2B (Part 2 of Mayo test) follows. It reads: 'Does the claim recite additional elements that amount to significantly more than the judicial exception?' If the question can be answered with yes, the claimed subject matter is eligible for patent protection. The fulfilment of the other requirements will be determined afterwards. Otherwise, the subject matter is outside of patentable subject matter.

It should be noted that some court decisions designate step 2A as step 1 and step 2B as step 2 (cf. e.g. §8.08[B][1], *TDE Petroleum Data Solutions v. AKM Enterprise or Synopsis v. Mentor Graphics Corp.*).

Furthermore, examination guidance is provided based on hypothetical cases, older cases and recent court decisions. Examples are provided for abstract ideas, nature-based products, life sciences and business methods. These efforts are appreciated; however, major concerns have been expressed, for example by leading IT or Software companies as to the clarity of the general guidance.

Google's comments include that guidance is based on too much former case laws.[55] Technology continues to develop. Examination of applications directed to modern computing technologies is difficult with reference to older cases. It has been suggested that examiners are instructed to look for a 'technological solution to a technological problem, rather than having them apply §101 exclusively by analogizing to past cases'. This is in particular appropriate since positions taken in former case law were partly overruled.

A similar position is taken by IBM.[56] The 'abstract idea' exception limits innovation in several industry sectors and in particular in information technology. Patentability requirements should not be developed by courts but by the Congress. Patentability of computer-related inventions should be broadly eligible for patent protection. Guidance should be given which is 'clear, objective and repeatable'. All former and current tests should be dropped. A fresh start should be made. Eligibility to patent law should not be mixed with novelty, obviousness and other requirements.

AIPLA (American Intellectual Property Law Association) has commented that the test developed by the Supreme Court is seen to result in more restrictive legal practice.[57] The outcome of the test is not predictable in several areas of technology due to the lack of clear guidance.

55. USPTO, Comments received in response to the May 2016 Subject Matter Eligibility Update, *COMMENTS OF GOOGLE INC.* https://www.uspto.gov/sites/default/files/documents/comments_google_jan182017.pdf (accessed 7 March 2017).
56. USPTO, IBM Corporation's Comments on 'Notice of Roundtables and Request for Comments *Related to Patent Subject Matter Eligibility,'* 81 Fed. Reg. 71485 (17 October 2016) https://www.uspto.gov/sites/default/files/documents/comments_ibm_jan182017.pdf (accessed 7 March 2017).
57. Comments of the AIPLA on Notice of Roundtables and Request for Comments Related to Patent Subject Matter Eligibility, 81 Fed. Reg. 71485, 17 October 2016. https://www.uspto.gov/sites/default/files/documents/comments_aipla_jan182017.pdf (accessed 7 March 2017).

§8.07 CBM AND TECHNOLOGICAL INVENTION

Patentability of Business Methods was a major topic in the AIA. Major topics of discussions were:

- eligibility of pure business methods to patent law;
- business methods in the realm of modern information technology;
- finding prior art for business methods.

[A] CBM: Legal Basis

[1] AIA Section 18

The AIA indicates the transitional rules for CBMs in section 18.[58] Section 7 concerns the constitution of the Patent Trial and Appeal Board (PTAB). It regulates different review procedures. There is one important difference for CBM reviews compared to other reviews. A petition can only be filed if 'the person or the person's real party in interest or privy has been sued for infringement of the patent or has been charged with infringement under that patent.'.

A definition is given for the CBM. It reads:

> (1) IN GENERAL. – For purposes of this section, the term "covered business method patent" means a patent that claims a method or corresponding apparatus for performing data processing or other operations used in the practice, administration, or management of a financial product or service, except that the term does not include patents for technological inventions.
>
> (2) REGULATIONS. – To assist in implementing the transitional proceeding authorized by this subsection, the Director shall issue regulations for determining whether a patent is for a technological invention.

The definition restricts business methods to financial products or services. Claims are mentioned which relate to 'a method or corresponding apparatus for performing data processing or other operations'.

[2] 37 CFR Part 42

More detailed information on the transitional program for CBM patents and definitions of CBM patent and technological invention were published in 2012 by the USPTO.[59]

---

58. *LEAHY-SMITH AMERICA INVENTS ACT PUBLIC LAW 112-29 – SEPT. 16, 2011* https://www.uspto.gov/sites/default/files/aia_implementation/20110916-pub-l112-29.pdf (accessed 12 March 2012).
59. USPTO, 37 CFR Part 42 – Transitional Program for CBM Patents – Definitions of *CBM Patent and Technological Invention; Final Rule* https://www.uspto.gov/sites/default/files/ip/boards/bpai/cbm_definitions_77_fr_48734_081412.pdf (accessed 12 March 2017).

Specific rules and their background are discussed. The definition of CBM remains unchanged. The term '**technological invention**' is more detailed. It reads:

> Technological invention. In determining whether a patent is for a technological invention solely for purposes of the Transitional Program for CBMs (section 42.301(a)), the following will be considered on a case-by-case basis: whether the claimed subject matter as a whole recites a technological feature that is novel and unobvious over the prior art; and solves a technical problem using a technical solution.

A reader familiar with the legal practice of the EPO might see similarities to some 'technicality' requirements, in particular to the solution of a technical problem by technical means.

The Federal Register Notice of 2012 includes five comments on the definition of CBM. Some require a broad interpretation of 'financial product or service'. Others suggest further clarification on 'financial product and service'. Twelve comments were directed at the interpretation of 'technological invention'. Different views were expressed on the clarity of the definition itself. Some views were directed to the combination of 'technological' with novelty and nonobviousness. The 'case by case' approach was seen as a risk that could create legal uncertainty. Examples for CBM were required.

[B] Examples: Business Methods, CBM

A study on CBM outcomes was published by M. Schecter (IBM) et al. in winter 2017.[60] Differences between CBMs and IPRs are indicated. In total, 382 CBMs were reviewed. The grounds for petition were divided between abstract idea (a subset of §101), prior art (§§102/103), and written description (§112) challenges. Petitions were hardly ever based on the exceptions 'laws of nature' or 'natural phenomenon' (sometimes 'physical phenomenon'). The study includes data before 1 October 2015 (filing of petitions but also issuance of institutions and final decisions). After the **Alice** case most of the petitions are based on section 101 challenges (mainly abstract idea). In summary, 77 CBM final written decisions were issued by PTAB. In forty-four final written decisions at least one claim was invalidated based on §101. Furthermore, at least one claim was invalidated based on §§102/103. In ten cases at least one claim was invalidated based on §112.

The USPTO provides several examples for abstract ideas and business methods. In January 2015 a first document on abstract idea examples was published with eight examples.[61] Two clear e-commerce examples are included. One example relates to a game comprising security features during ticket purchases.

60. Schecter, M. et al. *The Effects of Alice on Covered Business Method (CBM) Reviews*, 14 Nw. J. Tech. & Intell. Prop. 381 (2017) http://scholarlycommons.law.northwestern.edu/cgi/viewcontent.cgi?article=1261&context=njtip (accessed 14 March 2017).
61. USPTO, Abstract Ideas Examples January 2015 https://www.uspto.gov/patents/law/exam/abstract_idea_examples.pdf (accessed 13 March 2017).

[1] DDR HOLDINGS, LLC, v. HOTELS.COM, et al.

In ***DDR HOLDINGS, LLC, v. HOTELS.COM, et al.*** the Federal Circuit came to the conclusion that the claimed subject matter in claim 19 of US 7,818,399 is **eligible for patent protection.**[62] DDR is the assignee of two patents: US 6,993,572 and US 7,818,399 which are both continuations of US No. 6,629,135 (priority 17 September 1998). The original application was PCT application WO 00 16/210. Six patent family members exist for US 7,818,399. It is entitled: 'Methods of expanding commercial opportunities for internet websites through coordinated offsite marketing.' The specification indicates a typical physical structure of computers connected over the Internet. The software architecture that is based on a layered view comprises '3 tiers: web server, application server and database server'. Each tier can comprise further software layers. Thus, this structure is the basis for an affiliate commerce system.

A typical prior art web shop might work as follows: There is a merchant (host) website. It includes advertisements from other sellers (third-party merchants). When a customer clicks on such an advertisement a connection to the website of the third-party merchant is created. On the one hand, the original merchant gets revenues if the customer clicks on the advertisement but on the other hand, the customer will not remain on the original website. Customers are lured away from the original website. The aim of the invention was to solve the 'problem of retaining control over the customers during affiliate purchase transactions. The solution consisted in the creation of a 'system for co-marketing the "look and feel" of the host webpage with the product-related content information of the advertising merchant's web page'. This was achieved by adding a 'third-party outsource provider, who acts as a broker between multiple hosts and merchants'. The 'look and feel' of the host's webpage is stored at the outsource provider system. 'Look and feel' includes 'visually perceptible elements such as logos, colors, page layout, navigation system, frames, mouse-over effects or other elements that are consistent through some or all of each host's respective web pages'.

Thus, when a customer clicks on an advertisement a composite webpage is created by the third-party outsource provider's server. It comprises the visual perceptible elements of the host and another merchant's offer. The customer is not lured away. The impression is given that the customer is still on the host's webpage. Furthermore, the host receives the same advertising revenues as in the old system.

The specification indicates more detailed information on the implementation of the invention by software means. Thus, 'the business functionality is provided via "application servers"' e.g. with the basic software functionalities like Java Remote Method Invocation (RMI).

The original application filed under the Patent Cooperation Treaty (PCT) had fourteen claims. One process and one system claim for an outsource provider serving web pages offering commercial opportunities, a process and a system claim for capturing a look and feel description, both pairs of process and system claims had

62. DDR HOLDINGS, LLC, *Plaintiff–Appellee, v. HOTELS.COM* et al. No. 2013-1505. Decided: 5 December 2014 http://caselaw.findlaw.com/us-federal-circuit/1685815.html (accessed 13 March 2017).

dependent claims. Claim 13 was directed to a system for serving pages containing dynamically selected content. The final claim 14 was directed to a cost effective, scalable system for serving dynamically constructed Web pages.

In the course of the procedure the relevant claim was the following system claim:

> 19. A system useful in an outsource provider serving web pages offering commercial opportunities, the system comprising:
>
> (a) a computer store containing data, for each of a plurality of first web pages, defining a plurality of visually perceptible elements, which visually perceptible elements correspond to the plurality of first web pages;
> (i) wherein each of the first web pages belongs to one of a plurality of web page owners;
> (ii) wherein each of the first web pages displays at least one active link associated with a commerce object associated with a buying opportunity of a selected one of a plurality of merchants; and
> (iii) wherein the selected merchant, the out-source provider, and the owner of the first web page displaying the associated link are each third parties with respect to one other;
>
> (b) a computer server at the outsource provider, which computer server is coupled to the computer store and programmed to:
> (i) receive from the web browser of a computer user a signal indicating activation of one of the links displayed by one of the first web pages;
> (ii) automatically identify as the source page the one of the first web pages on which the link has been activated;
> (iii) in response to identification of the source page, automatically retrieve the stored data corresponding to the source page; and
> (iv) using the data retrieved, automatically generate and transmit to the web browser a second web page that displays: (A) information associated with the commerce object associated with the link that has been activated, and (B) the plurality of visually perceptible elements visually corresponding to the source page.

The Federal Circuit gave a majority decision that the subject matter is eligible for patent protection for the following reasons:

> Step 1: Is the claimed subject matter directed to one of the four fundamental claim categories? YES: 'The claim recites a system comprising a computer server and computer store. The system comprises a device or set of devices and, therefore, is directed to a machine which is a statutory category of invention'.
>
> Step 2: Does the claimed subject matter belong to the judicially accepted exceptions: abstract idea, law of nature, natural phenomenon? NO: The claim is directed to a system. It 'is directed to automatically generating and transmitting a web page in response to activation of a link using data identified with a source web page having certain visually perceptible elements'. The claim does not comprise a mathematical algorithm. It does not show a well-known 'fundamental economic or longstanding commercial practice'. It does not indicate a simple combination of a fundamental economic practice with the Internet. The claimed subject matter has an economic aim, i.e. primarily to retain customers on the host website. Some basic economic activities are indicated. However, the invention achieves the general aim by using computer networks. Step 2A results in eligibility to patent law.

Step 2B was answered with YES. The claim included additional limitations, in particular the limitations in part b) of claim 19 which indicate the specific functionality of the outsource provider's system. Thus, taken as a whole, there is more than an abstract idea. The claim is eligible for patent protection.

[2] buySAFE, Inc. v. Google, Inc

In ***buySAFE, Inc. v. Google, Inc.***, 765 F. 3d 1350 (3 September 2014) the Federal Circuit decided that a method directed to a safe transaction guaranty is not eligible for patent protection.[63] The PCT application WO2004095164 (A2) (PCT/US2004/010109) indicated 115 patent claims with claims relating to a method, a system and machine readable media encoded with instructions which are executed by a machine. The number of claims was reduced to fifty-two claims in US7644019 (B2). The whole patent was directed to an e-commerce system. Goods are offered on an Internet website. Customers purchase goods by clicking on respective offers on the webpage. Conventional processes of interacting with a human being are replaced by technology. The aim of the invention is to avoid fraudulent transactions. As indicated in the specification: 'For example, a seller may post an item for sale on one of the many auction sites. After receiving payment from a successful bidder, the seller may fail to deliver the item purchased at auction. Likewise, a buyer may make no payment when due after an ordered product has been shipped by the seller and received by the buyer'. The basic solution consists in that the buyer and seller interact over a third party – a safe transaction service provider. Simplified, this is primarily done in order to avoid a buyer paying for goods without receiving those goods. An underwriter may be part of the safe transaction service provider or it may be a separate unit. The specification discloses: 'The underwriter may be a person, a corporation that carries out the underwriting process either manually or automatically through a computer application program or semi-automatically'. The relevant claim reads:

1. A method, comprising:

   receiving, by at least one computer application program running on a computer of a safe transaction service provider, a request from a first party for obtaining a transaction performance guaranty service with respect to an online commercial transaction following closing of the online commercial transaction;
   processing, by at least one computer application program running on the safe transaction service provider computer, the request by underwriting the first party in order to provide the transaction performance guaranty service to the first party,
   wherein the computer of the safe transaction service provider offers, via a computer network, the transaction performance guaranty service that binds a transaction performance guaranty to the online commercial transaction involving the first party to guarantee the performance of the first party following closing of the online commercial transaction.

63. US, *buySAFE, Inc. v. Google, Inc.*, 765 F. 3d 1350, 2014 http://www.bitlaw.com/source/cases/patent/buySAFE.html (accessed 13 March 2017).

> Step 1: Is the claimed subject matter directed to one of the four fundamental claim categories? YES: It is directed to a process; i.e. a series of steps or acts, for providing a performance guaranty.
> Step 2A: Does the claimed subject matter belong to the judicially accepted exceptions: abstract idea, law of nature, natural phenomenon?

The claim is considered to represent 'the creation of a contractual relationship, which is a commercial arrangement involving contractual relations similar to the fundamental economic practices found by the courts to be abstract ideas (e.g. hedging in Bilski).' The claim is directed to an ineligible abstract idea.

In step 2B the claim is analysed to determine if there is more than the abstract idea. There are some limitations but they just indicate that there is a computer application running on a computer and the computer network. The generic computing means perform what they are usually are supposed to perform. Thus, the generic computing elements do not transform the abstract idea into subject matter eligible for patent protection.

[3] Ultramercial v. Hulu and WildTangent

Ultramercial v. Hulu and WildTangent, 2014 U.S. App. LEXIS 21633 (Fed. Cir. 2014), decided by the Federal Circuit is another example for ineligibility among the examples provided by the USPTO.[64] Patent US7346545 is directed to a method and system for distributing or obtaining intellectual property products by an interposed sponsor paying royalties on behalf of consumer via a telecommunications network. Such intellectual property might be represented as music, literature, visual arts (painting, photography, etc.) and motion pictures in a digital form. It can be easily copied and distributed over the Internet. The general problem consists in the loss of money for copyright holders. Traditional channels of monitoring distribution of copyrighted topics are no longer reliable. The same is true of payment for such digital media. A further general problem was the shift from traditional channels of advertisement to advertisement over the Internet.

The basic idea of the patent consists in offering 'people a legitimate and cashless way to obtain copyrighted music or other forms of intellectual property, while still delivering a royalty to the intellectual property rights holder'. The general solution was seen in a system in which the potential consumer of copyrighted media does not pay immediately with cash or credit card but first has to look at several advertisements indicated on the webpage offering the copyrighted material. According to one embodiment indicated in the specification, 'a consumer may obtain the right to download a musical composition if he or she agrees to first view an advertisement presentation, such as a multimedia video commercial, by an automobile manufacturer, who thereafter pays the royalties to the holder of the intellectual property product on behalf

64. US, *Ultramercial v. Hulu and WildTangent*, 2014 U.S. App. LEXIS 21633 (Fed. Cir. 2014) http://www.fr.com/wp-content/uploads/2016/09/Ultramercial-v-Hulu-772_F_3d_709.pdf (accessed 13 March 2017).

of the consumer'. Thus, this basic relationship between consumer, advertiser and provider of copyrighted material was implemented by computing means connected over the Internet.

The specification discloses the implementation of the relationship on a high level of abstraction. Details of an implementation in software are not provided.

The original claim 1 of WO 01/93159 (PCT US01/17170) reads:

> 1. A method for distribution of products over a communication network, said method comprising the steps of: providing a product at a networking site, said product being covered by intellectual property; restricting access to said product; facilitating the display of a sponsor message to a consumer; and allowing said consumer access to said product after said step of facilitating the display of said sponsor message.

The relevant claim that was the basis for the procedure at the Federal Circuit reads:

> 1. A method for distribution of products over the Internet via a facilitator, said method comprising the steps of:
>
> > a first step of receiving, from a content provider, media products that are covered by intellectual-property rights protection and are available for purchase, wherein each said media product being comprised of at least one of text data, music data, and video data;
> > a second step of selecting a sponsor message to be associated with the media product, said sponsor message being selected from a plurality of sponsor messages, said second step including accessing an activity log to verify that the total number of times which the sponsor message has been previously presented is less than the number of transaction cycles contracted by the sponsor of the sponsor message;
> > a third step of providing the media product for sale at an Internet website;
> > a fourth step of restricting general public access to said media product;
> > a fifth step of offering to a consumer access to the media product without charge to the consumer on the precondition that the consumer views the sponsor message;
> > a sixth step of receiving from the consumer a request to view the sponsor message, wherein the consumer submits said request in response to being offered access to the media product;
> > a seventh step of, in response to receiving the request from the consumer, facilitating the display of a sponsor message to the consumer;
> > an eighth step of, if the sponsor message is not an interactive message, allowing said consumer access to said media product after said step of facilitating the display of said sponsor message;
> > a ninth step of, if the sponsor message is an interactive message, presenting at least one query to the consumer and allowing said consumer access to said media product after receiving a response to said at least one query;
> > a tenth step of recording the transaction event to the activity log, said tenth step including updating the total number of times the sponsor message has been presented; and
> > an eleventh step of receiving payment from the sponsor of the sponsor message displayed.

Step 1: Is the claimed subject matter directed to one of the four fundamental claim categories? YES: It is directed to a process; i.e. a series of steps for distributing media and advertisements over the Internet.

Step 2: Does the claimed subject matter belong to the judicially accepted exceptions: abstract idea, law of nature, natural phenomenon? The basic concept is seen in using advertising as an exchange or currency. Similarity exists to **Bilsky** where hedging is seen as abstract idea in that the concept involves human activity relating to commercial practices. This basic idea is limited by additional information: 'such as receiving copyrighted media, selecting an ad, offering the media in exchange for watching the selected ad, displaying the ad, allowing the consumer access to the media, and receiving payment from the sponsor of the ad, …'. The limitations are not sufficient to make the idea less abstract. Thus, the answer to the question of step 2A is: The claim is directed to an abstract idea.

In step 2B the claim is analysed to determine if there is more than the abstract idea (concept of using advertising as an exchange or currency). The claim comprises some more detailed activities like 'accessing an activity log to verify that the total number of times which the sponsor message has been previously presented is less than the number of transaction cycles contracted by the sponsor of the sponsor message', 'facilitating the display of a sponsor message to the consumer' or 'recording the transaction event to the activity log'. However, such limitations represent insignificant pre-solution activities. This is true for separate limitations and the combination of the limitations. General Internet limitations try to limit the abstract idea to a particular technological environment. Since the answer to the question of step 2B is NO the claimed subject matter is not eligible for patent protection.

[4] Planet Bingo, LLC v. VKGS LLC

The case ***Planet Bingo, LLC v. VKGS LLC,*** 576 Fed. Appx. 1005 (Fed. Cir. 2014) is another example in the January 2015 list of examples of abstract ideas. It is not primarily directed to a business method but to a computer game.[65] However, electronic games are very often combined with payment activities related to the rules of the game. US6398646 has the title 'Method and system for storing preselected numbers for use in games of bingo'. Computerized bingo games already exist. The general aim of the invention is to create a computerized system 'which allows players to select their own numbers and store their numbers in the automated system for use in later sessions of Bingo'. Furthermore, the system has the ability to print sets of numbers on tickets on site. The system uses a computer to print the tickets, track the sale of the tickets and to validate winning tickets. The relevant claim 1 reads:

> 1. A system for managing a game of Bingo which comprises:

65. US, Planet Bingo, *LLC v. VKGS LLC*, 576 Fed. Appx. 1005 (Fed. Cir. 2014) http://law.justia.com/cases/federal/appellate-courts/cafc/13-1663/13-1663-2014-08-26.html (accessed 13 March 2017).

(a) a computer with a central processing unit (CPU) and with a memory and with a printer connected to the CPU;
(b) an input and output terminal connected to the CPU and memory of the computer; and
(c) a program in the computer enabling:
   (i) input of at least two sets of Bingo numbers which are preselected by a player to be played in at least one selected game of Bingo in a future period of time;
   (ii) storage of the sets of Bingo numbers which are preselected by the player as a group in the memory of the computer;
   (iii) assignment by the computer of a player identifier unique to the player for the group having the sets of Bingo numbers which are preselected by the player wherein the player identifier is assigned to the group for multiple sessions of Bingo;
   (iv) retrieval of the group using the player identifier;
   (v) selection from the group by the player of at least one of the sets of Bingo numbers preselected by the player and stored in the memory of the computer as the group for play in a selected game of Bingo in a specific session of Bingo wherein a number of sets of Bingo numbers selected for play in the selected game of Bingo is less than a total number of sets of Bingo numbers in the group;
   (vi) addition by the computer of a control number for each set of Bingo numbers selected for play in the selected game of Bingo;
   (vii) output of a receipt with the control number, the set of Bingo numbers which is preselected and selected by the player, a price for the set of Bingo numbers which is preselected, a date of the game of Bingo and optionally a computer identification number; and
   (viii) output for verification of a winning set of Bingo numbers by means of the control number which is input into the computer by a manager of the game of Bingo.

According to step 1 the computerized system relates to one of the four categories of statutory matter. Step 2A results in the evaluation of the system as an abstract idea. Several elements of the claim relate to the human activity of how to organize a Bingo game. It is similar to the **Alice** case. Thus, the claim comprises an abstract idea. In step 2B the question has to be answered whether there are limitations which transform the abstract idea into subject matter eligible for patent protection. The claim indicates generic computer elements (CPU, memory, input/output means ...) to implement the functions of the Bingo game. No inventive concept can be recognized. The specification discloses the Bingo game on a higher level of abstraction without details of the implementation. The claim is not eligible for patent protection.

In July 2015 illustrative examples 21–27 were published by the USPTO.[66] Example 21 was directed to the transmission of stock quote data. Hypothetical claims were used. They were modelled after the CBM case ***Google Inc. v. Simpleair, Inc.***, CBM Case No. CBM 2014-00170 (22 January 2015). The decision itself can be found on the

66. USPTO *July2015 Update Appendix1: Examples* https://www.uspto.gov/sites/default/files/documents/ieg-july-2015-app1.pdf (accessed 13 March 2017).

PTAB trial blog.[67] The patent used for the modelled claims is US-7035914 entitled 'System and method for transmission of data'.

The relevant claim (version without modelling) reads:

> 1. A method for transmitting data to selected remote devices, comprising the steps of: transmitting data from an information source to a central broadcast server;
>
> preprocessing said data at said central broadcast server, further comprising the step of:
>
> parsing said data with parsers corresponding to said central broadcast server;
>
> transmitting said data to an information gateway for building data blocks and assigning addresses to said data blocks;
>
> transmitting said data blocks from said information gateway to a transmission gateway for preparing said data blocks for transmission to receivers;
>
> transmitting preprocessed data to receivers communicating with said devices; and instantaneously notifying said devices of receipt of said preprocessed data whether said devices are online or offline from a data channel associated with each device.

The claim indicates the functionality of a network for data transmission. No specific kind of data is indicated. The specification discloses that the data can 'include but is not limited to stock quotes, weather, lotto, E-mail, ...'. Depending on the kind of data the system allows the display of the respective data (e.g. stock data, football data, text of a newspaper).

Elements relating to stock data processing are added to the original claim in order to better discuss eligibility questions.

Modelled claim 1 – Ineligible:

> A method of distributing stock quotes over a network to a remote subscriber computer, the method comprising:
>
> receiving stock quotes at a transmission server sent from a data source over the Internet, the transmission server comprising a microprocessor and memory that stores the remote subscriber's preferences for information format, destination address, specified stock price values, and transmission schedule, wherein the microprocessor
>
> filters the received stock quotes by comparing the received stock quotes to the specified stock price values;
>
> generates a stock quote alert from the filtered stock quotes that contains a stock name, stock price and a universal resource locator (URL), which specifies the location of the data source;
>
> formats the stock quote alert into data blocks according to said information format; and
>
> transmits the formatted stock quote alert to a computer of the remote subscriber based upon the destination address and transmission schedule.

The claim is directed to one of the four allowed statutory categories. In step 2A the analysis of the claim results in that it represents an **idea of itself**. This is the

67. USPTO *PTAB Trial Blog* http://ptabtrialblog.com/ (accessed 14 March 2017).

organization and comparison of data that can be performed mentally. The steps like receiving, filtering, formatting and transmitting stock quote information are normal steps known from similar concepts (e.g. the cases Cyberfone or SmartGene). The claim is directed to an abstract idea.

The analysis of step 2B results in that there are no limitations which transform the abstract idea into something more. The claim indicates a transmission server with a memory, a transmitter, and a microprocessor. All the elements are described at a high level of generality. It is concluded that 'Generic computers performing generic computer functions, ...'. The Internet limitations are seen as 'an attempt to limit the abstract idea to a particular technological environment'. The limitations seen either individually or as an ordered combination do not amount to something that is significantly more than the abstract idea. The claim is not eligible for patent protection.

A rejection of claim 1 should indicate the respective steps. It should be explained that steps of 'comparing and formatting information is a **mental process** that is similar to the concepts that courts have previously found abstract'. The limitations by generic computer elements and functions do not make the claim eligible for patent protection.

Modelled claim 1 – Eligible:

> A method of distributing stock quotes over a network to a remote subscriber computer, the method comprising:
>
> providing a stock viewer application to a subscriber for installation on the remote subscriber computer;
>
> receiving stock quotes at a transmission server sent from a data source over the Internet, the transmission server comprising a microprocessor and a memory that stores the remote subscriber's preferences for information format, destination address, specified stock price values, and transmission schedule, wherein the microprocessor
>
> filters the received stock quotes by comparing the received stock quotes to the specified stock price values;
>
> generates a stock quote alert from the filtered stock quotes that contains a stock name, stock price and a universal resource locator (URL), which specifies the location of the data source;
>
> formats the stock quote alert into data blocks according to said information format; and
>
> transmits the formatted stock quote alert over a wireless communication channel to a wireless device associated with a subscriber based upon the destination address and transmission schedule,
>
> wherein the alert activates the stock viewer application to cause the stock quote alert to display on the remote subscriber computer and to enable connection via the URL to the data source over the Internet when the wireless device is locally connected to the remote subscriber computer and the remote subscriber computer comes online.

Step 1 is easy to overcome since the claim is directed to a process.

The analysis according to step 2A again results in the conclusion that there is a mental process similar to other concepts found to be abstract by the courts.

In step 2B the final evaluation of the first version of claim 1 differs from the evaluation of the second version. The claim indicates additional and more detailed limitations like 'a stock viewer application causes the stock quote alert to display on the subscriber computer and enables a connection from the subscriber computer to the data source over the Internet when the subscriber computer comes online'. It could be argued that the limitations when seen individually do not amount to significantly more than the abstract idea. However, it is necessary to look at the additional limitations as an *ordered combination*. It can be seen that there is more than just linking the abstract idea (the general concept of organizing and comparing data) to the Internet. An Internet-centric problem is solved with the claimed solution. It is rooted in computer technology. A similar situation is known from the case **DDR Holdings**. Unconventional steps confine the abstract idea to a particular useful application. As a result the claim is eligible for patent protection.

In December 2016 three further examples were published on subject matter eligibility in the area of business methods.[68]

[5] BASCOM Global Internet v. AT&T Mobility LLC

In ***BASCOM Global Internet v. AT&T Mobility LLC***, 119 USPQ2d 1236 (Fed. Cir. 2016) eligibility of a claim was granted.[69] The respective patent is US-5987606 entitled 'Method and system for content filtering information retrieved from an internet computer network'. The example provides explanations as to why the claim was seen as eligible for patent protection. Such explanations are usually not provided in USPTO Office actions when the claim is regarded as eligible subject matter.

The general topic of the patent relates to filtering information on the Internet. This is primarily done in order to block access to certain content by certain end users. Different systems existed, for example with specific software on the client side (end-user), with a filter at a local server, and even with a filter at a remote server. Such systems could be manipulated by the end user or they were difficult to install and maintain. It was difficult to adapt the filter to changing circumstances and several end users.

Simplified, the solution consisted in creating a remote Internet Service Provider (ISP) server with the association of each network account to one filtering scheme and one set of filtering elements. Each subscriber's filter can be individually customized. As indicated in the specification: ' The filtering scheme may consist of any type of code which may be "executed," including object codes, interpreted code, such as Java.TM. or JavaScript.TM., other high-level code, or combinations thereof. The filtering scheme may be customized by combining portions of other filtering schemes, such as through

68. USPTO *Subject Matter Eligibility Examples: Business Methods*, December 2016 https://www.uspto.gov/sites/default/files/documents/ieg-bus-meth-exs-dec2016.pdf (accessed 13 March 2017).
69. US, *BASCOM Global Internet v. AT&T Mobility LLC, 119 USPQ2d 1236 (Fed. Cir. 2016)* http://www.cafc.uscourts.gov/sites/default/files/opinions-orders/15-1763.Opinion.6-23-2016.1.PDF (accessed 14 March 2017).

a high-level language or visual editor.' When the end user logs in a request is sent to the ISP server and the respective filtering scheme with the respective elements is activated.

In one embodiment, a partial processing of the end user request while the ISP server uses the filter scheme to screen content for words or phrases. Data packets are sent to the end user according to a table with logged-in end users and respective filter elements.

Representative claim:

> 1. A content filtering system for filtering content retrieved from an Internet computer network by individual controlled access network accounts, said filtering system comprising:
>
> > a local client computer generating network access requests for said individual controlled access network accounts;
> > atleast one filtering scheme;
> > a plurality of sets of logical filtering elements; and
> > a remote ISP server coupled to said client computer and said Internet computer network, said ISP server associating each said network account to at least one filtering scheme and at least one set of filtering elements, said ISP server further receiving said network access requests from said client computer and executing said associated filtering scheme utilizing said associated set of logical filtering elements.

Eligibility of Claim 1

Step 1 is answered with YES since the claim category belongs to the allowable categories as a system with devices is a machine.

Step 2A analyses whether the subject matter belongs to the judicial exceptions. Here, the basic idea is filtering content. This idea is implemented by a computer and networking components.

Filtering content is a '**method of organizing human behaviour**' according to the courts. This was identified as abstract by the courts (cf. case *Intellectual Ventures I v. Capital One Bank*). Organizing information through mathematical correlations (cf. case Digitech) was also seen as an abstract idea. Here claim 1 describes an abstract idea (filtering content), unlike previous cases decided by the courts.

This analysis cannot be amended by the approach taken in the Enfish case. In that case it was stated that 'claims directed to improvements in computer-technology, including claims directed to software, are not necessarily abstract'. Such an improvement in computer-technology is not really visible in the case under discussion. Therefore, the final decision can only be provided in Step 2B.

In Step 2B (also called 'inventive concept inquiry'), the claim as a whole is analysed to determine whether any element, or combination of elements, is sufficient to ensure the claim amounts to significantly more than the abstract idea. The claim of the content filtering system comprises several elements performing generic computer and network functions at a high level of generality. When 'taken individually' these elements indicate 'generic computer, network and Internet components, none of which is inventive by itself'. However, the claim indicates an 'unconventional and non-generic ***combination*** of known elements'. That is 'the installation of a filtering tool at a specific location, remote from the end-users, with customizable filtering features specific to each end user'. The filtering tool is able to 'identify individual accounts that communicate with the ISP server, and to associate a request for Internet content with a specific individual account'. Separate benefits of earlier solutions (filter at local computer, filter on ISP server) are combined. Now, there is a particular, practical application of the abstract idea. The combination is not a routine or conventional activity. The abstract idea is not just combined with the Internet or with generic computer elements. As a result, the claim is eligible for patent protection.

The original example comprises further explanations with references to different cases which are not indicated here.

Examples 35 and 36 are hypothetical examples for business methods. One example relates to verifying a bank customer's identity to permit an **ATM transaction**. The other example relates to **tracking inventory**. Three claim versions exist for each example. The claims are analysed in that: 'Each claim is given the broadest reasonable interpretation in view of the specification as it would be understood by one of ordinary skill in the art'. In both examples the terms in the claims are given their plain meaning in the art. No special definitions exist in the specification.

[6] Hypothetical Example ATM Transaction

Example ATM transaction

Claim 1: Ineligible:

> 1. A method of conducting a secure automated teller transaction with a financial institution by authenticating a customer's identity, comprising the steps of:
>
> obtaining customer-specific information from a bank card,
> comparing by a processor, the obtained customer-specific information with customer information from the financial institution to verify the customer's identity, and
> determining whether the transaction should proceed when a match from the comparison verifies the authenticity of the customer's identity.

Claim 2: Eligible:

> 2. A method of conducting a secure automated teller transaction with a financial institution by authenticating a customer's identity, comprising the steps of:
>
> obtaining customer-specific information from a bank card,
> comparing by a processor, the obtained customer-specific information with customer information from the financial institution to verify the customer's identity, by
> generating a random code and transmitting it to a mobile communication device that is registered to the customer associated with the bank card,
> reading, by the automated teller machine, an image from the customer's mobile communication device that is generated in response to receipt of the random code, wherein the image includes encrypted code data,
> decrypting the code data form the read image, and

> analysing the decrypted code data from the read image and the generated code to determine if the decrypted code data from the read image matches the generated code data, and
> determining whether the transaction should proceed when a match from the comparison verifies the authenticity of the customer's identity.

Claim 3 is not indicated here. It is similar to claim 2 but the random code is combined with a customer confirmation code and a control signal controls access to a keypad. Finally, claim 3 is eligible for patent protection.

Analysis claim 1

According to Step 1 of the Two-Step test claim 1 belongs to the statutory categories. The analysis according Step 2A results in that claim 1 represents an abstract idea which is a judicial exception. The steps of method claim 1 describe 'a method of fraud prevention by verifying the authenticity of the customer's identity prior to proceeding with a banking transaction, which is a "long prevalent" business practice that bank tellers have used for many years'. It is fundamental to business (c.f. also cases Alice Corp., Bilski and CyberSource). The claim as a whole could be seen as an 'abstract mental process for detecting fraud by obtaining and comparing intangible data pertinent to business risks.' Claim 1 is directed to an abstract idea.

In Step 2B (also called 'inventive concept inquiry'), 'the claim as a whole is analysed to determine whether any element, or combination of elements is sufficient to ensure that the claim amounts to significantly more than the abstract idea. The additional elements of the claim are seen in 'obtaining customer-specific information from a bank card' and in a 'processor comparing data'. The first element is well-known from the prior art indicated in the specification. Furthermore, it is described at a high level of generality. Thus, it is seen as an 'insignificant pre-solution activity, e.g. a mere data gathering step necessary to use the abstract idea.' The processor is a generic computer component. The comparison function done by the processor belongs to typical functions of processors. Taken individually the additional claim elements of claim 1 do not add something to the claim which transforms the abstract idea into a patent eligible claim. The combination of the additional elements amounts to a 'mere automation of verification steps that were in years past performed mentally by tellers when engaging with a bank customer.' 'Mere automation of an economic process' does not add significantly more to the abstract idea. Therefore, claim 1 is ineligible.

Analysis claim 2

Step1 and Step 2A result in the same conclusions. Eligibility to patent law results from the evaluation according to Step 2B in which the combination of additional elements with the abstract idea is evaluated. The creation and combination of different codes and their analysis is viewed as something 'more than the conventional verification process employed by an ATM alone'. A sequence of events is set up that 'address unique problems associated with bank cards and ATMs'. Thus, a specific and discrete implementation of the abstract idea is given. An inventive concept is provided. Fraud prevention is done in a non-conventional and non-generic way. This is true even if single steps use well-known components. Finally, claim 2 is eligible for patent protection.

[7] *Hypothetical Example Tracking Inventory*

Example Tracking Inventory

The explanations follow the same pattern as the ATM example. No details are explained here. Hypothetical claim 1 describes a system on a high level of generality. A combination of non-obvious technological elements is added to the abstract idea of hypothetical claim 2 and of claim 3. Finally, claim 2 and claim 3 are eligible for patent protection. Only claim 1 and claim 2 are indicated here.

Claim 1: Ineligible:

> 1. A system for managing an inventory record comprising a memory and processor configured to perform the steps of:
>
> (a) creating an inventory record for an item of inventory comprising acquired images of the item;
> (b) adding classification data relating to the acquired image to the inventory record;
> (c) adding location data relating to each acquired image to the inventory record; and
> (d) updating the inventory record with a physical location of each item of inventory in the warehouse to thereby manage the items of the inventory.

Claim 2: Eligible:

> 2. A system for managing an inventory record by tracking the location of items of inventory in a warehouse:
>
> a high-resolution video camera array, each video camera positioned at pre-determined locations with overlapping views, for acquiring at least one high-resolution image sequence of each item of inventory;
>
> a memory and processor configured to perform the steps of:
>
> (a) creating an inventory record for an item of inventory comprising the acquired image sequence of the item from the video camera array;
> (b) adding classification data relating to the acquired image sequence to the inventory record;
> (c) adding location data relating to each acquired image to the inventory record; the location data providing a position of the item of inventory in the image sequence;
> (d) reconstructing the 3-D coordinates of an item of inventory using the location data form multiple overlapping images and prior knowledge of the location and field of view of the camera(s); and
> (e) automatically updating the inventory record with the 3-D coordinates of each item of inventory in the warehouse to thereby manage the items of the inventory.

[8] *Business Methods: Summary*

The main objective of the recent legal development after Myriad, Mayo and Alice can be seen in precluding the granting of patents for well-known business methods implemented by generic computing means. One problem as expressed by Hazel V. J.

Moir in the area of business methods is that 'knowledge and know- how in business is not documented'.[70] Thus, prior art is difficult for examiners to find. The normal, technology-directed patent documentation is not sufficient. This is seen as one reason for the granting of obvious patents.

Fundamental economic practices are regarded as one group of abstract ideas. Building blocks of human ingenuity should remain ineligible for patent protection. Such business methods are sometimes seen as mental acts or as an organizational activity of human beings. If they are expressed by a mathematical formula, they can be excluded from patentability as mathematical formula and are not eligible for patent protection. The institution of a CBM Patent Review can be requested in infringement proceedings if the claims in the granted patent do not show a technological invention. It is a transitional program. Simply combining generic computer hardware elements /and or basic computational functionality like reading, storing, processing data in combination with a basic and long-standing principle of economy on a high level of generality in a claim, does not make that claim eligible for patent protection. A claim can comprise a well-known business method which is seen as an abstract idea. However, if this abstract idea is transformed by non-obvious technological means to something more than an abstract idea, the claimed subject matter is eligible for patent protection under §101. A technical problem has to be solved by technical means. This is similar to the legal practice of the EPO. The legal development does not mean that patents for pure business methods are prohibited, or that software patents are not allowed. Discussions on the interpretation of the law continue.

§8.08 ABSTRACT IDEA

As indicated in §7.00 fundamental economic practices are seen as abstract ideas. Abstract ideas can also be seen in 'Mathematical Relationships/ Formulas', 'In Idea "Of Itself"' and in 'Certain Methods of Organizing Human Activities'. Short examples are given in 'December 2016: Interim Eligibility Guidance Quick Reference Sheet *Identifying Abstract Ideas*'.[71] During the USPTO's discussions with interested circles it became clear that the term 'abstract idea' is difficult to interpret. One reason might consist in a discrepancy between the general explanations of 'abstract' e.g. according to Merriam Webster dictionary and the interpretation in US legal practice.
The definition according to the Merriam Webster dictionary reads:

> Definition of ASTRACT
>
> 1 a: disassociated from any specific instance ... an *abstract* entity
>
> b: difficult to understand: abstruse ... *abstract* problems
>
> c: insufficiently factual: formal ... possessed only an *abstract* right

70. Moir, H.V.J, Patent Policy and Innovation: Do Legal Rules Deliver Effective Economic Outcomes? Edward Elgar Publishing 2013, 86.
71. USPTO *Decisions holding claims eligible and identifying abstract ideas (quick reference sheet issued December 2016)* https://www.uspto.gov/patent/laws-and-regulations/examination-policy/subject-matter-eligibility accessed 13 March 2017).

2 a: expressing a quality apart from an object the word *poem* is concrete, poetry is *abstract*

3 a: dealing with a subject in its abstract aspects: theoretical ... *abstract* science

b: impersonal, detached

the *abstract* compassion of a surgeon — *Time*

4 : having only intrinsic form with little or no attempt at pictorial representation or narrative content ... abstract painting.[72]

The discrepancy is that the dictionary definition states that abstract is something that is difficult to understand, more theoretical, a description of something that is more high level than concrete contrary to e.g. a business method that has been well understood for years, which is not theoretical but real and has been practised for years. In legal practice, the term 'abstract idea' is more the well-known building block of human ingenuity. The obviousness of business methods very often results from undocumented knowledge and human practice.

[A] Abstract Idea: Mathematical Relationships/Formulas

The Quick Reference Sheet (December 2016) indicates nine examples from decisions of the past: '

- A formula describing certain electromagnetic standing wave phenomena (*Mackay Radio*)
- A formula for computing an alarm limit (*Flook*)
- A mathematical formula for hedging (*Bilski*)
- An algorithm for calculating parameters indicating an abnormal condition (*Grams*)
- An algorithm for converting BCD to pure binary (*Benson*)
- An algorithm for determining the optimal number of visits by a business representative to a client (*Maucorps*)
- Calculating the difference between local and average data values (*Abele*)
- Managing a stable value protected life insurance policy by performing calculations and manipulating the results (*Bancorp*)
- The Arrhenius equation (*Diehr*)'.

The Update on Subject Matter Eligibility of July 2015 provides some explanation of the different exceptions.[73] The examples 'A formula for computing an alarm limit (Flook)' and 'The Arrhenius equation (Diehr)' are explained in more detail below. Mathematical formulas are exceptions because they are 'basic tools of scientific and technological work' that lie beyond the domain of patent protection. Thus, there is the concern that

72. Merriam Webster Dictionary, *definition: abstract* https://www.merriam-webster.com/dictionary/abstract (accessed 15 March 2017).
73. USPTO *July 2015 Update: Subject Matter Eligibility* https://www.uspto.gov/sites/default/files/documents/ieg-july-2015-update.pdf (accessed 17 March 2017).

patents for such basic tools, even if new, could 'inhibit future innovation premised upon them'.

The 2015 document explains '"mathematical relationships/formulas" is used to describe mathematical concepts such as mathematical algorithms, mathematical relationships, mathematical formulas, and calculations'. The term 'algorithm', as it is used in computer science, is not discussed.

[1] A Formula for Computing an Alarm Limit (Flook)

This 1987 decision has already been briefly mentioned in the historical overview of §8.05[A]. At that time, this Supreme Court decision resulted in no patent being able to be granted for a well-known mathematical algorithm.

The application dealt with the repeated determination of an alarm limit in an industrial chemical system (catalytic conversion processing system). The alarm limit is expressed as a number. Important data in the process such as temperature, pressure, and flow rate is measured and monitored. If a specific value – the alarm limit – is exceeded, an alarm signal will be created. It could mean danger, inefficient process, or an abnormal condition. The value of the alarm limit is regularly updated.

The basic three steps (measure process value, calculate updated alarm limit, adjust alarm limit to the new value) were known from the prior art. However, the applicant discovered the specific formulae, the calculation of the alarm value. This was used for the second step and is done by a computer. Claim 1 reads:

> Claim 1
>
> 'A method for updating the value of at least one alarm limit on at least one process variable involved in a process comprising the catalytic chemical conversions of hydrocarbons wherein said alarm limit has a current value of $B_0 + K$ wherein B_0 is the current alarm base and K is a predetermined alarm offset which comprises:
>
> (1) Determining the present value of said process variable, said present value being defined as PVL;
> (2) Determining a new alarm base B_1, using the following equation:
> $B_1 = B_0 (1.0\text{-}F) + PVL(F)$
> where F is a predetermined number greater than zero and less than 1.0;
> (3) Determining an updated alarm limit which is defined as$B_1 + K$; and thereafter
> (4) Adjusting said alarm limit to said updated alarm limit value.'

Here the claim is interpreted according to the new two-step test. The claim is analysed with the broadest reasonable interpretation. This means that the updating method can be performed by hand or by a computer. The description of the example does not mention whether the specification discloses the execution of the method by hand. The use of a computer is disclosed.

The claim category method or process is one of the four allowable categories in §101. Thus, the hurdle of Step 1 is overcome.

Step 2A determines if there is a judicial exception. An exception does exist since there is a mathematical formula which was considered by the courts as an abstract idea. It remains an abstract idea even if the formula is new.

Step 2B analyse if there is something more in the claim than just the abstract idea (mathematical formulae). The additional elements, like determining the value of an unspecified process variable, taken alone or in combination do not amount to something which is significantly more than the exception. The claim does not indicate the meaning of the variables in the chemical process of catalytic conversion of hydrocarbons. It cannot be seen from the claim how a specific technological field (catalytic chemical conversion) is improved.

There is neither an improvement in the field of chemistry nor in the field of computing. Even if the claimed method were interpreted as executed by a computer this would not transform the abstract idea into something more. A generic computer is indicated as a means for implementing the method. This is obvious and conventional.

Thus, the claim is not eligible for patent protection under §101.

The example shows that the claim is overly broad in that the new mathematical formulae cannot be seen in the specific context of chemistry. Which chemical or physical value does the alarm base represent? Which kind of alarm (e.g. too hot, high pressure) is important for the chemical system?

Furthermore, the claim does not show whether the steps are done by a human being or by technological means. The formula is not complicated. Therefore, it could be assumed that an employee regularly reads values on measurement instruments, calculates a new value with paper and pencil and updates the alarm limit on another instrument.

The claim does not show a limitation by computer details. Even the indication of a generic computer would amount to nothing more than a mere automation of a process (e.g. done by hand in the past). Implementing the formula by a computer did not necessitate solving a specific computer hardware or software problem.

Thus, even if the mathematical formula is new, its specific use in a specific area has to be clear from the claim. The general combination of the formula with a field (here catalytic conversion of hydrocarbons) and/or with a generic computer remains at a high level of generality and does not show an inventive concept.

[2] The Arrhenius Equation (Diehr)

This 1981 decision was already briefly mentioned in §5.00, [B]. At that time the claimed subject matter was seen as patentable subject matter.

Here two versions of a *hypothetical claim* are interpreted according to the new two-step test. They are examples for claims eligible for patent protection despite the appearance of a mathematical formula in the claim.

The hypothetical claims are based on the **Diehr** decision. The example with the hypothetical claims is indicated in the July 2015 update of the list of examples.[74] One hypothetical claim is directed to a method of operating a computer. The second hypothetical claim is directed to a non-transitory computer readable medium.

74. USPTO *July 2015 Update Appendix 1: Examples* https://www.uspto.gov/sites/default/files/documents/ieg-july-2015-update.pdf (accessed 17 March 2017).

The real patent claims can be found in the patent US-4344142 entitled 'Direct digital control of rubber molding presses'. It was granted after the decision of the Supreme Court in **Diehr**.

The whole application (earliest priority 1973) was directed to the production of synthetic rubber. Uncured rubber had to be loaded by an operator into a rubber-moulding press. The heat of the press transforms uncured rubber into cured rubber with desired properties. The press was closed for a predetermined time set by a timer. The temperature of the press was monitored. After the predetermined time the press was opened by the operator. It could happen that the synthetic rubber did not possess the desired properties. It was possible that the synthetic rubber could be over- or undercured. The temperature inside the press could vary, for example because of the press being open for a long time. A major problem at this time was the difficulty in determining the actual temperature inside the hot rubber mould. This problem was solved by the use of thermocouples, or other temperature detecting devices which could be located directly within the mould cavity. The temperature could be read at the surface where the moulding compound touches the mould. This allowed a more accurate determination of the actual temperature that could be used by a standard computer to determine a more exact curing time. The temperature data is permanently transmitted to the computer, e.g. every ten seconds. The mould is not opened after a predetermined time but after a time during which the synthetic rubber is supposed to have achieved the desired properties. The computer is programmed to calculate the cure time based on the Arrhenius equation which was well-known at that time. The specification does not further specify the kind of computer. A flowchart is indicated which describes the sequence of steps executed by the computer. A possible programming language was not indicated. The Arrhenius equation is a formula for the temperature dependence of reaction rates.[75] The calculation is triggered by the press closing. The computer's processing performance allows several rubber-moulding presses to be operated simultaneously.

Hypothetical claim 1 (last three paragraphs are modified compared to granted claim 1):

> 1. A method of operating a rubber-molding press for precision molded compounds with the aid of a digital computer, comprising:
>
>> providing said computer with a data base for said press including at least, natural logarithm conversion data (1n),
>> the activation energy constant (C) unique to each batch of said compound being molded, and a constant (x) dependent upon the geometry of the particular mold of the press,

75. *Arrhenius equation* The equation was proposed by Svante Arrhenius in 1889, based on the work of Dutch chemist Jacobus Henricus van 't Hoff who had noted in 1884 that Van 't Hoff's equation for the temperature dependence of equilibrium constants suggests such a formula for the rates of both forward and reverse reactions. This equation has a vast and important application in determining rate of chemical reactions and for calculation of energy of activation. Arrhenius provided a physical justification and interpretation for the formula. https://en.wikipedia.org/wiki/Arrhenius_equation (accessed 17 March 2017).

> initiating an interval timer in said computer upon the closure of the press for monitoring the elapsed time of said closure,
> constantly determining the temperature (Z) of the mold at a location closely adjacent to the mold cavity in the press during molding,
> constantly providing the computer with the temperature (Z),
> repetitively calculating in the computer at frequent intervals during the each cure, the the Arrhenius equation for reaction time during the cure, which is ln v = CZ + x
> where v is the total required cure time,
> repetitively comparing in the computer at said frequent intervals during the cure each said calculation of the total required cure time calculated with the Arrhenius equation and said elapsed time, and
> opening the press automatically when a said comparison indicates equivalence.

Step1 of hypothetical claim 1 is answered with yes since it is directed to a process.

In Step 2A three judicial exceptions are found which can have different reasons depending on their interpretation.

The claim comprises the Arrhenius equation which describes a specific mathematical relationship. This represents a judicial exception which is seen as a **law of nature**. Mathematical relationships are also seen as an **abstract idea**. Thirdly, when the focus is on the sequence of steps, the sequence of performing repetitive calculations and the comparison between calculated and elapsed time could be seen as an activity of 'a **human being using mental steps** or basic critical thinking, which are types of activities that the courts have also found to represent abstract ideas. Thus, Step 2A is answered with yes: The claim is directed to a judicial exception.

The additional elements of the claim are analysed in Step 2B. As well as the mathematical relationship, the claim indicates several elements of a computer with a data base of values and other functions partly executed by the computer program running on the computer. Some of the elements/steps of the computer are seen as routine computer activities or generic functions performed by a computer when viewed alone. The limitations are indicated on a high level of generality (or level of abstraction). They are well-understood and correspond to the normal activities of a computer. Furthermore, elements like 'initiating a timer and determining a temperature' are when viewed in isolation mere data gathering steps that are necessary for the Arrhenius equation.

When the combination of the abstract idea with all the additional elements is seen as a whole it becomes evident that all the ideas are combined to improve the moulding process. Thus, the technical field of rubber moulding is improved. Furthermore, the steps taken together result in transforming the raw rubber 'into a different state or thing, i.e. a cured and moulded rubber product'. The claimed subject matter amounts to something more than the mathematical relationship.

The additional elements also result in something that is significantly more than steps of critical thinking.

Finally, hypothetical claim 1 is eligible for patent protection according to the two-step test.

Hypothetical claim 2 (the method claim is transformed into a computer readable medium claim):

> 2. A non-transitory computer readable medium with computer executable instructions stored thereon executed by a processor to perform the method of controlling a rubber-molding press having a mold with a cavity for precision molded compounds, the method comprising:
>
>> accessing a data base in the computer including at least, natural logarithm conversion data (ln), the activation energy constant (C) unique to each batch of said compound being molded, and a constant(x) dependent upon the geometry of the particular mold of the press,
>> initiating an interval timer in said computer upon the closure of the press for monitoring the elapsed time of said closure,
>> constantly receiving data relating to the temperature (Z) of the mold at a location closely adjacent to the mold cavity in the press during molding,
>> repetitively calculating in the computer at the frequent intervals during earch cure, the the Arrhenius equation for reaction time during the cure, which is 1n v = CZ + x
>> where v is the total required cure time,
>> repetitively comparing in the computer at said frequent intervals during the cure each said calculation of the total required cure time calculated with the Arrhenius equation and said elapsed time, and
>> initiating a signal that controls the press to open when the comparison indicates equivalence, meaning that the molded product is cured.'
>
> The original application did not comprise a medium claim storing a computer program since such claims were not allowed at that time.
>
> Eligibility of hypothetical claim 2 was also accepted. The claim relates to a manufacture (an article produced from materials). It is a statutory category under §101. It is underlined, that the medium has to be characterized as a non-transitory medium. This has to be done to make sure that 'the claim does not encompass signals and other non-statutory forms of signal transmission.

For Step 2A and Step 2B similar arguments are given as for hypothetical claim 1. It is explained that the software as an implementation of the sequence of steps improves the technical field of precision rubber moulding. The software controls the press so that it opens at the optimal time. The additional elements do not just indicate instructions for performing calculation/comparing steps in isolation.

The argumentation concerning the medium claim shows that claim interpretation is done within the limits of traditional patent law. The claim has to be a manufacture, an article, something tangible. However, from the practical perspective of a computer professional the relevant element or economic value is not the manufacture (e.g. the empty flash memory) but the computer program stored on the medium. One could argue that the specifics of software are not sufficiently taken into account. In a recent publication on protection of software-related inventions a reference was made to the European Patent Office's legal practice, in particular to decision T 1173/97- ((Computer program product/IBM) of 1 July 1998) which allowed claims for computer programs including signal claims. The decision indicates: 'it does not make any difference whether a computer program is claimed by itself or as a record on a carrier'.[76]

Furthermore, the term 'non-transitory' has to be added to the claim in order to avoid signals. Here again, patent law is not adapted to modern network technology which increasingly allows the transmission of software and all kinds of digital data over wireless networks. In re Nuijten (cf. §5.00, [C]) the patentability of a signal was not allowed.

The granted claim 1 reads:

> 1. A method of operating a rubber-molding press for precision molded compounds with the aid of a digital computer, comprising:
>
> > providing said computer with a data base for said press including at least, natural logarithm conversion data (1n),
> > the activation energy constant (C) unique to each batch of said compound being molded, and a constant (x) dependent upon the geometry of the particular mold of the press,
> > initiating an interval timer in said computer upon the closure of the press for monitoring the elapsed time of said closure,
> > constantly determining the temperature (Z) of the mold at a location closely adjacent to the mold cavity in the press during molding,
> > constantly providing the computer with the temperature (Z),
> > repetitively performing in the computer, at frequent intervals during each cure, integrations to calculate from the series of temperature determinations the Arrhenius equation for reaction time during the cure, which is
> > $1n\ v = CZ + x$
> > where v is the total required cure time,
> > repetitively comparing in the computer at frequent intervals during the cure each said calculation of the total required cure time calculated with the Arrhenius equation and said elapsed time, and
> > opening the press automatically when a said comparison indicates completion of curing.

To sum up, mathematical formulas and patents remain a field where the borderlines are not easy to determine. In applied mathematics, mathematical formulas are a means to express relationships between items of the real world compared with abstract mathematics. It can be seen from the case law that the mathematical formulas can relate to many different application areas like business methods (Bilski), to an application in core computing (number conversion in Benson) or to a technological process (curing rubber in Diehr). Thus, the claims do not usually show just a mathematical formula with variables or data without any relationship to a real-world procedure. However, due to Step 2A of the two-step test the claim has to be analysed to see if it is only an abstract idea. If only a mathematical formula is found then it is only an abstract idea. If there is more in the claim than the abstract idea eligibility to patent law is possible.

76. Jedrusik, A. et al. *Patent protection for software-implemented inventions* WIPO Magazine, February 2017, No. 1.

Mathematical formulas are very often executed by computer programs running on a computer/computer network. Here again, a claim formulation that just indicates the execution of a mathematical formula by a generic computer (hardware and/or software) is not sufficient to transform the abstract idea into subject matter which is eligible for patent protection. Eligibility to patent law for a mathematical formula can be achieved if the claim indicates non-obvious elements (e.g. functional elements of a computer program) which transform the judicial exception – here the mathematical formula – into something more – e.g. the solution of a problem in different fields of technology.

[B] Abstract Idea: An Idea 'Of Itself'

The 'July 2015 Update on Subject Matter Eligibility' uses the phrase 'an idea of itself', 'to describe an idea standing alone such as an uninstantiated concept, plan or scheme, as well as a mental process (thinking) that "can be performed in the human mind, or by a human using pen and paper"' Sometimes, the idea of itself can fall under other categories.

The following examples of an 'Idea "Of Itself"' are listed in the Quick Reference Sheet of December 2016: '

- Anonymous loan shopping (*Mortgage Grader*)
- Assigning hair designs to balance head shape (*Brown*)†
- Collecting and analysing information to detect misuse and notifying a user when misuse is detected (*FairWarning v. Iatric*)
- Collecting and comparing known information (*Classen*)
- Collecting information, analysing it, and displaying certain results of the collection and analysis (*Electric Power Group*)
- Comparing data to determine a risk level (*Perkin-Elmer*)†
- Comparing information regarding a sample or test subject to a control or target data (*Ambry/Myriad CAFC*)
- Comparing new and stored information and using rules to identify options (*Smartgene*)†
- Data recognition and storage (*Content Extraction*)
- Delivering user-selected media content to portable devices (*Affinity Labs v. Amazon.com*)
- Determining a price, using organizational and product group hierarchies (*Versata*)
- Diagnosing an abnormal condition by performing clinical tests and thinking about the results (*Grams*)
- Displaying an advertisement in exchange for access to copyrighted media (*Ultramercial*)
- Generating a second menu from a first menu and sending the second menu to another location (*Ameranth*)

- Mental process for logic circuit design (*Synopsys*)
- Migration or transitioning of settings (*Tranxition*)†
- Obtaining and comparing intangible data (*CyberSource*)
- Organizing information through mathematical correlations (*Digitech*)
- Providing out-of-region access to regional broadcast content (*Affinity Labs. v. DirecTV*)
- Retaining information in navigation of online forms (*Internet Patents*)
- Storing, gathering, and analysing data (*TDE Petroleum*)†
- Using categories to organize, store and transmit information (*Cyberfone*)†† indicates a non-precedential decision'.

The name of the respective decisions is shown in brackets. The case Ultramercial is explained in more detail in §7.02 [C]. It is assumed that it is difficult for patent professionals to determine whether there is an idea of itself or not. The examples are directed to different areas of technology. The activities very often relate to one or several of the activities of collecting, storing, recording, transmitting and comparing of information and/or data irrespective of whether the activities are done by a human being or something else e.g. a digital computer. It is also not relevant whether the activities are executed in a medical field, in telecommunications, computing or in business methods.

[1] TDE Petroleum Data Solutions v. AKM Enterprise

The case ***TDE Petroleum Data Solutions v. AKM Enterprise*** (2015) of the Federal Circuit is given as an example of an abstract idea, i.e. for 'An Idea 'Of Itself''. The Federal Circuit decided that claim 1 of the patent US6892812 entitled 'Automated method and system for determining the state of well operations and performing process evaluation' is not eligible for patent protection.[77]

The patent relates to drilling systems. Drilling rigs are typically rotary-typed rigs that use a sharp bit to drill through the earth. At the surface, a rotary drilling rig often includes a complex system of cables, engines, ... Underneath the surface, the bit is attached to a long drill pipe which carries drilling fluid to the bit. As indicated in the specification:

> Automated management of drilling rig operations is problematic because parameters may change quickly and because down hole behaviour of drilling elements and down hole conditions may not be directly observable. As a result, many management systems fail to accurately recognize the presence and/or absence of important drilling events, which may lead to false alarms and unnecessary down time.

77. United States Court of Appeals, Federal Circuit.
TDE PETROLEUM DATA SOLUTIONS, INC., v. AKM ENTERPRISE, INC., DBA MOBLIZE, INC., (2016) http://caselaw.findlaw.com/us-federal-circuit/1746153.html (accessed 18 March 2017).

Thus, the general aim is the improvement of the system for managing a drill system. According to the specification the monitoring system comprises a sensing system and a monitoring module for drilling operations of the rig. Furthermore:

> In a particular embodiment, the monitoring module ... may comprise logic encoded in media. The logic may comprise software stored on a computer-readable medium for use in connection with a general purpose processor, or programmed hardware such as application-specific integrated circuits (ASIC), field programmable gate arrays (FPGA), digital signal processors (DSP) and the like.

Claim 1 reads:

> 1. An automated method for determining the state of a well operation, comprising:
>
> > storing a plurality of states for a well operation;
> > receiving mechanical and hydraulic data reported for the well operation from a plurality of systems; and
> > determining that at least some of the data is valid by comparing the at least some of the data to at least one limit, the at least one limit indicative of a threshold at which the at least some of the data do not accurately represent the mechanical or hydraulic condition purportedly represented by the at least some of the data; and
> > when at least some of the data are valid, based on the mechanical and hydraulic data, automatically selecting one of the states as the state of the well operation.

The Federal Circuit decided that claim is not eligible for patent protection because:

> the steps of claim 1 recite operations performed by any general-purpose computer. ..., claims generally reciting "collecting information, analysing it, and displaying certain results of the collection and analysis" are 'a familiar class of claims "directed to" a patent-ineligible concept.' Claim 1 recites all but the 'displaying' step. Therefore, it is evident from our precedent that claim 1 is the sort of data gathering and processing claim that is directed to an abstract idea.

Additionally, the court concluded that there is 'nothing in claim 1 that adds anything more to the abstract idea of storing, gathering, and analyzing data'. The applicant could not show 'that storing state values, receiving sensor data, validating sensor data, or determining a state based on sensor data is individually inventive'. The specification shows several details of the system. However, no inventive concept arises from the ordered combination of all the steps in claim 1. It was underlined that: 'claim 1 simply recites generic computer functions that amount to nothing more than the goal of determining the state of an oil well operation'. The additional elements do not turn the abstract idea into subject matter eligible for patent protection. In the decision, Step 1 of the test relates to the determination if there is an abstract idea. Step 2 relates to the question whether there is additional subject matter which transforms the ineligible abstract idea into eligible subject matter.

[2] Synopsys v. Mentor Graphics Corp.

The case ***Synopsys v. Mentor Graphics Corp.*** is indicated as an example for an abstract idea, in particular of 'An Idea "Of Itself"'. The case concerned three patents (US5530841; US5680318; and US5748488) which related to the design process of a logic circuit.[78] Such a design was done with the support of hardware description languages. It provided the designer with a means for describing the operation of the desired logic circuit that is at least one level of abstraction removed from a schematic diagram or a set of Boolean logic equations. Unfortunately, hardware description language generally permitted only an operational description of simple circuit elements. For many circuit elements, such as high impedance drivers, level sensitive latches and edge sensitive flip-flops, the designer was required first to specify the specific circuit element and then the desired connection of that element using the Hardware Description Language (HDL). The synthesizer of the invention created a logic network not as in the prior art systems where the choice of logic components was stated at least partially explicitly, but rather where the choice of logic components was implied by the signals and structure specified by the user. The specification included an Appendix with a listing of computer programs and related data for one embodiment of the logic synthesizer of the invention.
The representative claim 1 reads:

> 1. A method for converting a hardware independent user description of a logic circuit, that includes flow control statements including an IF statement and a GOTO statement, and directive statements that define levels of logic signals, into logic circuit hardware components comprising:
>
>> converting the flow control statements and directive statements in the user description for a logic signal Q into an assignment condition AL(Q) for an asynchronous load function AL() and an assignment condition AD(Q) for an asynchronous data function AD(); and
>> generating a level sensitive latch when both said assignment condition AL(Q) and said assignment condition AD(Q) are non-constant;
>> wherein said assignment condition AD(Q) is a signal on a data input line of said flow through latch;
>> said assignment condition AL(Q) is a signal on a latch gate line of said flow through latch; and
>> an output signal of said flow through latch is said logic signal Q.

The Federal Circuit followed a test which slightly differs from the test published in the Federal Register of December 2014 (cf. §6.00) in that Step 2A of the test published in the notice of the Federal Register is seen as Step 1 and Step 2B is seen as Step 2. Step 1 of the test as published in the notice of the Federal Register asked whether the claim is directed to one of the four statutory categories (process, machine, manufacture,

78. United States Federal Circuit *Synopsis, Inc. v. Mentor Graphics Corp.* 2015-1599 Decided: 17 October 2016 http://caselaw.findlaw.com/us-federal-circuit/1751051.html (accessed 18 March 2017).

composition of matter). This requirement is fulfilled in most of the cases. Thus, the crucial questions remain but the steps are numbered differently.

The court discussed whether the claim is directed to a mental process, a subcategory of an abstract idea. The patentee argued against this because the steps are performed by a computer. The program of one embodiment was appended to the specification. Furthermore, the method could not be done by paper and pencil due to the complexity of the whole design process. The aim was to improve existing computing systems. The court could not find any limitations directed to an implementation by computing means.

The claims 'make no mention of employing a computer or any other physical device, they are so broad as to read on an individual performing the claimed steps mentally or with pencil and paper'.

Concerning the mental process it turned out that 'the limited, straightforward nature of the steps involved in the claimed method make evident that a skilled artisan could perform the steps mentally. The inventors ... confirmed this point when they admitted to performing the steps mentally themselves.'

The claim cannot be made eligible for patent protection, either by adding generic computer features to the claim or by adding program code from the appendix of the specification. Thus, the court concluded: 'the Asserted Claims are drawn to the abstract idea of: translating a functional description of a logic circuit into a hardware component description of the logic circuit. ... this translation is a mental process.'.

In Step 2 (or Step 2B) the question was raised whether the claims include an inventive concept. The court referred to the Alice case that indicated:

> an 'inventive concept' as 'an element or combination of elements that is 'sufficient to ensure that the patent in practice amounts to significantly more than a patent upon the [ineligible concept] itself.

It was argued that the claimed subject matter is new and not known from the prior art. The court counter argued that a new abstract idea remains an abstract idea since 'The search for a §101 inventive concept is thus distinct from demonstrating §102 novelty.' The additional elements in the claim are: 'the use of assignment conditions as an intermediate step in the translation process.'. Because 'the claims are for a mental process, assignment conditions, which merely aid in mental translation as opposed to computer efficacy, are not an inventive concept that takes the Asserted Claims beyond their abstract idea.'. No technical improvement can be seen by the additional element.

As a result, the claims are not eligible for patent protection.

[C] Abstract Idea: Certain Methods of Organizing Human Activity

According to the Interim Eligibility Guidance Quick Reference Sheet on Identifying Abstract Ideas of December 2016 'certain methods of organizing human activity is another topic of an abstract idea. Such methods describe 'concepts relating to interpersonal and intrapersonal activities, such as managing relationships or transactions between people, social activities, and human behaviour; satisfying or avoiding a legal obligation; advertising, marketing, and sales activities or behaviours; and managing human mental activity'. The term 'certain' reminds examiners to bear in mind that not all methods of organizing human activity are abstract ideas. The following list provides examples:

- Arbitration (*Comiskey*)
- Budgeting (Int. *Ventures v. Cap One Bank*)
- Cataloging labour data (*Shortridge*)†
- Classifying and storing digital images in an organized manner (*TLI Comms.*)
- Creating a contractual relationship (*BuySAFE*)
- Filtering content (*BASCOM*)
- Generating menus on a computer (*Ameranth*)
- Generating rule-based tasks for processing an insurance claim (*Accenture*)
- Hedging (*Bilski*)
- Managing a game of bingo (*Planet Bingo*)†
- Managing an insurance policy (*Bancorp*)
- Mental process that a neurologist should follow when testing a patient for nervous system malfunctions (*Meyer*)
- Mitigating settlement risk (*Alice*)
- Processing loan information (*Dealertrack*)
- Receiving, screening, and distributing e-mail (*Int. Ventures v. Symantec*)
- Structuring a sales force or marketing company (*Ferguson*)
- Tax-free investing (*Fort Properties*)
- Testing operators of any kind of moving equipment for any kind of physical or mental impairment (*Vehicle Intelligence*)†
- Using advertising as an exchange or currency (*Ultramercial*)
- Using an algorithm for determining the optimal number of visits by a business representative to a client (*Maucorps*)
- Virus screening (Int. *Ventures v. Symantec*)

  † indicates a non-precedential decision.

It can be seen that there is an overlap with business methods in the broader sense. Managing a game of bingo, Ultramercial, buySafe and BASCOM were explained in more detail in §7.00 under Business Methods. Bilski and Comiskey are explained in §5.03[B]. Alice is explained in §5.04[C].

[1] Apple v. Ameranth

The case ***Apple v. Ameranth*** (November 2016) relates to three patents directed to information management and synchronous communications systems for generating and transmitting menus, in particular for use in restaurants.[79] Eligibility to patent law was analysed for certain claims of the patents US 6384850, US 6871325 and US 6982733

79. US Federal Circuit *Apple Inc. v. Ameranth, Inc.* 15-1703 http://www.cafc.uscourts.gov/sites/default/files/opinions-orders/15-1703.Opinion.11-28-2016.1.PDF (accessed 19 March 2017).

under CBM. The Federal Court partly confirmed and partly reversed the earlier decisions.

The patents have priority dates from 1999. At that time, it was usual for restaurants to use paper and pencil for taking meal orders and managing waiting lists. The first digital systems of the time (e.g. personal digital assistants (PDAs)) had several drawbacks for restaurant use, for example the quality of the display properties, the connection to remote systems and the usability of the display of a handheld device for the purposes of managing customer orders. The aim of the invention was to provide a system which overcomes the disadvantages of the known systems. Claim 1 of US6384850 reads:

> 1. An information management and synchronous communications system for generating and transmitting menus comprising:
>
> a. a CPU,
> b. a data storage device connected to said CPU,
> c. an operating system including a graphical user interface,
> d. a first menu consisting of menu categories, said menu categories consisting of menu items, said first menu stored on said data storage device and displayable in a window of said graphical user interface in a hierarchical tree format,
> e. a modifier menu stored on said data storage device and displayable in a window of said graphical user interface,
> f. a sub-modifier menu stored on said data storage device and displayable in a window of said graphical user interface, and
> g. application software for generating a second menu from said first menu and transmitting said second menu to a wireless handheld computing device or Web page,
>
> wherein the application software facilitates the generation of the second menu by allowing selection of catagories [sic] and items from the first menu, addition of menu categories to the second menu, addition of menu items to the second menu and assignment of parameters to items in the second menu using the graphical user interface of said operating system, said parameters being selected from the modifier and sub-modifier menus.

Claim 1 of the other two patents is nearly identical to this claim. The menu can be created at a desktop computer and downloaded onto the handheld device. This menu can be modified according to user input (selection of specific items). As a result, another menu is created which corresponds to the customer orders.

The Federal Circuit went through the argumentation that was made by PTAB during the CBM review. Before eligibility was analysed, claim construction, i.e. the meaning of several elements of the claim, was discussed. The court confirmed PTAB's interpretation of 'menu' as 'a list of options available to a user displayable on a computer. The court also agreed to the interpretation of 'synchronous communication system' that does not necessarily include 'a central back-office server that communicates data updates to and from multiple client devices' according to the knowledge of a person of ordinary skill in the art. The court confirmed the interpretation of 'CPU' as 'the computational and control unit of a computer'. The patentee had argued that the CPU is not a generic one. It is special in that application software for generating second menus runs on the CPU. Furthermore, the patentee argued that dependent claim 5 indicated a 'microprocessor'. The board concluded that 'although claim 5 recites "microprocessor" and the other claims recite "CPU," this does not necessarily mean that the two terms must have a different meaning'.

The court agreed with PTAB's opinion that all three patents are CBM patents. The patentee agreed to the fact that the patents relate to a 'financial service or product' but additionally, they relate to technological inventions. The court agreed that it was difficult to define 'technological invention' but that an evaluation of the claimed subject matter could be made without a complete definition. The claims and the specification did not indicate new and unobvious technological features. The specification indicated the use of typical hardware and commonly known programming steps. Furthermore, the invention did not solve a technical problem using a technical solution. A problem was indicated, i.e. 'how to display and synchronize computerized menus on non-standard devices/interfaces'. In the Board's view no solution to this problem was indicated in the claims. Descriptions on menu generation do not provide a technological solution.

The Federal Circuit agreed with PTAB's opinion that the claims of all three patents are directed to the abstract idea of 'generating a second menu from a first menu and sending the second menu to another location'. Thus, the claims are directed to a judicial exception. The claims do not claim 'a particular way of programming and designing the software to create menus that have these features but instead merely claim the resulting systems'. A specific improvement in the way computers operate could be seen

The next step analysed whether the claims comprise features that transform the abstract idea into something more. Again, it became evident from the specification that 'discrete programming steps were commonly known'. The patentee argued that claim 1 of US6982733 points out 'second menu is manually modified after generation'. Furthermore, if the server selects e.g. 'Iced Tea' from the menu on the screen the restaurant server triggers the appearance of 'with lemon' on the screen. It was counter argued that 'manual modification of a menu and then writing on it with a pen' could be included in the manual modification of a menu.

The patentee went on to indicate several aspects (synchronization, printing of menus, specific types of ordering) of the claim elements as a basis for an inventive concept. The manual modification and the remaining aspects were evaluated as 'insignificant post-solution activities that do not support the invention having an "inventive concept.".' Thus, 'the claimed invention replaces a server's notepad or mental list with an electronic device programmed to allow menu items to be selected as a customer places an order'. Conventional computer components are added to well-known business practices.

The patentee argued that programming the software was difficult. Thus, the claimed subject matter could not be seen as an abstract idea. However, the difficulties are not recognisable from the claim. Additionally, 'The degree of difficulty in implementing an abstract idea in this circumstance does not itself render an abstract idea patentable'.

The Federal Circuit confirmed PTAB's view that the additional elements of the claims '- both individually and when combined – do not transform the claimed abstract idea into a patent-eligible application of the abstract idea'.

Finally, the court reversed PTAB's decision to allow some dependent claims as patentable subject matter. Thus, adding features like 'linking the second menu to a specific customer at a specific table' or the 'manual modification by handwriting or voice recording' did not transform the abstract idea into eligible subject matter. Linking an order to a customer and/or table is a 'classic example of manual tasks that cannot be rendered patent eligible merely by performing them with a computer'. Furthermore, the specification did not indicate how the use of handwriting and voice recording was implemented. The patentee explained that known technologies were used.

Thus, the decision of the Federal Circuit resulted in a stricter view on eligibility to patent law.

[2] Intellectual Ventures I v. Symantec Corp.

The case ***Intellectual Ventures I v. Symantec Corp.*** (September 2016) relates to three patents: US6460050, US6073142 and US5987610. All were filed at the end of the 1990s.

US6460050 relates to screening emails and other data files for unwanted content. US6073142 relates to routing of e-mail messages based on specific criteria. US5987610 is directed to using computer virus screening in the telephone network. The Federal Circuit confirmed two, and reversed one lower court decision. Circuit Judge Stoll wrote an opinion dissenting in part. Circuit Judge Mayer wrote a concurring opinion.

Relevant claim 9 of US6460050:

> 9. A method for identifying characteristics of data files, comprising:
>
> receiving, on a processing system, file content identifiers for data files from a plurality of file content identifier generator agents, each agent provided on a source system and creating file content IDs using a mathematical algorithm, via a network;
> determining, on the processing system, whether each received content identifier matches a characteristic of other identifiers; and
> outputting, to at least one of the source systems responsive to a request from said source system, an indication of the characteristic of the data file based on said step of determining.'
> It was held that the patent combines a long-prevalent practice for people receiving paper mail with a computer. When people receive paper mail they discard the ones from sources from which they do not want to receive mail. The claim was seen as similar to the claim of BASCOM on filtering content retrieved from the Internet. However, the claim does not provide limitations which transform the abstract idea into eligible subject matter. Improving speed or efficiency as a result of implementation by a generic computer is not efficient in order to provide an inventive concept. Furthermore, the functioning of the computer itself is not improved. The Federal Circuit emphasized that 'when a claim directed to an abstract idea "contains no restriction on how the result is accomplished ...[and] [t]he mechanism ... is not described, although this is stated to be the essential innovation[,]"..., then the claim is not patent eligible.

Relevant claim 1 of US6073142:

> 1. A post office for receiving and redistributing e-mail messages on a computer network, the post office comprising:
>
> > a receipt mechanism that receives an e-mail message from a sender, the e-mail message having at least one specified recipient;
> > a database of business rules, each business rule specifying an action for controlling the delivery of an e-mail message as a function of an attribute of the e-mail message;
> > a rule engine coupled to receive an e-mail message from the receipt mechanism and coupled to the database to selectively apply the business rules to the e-mail message to determine from selected ones of the business rules a set of actions to be applied to the e-mail message; and
> > a distribution mechanism coupled to receive the set of actions from the rule engine and apply at least one action thereof to the e-mail message to control delivery of the e-mail message and which in response to the rule engine applying an action of deferring delivery of the e-mail message, the distribution engine automatically combines the e-mail message with a new distribution list specifying at least one destination post office for receiving the e-mail message for review by an administrator associated with the destination post office, and a rule history specifying the business rules that were determined to be applicable to the e-mail message by at least one rule engine, and automatically delivers the e-mail message to a first destination post office on the distribution list instead of a specified recipient of the e-mail message.

This was seen as being analogous to corporate mailrooms. This is also indicated in the specification. Thus, there is the abstract idea, i.e. a method of organizing human activities. Such methods represent 'fundamental … practice[s] long prevalent in our system'. Such activities could be done by a human, mentally or with paper and pencil. The claim could also be seen as a conventional business method.
In the next step the court determined whether there are additional elements in the claim which are a basis for an inventive concept. The patent discloses generic computers performing generic functions. Servers operate with conventional operating systems. Thus, the specification confirms that the implementation of the abstract idea is conventional. It was argued that computers or the Internet do not have 'rule engines' with business rules. However, the court pointed out that 'we determine whether "each step does *no more than require* a generic computer to perform generic computer functions.".'
Thus, the claim is not eligible for patent protection.

Relevant claims 1 and 7 of US5987610:

> 1. A virus screening method comprising the steps of:
>
> > routing a call between a calling party and a called party of a telephone network;
> > receiving, within the telephone network, computer data from a first party selected from the group consisting of the calling party and the called party;
> > detecting, within the telephone network, a virus in the computer data; and

> in response to detecting the virus, inhibiting communication of at least a portion of the computer data from the telephone network to a second party selected from the group consisting of the calling party and the called party.
>
> 7. The virus screening method of claim 1 further comprising the step of determining that virus screening is to be applied to the call based upon at least one of an identification code of the calling party and an identification code of the called party.

Virus screening is an idea that comes from computing. The patent specification indicates briefly in the background of the invention that virus screening was done with software installed on the computer. Thus, 'by itself, virus screening is well-known and constitutes an abstract idea'.

The court went on to explain that an abstract idea remains abstract even if limited to the Internet or a telephone network. No details of an implementation are in the claims. Claim 7 steps are executed by different computers; the sending computer, the virus scanning computer and the receiving computer. The sending and receiving computers perform generic functions, i.e. sending and receiving functions. The function of the virus scanning computer is indicated in the specification: '[v]irus screening can be facilitated in the telephone network using either a *conventional* telephone network processor adapted to run associated virus screening software or an additional processor which runs virus screening software.... The processor can augment *conventional* circuit-switched network elements ... '. Thus, there are no additional elements which show an inventive concept. It was argued that the use in a telephone network was a specific solution in that an intermediate computer was used. However, this argument was not convincing. The claims were ineligible for patent protection.

An opinion dissenting in part was given by Circuit Judge Stoll. He saw the invention as a shift of virus scanning at the user's computer (locally) to a central solution. Furthermore, in the past each user had to regularly update virus software. This was no longer necessary by means of the central solution with the virus-scanning computer. Judge Stoll agreed to the abstract idea of virus scanning. However, he did not agree to the outcome of step 2. Elements might be well-known when seen individually but in combination the arrangement is not conventional and not generic. A so called protection gap problem was solved. The likelihood that a computer of an end user receives a virus is reduced. Similarity to the BASCOM case was discussed. Claim 7 is regarded as improving the computer itself or at least the Internet.

A concurring opinion was given by Circuit Judge Mayer. It indicated several objections raised by opponents of software patents. Point I related to the possible implication of patents upon the right to receive information and ideas as pointed out in the Constitution. Point II is directed to the opinion that patents are not eligible for patent protection when they are directed to software implemented on generic computers.

Regarding Point I

Patents which restrict the information channels contradict the First Amendment of the Constitution. Monopolies given by patents 'obstruct the essential channels of scientific, economic, and political discourse'. Claims are directed to new technology but the claims are very broad, they are worded 'in vague and functional language ...'. Freedom of speech and the press should exist irrespective of communication technology. The First Amendment circumscribes the power to issue patents and copyrights. Reference was made to copyright. The idea/expression dichotomy allows a balance between the First Amendment and the Copyright Act in that a free communication of facts is allowed but the author's expression is protected. Section 101 of patent law creates a 'patent-free zone'. Building blocks of human ingenuity are not eligible for patent protection (cf. Alice). The proper application of Section 101 'can preserve the Internet's open architecture and weed out those patents that chill political expression and impermissibly obstruct the marketplace of ideas'. The determination of eligibility for patent protection has to be done before analyzing non-obviousness (35USC §103) or adequate written description (35USC §112). A robust application of Section 101 is required for litigation cases in order to keep essential channels of online communication free.

Regarding Point II

The Alice decision should be seen as the 'death knell for software patents'. The decision was directed to a computer-implemented system for mitigating risk settlement. The use of a generic computer for implementing the business method did not render the claim eligible for patent protection.

Judge Mayer went on to express the view that software is a kind of language – a 'set of instructions, known as code that directs a computer to perform specified functions or operations'. It was argued that 'It is inherently abstract because it is merely "an idea without physical embodiment"'. For this reason software implemented on a standard computer should remain outside of section 101.

Unfortunately, as pointed out in The Guide to the Software Engineering Body of Knowledge (SWEBOK® V3.0, cf. also Chapter 2, §2.07)), this view ignores what happens with instructions: 'To the discipline of software engineering, the ultimate objective of problem solving is to transform a problem expressed in natural language into electrons running around a circuit'. It is often forgotten that, when executed, software determines functionality of complex systems and single devices.

Judge Mayer explains that modern computers are a basic tool of modern life. They should not be subject to patent monopoly. Furthermore, 'generally implemented software is an "idea" insufficiently linked to any defining physical structure other than a standard computer; it is a precursor to technology than technology itself'. Protection by copyright remains the only reasonable means of protection. Software was developed without patent protection. Open source communities exist which successfully develop software without patent protection. Many software start-ups do not have patents.

Four insurmountable problems are pointed out:

> First, the scope of software patents 'is generally vastly disproportionate to their technological disclosure'. The real code is not part of the disclosure. An 'intentionally vague and broad language' is used to describe 'a particular goal or objective'. Source code is usually kept secret. Little or no details about the programs are disclosed to the public.
>
> Second, software patents are obtained at the 'idea' stage. They can be easily obtained without indicating that any real development occurred. A 'minefield of abstract patent claims for others who actually deploy software' is created. It results in negative implications in litigation. Patent thickets arise from the pressure to patent early, at a time before any work is done. Reference was made to statistics which show: 'between 2007 and 2011, 46% of lawsuits involved software patents, ...'.
>
> Third, the sheer number of software patents is an enormous problem. Computer products are complex products. As a result 'any given product is potentially subject to a large number of patents'. Overlapping patent rights impede innovation. Companies have to expend exorbitant sums on infringement suits. This harms the economy.
>
> Fourth, 'generically implemented software invariably lacks the concrete borders the patent law demands'. A patent should provide a clear notice of what is claimed. The public can recognize what remains free. Additionally, a contradiction is seen between the territory principle of patent law and the lack of territorial boundaries of the Internet. Software is seen as a kind of music or literature or as too abstract.

It was summarized that generically-implemented software patents should be eliminated in to clear patent thickets.

[D] Judicial Exceptions and Evidence?

As can be seen by the examples on eligibility for patent protection, the basic test includes the determination of an abstract idea without evidence. The analysis is done prima facie. This has resulted in some concerns among interested circles. The USPTO explained its approach in the document 'July 2015 Update: Subject Matter Eligibility', Part IV Requirements Of A Prima Facie Case.[80]

The courts do not rely on evidence (publications, prior use ...) that a claimed concept is a judicial exception (for instance an abstract idea). It is seen as a question of law. In some cases documents are used but very often they do not fulfil the requirements of normal prior art since they were published after the priority date or after the filing date. The examiner will not always provide documents as evidence. Their argumentation 'may rely, where appropriate, on the knowledge generally available to those in the art, on the case law present, on applicant's own disclosure, or on evidence'. Training material is provided for examiners. The July 2015 document

80. USPTO *July 2015 Update: Subject Matter Eligibility* https://www.uspto.gov/sites/default/files/documents/ieg-july-2015-update.pdf (accessed 21 March 2017).

explains: 'Once the examiner has satisfied her initial burden, the burden then shifts to the applicant'.

The collection of examples based on real and hypothetical claims is seen as a basis to help examiners and the public to determine subject matter eligibility. The initial burden is on the examiner.

The courts' decisions were analysed to find out which computer functions are regarded to be 'well-understood, routine, and conventional functions when they are claimed in a merely generic manner'. The following computer functions are indicated (the references are not indicated):

- 'performing repetitive calculations,
- receiving, processing, and storing data,
- electronically scanning or extracting data from a physical document,
- electronic recordkeeping,
- automating mental tasks, and
- receiving or transmitting data over a network, e.g. using the Internet to gather data'.

The list does not mean 'that all computer functions are well-understood, routine and conventional, or that a claim reciting a generic computer component performing a generic function is necessarily ineligible'. In general, when the claim as a whole amounts to nothing more than generic computer functions merely used to implement an abstract idea, the claim will be ineligible.

Court practice did not require evidence to indicate that 'additional elements were well-understood, routine or conventional'. If the additional elements seen in combination amount to significantly more than the abstract idea, the claim will be eligible for patent protection.

[E] Abstract Ideas: Summary

The USPTO identified four basic groups for abstract ideas: mathematical relationships/formulas, fundamental economic practices, and idea 'Of itself' and certain methods of organizing human activity. These groups overlap. Thus, a mathematical method could be part of a business method. The examples are mainly based on case law. Thus, legal practice depends heavily on the concrete example of the respective case. The judicial exception of 'abstract idea' can also overlap with other exceptions. Thus, a mathematical relationship could be seen as a law of nature (Arrhenius equation). Many examples of an abstract idea relate to business methods implemented by a generic computer which is used to perform the normal functions of a computer. Most of the examples indicate when a claim is not eligible for patent protection. Only a few examples show when an abstract idea was transformed by non-generic computing means into a claim eligible for patent protection.

A two-step test is applied to the subject matter of a claim. In the form published by the USPTO the first step consists in determining whether the claim form belongs to one of the four categories: process, article, manufacture, composition of matter. In step

2A it is determined whether the claim comprises a judicial exception. If yes, it is analysed in step 2B if there are additional elements in the claim which, when seen as a whole, transform the abstract idea into subject matter eligible for patent protection. If this is not the case the claimed subject matter is not eligible for patent protection under section 101. Some courts *see* step 2A as step 1 and step 2B as step 2. This does not change the fundamental principles for determining eligibility to patent law.

The claims are interpreted with reference to the specification and the knowledge of a person skilled in the respective art. No specific prior art document seems to be necessary as evidence for abstract ideas.

As stated in Alice, the major aim of legal practice is that the building blocks of human ingenuity should not be patented. Determining this is difficult because technology is changing.

§8.09 SOFTWARE AND THE NEW LEGAL PRACTICE

US law does not include a specific passage on computer programs. Consequently, both the law and legal practice are applied to software-related inventions in the same way as they are to other fields.

In addition, the law does not indicate exclusions of specific topics that go with exclusions from patentability in other countries/regions. For instance, the EPC (Article 52(2, 3)) includes a non-exhaustive list of topics (mathematical methods, business methods, aesthetic creations ...) which when claimed *as such* are excluded from patentability.

As in other jurisdictions, the complete computer program as a set of instructions in a programming language, as opposed to an expression in human language on a high level of abstraction, cannot be part of the patent claim. It is protected by copyright. In the past, patent applications sometimes included the source code in an appendix. However, such appendices were never published as part of the official patent document. The specification may include passages of source code or pseudocode and/or other forms to describe a process or an algorithm as the basis for a patent claim.

Depending on the individual´s perspective there was either the fear or the hope that the new legal practice could be 'the end of software patents'. This cannot be completely confirmed. The new approach is stricter in that 'building blocks of human ingenuity', or in other words well-known procedures (abstract ideas, laws of nature, product of nature) are not eligible for patent protection. Furthermore, as expressed in the dissenting opinions of some decisions there is the general feeling that certain areas should remain outside of patent protection for political reasons. Thus, the focus is on the evaluation of a certain product or procedure as fundamental knowledge that should not be blocked by patents. This holds true if a building block is implemented by generic computing means. Several publications see major difficulties for the whole amount of software patents in the US (e.g. 'THE U.S. SUPREME COURT'S 'ALICE' DECISION HAS

MADE IT CUMBERSOME FOR COMPANIES TO GET SOFTWARE PATENTS').[81] Such statements ignore the large amount of software inventions that are patentable without any problem after Alice in the US. Computer-implemented business methods (like in Alice) are an important area but they are only one area among others in the enormous range of the use of software.

In the application software area, the building blocks can relate to different application areas (economy, medical, chemistry, law, social sciences ...). Thus, a mathematical formula, a business method, a legal contract, a human behaviour etc. which are supposed to be implemented as a computer program, can be regarded as something not eligible for patent protection. Eligibility cannot be obtained by adding generic computer features.

In application software, this particularly relates to areas outside the traditional fields of natural science and technology that were the areas of the traditional patent system. Modern software technologies allow the implementation of relationships not only in technological areas (software controls technological functionality in a car), but also in areas of social sciences (business including finance, law, education, human relationships ...). Thus, automation of procedures previously done by human beings by conventional means (e.g. paper documents, telephone calls) continues in such areas. This is in particular true if the claim just indicates a well-known concept implemented by generic computing means. Specifics of the software implementation are not shown. Very often it is assumed that the abstract concept (e.g. a mathematical method or a business method) is completely or partly implemented as a computer program.

From the perspective of a system analyst or of a software engineer, the claims of several landmark decisions indicate only the basic procedures (early stage of software development) of a certain application area without indicating the more detailed implementation as computer program and its functionality. Very often, the description does not show the programming language used, the kind of computer/processor or logic array, the concrete communication means. This might because of the fear that fast technological developments in IT might lead to the replacement of certain features of a specific technology within a short time limit (e.g. five years). Another reason might be the complexity and modularity of modern IT systems. A device will be part of a larger system which is not known and must not be known in detail by the producer of a device with features implemented in software. This relates to the lower level of abstraction: the code might include components of libraries created by others. It also relates to a higher level of abstraction: systems are heterogeneous and work with agreed interfaces. Thus, the device might be connected over the Internet with other elements that are not known in detail.

The challenge of the patent system is in finding the right balance between overly broad formulations which on the one hand only show the basic procedure either with no details or with generic implementation details, and on the other hand a satisfying

81. Chartier, D. *Software Patent Claims Get Post-Alice Clarity, Federal Circuit decision gives software patent holders more room to dodge the 'abstract concept' bullet* Law week Colorado, VOL. 14 NO. 40 3 October 2016.

level of detail for software implementation features. In the extreme case this could include the disclosure of a source code which does not yet exist. The cases **DDR Holdings** and **Enfish** can be seen as positive examples in which the additional elements of the claim transform the abstract idea into subject matter eligible for patent protection. A technological problem is solved by means of technology (including software). The elements implementing the abstract idea and their combination are described on a level of detail that indicates more than a conventional implementation.

Without giving any statistics, experience shows that legal practice in the area of computing system software (like operating systems, databases, distributed computing, graphical user interfaces ...) is very liberal.

The high complexity of modern systems allows the combination of areas which were previously separate (e.g. chapter 2, §2.07 - petrol pump with payment functionality). This is triggered by modern information technology. Thus, the question that many others have already posed is: Can the patent system adapt to technological development — to a kind of extension to traditional non-technological areas outside of physics, chemistry, electrical engineering ...?

A stricter evaluation of claims has been driven by dissatisfaction with overly broad claims and obvious patents, mainly in the area of well-known business methods implemented by computing means, and their negative implications for competitors. Patent claims in the field of core computing and computer networks are less often seen as abstract ideas. The same is true if the claim shows an abstract idea in combination with a non-obvious technological implementation of that abstract idea. The technological implementation is shown at a level of abstraction which cannot be regarded as a generic functionality of a computer or a computer network (Internet).

The new approach is heavily discussed in interested circles. The USPTO arranged roundtable discussions. The outcomes can be found on the website of the USPTO. Roundtable two took place in December 2016.[82] Major concerns result from the following topics:

- There is a lack of evidence for an exception as a building block of human ingenuity.
- Eligibility to patent law is mixed with novelty.
- The borderlines in the determination what are abstract ideas and what are not abstract ideas? - are unclear and blurred. There is the fear of an arbitrary interpretation. For example interpretation might depend on the level of knowledge of a patent professional, the respective time (what was new at the filing date might be seen as a building block after twenty years).
- The view on software technology as something abstract, purely mathematical and outside of 'real life' is outdated since software represents more and more essential functional parts of devices, systems and equipment increasingly connected by modern communication technologies.

82. USPTO *Roundtable Two* https://www.uspto.gov/patent/initiatives/patent-subject-matter-eligibility-roundtable-2 (accessed 20 March 2017).

- It is difficult to transform the legal language into a language understandable to the scientist, software engineer, programmer ..., in particular in information technology.

The future will show how the patent system can adapt to new technologies.

CHAPTER 9

China

§9.01 LEGAL ASPECTS

China's economy is emerging fast to being now the second largest economy in the world. This development coincides with a massive governmental campaign and with continuous and important changes in patent law, now leading to the third amendment of the Patent Law of the People's Republic of China (hereinafter referred to as the 'Chinese Patent Law').[1] The Chinese government has released a national innovation policy for the country. A specific strategy was published in order to foster innovation. National patent applications should reach a certain level. A WIPO paper gives statistics over the past years and emphasizes the strong growth in China:[2]

> While Chinese innovators filed the most patent applications (1,010,406) in 2015, followed by those from the United States of America (526,296) and Japan (454,285), they are comparatively home-focused: Innovators based in China filed 42,154 applications for patents outside their own borders, while U.S.-based innovators were the most outward-looking, with 237,961 patent applications filed abroad.

The WIPO paper further goes on to mention concrete application figures:

> China's patent office received 1,101,864 filings in 2015, making it the first office to receive more than a million applications in a single year – including both filings from residents in China as well as from overseas innovators seeking patent protection inside China.

1. B. Love, C. Helmers & M. Eberhardt, *Patent Litigation in China: Protecting Rights or the Local Economy?* (2016), available at: http://digitalcommons.law.scu.edu/facpubs/918 (accessed 11 March 2017).
2. WIPO, *Global Patent Applications Rose to 2.9 Million in 2015 on Strong Growth From China; Demand Also Increased for Other Intellectual Property Rights*, Press Release PR/2016/802, Geneva (23 November 2016).

According to WIPO statistics for 2016, the top IP offices in the world are headed by the Chinese Patent Office.[3]

Two Chinese companies, ZTE Corporation and Huawei Technologies, are among the top five applicants using the PCT route.

A white paper on China's intellectual property rights (IPRs) protection states:[4]

> China has constantly enhanced its patent examination capacity. 2,083,000 patent applications were examined, with a year-on-year increase of 10.3%, of which the number of patents for invention reached 558,000. While the number of patent applications was increasing, the pendency for patent examination decreased steadily. The pendency for invention patents examination was controlled within 21.9 months.

As in many other jurisdictions, there are discussions in China[5] as to how to adopt the Chinese Patent Law to take into account computer technology and information science and whether protection should be handled under copyright or patent law.[6]

Article 1 of the Chinese Patent Law states that:

> the Patent Law is enacted to protect patent rights for inventions-creations, to encourage invention-creation, to foster the spreading and application of inventions-creations, and to promote the development and innovation of science and technology, for meeting the needs of the construction of socialist modernization.

However, Article 25(2) of the Chinese Patent Law states that patent rights shall not be granted for rules and methods for intellectual activities. This section of Article 25 is often used by examiners as a basis for rejecting computer implemented or business method related inventions.

In a Q&A[7] panel the Chinese State Intellectual Property Office (SIPO) announced that computer programs as such cannot be patented, but may be protected under the 'Regulations on Computers Software Protection', formulated in accordance with the Copyright Law.

However, SIPO also states that an invention containing a computer program may be patentable if the combination of software and hardware as a whole can really improve prior art, bring about technical results and constitute a complete technical solution.[8]

3. *A one-minute tour of key IP filing trends in 2015* (video), accessible via WIPO website http://www.wipo.int/pressroom/en/articles/2016/article_0017.html (accessed on 3 March 2017).
4. *2015 Intellectual Property Rights Protection in China*, http://english.sipo.gov.cn/laws/whitepapers/201607/P020160721403876149335.pdf, 5 (accessed 11 March 2017).
5. *See* for example Z. Yan & L.Xiaoyu, *Patent Protection for Computer Software in China*, 1 China Patents & Trademarks 77 (2015), IP Protection System.
6. J. Zhou, *A Study of Patentability of Computer Software -Related Inventions – Practice in U.S., Europe and Japan and Outlook for China*, IIP Bulletin 130 (2008).
7. At http://english.sipo.gov.cn/FAQ/200904/t20090408_449722.html (accessed on 3 March 2017).
8. At http://english.sipo.gov.cn/FAQ/200904/t20090408_449722.html (accessed on 3 March 2017).

Generally speaking, we have the same situation as in other jurisdictions all over the world, where legislation provides very abstract rules for dealing with software related inventions, which in practice give little guidance and which need to be interpreted on a case-by-case basis, although China is not case law country.

§9.02 LEGAL REQUIREMENTS

Unlike in Europe, Chinese Patent Law does not expressly exclude 'programs for computers' as such from patentability. Nevertheless, Article 2 of the Chinese Patent Law requires an invention to be a technical solution. According to Article 2, section 2 of the Chinese Patent Law, the term 'invention' is defined:[9]

> Inventions mean new technical solutions proposed for a product, a process or the improvement thereof.

Article 20 of the Implementing Rules states in its second sentence:[10]

> The independent claim shall outline:
>
> - the technical solution of an invention or utility model and
> - state the essential technical features necessary for the solution
> - of its technical problem.

For this reason, 'technicity' may be defined as implicit requirement in Chinese Patent Law.

This general approach is also reflected in the 2010 Guidelines.[11] In particular, in Chapter 9, Section 2 it is explained that if the claim merely consists of algorithms or rules and mental activities without any technical feature, this claim will be rejected as it does not constitute the subject matter of patent protection. However, if the claim refers to a mixture of technical and algorithmic or non-technical features, it may be patent protectable. The 2010 Guidelines point out:

> if the contents of a claim include not only rules and methods for mental activities but also technical features, for example, the contents defining the devices for computer games including rules for games and technical features as well, then the claim is not wholly rules and methods for mental activities, and shall not be excluded from patentability in accordance with Article 25.

In the 2010 Guidelines the term computer program is defined:[12]

> Computer programs per se as described in this Chapter mean a coded instruction sequence which can be executed by a device capable of information processing, e.g. a computer, so that certain results can be obtained, or a symbolized instruction sequence, or a symbolized statement sequence, which can be transformed

9. Patent Law of the People's Republic of China, Article 2 http://english.sipo.gov.cn/laws/lawsregulations/201101/t20110119_566244.htm (accessed on 4 March 2017).
10. Rules for the Implementation of the Patent Law of the People's Republic of China, Article 20.
11. *Guidelines for Patent Examination* (2010).
12. *Guidelines for Patent Examination*, Part II, Chapter 9, 305 (2010).

automatically into a coded instruction sequence. Computer programs per se include source programs and object programs.

§9.03 PROCEDURAL AND FORMAL ASPECTS

As in Germany and other countries, patents are examined by SIPO and a deadline must be met for filing a request for examination. The examination request has to be submitted within three years of the filing date or, if priority is claimed, within three years of the priority date. If no request is filed within this time limit, the application is deemed to be withdrawn.

It is possible to request that application is published earlier than eighteen months from the filing date. In this case SIPO will conduct a preliminary examination and publish the application immediately afterwards (provided it is not rejected).

As in Europe, it is possible to withdraw an application at any time before grant by filing a request even before it is published.

Also, as in Europe, any person may submit observations on the lack of conformity of an application with the provisions of the patent law to SIPO as a third party observation. This can be done at any time from the date of publication of the application to the announcement of the decision to grant.

After grant, the validity of a patent may only be challenged by an invalidation procedure, because the opposition system was abolished in China in 2001. Requests for invalidation can be filed at any time, even after the patent has expired.[13]

If SIPO refuses to grant a patent right, the applicant may request a re-examination by the Patent Re-examination Board (PRB). If the rejection decision is upheld by the PRB, the applicant may file a lawsuit with the Beijing Intellectual Property Court. The decision of the Beijing Intellectual Property Court may be further appealed to the highest legal instance, the Beijing High People's Court.

[A] Assessment of Novelty

With effect from October 2009, the Chinese Patent Law has been amended. One major change relates to the implementation of an absolute novelty regime as in Europe. Under the new Chinese Patent Law any public disclosure of any kind anywhere in the world prior to the filing date (or the priority date if any) of a Chinese patent application will count against it. Before this amendment was implemented it was possible to apply for a patent in China, even though the application had been disclosed outside China (e.g. at a trade fair). This amendment is especially important for attacking a competitor's patent in infringement suits. All state of the art and evidence published or produced outside of China, including public use and public knowledge, can now be used to challenge a patent.

13. *See The patentability criterion of inventive step/non-obviousness*, AIPPI (21 April 2001) https://aippi.org/download/commitees/217/GR217china.pdf (accessed 11 March 2017).

[B] Assessment of Inventive Step

Article 22 of the Chinese Patent Law stipulates: 'Inventions and utility models for which patent rights are to be granted shall be novel, creative and of practical use.'

And paragraph three of this Article defines 'creativity' or 'inventiveness':

> Creativity means that, compared with the existing technologies, the invention possesses prominent substantive features and indicates remarkable advancements, and the utility model possesses substantive features and indicates advancements.

For assessing inventive step, the claims have to be construed in light of the description. However, if an abstract term is used in the claims (e.g. computing entity) and the description mentions limited embodiments thereof (e.g. cell phone) the claims have to be construed in the general, literal meaning as a computing entity, which may thus include non-cellphone computing entities.

The Guidelines mention that if a claim is directed to a combination or juxtaposition of known features, and the technical features are the sum of the technical features of the combined parts without any additional functional interaction, then the claim will be judged to be not inventive.[14]

According to the 2010 Guidelines, to determine whether an invention has prominent substantive features is to determine whether the claimed invention is inventive to the person skilled in the art as compared with the prior art. Usually and in correspondence with the Guidelines, the following three steps are followed to determine whether a claimed invention is inventive as compared with the prior article:[15]

(1) determining the closest prior art;
(2) determining the distinguishing features of the invention and the technical problem actually solved by the invention;
(3) determining whether or not the claimed invention is obvious to a person skilled in the article.

To be specific, when determining the distinguishing feature, an assessment of technical character of these features seems to be implied. The examples given in the Guidelines suggest that the distinguishing feature should be a technical feature solving a technical problem.

China is not a case law country. That is why the SIPO Guidelines are actually the only resource available for determining inventive step during examination, invalidation and litigation. There is no other jurisprudence or authoritative literature further interpreting the meaning of such a test.

---

14. *See Guidelines for Patent Examination*, Part II, Chapter 4, 4.2 (2010).
15. *Guidelines for Patent Examination*, Part II, Chapter 4, 3.2.1.1 (2010) http://www.sipo.gov.cn/zhfwpt/zlsqzn/sczn2010eng.pdf (accessed 11 March 2017).

In practice and according to the Guidelines, a key factor for assessment of inventive step therefore is evaluating whether or not the invention produces advantageous technical effects.

As in other jurisdictions (Germany, European Patent Office) in assessing whether a software-related invention solves a technical problem and provides a technical effect, the claimed invention must be considered as a whole. Therefore, for example, if an invention concerns a computer program that is employed together with known hardware, the patentability of the invention should not be examined by way of considering the computer program and the known hardware separately. Rather, the invention should be looked at in its entirety.

As a general rule, the drafter should consider whether the invention's contribution to the current technology comes only from the mental activity elements. If so, further technical claim limitations should be added, so that the invention might be considered as patentable subject matter.

[C] Clarity of the Disclosure and Conciseness of the Claims

Article 26, paragraph 3 of the Chinese Patent Law prescribes that the description shall set forth the invention (or utility model) in a manner that is sufficiently clear and complete so as to enable a person skilled in the relevant field of technology to carry it out.

In particular the Guidelines to Preliminary Examination of the PCT point out:

> The description should be clear and specific, avoiding the unnecessary use of technical jargon.[16]

Acknowledged technical terms may be used. Technical terms that are not commonly used may also be used, provided that they are appropriately defined and there is no acknowledged and identical concept having the same meaning.

With regard to the clarity of the description, paragraph 2.1.1 of Part 2, Chapter 2 of the SIPO Guidelines provides the following information:

> the description should use technical terms of the technical field to which the invention or utility model belongs. The terms in the description should express precisely the technical content of the invention or utility model, they should not be so vague or ambiguous as to make a person skilled in the art fail to understand the invention clearly and correctly.[17]

This regulation comes into particular consideration for computer implemented invention (CII) applications, because these types of applications often use non-standard technical terms. The meaning of the term only according to the literal interpretation may be vague.

16. *See PCT International Search and Preliminary Examination Guidelines*, Part II, 4.22 (as in force from 15 December 2016); p. 33.
17. At http://english.sipo.gov.cn/examination/topics/201108/t20110802_614222.html (accessed 2 March 2017).

Thus, the person making the assessment of whether the description is clear or not should be 'one skilled in the technical field to which the invention belongs', and the criterion for making the assessment should be whether the technical solution can be carried out.

Therefore, claim features and important fallback positions, which may be used for amended claims in later stages of the proceedings, should be contained literally in the application as filed, because generalizations or intermediate generalizations of a claim features are generally not allowable. It is also helpful if the wording of the claims is mirrored in the description.

In practice, clarity issues are key aspects in examination of CIIs.

With respect to technicity, it has to be emphasized that the technical problem must be clearly and objectively described in the description.

With respect to the figures, it is a requirement to include a general flowchart of the computer program in the drawings. Each step of the computer program should be explained in the description based on the flowchart in time-based order using natural language.

It is possible to include a section of the program with source language or code or in abstracted pseudo code, if necessary. But it is neither required nor useful to provide the whole source code program.

[D] Infringement Aspects

In China, two kinds of actions are available to the owner of a technical IP right against infringement of for example a patent, namely a judicial action and an administrative action.

The only authority that grants patents is SIPO, which makes harmonization easy. Patent validity proceedings are dealt with at first instance by the Patent Review and Adjudication Board of SIPO, which is based in Beijing. Generally, China has adopted bifurcated system, where patent invalidation actions are heard by the Patent Review and Adjudication Board and patent infringement cases are handled by the Courts.[18]

The Chinese court system consists of several basic courts at county level, intermediate courts, high courts and the Supreme Court. In 2014 three specialized Courts for IP were established in Beijing, Shanghai and Guangzhou, which serve as intermediate courts in China and will hear both civil and administrative IP cases.

As in other jurisdictions, patent infringement in China may be direct or indirect. Direct infringement is established if all the features in a patent claim (apparatus or method) are realized in the alleged infringing product and are implemented by a single party. The single party is the direct infringer. Indirect infringement is officially referred to as joint infringement in China.

18. An overview is given at http://limegreenip.hoganlovells.com/article/22/patents-patent-litigation-china#sthash.m1FjlI4S.dpuf (accessed 9 March 2017).

As well as with respect to patent application filing figures, China has also become the global leader in patent litigation cases with 9,680 suits filed in 2012, which was 80% more than the total number in the USA.[19]

For example, Apple has been sued for allegedly infringing Chinese patent rights that cover virtual assistant Siri, the videotelephony service FaceTime, and aspects of the famously sleek designs of the iPod, iPad, and iPhone.[20]

Chinese Courts recognize the doctrine of equivalents by stressing the technical character of the equivalent features.[21]

§9.04 CLAIM FORMATS FOR CII

According to the newly published draft revision of the Examination Guidelines[22] the following claim categories are available in China:

(1) method/process;
(2) apparatus/product/device/system;
and according to the new 2017 Guidelines also;
(3) data carrier type claims ('A computer readable medium, including computer program stored thereon for, when executed on a computer device, causing the computer device to carry out the following steps of method of claim 1: with steps A, B, C, etc.') is now allowed.

According to the new 2017 Guidelines, software related inventions may be claimed by process, apparatuses/systems and computer readable media/data carriers. According to initial comments, SIPO appears to be moving towards the approach of the USPTO and the EPO, where data carrier claims are also allowed.

This liberalization was motivated by making patent enforcement much easier for software related patents. For enforcing method claims for software it is necessary that the software is executed in a computing entity. If the software is only loaded or imported but not executed, the courts will generally decline a direct patent infringement. This situation changes if a storage medium or data carrier is claimed. Then, it is no longer required that the software is executed.

Under the new 2017 Guidelines, computer software drafted as an apparatus claim in 'means-plus-function' format is allowable.

---

19. Erin Coe, *5 Tips in the Art of Patent War in China*, LAW 360 (29 May 2014); *see also* Yan Zhao, DLA Piper, *China's Patent Litigation Landscape Shifts* (2012), available at https://www.dlapiper.com/en/us/insights/publications/2012/09/chinas-patent-litigation-landscape-shifts/ (reporting an emerging trend for filing patent suits in China and that Chinese courts saw 7,819 new patent suits in 2011 and 5,785 in 2010, accessed 11 March 2017).
20. A summary of the lawsuits may be found at http://www.ipwatchdog.com/2013/04/04/chinas-great-leap-forward-in-patents/id=38625/ (accessed 11 March 2017).
21. *The role of equivalents and prosecution history in defining the scope of patent protection*, AIPPI Report Q175, available at https://aippi.org/download/commitees/175/GR175china.pdf (accessed 5 February 2017).
22. In October 2016.

Prior to the amendment of the Guidelines, it was necessary to provide a very strict correspondence between method and apparatus claims and the respective figures (block diagram and flow chart). In particular, each component/module of the apparatus has to fully correspond to each step in the computer program flow. Also, each step in the method claim was to reflect the computer program flow. If an apparatus claim was limited with functional features (as typical with 'means plus function' language – 'terminal, constructed to receive data...'), the courts tended to construe this by referencing the specific embodiment and its equivalent embodiment(s) as described in the description. If no such embodiments were included, it was not possible to determine the scope of the claim and thus an alleged infringement.[23] With the new Guidelines, commentators say, that the situation seems to become less stricter now.

In contrast to the approach of the EPO, claims directed to a computer program or a program signal or a data signal is still not allowed under the Chinese Patent Law.

§9.05 GUIDELINES FOR CII

In October 2016, SIPO published the Draft (for Public Comment) of Revisions to the Patent Examination Guidelines. The revised Guidelines are expected to be officially released in April 2017.

According to initial comments, the new Guidelines appear to loosen the standards for obtaining software enabled and business method related inventions.

Claims related to business methods that contain both business rules/methods and technical features in the claim as well, shall no longer be excluded from patent protection according to Article 25 of the Chinese Patent Law. With this change, China seems to be the first country worldwide to ease the patent protection of business methods.

As suggested in a blog,[24] 'SIPO welcomes and encourages inventions in the fields of finance, insurance, bond/securities, leasing, auction, investment, marketing, advertising, and management, which all clearly fall in the "business" category.' The blog statement ends by assuming that this 'pioneering statement has no precedent in the US or Europe'.

According to the new 2017 Guidelines a major trend for further liberalization with respect to CIIs is noted:

- a computer readable medium plus computer program flow is patentable (previously it was not);
- an apparatus claim defined as combination of software and hardware is patentable;

23. *See* the case in Shanghai High People's Court on 24 February 2014 – *Nokia v. Huaqin* (HuGaoMin San (Zhi) ZhongZi No. 96 (2013)); this decision was reported at http://www.mondaq.com/china/x/381748/Patent/Patenting+Software+In+China+The+Challenges+Of+Drafting (accessed 12 March 2017).
24. At http://www.rcip.co.il/en/article/china-may-become-more-liberal-towards-business-method-and-software-related-patents/ (accessed on 10 February 2017).

- the 'software part' or the functional module in an apparatus claim will be construed as only relating to a program, rather than to a functional technical feature.

Moreover, Part II, Chapter 9, § 2 of the 2010 Guidelines defined three requirements for the eligibility of software inventions:

(i) the invention solves a technical problem;
(ii) the invention uses technical means following the laws of nature to control and to process external or internal objects; and
(iii) the invention achieves a technical effect in conformity with the laws of nature.

Regarding the threshold of patentable subject matter, the 2010 Guidelines provided four examples to illustrate eligible software inventions:

- to control an industrial process, e.g. a method for controlling a die forming process of rubber;
- to improve the internal performance of computer-related product, e.g. a method for expanding the storage capacity of movable computer device;
- to measure or test, e.g. a method for measuring liquid viscosity by computer program;
- to process external data, e.g. a method for removing image noise in digital image processing.

In the following, passages of the 2017 Guidelines are specified, which show amendments in relation to the 'old' 2010 Guidelines (changes in *italic*):

GL-B-I 4.2:

(2) Except in the cases described above in point (1), if a claim in its entirety contains not only matters of rules or methods for mental activities but also technical features, then the claim, viewed as a whole, is not a rule or method for mental activities, and shall not be excluded from patentability under Article 25.

[Example]

For claims relating to business models, they should not be precluded from possibility of being granted a patent under Article 25 of the Patent Law if the claims comprise both subject matter of business rules and methods, and technical features.

GL-B-IX 2:

If a claim merely relates to an algorithm, or mathematical computing rules, or computer programs per se, or computer programs per se recorded on media (such as tapes, discs, optical discs, magnetic optical discs, ROM, PROM, DVD, or other computer-readable media), or rules or methods for games, etc., it falls under the scope of rules and methods for mental activities and does not constitute the subject matter for which patent protection may be sought.

For example, a computer-readable storage medium or a product of computer program that is merely defined by a recorded program per se, or a device for computer games, etc., which is merely defined by game rules and does not include any technical features, e.g., does not include any physical entity, does not constitute the subject matter of patent protection because it essentially merely relates to rules and methods for mental activities. However, the claimed medium in a patent application relating to physical characteristics improvement thereof, for example, layer composition, magic channel spacing, materials, etc., does not fall under the cases mentioned above.

GL-B-IX 3:

This passage was deleted.

GL-B-IX 5.2:

A claim for an invention application relating to computer programs may be drafted as a process claim or product claim, e.g. the apparatus for executing the process. No matter what kind of claim it is drafted as, the claim shall be supported by the description, represent the technical solution of the invention in its entirety and outline the essential technical features for resolving the technical problems, and not describe resumptively the functions of the computer program and the effects those functions can produce only. If it is drafted as a process claim, the various functions to be performed by the computer program and the way to perform the functions shall be described in detail according to the steps of the process. If it is drafted as an apparatus claim, the various component parts and the connections among them shall be specified, and a detailed account shall also be given of the component parts by which the various functions of the computer program are performed, and of how these functions are performed, *the said component parts may comprise not only hardware but also software.*

If an apparatus claim is drafted on the basis of a computer program flow completely and completely identical with and corresponding to each step in the said computer program flow, or completely identical with and corresponding to the process claim reflecting the said computer program flow, i.e. each component in the apparatus claim completely corresponds to each step in the said computer program flow or each step in the said process claim, then each component in the apparatus claim shall be regarded as a *program* module which is required to be built to realize each step in the said computer program flow or each step in the said method. The apparatus claim defined by such a group of *program* modules shall be regarded as the *program* module architecture to realize the said solution mainly through the computer program described in the description rather than entity devices to realize the said solution mainly through hardware.

§9.06 BEST PRACTICE

It is helpful to include technical features in the claims supported by the description. It is important to include as many concrete technical embodiments as possible in the description. Claims have to be concise and be supported by the description and the description has to be clear. In China, a best mode requirement does not exist as it does in the USA.

Claims may be directed to methods, apparatuses and data carriers.

The claims:

- shall outline the technical solution of an invention; and
- state the essential technical features necessary for the solution;
- of its technical problem.

Prior to implementation of the new Guidelines in 2017, business methods were usually not patentable and were only eligible for patent protection if they were claimed in combination with physical or hardware features.

§9.07 SUMMARY

In general, the practice in China is similar to the European situation. Although there is no explicit technicality requirement as in Europe, there is indeed a reference to the field of technology in the definition of an invention (which is based on a technical idea).

In sum, according to the Chinese Patent Law the following requirements are listed, which must be met from a practical point of view:

- Existence of an 'invention' – Article 25.1 (2) of the Chinese Patent Law, requiring a technical solution (according to the Guidelines, Part II; Chapter 9, section 2).
- Novelty – Article 22.2 of the Patent Law (Guidelines, Part II; Chapter 3).
- Inventive step – Article 22.3 of the Patent Law (Guidelines, Part II; Chapter 4).
- Practicable applicability – Article 22.4 of the Patent Law (relevant for medical and surgical methods, Guidelines, Part II; Chapter 5).
- Sufficiency of disclosure and support of the claims in the description – Articles 26.3, 26.4 of the Patent Law.
- Conciseness of the claims – Article 26.3 of the Patent Law.

§9.08 EVALUATION OF CASE LAW

[A] Supreme Court Decision: Doctrine of Extra Limitation

The case *Xinyi Construction Material v. Renda New Wall Construction Material* concerned an application in the field of mechanics. It dealt with evaluation of the scope of protection in infringement proceedings.

Rules 20, 21 of the Implementing Regulation of the Chinese Patent Law provide that claims should clearly, concisely define the invention for which protection is sought, and that an independent claim should recite all essential features defining the claimed invention. For this reason, all features in independent claim should be deemed indispensable and cannot be omitted (during both prosecution and litigation). As a result, the application of the so-called 'Doctrine of Extra Limitation' should be restricted in determination of patent infringement.

In particular, the term 'at least two layers of glass fibre cloth' had to be construed in the light of the description and in view of the alleged infringing product.

In this 2005 case the Supreme Court overturned the lower court's judgment and issued a final judgment in favour of Xinyi of non-infringement literally and under the doctrine of equivalents.

[B] Supreme Court Decision: The Patent Office Must Prove Common Knowledge[25]

A recent case, decided in 2015 by the Supreme Court, dealt with the Patent Office's burden of proof of common knowledge during assessment of inventiveness according to Article 22(3) Patent Law in patent examination, which is a typical objection in practice from examiners.

The decision concerns Huawei Patent No. 200810132469.5 entitled 'A CRBT Selection Method, System and Related Device' and the technology concerns telecommunications.

The revised claim 1 reads as follows:

> A ring tone selection method, comprising: the calling party initiating a call request including a ring tone required by the calling party; the type of ring tone required by the calling party includes the calling party's needs; the calling party obtains the ring back tone information sent by the ring back tone server according to the type of ring tone required by the calling party; and the ring back tone information includes called information.

Further independent claims concern a system, a terminal, and a server.

The application was first rejected by the Chinese Patent Office due to a lack of inventiveness/creativity. The distinguishing features over prior art were not disputed by the applicant but the proof of common knowledge which – according to Huawei's position – should have been given by the PRB, was disputed.

On 9 March 2016, the Supreme Court held a public hearing in accordance with the law.

In its decision, the Supreme Court confirmed the burden on the PRB to state reasons or provide corresponding evidence for proof of common knowledge, if the interested party disputes or has objections to it.

In the previous instance, the PRB identified a patent as the closest prior art and determined that: the distinguishing features of the current invention were that the calling party's call request includes its CBRT ordering information and through this CBRT ordering information the calling party can request and consequently receive, among other things, the called party's information.

The technical problem solved by the invention is to enable the calling party to select a CBRT in the course of initiating a call request and receive the called party's

25. The full decision (in Chinese) can be accessed at http://www.chinaiprlaw.cn/index.php?id=4448 (accessed 3 March 2017 and translated with Googletranslate); a report on this decision may be found at http://trustinip.com/a-recent-case-in-china-concerning-the-patent-offices-burden-to-prove-common-knowledge-in-patent-examination/ (accessed 12 March 2017).

information, thus to improve the user experience. Huawei had no objection to this analysis.

It was disputed whether the above mentioned distinguishing features were known technical means in the art to solve the said technical problem, thus qualifying as common knowledge. If so, there would exist a technical solution in the prior art and the invention would lack inventiveness.

According to the Supreme Court, the burden should not be lowered with respect to the telecommunications field, where technologies are updated rapidly, and many emerging technologies are widely used in the industry but may not yet be included in textbooks, technical manuals or technical dictionaries. The Court referred to applying the Guidelines and considering the technological development level of the telecommunications field at the given time and the degree to which persons skilled in the art had accepted and applied the technical features in question. In particular, the Supreme Court found the two patent documents submitted by the PRB not sufficient to show that the distinguishing features in question were customary means in the art.

[C] Supreme Court: Order for Full Compensation in IPR Infringement Cases[26]

In 2008 it was reported that the Supreme Court had ordered courts at all levels to adhere to a 'full-compensation' principle when dealing with IPR cases.

'Courts should fully apply logical reasoning and everyday life experiences, and comprehensively and objectively examine the evidence for calculating the amount of compensation,' Supreme Court vice-president Cao Jianming told a national work conference on IPR trials in Jinan:

> Courts should avoid applying simple methods of legal compensation when handling IPR infringement cases. Instead, they should try to guide parties involved to calculate the amount, using methods of infringement damages and infringement gains.

[D] Clarity of Claim Features

The decision *BAI Wanqing v. Chengdu Hard-To-Find Items Marketing Services Center et al.* relates to determining an infringement analysis based on unclear claim features.[27]

The Court held that the scope of protection of a patent should be clear. If there is an obvious error in the statements of a patent claim and the specific meaning of the technical terms in the claim cannot be determined by combining the specification of the patent involved in a case, attached figures, common knowledge in the art, relevant existing technology, etc., resulting in the scope of protection of the patent being

26. Available at http://www.china.org.cn/english/government/243500.htm (accessed 12 March 2017).
27. A report of this decision may be found at https://cgc.law.stanford.edu/guiding-cases/guiding-case-55/ (accessed 9 March 2017).

obviously unclear, then the Court cannot determine whether the allegedly infringing technical solution constitutes an infringement of rights because there is no way to conduct a substantively meaningful infringement comparison of the claim with the allegedly infringing technical solution.

This once again, emphasizes the need to specifically define claim features and fallback positions.

CHAPTER 10
Korea

§10.01 LEGAL ASPECTS

Discussions about the patentability of computer implemented inventions (CII) have a long tradition in Korea, because large Korean corporations dealing with software, such as KT, Samsung Electronics and LG Electronics, filed the most patent applications, constituting 60% of all applications. This indicates that large corporations have shifted their attention to new computer science technologies, in an effort to generate new profits in the stagnating smartphone market.

In recent years, particularly during 2014 and 2015, the number of patent applications related to computer communication networks for information exchange in various technological fields, also called as 'Internet of Things' (IoT), has increased. The subject matter typically comprises software, typically embedded within electronics, sensors and connectivity entities. Applications in the fields of access control, resource allocation, and power reduction occupied the largest portion with 68.0% of the total. Other classes of patent applications relating to servicing technologies in different technical fields such as smart cars, healthcare, and smart home technologies, accounted for 16.5%, followed by the network control and management technologies. According to the Korean Intellectual Property Office (KIPO), the number of patent applications for IoT technology has increased nearly seven-fold over the last four years, increasing from thirty-three cases in 2009 to over 220 cases in 2013.

This phenomenon is a result of the development of international standards for IoT technology and the Korean government's active promotion of the IoT industry.

For example, the Korean law firm Lee International refer to a new technology, called Zing.[1] In 2016 the Korean Electronics and Telecommunications Research Institute (ETRI) developed and announced Zing as a new high-speed close proximity

1. At http://www.leeinternational.com/plaza/letter/view.php?letterContentsSeq=3088 (accessed *28 March 2017*).

technology. Zing enables users to easily and rapidly send and receive gigabytes of content when their devices are within 10 cm of each other, with a transmission rate which is approximately 8,000 times faster than the current near field communication (NFC) technology. It can be used only in extremely limited areas, but the technology can be applied to a variety of products and services, such as smart home appliances including TVs and refrigerators, in-vehicle infotainment and IoT advertisements. Zing is expected to be established as an international standard in the first half of 2017, which will provide a relevant factor for its commercialization. ETRI's research team has filed twenty-seven patent applications in Korea and overseas for Zing technology, including essential patents, and published thirty-eight treatises.

Another emerging field relates to mobile biometric authentication technology. According to a report from the KIPO on recent patent filing trends, the number of patent applications related to this technology has increased from a total of seventy-six in 2011 to 178 in 2015.[2]

Since the Patent Act of South Korea does not explicitly prescribe the patentability of CII, this issue is subject to major decisions and is still discussed in the patent community. Examination is based on the requirements of the existence of an invention, novelty and inventive step.

[A] Legal Requirements

In contrast to European Patent Office (EPO) and German patent law, the Korean Patent Act defines the term 'invention' under Article 2, paragraph 1[3] as:

> the highly advanced creation of a technical idea using the laws of nature.

To make use of 'the laws of nature' means to apply the law of cause and effect in the context of natural science.

The invention is to be based on a technical idea. However, the technical idea shall not be abstract, but shall be a concrete solution to a problem.

Thus, the definition of patentable inventions in the Korean statutes is clear in its reference to technology. 'Technicality' may also be specified as an implicit criterion for patentability in Korea.

A new revision of the Korean Patent Act came into force on 1 March 2017. Based on this revision, post grant cancellation or opposition proceedings will now be introduced. In parallel an interested party may file a request for invalidation without a time limit after grant of the patent. Thus, granted patents could now be challenged by invalidation and by a post grant opposition procedure (from 1 March 2017). Third party observations are possible during the period pending grant but only after publication. This introduction was motivated by the finding that about 40% of all Korean patents

2. Lee International, *Newsletter* (Winter 2016), 3.
3. At http://www.kipo.go.kr/upload/en/download/PatentAct.pdf and http://www.wipo.int/wipolex/en/text.jsp?file_id=214534 (both accessed 13 March 2017).

are granted before they are published. According to statistics there is a relative high success rate of invalidation cases (one in two are successful).

The time limit for requesting examination is reduced to only three years (from five years) to adapt the Korean system to those of Japan and China and to reduce the time period of uncertainty. If this deadline is missed, the application will be deemed to be withdrawn. Ex officio re-examination proceedings are introduced as a last option for the patent examiner to reject the patent application even after an examiner's decision to grant the application. This is, however, only admissible if the applicant has not paid the first annual fee.

[B] Procedural and Formal Aspects

Generally, international applicants should note that the revised Patent Act became effective in Korea as of 1 January 2015. From January 2015, an applicant can submit the specification, claims and drawings in English when filing a Korean patent application in order to secure an effective filing date for the application. A Korean translation of the specification, claims and drawings must be submitted within fourteen months after the earliest priority date. Patent applications may be filed simply with 'idea description data' consisting of articles published in Korean or foreign journals or research notes, without complex restrictions as to the filing format.

Under the revised Patent Act, amendments to the specification of a Korean national phase application or a Korean patent application filed in English can be made within the scope of a Patent Cooperation Treaty (PCT) application or original application in English. An applicant will be allowed to correct translation errors found in the Korean translation of a PCT application entering into the national phase or the Korean translation of a Korean patent application filed in English within the scope of the English specification during the prosecution.

Based on its Examination Guidelines as revised on 31 December 2014, the KIPO will initiate a prior review procedure for discussion of draft amendments to patent applications prior to formal submission of the amendments.

On 28 January 2015, a revision to the Patent Act regarding the twelve month novelty grace period and the filing of a divisional application was promulgated. The revision became effective on 29 July 2015.

Further, in 2015 regulatory criteria for preventing patent trolls and abuse of standard-essential patents were provided. The revisions relate to general examination rules on the exercise of IP rights.

[1] Disclosure of the Invention

According to Article 42(4)2 of the Korean Patent Act, the claims shall be supported by a detailed description of the invention and shall define the invention clearly and concisely.

Article 42(3) of the Korean Patent Act provides that the detailed description of the invention shall be provided in accordance with the methods prescribed by Ordinance of the Ministry of Knowledge Economy in a clear and detailed manner to ensure that any person with ordinary knowledge in the technology sector to which the relevant invention belongs can easily carry out the invention. Thus, the specification should provide examples describing the claimed invention sufficiently to enable one skilled in the art to easily carry out the invention.

It should be defined which of the method steps is performed on which computer entity. Thus, a claim will usually be deemed to be unclear if it is only specified that the plurality of the method steps be performed on a computer.

The underlying algorithm or computer processing has to be defined and explained as well.

Relating to the description, the enablement requirement has to be met.

The specification should clearly describe the prior art, the problem to be solved with the application, and the concrete (technical) means to solve said problem.

The Examination Guidelines for CII applications (last amended 1 July 2014) state that if claim features are defined by functions and corresponding flowcharts are provided, the functions in the claims should consistently correspond to the flowcharts in the specification. Otherwise, the invention cannot be carried out.

The scope of a claim needs to be clear and definite. If 'result to be achieved' language is used, then this requirement will usually not be met. As an example, the Guidelines refer to the wording 'an aircraft-controlling computer or previously predicting an occurrence of turbulence' without giving any further technical details in the description, this feature would be judged as an indefinite description of the invention.

[2] Assessment of Inventive Step

For the assessment of inventive step it has to be noted that commercial success or its equivalent may be considered in determining inventive step. This is different to the EPO approach.

Combining different technologies is usually not considered as involving an inventive step. The same holds for applying known approaches, such as known in computer science, to another field. For example, to apply an encryption technique known in the field of medical technology and apply this encryption technique to medical images would be judged to be obvious for a person skilled in the art.

In a recent decision[4] the Korean Supreme Court held:

> In determining the non-obviousness of an invention, the court shall: (a) based on the evidence and the record on the scope and content of prior art, ascertain, at a minimum, the distinction between the subject matter and the prior art and the level of technology of the person having ordinary skill in the art to which the subject matter pertains (hereinafter 'ordinarily skilled person'); and, on that basis, (b) determine whether, in light of the level of technology at the time of patent application, the subject matter is obvious to an ordinarily skilled person, notwithstanding its distinction from prior art. In such cases, it is impermissible to

4. At http://library.scourt.go.kr/SCLIB_data/decision/73-ph-2014Hu2184_Nov.25.2016_(Patent NonObviousness).htm (accessed 12 March 2017).

> determine the obviousness of the subject matter to an ordinarily skilled person ex post, on the assumption that the art disclosed in the specification was known (see, e.g., Supreme Court Decisions 2006Hu138, 24 August 2007; 2007Hu3660, 12 November 2009).

According to the Guidelines the following assessment should be used:

> Step 1: identify the invention defined in the claims;
>
> Step 2: identify the prior art;
>
> Step 3: select the closest prior art; compare the claimed invention and the prior art; and clarifying the differences between the two;
>
> Step 4: assess whether arriving at the claimed invention, overcoming the above differences, from the prior art would have been easy to the person skilled in the art; while
>
> Step 5: taking the following three factors into account in the above assessment: motivation, exercise of ordinary creativity, advantageous effect.

[3] Assessment of Novelty

With reference to subject matter relating to known principles and algorithms that are applied to a new field or technology, it has to be mentioned that in case the only difference between claimed invention and state of the art lies in the content of data, such difference does not make the claimed invention novel.

[4] Scope of Protection for Non-literal Equivalents

Korean Courts recognize the doctrine of equivalents.

[5] Invalidation Actions

Anyone may file an invalidation action against an issued patent within a term of three months. For CII in particular, the action may *inter alia* be based on the grounds that the claims do not refer to an invention, do not comply with inventive step or novelty requirements, do not clearly and concisely define the invention, or are not supported by the specification, or where the specification does not describe the invention in a manner sufficiently clear and complete and in sufficient detail to render it apparent to the skilled person how to carry out the invention. The above-mentioned list is of course not exhaustive and an invalidation action may also be based on other grounds.

Generally, IP litigation is a bifurcated system in Korea.

[C] Claim Formats

According to the newly released Guidelines, the following claim categories are available in South Korea:

(1) method;
(2) apparatus/device;
(3) program recorded medium ('A computer-readable medium having a program recorded thereon for executing, by a computer, the steps A, B, C, etc.');
(4) data recorded medium ('A computer-readable medium having data recorded thereon having structures A, B, C, etc.');
(5) computer program ('A computer program stored on a medium for solving a specific task in combination with hardware'). This category will be deemed to be allowed for applications filed on or after 1 July 2014, the entry into force of the Guidelines. It should be noted that a claim relating to a computer program which is not stored on a medium is not allowed because such a claim is related to a program per se.

Claims relating to a program signal or a data signal are not allowed under the Korean Patent Act. Further, claims relating to pure business methods, mental or economic rules will probably be rejected.

[D] Guidelines for CII

On 1 July 2014, the KIPO published specific Guidelines for examination of software-related inventions. In these Guidelines the KIPO explains the matters that require special judgment and treatment for examination. Moreover, they state that software may also be claimed as a computer program (and not – as before – as a method or apparatus). However, as a first further requirement, the computer program has to be stored on a medium, and as a second further requirement it has to solve a specific problem in combination with hardware.

In general, the Guidelines say that for evaluating whether or not an invention meets the requirements for patentability, it is inadmissible to split the invention into parts and to evaluate them separately. Therefore, the whole combination of the elements of the CII has to be analysed and examined, *inter alia* with respect to utilizing the laws of nature.

The mere fact that a computer is used for implementation of the claimed method generally does not render the claimed method patent eligible. It has to be evaluated whether the claimed method solves a given problem with technical features and is based on the laws of nature.

Pure economic principles, artificial decisions, mathematic formulae, and/or mental activities are usually not judged to be a technical idea using the rules of nature.

Mere presentation of information where the technical feature resides solely in the content of the information and its main objective is to present the information is not considered a legitimate invention. However, if the technical feature resides in the presentation of information, the presenting per se, the means for presentation and the method of presentation, might be considered as a legitimate invention.

A computer program is a mere list of instructions to be executed on a computer. Therefore, a computer program is not considered a legitimate invention. However, in the case of an invention where data processing with a computer program is specifically executed using hardware, the invention is viewed as a legitimate invention.

In general, the inventiveness of an invention should be judged on whether the claimed invention could have been easily conceived by those skilled in the art in view of the cited reference(s). Combining different technologies usually will be judged to be non-inventive, provided that the combination does not involve any technical difficulties. A computer implementation of well-known phenomena or procedures that formerly have been executed by humans will usually be judged as non-inventive. Commercial success or its equivalent may be considered in determining inventive step, only if the examiner accepts the applicant's arguments and proof that such commercial success is not a result of marketing, advertising and so on, but a result of the characteristic features of the claimed inventions.

If the only difference between the claimed invention and the cited prior art lies in the contents of data, such difference does not make the claimed invention novel.

According to Article 42(4) of the Korean Paten Act the claims shall define the invention clearly and concisely and according to Article 42(3) the detailed description of the invention shall state the purpose, construction, and effect of the invention in such a manner that it may easily be carried out by a person having ordinary skill in the art to which the invention pertains.[5] In the Guidelines the following example is given for an indefinite description 'a computer for solving a puzzle with a right brain rule' without defining the right brain rule in the description.

Further, the Guidelines emphasize the necessity to define the meaning of technical terms which are neither generally used nor separately defined in the description. For software, it is not sufficient to mention modules or entities in the claims in a means plus function language without a concrete description how to implement the functions ('graphical user interface (GUI) for receiving input data' without concretely figuring out how to configure the GUI for reception of the input data).

Where claims include functional expressions describing the function or effect of an invention, but if the composition or structure of the invention is not deemed to be clear even with such descriptions, the claims cannot be allowed (refer to Supreme Court Case No. 97 Hu 1344, 18 October 1998).[6] However, cases where the structure of the invention is deemed to be clear even with functional expressions refer to:

- where expressing claims functionally is necessary since the technical idea of the invention cannot be clearly disclosed with only the existing technical structure (there are cases where the claims cannot be expressed with only the detailed description of the structure due to the characteristics of the technical field to which the concerned invention pertains such as business method related inventions or computer related inventions, etc.);

5. *See* Korean Patent Act, http://www.wipo.int/wipolex/en/text.jsp?file_id=128468 (accessed 28 March 2017).
6. At http://www.wipo.int/edocs/lexdocs/laws/en/kr/kr199en.pdf, 158 (accessed 13 March 2017).

- where the meaning of the functional expressions is clearly specified by the detailed description of the invention and in drawings (refer to Patent Court Case No. 2005 Heo 7354, this case was decided in 2006 and relates to a pharmaceutical injector).[7]

Where claims include functional expressions, the examiner shall determine whether the subject matter for which patent protection is sought is clearly understood from the perspective of a person skilled in the technical field to which the invention pertains considering the detailed description of the invention or the description in the drawings and the level of technology at the time of application filing. If deemed otherwise, the examiner shall notify grounds for rejection citing the violation of Article 42(4)(ii) of the Patent Act (refer to Supreme Court Case No. 2005 Hu 1486, 6 September 2007. The application relates to a tray for storing integrated circuits. The decisions dealt with the question how to interpret a functional claim language if specific embodiments are given in the description.).[8]

[E] Best Practice

In Korea, CII applications are subject to the same statutory patentability requirements that apply to patent applications in general (novelty, inventiveness and description requirements). There are no specific regulations for CII in the South Korean Patent Act.

Under the current examination practice in Korea, a software-related invention is patentable if hardware or other technical/apparatus limitations are included in the claim.

Practitioners in the field of CII are recommended to recite concrete technical means in the claim (e.g. server, memory, means for performing a specific function) and their interrelation or interaction. Further, care should be taken in order to exclude mental steps executed by humans (which corresponds to a former legal requirement in Germany but which no longer applies in Germany). Claims, therefore, should not involve human activities (as opposed to software processing). [9,10] A typical examiner's reasoning is that when a step is executed based on an artificial decision or the mental activity of a human, and the hardware or software components are simply recited as an instrument for human mental activity (and not as a specific means for realizing the invention), the invention is not deemed to be concretely realized through a cooperation of hardware and software and is not deemed to be patentable.

According to the examples given in the Guidelines, it seems to be easy to fulfil this requirement simply by adding computer nodes which are used to execute the respective method step.

7. At http://www.wipo.int/edocs/lexdocs/laws/en/kr/kr199en.pdf, 158 (accessed 13 March 2017).
8. At http://www.wipo.int/edocs/lexdocs/laws/en/kr/kr199en.pdf, 158 (accessed 13 March 2017).
9. At http://www.internationallawoffice.com/Newsletters/Intellectual-Property/South-Korea/Kim-Chang/Patent-protection-of-computer-program-inventions# (accessed 13 March 2017).
10. At http://www.iam-media.com/Magazine/Issue/80/Management-report/South-Korea (accessed 13 March 2017).

Therefore, Stephan T. Bang at Kim & Chang considers the eligibility test in South Korea as being 'lenient' as it focuses on more formal issues.[11]

Business methods are usually not patentable and may only be eligible for patent protection if they are claimed in combination with physical or hardware features.

[F] Summary

In general, the practice in Korea is similar to the European situation. Although there is no explicit technicality requirement as in Europe, there is indeed a reference to the field of technology in the definition of an invention (which is based on a technical idea).

In sum, according to the Korean Patent Act the following requirements are listed, which must be met from a practical point of view:

- existence of an 'invention' – Article 2.1 of the Patent Act;
- novelty – Article 29.1 of the Patent Act;
- inventive step – Article 29.2 of the Patent Act;
- industrial applicability – Article 29.1 of the Patent Act (relevant for medical inventions);
- enablement requirement – Article 42.3 of the Patent Act;
- sufficiency of disclosure – Article 42 of the Patent Act.

§10.02 LANDMARK DECISIONS

[A] Supreme Court Decision 2008 Hu 4998, Decided 19 August 2010 (Invalidity of Registration (Patent))[12]

This decision relates to the use of functional features and the assessment of inventive step, in particular of an invention which uses specific numerical values to express the scope of elements for a publicly known invention. Such a constellation might also exist for CII applications or may be transferred correspondingly.

The Court held that claims 1–17 of the patented invention entitled 'Electrodeless, Low- Pressure Light Source of High Brightness and Operation Method Thereof' could not be easily invented by a person skilled in the art using comparable inventions, thus satisfying the inventive step requirement. The appeal was dismissed.

In general, a claimed invention derived from experimental optimization of a numerical limitation is considered as an exercise of ordinary creativity. It may have inventive step if it secures remarkable advantageous effect in comparison with the prior art over the selected range. If the advantageous effect is of the same kind as in the prior art, a remarkable effect is required. In particular, in the case of a patented invention which uses specific numerical values to express the scope of claim features

11. At http://www.internationallawoffice.com/Newsletters/Intellectual-Property/South-Korea/Kim-Chang/Patent-protection-of-computer-program-inventions# (accessed 13 March 2017).
12. At http://library.scourt.go.kr/SCLIB_data/decision/6.Supreme%20Court%20Decision%202008Hu4998%20Decided%20August%2019.htm (accessed 13 March 2017).

for an invention already publicly known at the time of application, if there is a difference only in the numerical limitation while the object and functional effects of the patented invention are in line with those of publicly known inventions, and if no substantial difference in functional effect occurs within the limited numerical range, the patented invention lacks the requisite 'inventive step' since it is no more than a simple numerical limitation that a person having ordinary skill in the art can properly derive through ordinary and repetitive experimentation. However, if the numerical limitation has significance as a technical means for achieving an object other than that of the publicly known inventions and the functional effects are also different, the patented invention cannot be found to lack the requisite 'inventive step' merely because there is no critical significance in the numerical limitation.

Thus, the Supreme Court confirmed that if the numerical limitation is employed to solve a technical problem distinguished from that of the prior art and achieves a unique effect, the numerically limited invention can be deemed inventive even in the absence of any criticality shown at the boundary of the numerical limitation.

[B] Supreme Court Decision 2006 Hu 138, Decided 24 August 2007 (Invalidity of Registration)[13]

This decision relates to criteria for assessment of inventive step of an invention, relating to eavesdropping of data and to the legal question of whether it is permissible to determine inventive step based on commercial success.

The Supreme Court took up the clear position that inventive step cannot be recognized only based on commercial success itself (Supreme Court Ruling of 2004 HU 3546 (10 November 2005).

The Korean Examination Guidelines prohibit hindsight reasoning in determining inventive step of an invention and the Korean Supreme Court has clearly declared in this decision that hindsight reasoning should be prohibited in judgments on inventive step.

In order to determine whether to deny inventive step under Article 29(2) Patent Act, a check is required to determine whether the invention can be easily made, by the standards of an ordinary technician, from publicly known inventions at the time of the filing of the application of the invention, and such judgment shall not be made on the basis of whether an ordinary technician can easily make the invention after filing, on the grounds that he or she knows the technology disclosed in the specification of the invention subject to the determination of whether to deny its inventive step.

In determining whether to deny inventive step for a patent invention called a 'Device and Method to Process Emergency Calls Using Mobile Communications Networks' characterized by the 'controlling means that blocks the reception of receiving voice signals and only permits the transmission of the caller's voice by implementing the eavesdropping mode according to an emergency signal sent from

13. At http://library.scourt.go.kr/SCLIB_data/decision/4-58%20Supreme%20Court%20Decision%202006Hu138%20Decided%20August%2024.htm (accessed 13 March 2017).

emergency contacts', it is not permissible to determine that the patent invention can be easily made from the 'composition where a subscriber presses the emergency button on a terminal to record the sound of the situation' or the 'composition where a security centre receives a non-sound signal onto a terminal to record the sound of the situation' of the invention in comparison since it amounts to an ex post facto determination as to inventive step of invention on the basis of the knowledge of the contents disclosed by the specification of the above-mentioned patent invention.

The decision of the lower court was reversed, and the case remanded to the Patent Court.

The Reasons for Appeal are examined below (as for the supplementary Reasons for Appeal submitted after the relevant deadline, the examination is limited to those parts that complement the Reasons for Appeal).

According to the reasons provided in the lower court judgment, in determining inventive step of the claims by comparing the invention in this case (submitted 10 September 2001 and registered 31 March 2003 as No. 379,946) with the inventions 1 and 2 in the comparison cited in the judgment, the lower court divided the invention into the preamble and features 1 through 4. It determined that the preamble has no technological uniqueness in that it only illustrates the composition of an ordinary mobile communication terminal. It then determined that features 1 through 3 are easily derivable from inventions 1 and 2. The court acknowledged that component four characterized by 'controlling means that blocks the reception of receiving voice signals and only permits the transmission of the caller's voice by implementing the eavesdropping mode according to emergency signals sent from emergency contacts.' It then determined that implementing demonstration 1 of invention 1 in the comparison cited in the judgment is a case where a subscriber presses the emergency button on a Personal Handy-Phone System (PHS) terminal to record the sound of the situation, while implementing demonstration 2 is a case where a security centre receives a non-sound signal onto a PHS terminal to record the sound of the situation because the subscriber cannot operate the terminal for reasons such as not being present. As such, the court determined, implementing demonstration 1 is based as a matter of fact on the premise of the function that blocks the receiver's voice signals while the 'reception of non-sound signals' in implementing demonstration 2 means that when it is sent to a PHS terminal from a security centre, not only the calling sounds but also the receiver's voice signals are blocked, and component four of the invention is either identical or similar to the composition of implementing demonstration 2 of invention 1 in the comparison such that 'when a signal input from a security centre is distinguished as an order to be sent to a certain PHS terminal, it is sent to the designated PHS terminal to be received as a non-sound signal, and the PHS terminal gathers and transmits the sound from the surrounding situation so that the recording device at the security centre can record it,' so it is difficult to decide that it has technological uniqueness. Therefore, the court determined that the invention shall be denied inventive step with regard to inventions 1 and 2 cited in the judgment thereby failing to satisfy the independent patent requirements.

However, it is difficult to agree with the decision of the lower court for the following reasons.

According to the foregoing legal reasoning, and the record, the composition of invention 1 demonstrates the reception of a non-sound signal, but it is a matter of principle to interpret the terms of the specification with their ordinary meaning first. In this case the dictionary meaning of the reception of a signal is 'arrival of communication'. So, the reception of a non-sound signal means nothing more than 'arrival of communication with no sound.' Furthermore, invention 1 stipulates that it 'sends signals including an instruction to change the process of calling so that the call is made silently' and 'without the intervention or notice of a person' which means that the composition of invention 1 only demonstrates a composition to connect the conversation without the notice of other people by making a call soundless to avoid receiving signal sound and making a signal connected without separate human action such as pressing a button on the terminal in case the terminal cannot be operated for reasons such as the owner of the terminal being absent, and does not demonstrate a composition to send voice only to a security centre from a PHS while blocking the voice that is received on a PHS at the security centre. Therefore, it is difficult to deduce from the structure of invention 1, the demonstration of a controlling means performing the so-called eavesdropping mode which blocks the reception of the receiver's voice signals. The terminal only permits the transmission of the caller's voice when there is an emergency call from an emergency contact (upon an emergency call from the terminal owner). No data has been submitted regarding publicly known preceding inventions that imply an eavesdropping mode such as detailed above before the filing of the application of the patent invention in this case. In addition, in this case there is no evidence to acknowledge the circumstances that an ordinary technician must think of the above feature four from the above composition of invention 1 in comparison cited in the judgment below. Consequently, unless a judgment is made afterwards on the premise that an ordinary technician knows the contents disclosed by the specification of the patent application in this case, it shall not be deemed that he or she could easily produce the invention, which is not permitted.

Nevertheless, the lower court determined that the invention in paragraph 3 shall be denied its inventive step by inventions 1 and 2 in comparison mentioned in the judgment of the lower court, which affected the result of the judgment because it misapprehended the legal principles concerning inventive step of invention. As such, the argument in the Reasons for Appeal that points out the above is reasonable.

Therefore, with no need to determine the rest of the Reasons for Appeal, by the unanimous assent of all participating Judges, the judgment of the lower court is reversed and the case is remanded to the lower court for further deliberation and determination.

[C] Patent Court Decision, 2005 Heo 11094, Decided 21 December 2006 (Cyworld Case)[14]

For a business method invention, information processing by software on a computer should be particularly embodied using hardware, by using a particular information processing apparatus or operating process for the purposed utility via a specific inter-cooperative means.

Generally, a mere business method in itself is not regarded as patentable. Simple automation of a known business method using known automation techniques does not make it patentable, because it still lacks inventive step. However, novel business method inventions using automation systems having improved technical features may be patentable in South Korea.

Cyworld Co., Ltd. filed Korean Patent Application (No. 10-200221391) in 2002, entitled 'Method for Managing Mini-rooms for Use in Internet Community'. The KIPO examiner rejected the application because of ineligibility as the application did not specifically describe a method embodying the steps of creating and managing mini-rooms on a computer. The Intellectual Property Tribunal and Appeal Board (IPTAB) reviewed the case and decided to dismiss the appeal. They argued that the invention violates the main text of Article 29(1) of the Korean Patent Act because it does not utilize the laws of nature. In particular, a business method invention, using information technology or information processing by software on a computer should be claimed by using hardware (*see* Supreme Court Decision 2001Hu3149 rendered on 16 May 2003).

In this respect, reference should be made to the Patent Court Decision, 2000 Heo 5438, decided 21 September 2001 (Household Garbage Recycling Case).[15] The application relates to management of household garbage by using a barcode to be added to the garbage bag for selecting an appropriate garbage category and for preventing misallocation. The Court evaluated whether or not the application refers to a (technical) invention. According to this decision, a claim which does not use laws of nature, such as an artificial decision or agreement, a mathematical formula, or mental activities of a human being, does not fall within the scope of an invention under the Patent Act.

Thus, similar to the approach taken by the EPO, if the software is part of an otherwise patentable invention or if the software is combined with hardware or other technical features and the combination meets the requirements of patentability, a patent can be obtained for the invention in South Korea.

14. At http://ebook.scourt.go.kr/ebook/ebook_detail.asp?goods_id=100000346 (accessed 13 March 2017).
15. At http://ebook.scourt.go.kr/ebook/ebook_detail.asp?goods_id=100000346 (accessed 13 March 2017).

[D] Supreme Court Decision 2001 Hu 3149, Delivered on 16 May 2003 (Rejection Decision (Patent))[16]

This Supreme Court decision deals with the question of whether a patent application should be refused where the subject matter refers to a combination of hardware and software and does not involve rules of nature (in this case, this question was answered to the affirmative).

It was held that a patent application entitled the 'Total Management System for Recycling Household Garbage' is not an invention utilizing rules of nature.

It was held that the patent application cannot be viewed as an 'invention having intellectual applicability' as stipulated by Article 29(1) of the Patent Act on the grounds that it cannot be implemented by itself, considered as a whole, unless relevant regulations are provided; it does not utilize rules of nature as a mere man-made decision rendered by agreement among the pertinent authorities, garbage producers, and garbage collectors, or as a follow-up decision at the discretion of the above pertinent authorities; each step is performed off-line, not on-line on the internet; also, it cannot be viewed as belonging to the category of a business model since the system linking software and hardware is not yet specifically realized.

Article 2(1) of the Patent Act defines the term 'invention' as the highly advanced creation of technical ideas utilizing rules of nature. There are no grounds for regarding Article 2(1) as a mere instructive provision. Thus, in a case where a patent application is for an invention that does not utilize rules of nature, the application is refused pursuant to Article 62 of the Patent Act on the grounds that an invention does not satisfy the element of 'inventions having intellectual applicability,' under Article 29(1) of the Act (*see* Supreme Court Decision 98Hu744 delivered on 4 September 1998).

The lower court decided that the invention set forth in the patent application cannot be viewed as 'inventions having intellectual applicability' as stipulated by Article 29(1) of the Patent Act, on the following grounds. Each procedural step comprising the plaintiff's invention entitled 'Total Management System for Recycling Household Garbage' cannot be viewed as utilizing rules of nature. Although the invention as a whole includes hardware and software means such as bar code stickers, calendar papers, garbage bags and bar code decoding, each of said means does not contain any specific way of combining the above-mentioned hardware and software; rather, they involve human mental activities using those means as instruments.

In light of the record and the legal principles set out above, the lower court's acknowledgment and judgment are justified, and there were no errors of misinterpretation of the legal principles with regard to Articles 2(1), 29(1) and 62 of the Patent Act, as asserted in the grounds for appeal.

Therefore, the appeal was dismissed, and all costs of the appeal were assessed against the losing party. This is per the disposition by the assent of all Judges who reviewed the appeal.

---

16. At http://library.scourt.go.kr/SCLIB_data/decision/2-32%20Supreme%20Court%20Decision%202001Hu3149%20Delivered%20on%20May%2016.htm (accessed 13 March 2017).

In this respect, reference should be made to an older appeal decision relating to business methods, in particular to the court decision dated 18 December 2002.[17] The application refers to a client-server based tele-education system with two independent claims and dependent claims which claim a tele-education method and its apparatus. Jinbo Network took legal proceedings against the proprietor Samsung to invalidate the patent arguing that the invention has no statutory subject matter, because the invention is purely based on artificial agreements among people and mental activity, and thus it does not utilize any laws of nature. The Industrial Property Tribunal (lower instance) recognized the invention as utilizing laws of nature. However, the Court decided that the invention has no inventive step.

17. At http://s-space.snu.ac.kr/bitstream/10371/85074/1/4.%20Business%20Method%20Patents%20in%20Korea.pdf (accessed 13 March 2017).

CHAPTER 11

Japan

§11.01 LEGAL REQUIREMENTS

[A] Patent Act

The fundamental requirements for patents are defined in the Patent Act of 1959.[1] The Patent Act has been revised several times. The latest version incorporates amendments up to Act No. 55 of 10 July 2015, which came into force on 1 April 2016. In this book the explanations of legal requirements are based on the English translation. The text in Japanese takes precedence over the English translations. Article 2 of the Patent Act explains the invention:

> Article 2
> (1) 'Invention' in this Act means the highly advanced creation of technical ideas utilizing the laws of nature.
> (2) 'Patented invention' in this Act means an invention for which a patent has been granted.
> (3) 'Working' of an invention in this Act means the following acts:
>   (i) in the case of an invention of a product (including a computer program, etc., the same shall apply hereinafter), producing, using, assigning, etc. (assigning and leasing and, in the case where the product is a computer program, etc., including providing through an electric telecommunication line, the same shall apply hereinafter), exporting or importing, or offering for assignment, etc. (including displaying for the purpose of assignment, etc., the same shall apply hereinafter) thereof;
>   (ii) in the case of an invention of a process, the use thereof; and
>   (iii) in the case of an invention of a process for producing a product, in addition to the action as provided in the preceding item, acts of using, assigning, etc., exporting or importing, or offering for assignment, etc. the product produced by the process.

1. WIPO *Patent Act Japan (Act No. 121 of 1959)* unofficial English translation http://www.wipo.int/edocs/lexdocs/laws/en/jp/jp206en.pdf (accessed 4 April 2017).

(4) A 'computer program, etc.' in this Act means a computer program (a set of instructions given to an electronic computer which are combined in order to produce a specific result, hereinafter the same shall apply in this paragraph) and any other information that is to be processed by an electronic computer equivalent to a computer program.

[B] Guidelines and Handbook

Reference is made to the 'Examination Guidelines for Patent and Utility Model in Japan' ('Examination Guidelines' that came into force on 1 October 2015.[2] There is also an 'Examination Handbook for Patent and Utility Model in Japan' ('Examination Handbook' - without a date in the English version).[3] The Examination Guidelines provide a summary of the application of the law such as the Patent Act. The Examination Handbook gives guidance for examination. The application of law is explained based on several examples and court precedents. The relationship between the Examination Guidelines and the Examination Handbook is explained in the 'Outline of the Examination Guidelines for Patent and Utility Model'.[4]

A new document 'Case examples pertinent to IoT related technology, etc.' (added to the webpage in March 2017) relates to new technologies. Examples are provided for inventions in the area of Internet of Things (IoT), artificial intelligence (AI) and 3D-printing. The document complements examples given in the Examination Guidelines and in the Examination Handbook.

The JPO website indicates a document 'Policies on business method patents' last updated 30 November 2000. It seems that there are currently no further specific activities relating to that document.

The Examination Guidelines (1 October 2015) indicate in Part III, Chapter 1, section 2.1 the list of subject matter not corresponding to statutory 'inventions':

'(i) A law of nature as such';
'(ii) Mere discoveries and not creations';
'(iii) Those contrary to a law of nature';
'(iv) Those in which a law of nature is not utilized ';
'(v) Those not regarded as technical ideas';
'(vi) Those for which it is clearly impossible to solve the problem to be solved by any means presented in a claim'.

A 'law of nature as such' does not constitute statutory subject matter. A claimed invention is not deemed to utilize a 'law of nature' if it is directed to:

(i) Any laws other than a law of nature (e.g. economic laws)

2. Japan Patent Office (JPO) *Examination Guidelines for Patent and Utility Model in Japan* http://www.jpo.go.jp/tetuzuki_e/t_tokkyo_e/1312-002_e.htm (accessed 11 April 2017).
3. JPO *Examination Handbook for Patent and Utility Model in Japan* http://www.jpo.go.jp/tetuzuki_e/t_tokkyo_e/handbook_sinsa_e.htm (accessed 11 April 2017).
4. JPO, *Outline of the Examination Guidelines for Patent and Utility Model* 2016.05 http://www.jpo.go.jp/tetuzuki_e/t_tokkyo_e/pdf/outline_guideline_patents/outline.pdf (accessed 13 April 2017).

(ii) Arbitrary arrangements (e.g. a rule for playing a game as such)
(iii) Mathematical formula
(iv) Mental activities of humans
(v) Those utilizing only (i) to (iv) (e.g. methods for doing business as such).

Examples are provided for the respective topics. Furthermore, the Examination Guidelines relate to claimed subject matter that can be a mixture of parts utilizing a law of nature or not utilizing a law of nature. In such a situation, the 'claim as a whole' has to be evaluated. An invention can be judged as an invention which uses a law of nature or not. Finally, it reads: 'The characteristic of the technology is to be considered in judging whether a claimed invention as a whole utilizes a law of nature.'

The Examination Guidelines (1 October 2015) Part II, Chapter 1, Section 2 state that an invention is 'a creation of a technical idea'. The invention should show the technical significance of the invention compared to the prior art. The technical problem which is solved should be indicated. Here one can see some similarity to the understanding of an invention in Europe. In contrast, the indication of advantageous effects over prior art are not necessarily required but can support the explanation of the invention.

The Examination Handbook, Annex B has three chapters about 'Application examples of the specific technical fields': 'Computer Software related Inventions', 'Biological Inventions' and 'Medicinal Inventions'. Examples relating to computer programs or software will be explained later in Chapter 11, §11.04 Guidelines for Computer Implemented Invention (CII).

§11.02 PROCEDURAL AND FORMAL ASPECTS

Information on intellectual property (law, guidelines, decisions) is published in Japanese on the JPO and Intellectual Property High Court (IPHC) websites, as well as an ever-increasing amount of information in English and some other languages. However, the documents in Japanese language are decisive for legal procedures.

Prior art searches are outsourced by the JPO. After the submission of a patent application, a search organization can be selected from the ones that are registered at the JPO.[5]

The Japanese patent system has developed a special patent classification based on the International Patent Classification (IPC). A special search system had already been developed in the 1980s, that is the FI/F-term system (FI – file index).[6] This system allows an improved electronic search. A major advantage is that one can create 'multiple viewpoints' in a search and cover several IPC sub groups in an efficient way. This is advantageous for covering technologies that might appear in many IPC sub groups.

5. JPO *Applicants can obtain high quality search reports before publication* http://www.jpo.go.jp/tetuzuki_e/t_tokkyo_e/touroku_chousa_e.htm (accessed 10 April 2017).
6. JPO *Outline of FI/F-term* http://passthrough.fw-notify.net/download/874359/http://www.jpo.go.jp/torikumi_e/searchportal_e/pdf/classification/fi_f-term.pdf (accessed 10 April 2017).

§11.03 CLAIM FORMATS

Article 2(3) of the Patent Act shows different ways in which an invention could work: the invention could be a product (including computer programs), a process or a process for producing a product.

The Examination Guidelines (Part II, Chapter 1, Section 1) indicate a few specific types of process in the context of enablement: a method for using a product, a measurement method, and a controlling method, etc. The same holds for a process for producing a product: a method for manufacturing a product, a method for assembling a product, and a method for processing a product, etc. Furthermore: 'Any of these methods consists of three factors of (i) a starting material, (ii) process steps therefor, and (iii) a final product'. Special claim formulations like Markush type claims might exist, in chemistry for example.

The Examination Guidelines (Part II, Chapter 2) are about 'Requirements for Claims'. Section 1 (3) reads: 'The technical scope of the patented invention is determined based on the statement of the claim (Article 70(1)), and that the subject of the examination is the invention identified based on the statement of the claim'.

The category of software-related inventions is explained in the Examination Handbook, Annex B, Chapter 1.[7] Primarily a software-related invention can be claimed as a product or as a method. A product is characterized by the function which results from the software. Different claim formulations are allowed for a program and related digital information:

- 'Program for causing a computer to execute a step A, a step B, a step C, ...'.
- 'A program for causing a computer to function as means A, means B, means C, ...'.
- 'Structured data including a data element A, a data element B, a data element C, ...'.
- 'A data structure including a data element A, a data element B, a data element C,...'.

Claims for a computer readable recording medium can focus on a program or on structured data. They are considered as an invention of a product. Signal claims that might be directed to the transmission of a program and/or data over a wireless connection are not mentioned.

The claim formulation should make clear whether the claim is a product or a method claim. It is not necessary to include 'program' in the claim. If a claim for a software-related invention uses terms 'for example "module", "library", "neural network", "support vector machine" or "model"', such terms should be interpreted in the context of software.

7. JPO, *Examination Handbook, Annex B, Chapter 1 Computer Software Related Inventions* http://www.jpo.go.jp/tetuzuki_e/t_tokkyo_e/files_handbook_sinsa_e/app_b1_e.pdf (accessed 13 April 2017).

The following claim lacks clarity. It does not indicate whether it relates to a product or to a method:

> A program signal array for causing a computer to execute a step A, a step B, a step C.

A huge variety of claim formulations is available for the formulation of software-related inventions.

§11.04 GUIDELINES FOR CII

The JPO had already developed guidelines for computer software-related inventions in the 1990s. The Examination Guidelines valid until 30 September 2015 included Part VII with three guidelines for computer software-related inventions, for biological inventions and for medical inventions. Now, respective parts have been transferred to the Examination Handbook which gives plenty of examples in all three areas. The Examination Guidelines comprise some general examples relating to computer software.

[A] Examination Guidelines

Section 2.1 (Subject Matter not Corresponding to Statutory 'Inventions') relates in part to inventions relating to computing.

Inventions are non-statutory if **a law of nature is not utilized**. This is the case for computer programming languages. A claim can be regarded as non-statutory even if it indicates a computer or means which implicitly relate to software.

This is the case for a method of playing 'shogi' (Japanese chess) which uses the technical means of a 'chat system' to allow the transmission of a move to another player. It is not an invention according to the Patent Act despite the 'chat system'.

A method for playing a game (playing cards) in which a computer draws marks and the winner is determined based on the cards which have marks drawn on them is not an invention according to the Patent Act despite the technical means 'computer' in the claim.

Inventions which are **not regarded as technical ideas**. This can be the case for mere presentation of information and aesthetic creations. Computer software-related examples are only provided for presentation of information.

In the context of presentation of information, the following is seen as non-statutory subject matter:

- 'An image taken with a digital camera'.
- 'A program of an athletic meeting made by a word processor'.
- 'A computer program list (mere representation of computer programs by means of printing them on paper, displaying them on a screen, etc.)'.

Mere presentation of information does not exist if a technical feature resides in presentation of information. This is the case in the following example since 'A technical feature resides in the pattern per se':

> A test pattern for use in checking the performance of a television set.

The example does not indicate whether it relates to digital computing technology. However, it is assumed that the test pattern could represent a kind of digital test pattern.

Section 2.2. (Points to consider in examination of an invention utilizing computer software) provides some general explanations on software-related inventions.

It becomes clear that software can be used as a means to implement an invention for topics which do or do not correspond to statutory 'inventions'. For software used as a means to implement non-statutory topics the guidelines explain in paragraph (1):

> (1) For inventions relating to a method for doing business, playing a game or calculating a mathematical formula, since there are cases in which the claimed invention a part of which utilizes an article, apparatus, device, system, computer software, etc., is judged as not utilizing a law of nature when considered as a whole, whether they are 'creation of a technical idea utilizing a law of nature' shall be carefully examined.
>
> On the other hand, there is possibility for an invention to be considered as a 'creation of a technical idea utilizing a law of nature' where the invention is made having an intention of utilizing computer software such as software used in doing business, in playing a game or in calculating a mathematical formula as a whole, even though the invention is made related to a method for doing business, playing a game or calculating a mathematical formula.
>
> An examiner shall examine whether such an invention is to be considered as a 'creation of a technical idea utilizing a law of nature' from a viewpoint of computer software. On the whole.

Paragraph (2) is about inventions that are in the normal realm of statutory subject matter and that are implemented as software:

> (2) Those utilizing a law of nature as a whole and being considered as a 'creation of a technical idea utilizing a law of nature' irrespective of whether computer software is utilized (e.g., (i) or (ii) shown below) constitute a statutory 'invention' without being examined from a viewpoint of computer software.
>
> Computer software for causing a computer to execute a method, which is a 'creation of a technical idea utilizing a law of nature' and thus constitutes a statutory 'invention', or a computer or system for executing such method is normally a creation of a technical idea utilizing a law of nature as a whole, and thus, it constitutes a statutory 'invention'.
>
> (i) Those concretely performing control of an apparatus (e.g., rice cooker, washing machine, engine, hard disk drive, chemical reaction apparatus, nucleic acid amplifier), or processing with respect to the control
>
> (b) Those concretely performing information processing based on the technical properties such as physical, chemical, biological or electric properties of an object (e.g., rotation rate of engine, rolling temperature, relation between gene sequence

and expression of a trait in a living body, physical or chemical relation of bound substances).

The view expressed in Parts (1) and (2) of Section 2.2 seems to be similar to European practice. It is usually not a problem when an invention from a traditional technical area is implemented by software (Part (2)). If the invention implemented by software results from a traditional non-technical area (business, games, mathematics as such) the examiner has to carefully examine the invention as to whether the invention is an invention within the patent law under the requirements of Article 2(1) Patent Act.

[B] Examination Handbook, Annex B, Computer Software Related Inventions

The Chapter on 'Computer Software Related Inventions' provides detailed information relevant to computer software-related inventions. Examples of computer software-related inventions can also be found in other sections of the Examination Handbook e.g. under inventive step. The possible claim formulations have already been explained in §11.03 of this chapter.

A few general examples are indicated in the Examination Guidelines. The Chapter on 'Computer Software Related Inventions' starts with general explanations. The major part gives detailed examples. The claims, the description, prior art and the respective explanations are provided. The overview is as follows:

- Cases 1-1 to 1-2 are about clarity requirements for claims on storage or transmission medium.
- Cases 2-1 to 2-15 are about eligibility (mathematics, business, games, data structures, autonomous vehicle, training model (neural network), 3D printing).
- Cases 3-1 to 3-5 are about determination of inventive step (searching chemical material, business, data structure, 3D printing).

The **enablement** requirement is important for software-related inventions. Even if the claim indicates technical procedures or functions, the person skilled in the art has to be enabled to carry out the invention. It has to be shown how a technical procedure or function is implemented by means of hardware or software. Enablement is not satisfied for a claim with 'a step of operating a computer based on a display screen of a computer' for example, if the person skilled in the art with common knowledge does not know how 'operating' is implemented.

The enablement criteria might not be satisfied if the claim indicates functions or means defined just by a function of the claimed invention (e.g. 'calculation means configured to calculate …') that are only described by flow charts or functional block diagrams in the description. The skilled person cannot recognize how a function is really implemented.

The determination of **eligibility for patent protection** is a crucial topic. If the claimed subject matter relates to a 'creation of a technical idea utilizing a law of nature' irrespective of an implementation in software, the examiner will follow the normal examination procedures. Such areas relate to the control of machines and technical devices such as a rice cooker, the control of chemical reactions or information processing on 'technical properties such as physical, chemical, biological or electric properties of an object'.

If the claimed subject matter of a software-related invention does not relate to a 'creation of a technical idea utilizing a law of nature' as indicated earlier in this Chapter in §11.01, [B] a careful examination has to take place. It has to be determined whether the claimed subject matter as a whole does not utilize a law of nature. This is the case if the invention relates to economic laws, mental acts, mathematical formulas, methods of doing business, aesthetic creations and presentation of information for example. Examples for claimed subject matter outside the patent law have already been indicated in §11.01, [B] of this Chapter.

If the examiner cannot determine whether the claimed software-related invention falls under the 'creation of a technical idea utilizing a law of nature', the examiner will evaluate the invention as being software. The indication of hardware resources in a claim can be an indication for eligibility but not under all circumstances. No eligibility for patent protection is given in the following example:

> A computer comprising input means configured to input document data, processing means configured to process the inputted document data, and output means configured to output the processed document data, the computer for creating a summary of the document inputted by the processing means.

The processing of information by the software does not show a specific implementation for using the hardware resource. It is not an invention in the sense of the Patent Act despite 'computer'.

In general, a claim with generic hardware elements in combination with elements outside of a 'creation of a technical idea utilizing a law of nature' does not immediately result in eligibility for patent protection as at the European Patent Office (EPO). Here, the legal practice seems to follow the legal practice of the US. It reads:

> Even if the claims state such hardware resources as a 'computer (information processor), a 'CPU (calculation means)', or a 'memory (storage means)', the examiner should note that the claimed invention is not 'creation of a technical idea utilizing a law of nature' unless the claims state specific means or a specific procedure for implementing specific calculation or processing of information depending on intended use on which software and hardware resources cooperate'.
>
> This is because with a simple statement of hardware resources, it cannot be stated that a specific information processor or an operation method thereof depending on an intended use has been constructed through co-operation of software and the hardware resources, and that information processing by the software has been specifically implemented by using the hardware resources.

In the case of business methods the examiner should not look primarily at the business method but 'on whether or not information processing by software that said business-related invention utilizes is specifically implemented by using hardware resources'.

The determination of **novelty and inventive step** in the area of software-related inventions takes into account the fact that, for the person skilled in the art, the technologies of several areas are sometimes combined without any difficulty. Special circumstances might exist which result in a specific technical effect and justify an inventive step.

The Examination Handbook points out that there are **general issues common to computer technology.** This shows that there is an awareness of core computer science concepts that are sometimes not known to scientists in other fields. The Examination Handbook explains that the examiner should pay attention to the fact that 'Issues involved in software or computerization are often general issues common to computer technologies'. For example, they include 'sophistication of a determination through AI or fuzzy logic', 'facilitation of input through GUI' or the like. In this case 'The examiner shall make a determination on inventive step based on these general issues that have been known in the field of computer technology.'

The use of general computing procedures results in **general effects** that are foreseeable by the skilled person. Such effects are '"capable of processing fast," "capable of processing volume of data," "capable of reducing errors," "obtaining uniform results,"'.

Here, it is acknowledged that fundamental computing procedures are valid for a huge area of applications in different fields of technology. The same general effects are achieved without any inventive step.

The Examination Handbook indicates several examples in detail. Not inventive is usually:

- The use of a general principle of software in a specific field (a general file system used in a medical application).
- The use of well-known means or well-known equivalent means (adding input by a mouse to input over keyboard).
- A function implemented by hardware is implemented by software.
- Replacement of business functions by a newer technology (replacing an order by fax or phone by an order over Internet; replacement of trade information in a paper magazine by information on a webpage).
- Reproduction of a publicly known event in a computer virtual space.
- Design change based on a publicly known fact or custom (indication of an additional information on a screen 'Thank you for your purchase' after the purchase).

Inventive step is usually denied when the difference between the claimed subject matter and the prior art consists only in the content of data (e.g. 'computer readable recording medium in which music C' having a data structure B is recorded, is stored ...). The same is true if the claimed invention is only characterized by a function specific to a medium. The commercial success of a software implemented business method cannot be the basis for inventive step.

[C] Case Examples Pertinent to IoT, AI and 3D-Printing

The specific document with examples relating to the IoT, AI and 3D-printing gives an impression of how examination is done in modern software- related fields.[8] The document refers in part to examples given in other parts of the Examination Guidelines.

IoT means that former autonomous systems are connected over networks to remote processing means. New and more sensors can be used and allow the collection of huge amounts of data. Complex systems are usually the result. AI is very often based on neural network learning. 3D-printing (three-dimensional printing) requires prefabricated data representing the three-dimensional properties of an object. Based on this data objects can be created in a process similar to a former two-dimensional printing process.

In the following short example per IoT, AI and 3D-printing is indicated with respect to eligibility for patent protection. More details are given in the document on the case examples.

IoT and AI can be combined. Claim formulation has to be at a level of detail that is sufficient to consider the claimed subject matter as an invention according to the Patent Act.

Example 1 (IoT and AI)

[Claim 1] Does not fall under 'invention':

> Sugar content data of preharvest apples on trees measured by a portable sugar content sensor for apples which performs reflective near-infrared spectroscopic analyses.

[Claim 2] Does not fall under 'invention':

> The sugar content data of apples as described in Claim 1 received by a receiving unit of a server and stored in a memory unit of the said server.

[Claim 3] Falls under 'invention':

> A method for predicting sugar content data of apples comprising;
>
> a step in which an analysing unit of the server analyses the relationship between sugar content data of preharvest apples for specified periods and data on meteorological conditions, and sugar content data of apples at the time of their shipping, based on past performance;
>
> a step in which the receiving unit of the said server receives the sugar content data of apples for specified periods as described in Claim 1; and
>
> a step in which a prediction unit of the said server predicts and outputs sugar content data of apples at the time of future shipping using the said received sugar content data of apples for specified periods and data on past and future meteorological conditions as inputs, based on the said analysed relationships.

---

8. JPO *Case examples pertinent to IoT*, etc. *related technology* http://www.jpo.go.jp/tetuzuki_e/t_tokkyo_e/files_handbook_sinsa_e/app_z_e.pdf (accessed 19 April 2017).

Claims 1 and 2 are evaluated as 'mere presentation of information'. This holds true for claim 2 despite 'memory' and 'server'. Claim 3 is eligible. Computer software is used to predicting the sugar content data of apples. The description indicates that the prediction is done by machine learning based on deep learning with neural networks.

Example 2 (AI):

> *A trained model* for causing a computer to function to output quantified values of reputations of accommodations based on text data on reputations of accommodations, wherein; the model is comprised of a first neural network and a second neural network connected in a way that the said second neural network receives output from the said first neural network;
>
> the said first neural network is comprised of an input layer to intermediate layers of a feature extraction neural network in which the number of neurons of at least one intermediate layer is smaller than the number of neurons of the input layer, the number of neurons of the input layer and the number of the output layer are the same, and weights were trained in a way each value input to the input layer and each corresponding value output from output layer become equal;
>
> weights of the said second neural network were trained without changing the weights of the said first neural network; and
>
> *the model causes the computer function to perform a calculation based on the said trained weights in the said first and second neural networks in response to appearance frequency of specific words obtained from the text data on reputations of accommodations input to the input layer of the said first neural network and to output the quantified values of reputations of accommodations from the output layer of the said second neural network.*

The claim is patent eligible even if the claim starts with 'A trained model'. It falls under an 'invention' as a 'program' despite 'model'. The description provides details of information processing. The 'information processing by software is specifically implemented by using hardware resources, the trained model of Claim 1 is a creation of the technical idea utilizing a law of nature and thus falls under "invention"'.

Example 3 (3D printing):

> *3D printing data* used in a 3D printer which laminates model materials that finally constitute a 3D-modeled object and supporting materials that support the said model materials during modeling, wherein the 3D printing data has a structure comprising in each layer of the said 3D-modeled object:
>
> model material data indicating the quantity and position of dispensation of the said model materials;
>
> *a model material* pointer that points to data used for the following modeling of modeling based on the said model material data;
>
> supporting material data indicating the quantity and position of dispensation of the said supporting materials; and
>
> *a supporting material pointer that points to data used for the following modeling of modeling based on the said supporting material data;*

> wherein (a) the model material pointer is set (a1) to point to the supporting material data of the lowermost layer that is not modeled at the time when modeling of the model material of the layer in which the modeling material pointer is included completed,
>
> ...
>
> *wherein the 3D printing data is used by a control unit of the said 3D printer for processing to acquire the model material data or the supporting material data from a memory unit of the said 3D printer in accordance with the said model material pointer or the supporting material pointer after the modeling based on the said model material data or the supporting material data.*

This very long claim is an invention under the Patent Act. Other examples relate to robot technologies, drones and autonomous vehicles. The examples are a valuable source of information to understand examination in the fields of new technologies.

§11.05 HISTORICAL OVERVIEW

[A] General Development

The Japanese patent system has a long tradition. It was influenced by the German patent system and later by the US patent system.[9] As a result it has traditions both of common law and of civil law. Like in other countries, the intellectual property law was repeatedly amended following economic and technological developments. Major developments during the 1990s and the beginning of the twenty first century are pointed out in the article by Takenaka in 'Success or Failure? Japan's National Strategy on Intellectual Property and Evaluation of Its Impact from the Comparative Law Perspective'.[10]

The JPO is the organization which is responsible for the fundamental legal work on patents, utility models, designs and trademarks.[11] It is a governmental agency under the Ministry of Economy, Trade and Industry. There is both a trial and appeal department at the JPO.[12] Appeals can be submitted against the decision of examiners to refuse a patent application. A request for the invalidation of a patent can only be filed by interested persons even after the end of a patent's term. Third parties can oppose patents within six months of the publication date of the Gazette containing the patent.

The JPO participates in a Trilateral Co-operation (JPO, EPO, USPTO) which was set up in 1983.[13] Comparative studies on the examination of inventions in the fields of

9. Takenaka, T. et al. *Intellectual Property in Common Law and Civil Law* Edward Elgar 2013.
10. Takenaka, T. *Success or Failure? Japan's National Strategy on Intellectual Property and Evaluation of Its Impact from the Comparative Law Perspective,* 8 Wash. U. GlobalStud. L. Rev. 379 (2009). At http://openscholarship.wustl.edu/law_globalstudies/vol8/iss2/14 (accessed 6 April 2017).
11. JPO http://www.jpo.go.jp/ (accessed 10 April 2017).
12. JPO *Questions and Answers about Trial and Appeal System* http://www.jpo.go.jp/torikumi_e/t_torikumi_e/appeal_trial_qanda.htm (accessed 7 April 2017).
13. *Trilateral European Patent Office, Japan Patent Office, United States Patent and Trademark Office* http://www.trilateral.net/index.html (accessed 7 April 2017).

business methods and software were done in the 1990s. The result of that early comparative study on hypothetical inventions in the area of software can be found on the JPO website.[14] The co-operation of five patent offices began in 2008 - IP5 co-operation[15] when the Korean Intellectual Property Office (KIPO) and the State Intellectual Property Office of the People's Republic of China (SIPO) joined the trilateral group.

The protection of computer programs by copyright was introduced in 1986 by the amendment of the copyright law of 1970.[16] Article 10 (3) of the copyright law indicates that programming languages, rules for the use of a programming language and algorithms (methods of combining, in a program, instructions given to a computer) are not protected under copyright.

In 2002, Prime Minister Junichiro Koizumi's speech became the starting point to transform Japan into an 'IP-based nation'.[17] Several actions were taken to achieve this aim. Intellectual Property Headquarters were created as an organ of the Prime Minister and his Cabinet. The 'Headquarters' create annual Intellectual Property Promotion Plans which focus on the particularly relevant parts of intellectual property protection like copyright, patents, trademarks. Furthermore, the actions of ministries and agencies are regularly monitored.

Following the amendment of the Code of Civil Procedure in 2003, an IPHC was established in 2005.[18] The aim was more harmonized legal practice. The IPHC is a branch of the Tokyo High Court with own administrative power. Tokyo District Court and Osaka District Court are 'courts of first instance to have exclusive jurisdiction over lawsuits relating to technical intellectual properties, patent rights ..., as well as lawsuits relating to computer program copyrights'.[19] The Tokyo High Court is the court for infringement cases and for lawsuits on revocations made by the JPO. The number of suits against Appeal/Trial decisions was halved between 2005 and 2015.[20] The Supreme Court of Japan is the Court of final instance.

The JPO Status Report 2017 shows that the Fourth Industrial Revolution with new technological developments like IoT or AI is being taken into consideration to

14. *Report on Comparative Study Carried Out under Trilateral Project 24.2* http://www.jpo.go.jp/shiryou_e/toushin_e/kenkyukai_e/repo242.htm#repo1.2 (accessed 7 April 2017).
15. *Five IP offices – IP5 co-operation* http://www.fiveipoffices.org/about.html (accessed 7 April 2017).
16. Karjala, D. *Japanese Courts Interpret the 'Algorithm' Limitation on the Copyright Protection of Programs* 1990 https://www.researchgate.net/publication/228171993_Japanese_Courts_Interpret_the_%27Algorithm%27_Limitation_on_the_Copyright_Protection_of_Programs (accessed 6 April 2017).
17. *ID.* art. II. A.
18. Japan, *Intellectual Property High Court History* http://www.ip.courts.go.jp/eng/aboutus/history/index.html (accessed 6 April 2017).
19. Tamura, Y. *IP-based nation: Strategy of Japan* in 'Emerging Markets and the World Patent Order' edited by Abbott, F. M. et al, Edward Elgar, 2015.
20. IPHC *Number of Suits against Appeal/Trial Decisions made by the JPO Commenced and Disposed, and Average Time Intervals from Commencement to Disposition* http://www.ip.courts.go.jp/eng/documents/statistics/stat_02/index.html (accessed 13 April 2017).

further develop the system for protecting intellectual property.[21] Special actions are planned to improve the search in IoT areas and for search of non-patent literatures relating to computer software technologies.

[B] The 'Ichitaro' Decision

The **'Ichitaro' decision** (Tokyo High Court / Case H17 (Ne) 10040 (30 September 2005(H17)) is regarded as the first decision of the IPHC. It was famous not only because it was the first decision but also because it was a decision about software for text processing.[22] A patent (priority 1989) was granted to Matsushita in 1998. Simplified, the patent was about a graphical user interface that displayed functional descriptions of icons according to user selections. Matsushita filed an infringement lawsuit at the Tokyo District Court alleging that the company Justsystem Corporation infringed Matsushita's patent. Justsystem produced and sold the text processing software 'Ichitaro' and the graphic software 'Hanako'. The Tokyo District Court decided that a computer with the software of Justsystem infringed the patent indirectly. As a result, Justsystem was sued for injunctive relief and the court ordered the destruction of the software products 'Ichitaro' and 'Hanako'. Justsystem appealed the decision.

IPHC concluded that there was an indirect infringement of claims 1 and 2. No indirect infringement was seen for method claim 3. IPHC decided that Matsushitas patent was obvious in the light of prior art. The patent was to be invalidated according to invalidation procedures at the JPO. As a result, Matsushita was not allowed to exercise its patent right according to Article 104, Paragraph 1 of the Patent Act.

The IPHC demonstrated that software patents could be dealt with like 'normal' patents under the criteria of novelty and inventive step.

§11.06 CURRENT EXAMINATION PRACTICE

General practice has some facets of European and of US practice. The requirement of a technical idea using the law of nature seems to result to a certain degree from Europe (technical idea) and to a certain degree from Germany ('use of laws of nature' corresponds to 'Einsatz beherrschbarer Naturkräfte', cf. Germany, Chapter 5). Laws of nature as such are not patent eligible like in many other countries (cf. law of nature in the US, Chapter 8).

The proliferation of software technology over nearly all other technologies has resulted in the use of software not just in traditional technological areas that were previously the traditional areas of the patent system (physics, chemistry, electrical engineering ...), but also in areas of the social sciences. If processes and functions of

21. *JPO Status Report 2017* http://www.jpo.go.jp/english/reference_room/statusreport/status2017_e.htm (accessed 13 April 2017).
22. Beyerlein, T. *Die ‚Ichitaro ‚-Entscheidung des Obergerichtes für geistiges Eigentum (2005(Ne) 10040)* ZJapanR / J.Japan.L. 23 (2007) 241–245.

objects of such traditional areas are implemented by software, eligibility is usually no problem. Substantive examination is executed according to the normal requirements of novelty, inventive step and other requirements. Patent applications relating to core areas of computing (e.g. memory allocation, distributed computing, parallel processing) are treated in the usual way. They are not seen as a 'computer program as such'.

If software is used in areas that did not traditionally belong to core areas of the patent system (e.g. mental act, business method) of several countries, eligibility can become critical. The examiner has to evaluate the claim as a whole taking into account technology. A broad claim with a combination of non-technical topics (e.g. business method) with well-known general computer features might run the risk of not being eligible for patent protection. This holds true despite some features of a computer (e.g. processor, memory, server) in the claim. Here, the legal practice is similar to US practice. Exclusion from patentability can only be avoided if such a claim indicates the interaction of the software with the hardware on a level of detail that really shows the inventive features.

§11.07 SUMMARY AND BEST PRACTICES

The Japanese patent system provides several ways to protect inventions related to software (system software and application software) and digital data. Since it is accepted that an invention is a 'technical idea', limitations exist if software relates to non-technical ideas (e.g. business, games, presentation of information).

The Examination Guidelines and the Examination Handbook explain some fundamental terms of computing. This seems to reduce some confusion in the interpretation of software-related inventions and computer programs. The Examination Handbook states that, in the context of novelty and inventive step, there are general procedures and principles of computing including software that are usually applicable to several areas of technology without any inventive step. This clearly shows that the knowledge of a computer professional is the basis for the evaluation of novelty and inventive step in different application areas of software (e.g. a fundamental well-known file search system is used in a medical area as a medical file search system). Additionally, the normal use of software results in general effects (e.g. higher processing speed, processing more data, and reducing errors) which are not surprising for the skilled person.

In any specific case, it might still be difficult to determine if the claimed subject matter is eligible for patent protection despite several examples in the Guidelines and in the Handbook. This is due to the difficulty of determining whether a computer software-related invention represents a technical idea using the laws of nature.

The Examination Guidelines and the Examination Handbook which has a specific chapter on computer software-related inventions provide information in a bundled form and with plenty of examples. The examples relate in detail (claims, description, and explanation) to modern software-related technologies. Patent professionals are able to find better information on newer technologies. Applicants working in newer areas of technology can see the limits of patentability more clearly.

In summary, the Japanese patent system is liberal regarding software-related patents. Patent professionals have plenty of information for making applications and examining patents. This is provided based on modern and detailed examples of computing technology. They are not only described from the legal view but also from the view of a computer professional.

CHAPTER 12
India

§12.01 LEGAL REQUIREMENTS AND GENERAL DEVELOPMENT

A short overview will be given on the requirements for software patents in India. The Indian patent system has a long tradition. Act VI of 1856 was based on the British Patent Law of 1852. The Patent Act of 1970 has been amended several times.[1] Patents are managed by four branches of the patent office (Mumbai, Chennai, Kolkata, New Delhi). The Office of the Patent Information Centre is located in Nagpur. The offices are under the administrative control of the Controller General of Patents, Designs and Trademarks. The latter is monitored by the Ministry of Commerce and Industry. For the applicant, who is non-resident or has no domicile or has no place of business in India, the address for service in India or place of business of his patent agent determines the particular patent office where he can file patent applications.

Chapter II, 3 of the Patent Act of 1970 with all amendments up to 11 March 2015 indicates several inventions that are not patentable inventions in the sense of the Patent Act. Among these are:

> (k) a mathematical or business method or a computer programme per se or algorithms;
>
> (l) a literary, dramatic, musical or artistic work or any other aesthetic creation whatsoever including cinematographic works and television productions;
>
> (m) a mere scheme or rule or method of performing mental act or method of playing game;
>
> (n) a presentation of information;

1. *History of the Indian Patent System* http://www.ipindia.nic.in/history-of-indian-patent-system.htm (accessed 13 April 2017).

The list of excluded subject matter is similar to those under the patent systems of many countries in Europe and other Asian countries. Like in many other states patentability of software is a contentious topic in India.[2]

India is one of the very few countries (together with some states of the former Soviet Union) that consider not only computer programs per se as excluded subject matter but also algorithms.[3]

The Manual of Patent Practice and Procedure (22 March 2011) provides strict limitations for the topics under Section 3 (k) of the Patent Act.[4] Patent applications, with 'computer programme' as a subject matter, are first examined with respect to mathematical methods, business methods and algorithms. If the subject matter of an application does not fall under these categories, then, the subject matter is examined with a view to decide whether it is a 'computer programme' per se. Furthermore: 'Claims directed at "computer programme products" are computer programmes per se stored in a computer readable medium and as such are not allowable. Even if the claims, *inter alia*, contain a subject matter which is not a computer programme, it is examined to see whether such subject matter is sufficiently disclosed in the specification and forms an essential part of the invention.'

In 2013 'Draft guideline for Computer Related Inventions (CRIs)' appeared.[5] The public gave feedback.[6] In 2015 a first version was published. After several discussions among interested circles, a first revision of Guidelines for Examination of CRIs was released in February 2016.[7] A further revision of Guidelines for Examination of CRIs became effective on 30 June 2017.[8]

§12.02 CRI GUIDELINES OF JUNE 2017

The final version of the CRI Guidelines is more in line with the international legal practice. While the earlier version of 2016 included illustrative examples for unpatentable claims the new version refers only to a decision of the Hon'ble Supreme Court

2. Chingale, R. et al. *Software Patent in India: A Comparative Judicial and Empirical Overview* Journal of Intellectual Property Rights, Vol. 20, July 2015, 210–222.
3. WIPO *Standing Committee on the Law of Patents Exclusions from Patentability and Exceptions and Limitations to Patentees' Rights 2 September 2010* http://www.wipo.int/edocs/mdocs/scp/en/scp_15/scp_15_3-annex1.pdf (accessed 13 April 2017).
4. *Manual of Patent Practice and Procedure (22 March 2011)*, THE OFFICE OF CONTROLLER GENERAL OF PATENTS, DESIGNS & TRADEMARKS, BOUDHIK SAMPADA BHAWAN, S. M. ROAD, ANTOP HILL, MUMBAI (INDIA) http://www.ipindia.nic.in/writereaddata/Portal/IPOGuidelinesManuals/1_28_1_manual-of-patent-office-practice_and-procedure.pdf.
5. India, *Draft guideline for Computer Related Inventions (CRIs)*, 2013 http://www.ipindia.nic.in/guidelines-patents.htm (accessed 13 April 2017).
6. *Feedbacks/Comments on Draft guidelines for Computer Related Inventions(CRIs) 2013* http://www.ipindia.nic.in/CRI-Comments.htm (accessed 13 April 2017).
7. *Guidelines for Examination of Computer Related Inventions (CRIs)* 2016 http://www.ipindia.nic.in/guidelines-patents.htm (accessed 13 April 2017).
8. *Guidelines for Examination of Computer Related Inventions (CRIs) 2017* http://www.ipindia.nic.in/writereaddata/Portal/Images/pdf/Revised__Guidelines_for_Examination_of_Computer-related_Inventions_CRI__.pdf (accessed 14 July 2017).

of India and a decision of the Hon'ble Delhi High Court. The cases relate to general approaches on inventive step.

[A] Overview

The CRI guidelines use the term **Computer Related Invention**. It means 'inventions which involve the use of computers, computer networks or other programmable apparatus and include such inventions having one or more features of which are realized wholly or partially by means of a computer programme or programmes'. This definition seems to correspond to the term computer-implemented invention used at the European Patent Office (EPO).

Firstly, the legal provisions of the Patent Act of 2002 are indicated. The CRI Guidelines comprise a chapter with definitions of basic terms of computing and two legal terms (Manual, per se). Some definitions result from 'The Information Technology Act 2000 (no. 21 of 2000)', the Oxford Advanced Learners Dictionary or the Copyright Act 1957.

The following terms are defined: 'computer', 'computer network', 'computer system', 'hardware', 'firmware' and also 'algorithm', 'computer programme', 'data', 'function', 'information' and 'software'. While the definition of basic terms is helpful, those relating to computing terminology are not always exact. Unfortunately, terminology in computing is not as exact as in chemistry for example. Computing itself can be seen from different viewpoints and traditions (cf. Chapter 2, §2.05 [C]). General tools and principles of computing are used in different application domains. Vocabulary of the application domain (business, medical, chemical...) is merged with computing terminology. Section 4 of the CRI Guidelines explains the examination procedure. The CRI Guidelines of 2016 included Section 5 with a patentability test and Section 6 with fifteen examples for non-patentable claims together with the respective reasons why they are not patentable. The former content of Sections 5 and 6 was deleted.

[B] Algorithm

One critical term is 'algorithm'. Computer professionals very often use it both in a broader sense as well as in a very specific sense of computing (cf. Chapter 2 of this book, §2.06). Computer professionals use it for simple numerical calculations as well as for complex sequences. According to SWEBOK® Guide V3.0 (cf. Chapter 2 of this book, §2.07, [C]): 'Though there is no universally accepted definition, some agreement exists that an algorithm needs to be correct, finite (in other words, terminate eventually or one must be able to write it in a finite number of steps), and unambiguous'.[9]

9. Bourque, P. et al, eds., *Guide to the Software Engineering Body of Knowledge, Version 3.0*, IEEE Computer Society, 2014; 13-10 www.swebok.org. (accessed 13 April 2017).

The relationship between algorithm and computer program is explained in parts of section '4.4 Sufficiency of Disclosure' of the CRI Guidelines. Under '4.4.4 Form and substance' it reads:

> The sub-section 3(k) excludes mathematical methods or business methods or computer programme per se or algorithms from patentability. While the judgment of mathematical methods or business methods is comparatively easier, it is the computer programme per se or algorithms related inventions that require careful consideration of the examiner.

The following two sentences are very important in protecting of computer programs with patents:

> Computer programmes are often claimed in the form of algorithms as method claims or system claims with some 'means' indicating the functions of flow charts or process steps. The algorithm related claims are even wider than the computer programmes claimed by themselves as a single algorithm can be implemented through different programmes in different computer languages.

The first sentence shows the important difference between computer program and algorithm. It is not the computer program in the claim but a method or an algorithm. A formulation of the algorithm as a functional feature of a system claim is also possible. The second sentence indicates the reason: 'a single algorithm can be implemented through different programmes ...'. The CRI Guidelines do not mention that an algorithm could be implemented in hardware in principle.

Finally: 'If, in substance, claims in any form such as method/process, apparatus/system/device, computer program product/ computer readable medium belong to the said excluded categories, they would not be patentable'.

Section 4.5 is about the 'Determination of excluded subject matter relating to CRIs'. Section 4.5.3 is about '**Claims directed as "Algorithm"**'. Here it reads:

> Algorithms in all forms including but not limited to, a set of rules or procedures or any sequence of steps or any method expressed by way of a finite list of defined instructions, whether for solving a problem or otherwise, and whether employing a logical, arithmetical or computational method, recursive or otherwise, are excluded from patentability.

This section is difficult to understand in particular 'Algorithms in all forms including but not limited to, ... any method expressed by way of *a finite list of defined instructions* ... are excluded from patentability'. It seems, that here some characteristics of the algorithm in the narrow sense of computing were introduced. That is the *finite list of defined instructions*. However, under section 2 of the CRI guidelines the algorithm was defined (very broad) as 'a set of rules that must be followed when solving a particular problem'. One possible definition of an algorithm was provided by computer professionals Sedgewick/Wayne (cf. Chapter 2, §2.06, [D]). An algorithm in the context of computing allows 'describing a finite, deterministic, and effective problem-solving method suitable for implementation as a computer program'.

The question arises whether the applicant will formulate a claim with an algorithm in the narrow sense of computing, probably not. Even if this is done the next question is whether, in the normal course of his work and without a real computing system at his disposal, the examiner can really ascertain whether a method in a claim fulfils the requirements of an algorithm in the narrow sense of computing.

While the term algorithm is a fundamental term of computing it is difficult to bring the different facets into one definition. According to SWEBOK® V3.0: 'The attributes of algorithms are many and often include modularity, correctness, maintainability, functionality, robustness, user-friendliness (i.e. easy to be understood by people), programmer time, simplicity, and extensibility. A commonly emphasized attribute is "performance" or "efficiency" by which we mean both time and resource-usage efficiency while generally emphasizing the time axis. To some degree, efficiency determines if an algorithm is feasible or impractical....'. It follows that there is a grey zone between a normal method ('A particular procedure for accomplishing or approaching something, especially a systematic or established one')[10] and an algorithm that fulfils the requirements of computing.

If 'algorithm' is interpreted in a broad sense then there is the danger that traditional technical processes implemented in software or not, could be interpreted as algorithm and thus as excluded subject matter. A broad interpretation of 'algorithm' is apparently one means to strictly limit patents in the area of software. This could lead to a practice that was common in many countries in the past. Applicants disguised software as hardware.

[C] Mathematical Methods and Business Methods

The Indian Patent Act comprises the 'per se' wording (similar to the 'as such' wording in the European Patent Convention) only for a 'computer programme'.

Mathematics in a claim is not completely forbidden: 'mere presence of a mathematical formula in a claim, to clearly specify the scope of protection being sought in an invention, may not necessarily render it to be a "mathematical method" claim.'

The borderline between patentable and non-patentable subject matter might be difficult to determine since several technical advancements in specific areas of computing rely on mathematics (e.g. image/video compression methods, encryption methods for a secure and fast transmission of information). Such mathematical improvements very often facilitate an easier implementation as a computer program. Such programs become a part of a product (e.g. a TV apparatus).

Claims directly or not directly drafted as 'business method' 'but with some unspecified means are held un-patentable'. However, the appearance of business related words in a claim does not automatically lead to the evaluation of the claimed subject matter as a business method. If the claimed subject matter is not only a business method but 'specifies an apparatus and/or a technical process for carrying out the invention even partly, the claims shall be examined as a whole'. Here it seems that technical improvements for carrying out a business method can lead to a patentable

10. Oxford Dictionary *Definition of method in English* https://en.oxforddictionaries.com/definition/method (accessed on 19 April 2017).

claim. However, the meaning of 'technical' in the context of computing is not explained.

[D] 'Computer Programme'

The definition of 'computer programme' (CRI Guidelines use 'programme' contrary to 'program' used in computing publications) in the CRI guidelines is based on the Copyright Act of 1957. It means 'a set of instructions expressed in words, codes, schemes or in any other form, including a machine readable medium, capable of causing a computer to perform a particular task or achieve a particular result'.

Software is a broader term than computer program since it can comprise several programs and also digital data. It includes 'firmware' as a specific type of computer software that 'cannot be changed or lost'.

The CRI Guidelines require that claim interpretation should focus on the substance of the claim or on the underlying substance of the invention, not the particular form in which it is claimed. Exclusions of 'computer programmes' per se cannot be avoided by 'camouflaging the substance of the claim by its wording'. On the other hand it reads: '... it is important to ascertain from the nature of the claimed Computer-related invention whether it is of a technical nature involving technical advancement ...' and later 'if in substance, the claim, taken as a whole, does not fall in any of the excluded categories, the patent should not be denied.'.

Means plus function wording is allowed but if the specification of the invention shows that means plus function is an implementation solely by a computer program then the claim is a 'computer programme' per se.

Claims directed as 'Computer Programme *per se*' are according to the CRI Guidelines:

(i) Claims directed at computer programmes/ set of instructions/ Routines and/or Sub-routines.
(ii) Claims directed at 'computer programme products' / 'Storage Medium having instructions' / 'Database' / 'Computer Memory with instruction' i.e. computer programmes per se stored in a computer readable medium.

The 'per se' wording is explained as 'is "by itself" or "in itself" or "as such" or "intrinsically" – to show that you are referring to something on its own, rather than in connection with other things'.

Bearing in mind the additional 'per se' formulation it is not clear whether the exclusion avoids

- the exclusion of a claim comprising a real computer program as a set of instructions in a programming language (narrow interpretation) or in a broader sense a claim with method steps in a human language (which e.g. describe the function of a possible program);
- all kinds of computer programs even if they are directed to what is a traditional technical area in most international patent systems (e.g. the control of the temperature in a chemical process) and achieve a technical advancement;

- a claim formulation which begins with 'computer program ...', 'computer program product ...' or 'computer readable medium ...' contrary to product or process claims.

It will be seen later in Chapter 12, §12.03 that all three situations seem to be included.

The test for the determination of patentability of CRIs (Section 5. of the CRI Guidelines of 2016) no longer exists. This is appreciated since the patentability requirement of the combination of a computer program with a novel hardware is no longer indicated in the CRI Guidelines of 2017.

Even if the fifteen examples of former Section 6 of the CRI Guidelines 2016 are no longer part of the CRI Guidelines of 2017 one example is indicated here. It is now indicated in a footnote.

Decision ***Yahoo Inc. v. Rediff.com India Ltd.*** of the Intellectual Property Appellate Board (IPAB).[11] The only claim is about:

> A method of operating a computer network search apparatus for generating a result list of items representing a match with information entered by a user through an input device connected to the computer network, the search apparatus comprising a computer system operatively connected to the computer network and the method comprising.

Simplified the method was seen as a method in which advertisers pay for a better position of their advertisement on a webpage. The Board analysed decisions of foreign courts and came to the conclusion that the method is a business method which is not patentable.

[E] Examination Procedure

Section 4 of the CRI Guidelines of 2017 indicate:

> The examination procedure of patent applications relating to CRIs is the same as that for other inventions to the extent of consideration of novelty, inventive step, industrial applicability and sufficiency of disclosure etc. The determination that the subject matter relates to one of the excluded categories requires greater skill on the part of the examiner and these guidelines focus more on this aspect.

The difficulty for CRIs lies in the determination of the required 'technical advance' which is supposed to make the claimed subject matter not obvious.

Section 4.2 on Inventive Step refers to the decision of the Hon'ble Supreme Court of India in *Biswanath Prasad Radhey Shyam vs Hindustan Metal Industries Ltd* and briefly to the decision of the Hon'ble Delhi High Court in F.Hoffman la *Roche v. Cipla*.

---

11. India, *Intellectual Property Appellate Board* http://ipabindia.org/Jurisdiction.aspx (accessed 13 April 2017).

Determination of inventive step is discussed. The decision *Yahoo Inc. v. Rediff.com India Ltd* is also indicated.

Based on the decisions the determination of inventive step should be based on the following points:

> 1. Identify the "person skilled in the art", i.e competent craftsman or engineer as distinguished from a mere artisan;
> 2. Identify the relevant common general knowledge of that person at the priority date;
> 3. Identify the inventive concept of the claim in question or if that cannot readily be done, construe it;
> 4. Identify what, if any, differences exist between the matter cited as forming part of the "state of the art" and the inventive concept of the claim or the claim as construed;
> 5. Viewed without any knowledge of the alleged invention as claimed, do those differences constitute steps which would have been obvious to the person skilled in the art or do they require any degree of inventive ingenuity?

One has to look at the invention as a whole. Nevertheless, inventive step cannot result from an excluded subject itself.

§12.03 CURRENT EXAMINATION PRACTICE AND SUMMARY

The random selection of decisions of the IPAB shows that the Patent Office follows a strict application of the CRI Guidelines.[12] The decisions are usually very short. An in depth analysis is difficult because the claim is not included in the decision. Refusal based on excluded subject matter ('computer programme' per se, algorithm) is very common in the related fields of technology.

In patent application No. 8306/DELNP/2007 by Oracle Int. titled 'Techniques for handling lock-related inconsistencies' (priority of earlier US patent application No. 11/156,318 dated 16 June 2005) the decision dated 12 April 2017 referred to the test in the CRI guidelines of 2016. The patent application related to a processor system with several nodes. Each node maintains information on locks relating to a resource. Inconsistencies between lock information can be avoided by a method of correcting lock information. All the limitations of the claim were considered as software limitations. The contribution was seen only in the computer program and without specific hardware. The only hardware was the processor that worked in a conventional or normal manner.

It has to be seen if and how the the legal practice will change after the release of the CRI Guidelines of 2017. Patentability of a software related invention does no longer require a combination with new hardware in the claim. There are some cases where patents including software have been granted. The detailed criteria are difficult to find. The future will show how legal practice in the field of CRI will develop in India.

---

12. India, *Intellectual Property Appellate Board* http://www.ipabindia.in/ (accessed 19 April 2017).

CHAPTER 13
Patent Cooperation Treaty: PCT

§13.01 OVERVIEW

The Patent Cooperation Treaty (PCT) was founded in 1970. In a large number of countries patents can be obtained with one international patent application.[1] It is said that the PCT influenced the European Patent Convention wording with respect to excluded subject matter and in particular regarding computer programs.

Article 17 (2)(a) PCT indicates that there are situations where a search cannot be done. This can happen if a claim relates entirely to an excluded subject matter. The article reads:

> (2)(a) If the International Searching Authority considers
>
> (i) that the international application relates to a subject matter which the International Searching Authority is not required, under the Regulations, to search, and in the particular case decides not to search, or
> (ii) that the description, the claims, or the drawings, fail to comply with the prescribed requirements to such an extent that a meaningful search could not be carried out, the said Authority shall so declare and shall notify the applicant and the International Bureau that no international search report will be established.
>
> (b) If any of the situations referred to in subparagraph (a) is found to exist in connection with certain claims only, the international search report shall so indicate in respect of such claims, whereas, for the other claims, the said report shall be established as provided in Article 18.

The corresponding article for the examination is Article 34 (4).

1. WIPO *PCT- The International Patent System* http://www.wipo.int/pct/en/ (accessed 25 March 2017).

§13.02 PCT REGULATIONS

More detailed information is provided in the PCT Regulations (as in force from 1 July 2016).[2] Rule 39 (reference to Subject Matter under Article 17(2)(a)(i)) reads:

> 39.1 Definition
>
> No International Searching Authority shall be required to search an international application if, and to the extent to which, its subject matter is any of the following:
>
> (i) scientific and mathematical theories,
> (ii) plant or animal varieties or essentially biological processes for the production of plants and animals, other than microbiological processes and the products of such processes,
> (iii) schemes, rules or methods of doing business, performing purely mental acts or playing games,
> (iv) methods for treatment of the human or animal body by surgery or therapy, as well as diagnostic methods,
> (v) mere presentations of information,
> (vi) computer programs to the extent that the International Searching Authority is not equipped to search prior art concerning such programs.

There is some flexibility with respect to the search of subject matter which is excluded, if claimed 'as such' in many countries. In comparison to the European Patent Convention (EPC) the Rule does not comprise an 'as such' formulation in combination with points (i), (iii) to (vi). Mental acts which might be excluded from the search are 'purely mental acts'. Computer programs are mentioned without any further definition. The general interpretation and practice of the patent offices seems to be that computer programs are not collected. The computer program is understood as a complete list of instructions in a programming language. Furthermore, there is no systematic search in such program listings. It should be taken into account that a computer program can represent an implementation of excluded subject matter like 'presentation of information as such' or 'business methods as such'.

The corresponding Rule for the preliminary examination is Rule 67 which repeats points (i) to (vi) for examination.

§13.03 PCT INTERNATIONAL SEARCH AND PRELIMINARY EXAMINATION GUIDELINES

The PCT International search and the preliminary examination guidelines, as in force from 15 December 2016,[3] make the differences in the legal practice for excluded subject matter more evident.

The Guidelines point out that there are differences between the practices of the various PCT authorities with respect to excluded subject matter (PCT Guidelines, Part

2. WIPO *Regulations under the Patent Cooperation Treaty* (accessed on 25 March 2017).
3. WIPO *PCT INTERNATIONAL SEARCH AND PRELIMINARY EXAMINATION GUIDELINES* (accessed on 25 March 2017).

III, Chapter 9). The Guidelines still indicate the former US practice! Thus, two approaches are pointed out: the 'practical application' approach (mainly former US approach) and the 'technical character' approach which is used in Europe and to a certain degree in Asian countries.

[A] General Remarks on Software Related Inventions

Presentation of information is a field which is relevant for conventional technologies and for computing. Paragraph 9.11 of Chapter 9 indicates the distinction between claims 'directed to the presentation of the information per se (e.g. by acoustical signals, spoken words, visual displays), to information recorded on a carrier (e.g. books characterized by their subject, ..., magnetic computer tapes characterized by the data or program recorded), or to processes and apparatus for presenting information (e.g. indicators or recorders characterized solely by the information indicated or recorded)'. Unfortunately, several examples relate to conventional or nearly outdated computing technology.

Paragraph 9.12 of Chapter 9 relates to some aspects of computing, i.e. collections of data and listings of computer programs. It reads:

> Mere arrangements or compilations of data are generally excluded subject matter unless the arrangement or manner of presentation has technical character or a practical application. For example, a mere program listing itself is not capable of execution and represents merely the expression of the underlying idea rather than the application of that idea, and would thereby fall within this exclusion. A disembodied data structure that has no interaction with an underlying program would not require international search and examination, while a data structure embodied in a tangible medium that has a technical character or has a practical application should be subject to international search and examination.

Sentence two indicates the important difference between the 'underlying idea' which is usually the algorithm as a basis for the computer program and the 'expression of the underlying idea' which is the computer program itself in a programming language. Thus, if somebody claimed a program listing it seems that it could be excluded from patentability as mere presentation of information. A practical application of the program is necessary.

However, as stated in Chapter 4 of the PCT Guidelines, parts of program listings can be indicated in the description:

> 4.23 In the particular case of inventions in the computer field, program listings in programming languages cannot be relied on as the sole disclosure of the invention. The description, as in other technical fields, should be written substantially in normal language, possibly accompanied by flow diagrams or other aids to understanding, so that the invention may be understood by those skilled in the art. Short excerpts from programs written in commonly used programming languages can be accepted if they serve to illustrate an embodiment of the invention.

Bioinformatics is an important field in computing. The PCT Guidelines comprise a few examples. Paragraph 9.12. reads:

> A computer system for searching gene sequences within a particular library of genetic data (the searching function goes beyond mere presentation of information) would have a technical character or a practical application as would a computer program capable of directing the display of three dimensional coordinates of a polypeptide and the atomic coordinates of a polypeptide Q. A computer readable media having the atomic coordinates of a polypeptide encoded thereon, however, would not have a technical character or practical application even though the data structure is embodied in a tangible medium.

Paragraph 9.13 indicates Example 1 which illustrates excluded subject matter for arrangements or compilations of data in the field of bioinformatics:

> Example 1: 3-D structural data of a protein per se
>
> Claim 1.
>
> A computer model of protein P generated with the atomic coordinates listed in Fig. 1.
>
> Claim 2.
>
> A data array comprising the atomic coordinates of protein P as set forth in Fig. 1 which, when acted upon by a protein modeling algorithm, yields a representation of the 3-D structure of protein P.

International search and examination are not required for claims 1 and 2. Both claims are directed to a disembodied data structure that has no interaction with an underlying program.

Paragraph 9.14 indicates a second example:

> Example 2: In silico screening methods directed to a specific protein
>
> Claim 1.
>
> A method of identifying compounds that can bind to protein P, comprising the steps of:
>
> applying a 3-dimensional molecular modeling algorithm to the atomic coordinates of protein P shown in Fig. 1 to determine the spatial coordinates of the binding pocket of protein P; and
>
> electronically screening the stored spatial coordinates of a set of candidate compounds against the spatial coordinates of the protein P binding pocket to identify compounds that can bind to protein P.
>
> Claim 2.
>
> A database encoded with data comprising names and structures of compounds identified by the method of claim 1.

It is explained: 'Claim 1 is directed to a method that has a technical character or practical application. Accordingly, international search and examination is required. Claim 2 is directed to a disembodied data structure that has no interaction with an underlying program. Thus, international search and examination is not required.'

Paragraph 9.15 relates to the exclusion of computer programs. Here, the general international practice is expressed: 'Normally, claims that merely recite program code are excluded subject matter'. According to the text computer programs can be expressed in several forms. One of these is seen in an expression in natural language.

In such a case it follows: 'However, to the extent that a natural language description of any computer-executable program, or a self-documented code, is included in the description and the claims, the Authority should be considered "equipped" to carry out a search and preliminary examination based on such a description subject to the relevant guidelines regarding the conditions as to exclusion'.

The PCT Guidelines apparently use a very broad interpretation of 'computer program'. The question arises from the perspective of a computer professional: 'When is a computer program a computer program?' In very unusual cases the natural language description can be identical to the source code in a specific programming language. In most cases, the description of the program in natural language relates to the fundamental idea (e.g. method, algorithm) of the program which has to perform a desired function. The view expressed in paragraph 9.15 of the PCT Guidelines is not in line with the generally accepted views of computer professionals in software engineering as expressed in SWEBOK® V3.0 (cf. Chapter 2, §2.07).[4] SWEBOK® Chapter 13 'Computing foundations' states: 'Programs must be written in some programming language .... To write any program, one must understand at least one programming language' and later in Chapter 13: 'Programs are not random pieces of code: they are meticulously written to perform user-expected actions. The guide one uses to compose programs are algorithms, which organize various functions into a series of steps and take into consideration the application domain, the solution strategy, and the data structures being used. An algorithm can be very simple or very complex'.

The 'application domain' is an important topic for the patent system. It is well-known that computer programs and in particular application programs are created for a specific 'application domain'. In other words, for processes in different scientific and technological areas and in daily life. As expressed in SWEBOK®: the knowledge of the application domain ('e.g., *aerospace v. hotel management*') has to be taken into account in software development. Computer programs are written for fields which are not traditionally considered to belong to the patent system. Here again, the patent system is faced with the question of whether a proper and efficient search can be done for the description of a program in natural language which relates to 'application domains' (e.g. hotel management) traditionally outside the realm of the patent system. As early as 2005, the Meeting of International Authorities decided to create a task force under the guidance of the European Patent Office (EPO) dedicated to the PCT minimum documentation. The topic included inclusion of Non-Patent Literature, electronic databases and traditional knowledge.[5]

It can be seen, that there are different interpretations of 'computer program' and different understandings of 'programming'. From the general perspective of software engineering as expressed in SWEBOK®, 'programming can be considered as the process of designing, writing, testing, debugging, and maintaining the source code. The source code is written in a programming language. ... *Writing* is the actual coding of the design

4. P. Bourque and R.E. Fairley, eds., *Guide to the Software Engineering Body of Knowledge, Version 3.0*, IEEE Computer Society, 2014; www.swebok.org.
5. WIPO *PCT Minimum Documentation Task Force*, 13 April 2016 http://www.wipo.int/edocs/mdocs/pct/en/pct_wg.../pct_wg_9_22.docx (accessed 29 March 2017).

in an appropriate programming language.' Conversely, this means that computer programs are normally not written in natural human language even if some higher programming languages use natural-language elements to make the program easier for humans to understand.

[B] Divergent Practices Between PCT Authorities

Chapter 9 of the PCT Guidelines has an 'Appendix to chapter 9' with two basic parts:

- 'Excluded Subject Matter Regarding Schemes, Rules or Methods of Doing Business, Performing Purely Mental Acts or Playing Games' and
- 'Excluded Subject Matter Pertaining to Programs for Computers'.

Each part shows the divergent practices of the PCT Authorities. When excluded subject matter regarding schemes, rules, or methods of doing business, ... are implemented by computing means the respective section on programs for computers must be considered. One section indicates the 'practical application' approach and the other the 'technical character' approach. The 'practical application' approach stems from the USA. It is unclear whether the current version (15 December 2016) of the PCT Guidelines reflects the new approach in the USA following the Alice decision.

Both approaches are more harmonized contrary to the past. Search and examination must be made for program-controlled manufacturing and control processes as well as for the program-controlled internal working of a computer. Search and examination have to be done when the subject matter provides a practical application or when the computer program has technical character. The text seems to have its roots in the EPO's decision T1173/97 (IBM- computer program product – 1998). In addition, the text gives an example of the program-controlled organization of a small, fast-working memory and a larger, but slower, further memory in a data-processing system. The effect of the program by virtually extending the working memory provides a practical application according to the 'practical application' approach, or a technical character for the 'technical character' approach. The paragraph relating to the 'technical character' approach states that search and preliminary examination will be done for a claim relating to the program. The claim can have different forms such as product, computer program product, process and use claim. The example with the virtual extension of a memory as an example of a program-controlled internal working of a computer seems to result from the amendment of the Guidelines by the EPO in 1985.[6]

The Appendix to Chapter 9 of the PCT Guidelines points out that for both approaches 'a data-processing operation can be implemented either by means of a computer program or by means of special circuits, and the choice may have nothing to do with the inventive concept but be determined purely by factors of economy or practicality'.

6. EPO, *Notices dated 6 and 26 March 1985 concerning amendment to the Guidelines for Examination in the European Patent Office* OJ, 6/1985, 179 http://archive.epo.org/epo/pubs/oj1985/p157_186.pdf (accessed 27 March 2017).

The passage with the 'practical application' approach states that: a 'mere program listing that describes an executable code that is not tangibly embodied as a record on a computer-readable carrier' and 'an executable program producing only an expression of an idea (such as a mathematical theory) even if tangibly embodied' are excluded. On the contrary, 'a program containing executable code tangibly embodied on a computer-readable carrier which when executed has a practical application' is not excluded. A search and a preliminary examination must be done.

§13.04 SUMMARY

The PCT route has advantages in the patenting strategy. The different practices among PCT authorities have to be considered for software related inventions.

CHAPTER 14

Unitary Patent and Unitary Patent Court

§14.01 OVERVIEW

A major development towards a more efficient protection of intellectual property in Europe is the creation of the Unitary Patent (European Patent with unitary effect) and of the Unified Patent Court (UPC) under the Guidance of the European Union (EU). After years of negotiations, European Union countries and the European Parliament agreed on a 'patent package' with the following three parts:[1]

- 'a Regulation creating a European patent with unitary effect ('unitary patent');
- a Regulation establishing a language regime applicable to the unitary patent;
- an Agreement between EU countries to set up a single and specialized patent jurisdiction (the 'Unified Patent Court')'- UPCA.

The Agreement on the UPC was signed by most of the EU Member States in February 2013. The EU now has twenty-eight Member States (including UK for the time being).[2] The whole package will come into effect when thirteen countries (among them France, Germany and the United Kingdom) have ratified the Unified Patent Court agreement (UPCA). Spain did not participate in the package and did not sign the UPCA. Poland participates in the enhanced cooperation but it did not sign the UPCA.[3] An overview on the new system is given from several perspectives in the book 'The Unitary EU Patent System' edited by J. Pila and C. Wadlow.[4]

1. European Union *Unitary Patent* https://ec.europa.eu/growth/industry/intellectual-property/patents/unitary-patent_en (accessed 13 April 2017).
2. European Union *Member States* https://europa.eu/european-union/about-eu/countries_en#tab-0-1 (accessed 18 April 2017).
3. European Union *2011/167/EU: Council Decision of 10 March 2011 authorizing enhanced cooperation in the area of the creation of unitary patent protection* http://eur-lex.europa.eu/legal-content/EN/TXT/?uri=CELEX:32011D0167 http://eur-lex.europa.eu/legal-content/EN/TXT/?uri=CELEX:32011D0167 (accessed 26 April 2017).
4. Pila, J. et al. *The Unitary EU Patent System* Bloomsbury Publishing, 26 March 2015.

§14.02 THE UNITARY PATENT

The unitary patent is a European Patent granted by the European Patent Office (EPO) according to the European Patent Convention (EPC). The effects of the unitary patent will be valid for the twenty-six Member States of the unitary patent system. In September 2015 Italy joined the Unitary Patent and became the twenty sixth Member State The EU Member States Spain and Croatia have not participated in the package and did not sign the UPCA.

In future applicants will have three options:

- the Unitary Patent with unitary effect;
- the European Patent (bundle of national patents according to the designated countries);
- the national patent.

The Unitary Patent is based on the procedure for a European Patent. It will allow one patent for all Member States. The European Patent Organization currently has thirty-eight Member States, two validation states and two extension states. Among the Member States are states like Norway, Switzerland or Turkey that are not members of the European Union.[5] The applicant designates the Member States, validation states and the extension states of a European Patent.

In order to get a Unitary Patent a patent application has to be filed at the EPO in one of the three official languages (English, French, German).[6] The patent application will be examined according to the EPC. As a result, software related inventions will be examined according to the EPO's legal practice. After the grant of a patent, the proprietor will have the option to file a request for unitary effect at the EPO. If the formal requirements are fulfilled a Unitary Patent will be created for all Member States which participate in the Unitary Patent scheme. The EPO will take over several tasks in the context of the Unitary Patent. Among them are the creation and maintenance of the 'Register for unitary patent protection', collecting of annual fees for unitary patents, distributing part of the annual fees to the participating Member States and several tasks in the context of translations. Details concerning the Unitary Patent can be found on the EPO's website 'Unitary Patent - frequently asked questions'.[7]

§14.03 THE UNITARY PATENT COURT

Basis for the creation of the UPC is the agreement on the creation of the Unitary Patent Court (UPCA).[8] The UPC will have several divisions. The central division will be

5. EPO *Member States* http://www.epo.org/about-us/organisation/member-states.html (accessed 18 April 2017).
6. European Patent Court *Enhanced European Patent System* https://www.unified-patent-court.org/sites/default/files/enhanced-european-patent-system.pdf (accessed 18 April 2017).
7. EPO *Unitary Patent – frequently asked questions* http://www.epo.org/law-practice/unitary/faq.html#faq-634 (accessed 18 April 2017).
8. *Agreement on a Unified Patent Court* https://www.unified-patent-court.org/sites/default/files/upc-agreement.pdf (accessed 18 April 2017).

located in Paris with sections in London and Munich, which will all deal with cases according to their patent classification area. There will also be local divisions and regional divisions. The court of Appeal will be located in Luxembourg.

In general, all matters of civil litigation will fall under the exclusive competence of the UPC. This concerns matters relating to European patents, European patents with unitary effect, supplementary protection certificates issued for a product covered by such a patent and European patent applications. Special rules have been drawn up for the transitional period. The competence of the divisions of the UPC's court of First Instance is indicated in Article 33 of the UPCA. It sets out different scenarios dependent on the location of infringement or the residence or location of the business. A counterclaim for revocation can be launched in the case of an action of infringement. In this situation 'the local/regional division may:

- proceed with both actions;
- refer the counterclaim for revocation to the central division (Bifurcation); or
- with the agreement of the parties, refer the whole case to the central division.
- parties may agree to bring actions before the division of their choice, including the central division'.

A more harmonized evaluation of validity is expected in the area of software related patents.[9] Some concerns are raised on actions taken by so called 'patent trolls'. The UPC webpage explains that several aspects known from the US patent litigation system will not exist under the UPC system.[10] Weak software patents could be more easily attacked than is possible by opposition procedures at the EPO.

Under 83(3) UPCA it is possible to opt out of the exclusive competence of the court. Different scenarios are discussed on the webpage of the UPC.

A Preparatory Committee will take care of all the necessary work (legal, financial, IT, facilities, human resources) until the court is established. A new version of the Draft Rules of Procedure was published in March 2017.[11] The Preparatory Committee announced that the phase of provisional application could start in the near future.

9. *Software & IP: Patent trolls in the UPC landscape* http://www.arnold-siedsma.com/news/news-and-articles/software-ip-patent-trolls-in-the-upc-landscape (accessed 18 April 2017).
10. *Impact of the UPC* https://www.unified-patent-court.org/faq/impact-upc-0 (accessed 18 April 2017).
11. UPC *Draft Rules of Procedure* https://www.unified-patent-court.org/sites/default/files/upc_rules_of_procedure_18th_draft_15_march_2017_final_clear.pdf (accessed 18 April 2017).

CHAPTER 15
Summary: International Comparison

§15.01 INTERNATIONAL DIFFERENCES

As can be seen from the analysis given in Chapters 4–12, there are national differences for the evaluation of patentability for computer implemented inventions.

A one size fits all approach will lead to unnecessary costs in prosecution. Therefore, it is necessary to get an overview of the different national requirements in order to include fallback positions in the original disclosure in the drafting phase of the application to safeguard the company's or the client's interests.

Software may be virtualized, cloudified and distributed over different computing entities which are located in or outside of patent-protected countries. These aspects need to be considered when drafting the claims. A method and apparatus claim will usually be accompanied by other claim formats, if admissible in the relevant jurisdiction. If not, at least a paragraph with an indication of said other claim formats should be included in the description as a fallback position for later examination stages of the application or in other jurisdictions. After grant, this patent helps to provide protection against an infringement scenario in which, for example, software or a digital message is transferred by means of a network interface via a propagation medium from one entity to another. The signal claim format may add value, but is only available in Europe.

The IP5 Offices have compiled a quick reference guide to the most important features of the patent systems in the IP5 regions.[1] This helps in getting an overview.

The following tables should be construed as a very brief summary of a complex legal situation. It should be emphasized, however, that the tables represent the legal situation in a very simplified manner. Therefore, in some cases the answer in practice might be less clear and somehow in between – 'it depends'. However, for giving some

1. At http://www.fiveipoffices.org/news.html (accessed 23 April 2017).

guidance, a binary classification is applied where possible. More specific details may be found in the respective chapters.

The following table summarizes possible claim formats in the different countries.

Table 15.1 Overview over Available Claim Formats in Selected Countries

Claim formats	*EPO*	*DE*	*USA*	*CN*	*KR*	*JP*	*IN*
Method	✓	✓	✓	✓	✓	✓	✓
Apparatus	✓	✓	✓	✓	✓	✓	✓
System	✓	✓	✓	✓	✓	✓	✓
Data carrier / computer readable medium	✓[2]	✓	✓- ⊘ - CRM: uncertain.[3] - If only with 'non-transitory' components.[4]	✓ (Guidelines 2017)	✓ (Guidelines 2014)	✓	⊘[5]
Computer program / Computer program product	✓[6]	✓[7]	⊘ for computer programs per se[8]	⊘	✓ (Guidelines 2014)	✓[9]	⊘[10]

2. *See Guidelines European Patent Office (EPO)*, F, IV, 3.9.1, available at: http://www.epo.org/law-practice/legal-texts/html/guidelines/e/f_iv_3_9_1.htm (accessed 19 March 2017).
3. Due to *Alice Corp. v. CLS Bank International*, available at: https://www.supremecourt.gov/Search.aspx?FileName=/docketfiles/13-298.htm (accessed 19 March 2017).
4. Ex parte *Mewherter*, Appeal No. 2012-007692, available at: https://www.uspto.gov/sites/default/files/ip/boards/bpai/decisions/prec/fd2012_007692_precedential.pdf (accessed 18 March 2017).
5. *Guidelines for Examination of Computer Related Inventions* (CRI), Intellectual Property Office (IPO) (2016), available at http://www.ipindia.nic.in/writereaddata/Portal/IPOGuidelinesManuals/1_83_1_Guidelines-for-Examination-of-CRIs-19-2-2016.pdf (accessed 23 April 2017).
6. *See Guidelines EPO*, F, IV, 3.9.1, available at: http://www.epo.org/law-practice/legal-texts/html/guidelines/e/f_iv_3_9_1.htm (accessed 19 March 2017).
7. For more details *see* Chapter 5, §5.03.
8. *Gottschalk v. Benson*, 409 U.S. at 72, 175 USPQ at 676–677.
9. For more details, *see* Chapter 11, §11.03.
10. *Guidelines for Examination of Computer Related Inventions* (CRI), IPO (2016), available at http://www.ipindia.nic.in/writereaddata/Portal/IPOGuidelinesManuals/1_83_1_Guidelines-for-Examination-of-CRIs-19-2-2016.pdf (accessed 30 March 2017).

Claim formats	*EPO*	*DE*	*USA*	*CN*	*KR*	*JP*	*IN*
Signal	✓[11]	✓[12,13]	⊘[14]	⊘	⊘	⊘	⊘[15]
Data structure	✓[16]	✓[17]	⊘	⊘	⊘	⊘	⊘[18]

The table below summarizes countries where amendments and delimiting claim features (features to be included in the claims for delimitation over prior art) have to be disclosed in the original application. This in turn emphasizes the need to think ahead during drafting of the original priority application and to include aspects in the application.

Table 15.2 Overview over Proof of Original Disclosure in Selected Countries

Jurisdiction	*EPO*	*DE*	*USA*	*CN*	*KR*	*JP*
Proof of original disclosure is required	✓[19]	✓[20]	✓[21]	✓[22]	✓[23]	✓[24]

11. The EPO applied a very liberal approach at a very early stage, e.g. taken in T 0163/85 (Colour television signal) of 14 March 1989, available at: https://www.epo.org/law-practice/case-law-appeals/recent/t850163ex1.html (accessed 19 March 2017).
12. For example claimed as 'method for transmission of digitalized audio signals...' in BGH, 3 February 2015 - X ZR 69/13 - Audiosignalcodierung; OLG Karlsruhe, available at: http://lexetius.com/2015,480 (accessed 19 March 2017).
13. For example claims relating to 'Method for coding /decoding ---' *see* BGH, 21 August 2012 - X ZR 33/10 - MPEG-2-Videosignalcodierung; OLG Düsseldorf, available at: http://lexetius.com/2012,4678 (accessed 18 March 2017).
14. Ex parte *Nuijten*, a 2007 Federal Circuit case.
15. *Guidelines for Examination of Computer Related Inventions* (CRI), IPO (2016), available at http://www.ipindia.nic.in/writereaddata/Portal/IPOGuidelinesManuals/1_83_1_Guidelines-for-Examination-of-CRIs-19-2-2016.pdf (accessed 30 March 2017).
16. *See Guidelines EPO*, G, II, 3.7.2, available at: https://www.epo.org/law-practice/legal-texts/html/guidelines/e/g_ii_3_7_2.htm (accessed 19 March 2017) and T 1194/97 (Data structure product/PHILIPS) of 15.3.2000, available at: http://www.epo.org/law-practice/case-law-appeals/recent/t971194ex1.html#q (accessed 19 March 2017).
17. In Germany, generally, the applicant is free to choose the appropriate claim format. Examination is based on the technical features of the respective claims. *See Guidelines for Examination of Patent Applications*, available at https://www.dpma.de/docs/service/formulare_eng/patent_eng/p2796_1.pdf (Chapter 4.3).
18. *Guidelines for Examination of Computer Related Inventions* (CRI), IPO (2016), available at http://www.ipindia.nic.in/writereaddata/Portal/IPOGuidelinesManuals/1_83_1_Guidelines-for-Examination-of-CRIs-19-2-2016.pdf (accessed 30 March 2017).
19. Article 123 (2) and (3) European Patent Convention (EPC).
20. Chapter 38 German Patent Law.
21. Support for Claim Changes, 35 U.S.C. §316(d)(3); 37 C.F.R. §42.121(a)(2)(ii).
22. Article 33 of the Chinese Patent Law.
23. KIPO Website: http://www.kipo.go.kr/kpo/user.tdf?a = user.english.html.HtmlApp&c = 30101&catmenuek30101 (accessed 30 March 2017).
24. Article 17bis(3) Japan Patent Law.

The analysis of case law provided in Chapters 4–12 reveals that if technical features are not properly elaborated or disclosed in the original disclosure, a significant risk may arise. In some jurisdictions (EPO, DE) it will be difficult to bring the application to grant because insufficient technical information in the original first filing.

Therefore, it is vital to incorporate as many technical considerations, features and aspects as possible in the first filed application.

Usually several independent claims in different and even in same claim formats are claimed. Unity issues are sometimes discussed.

Eligibility for patent protection for business related subject matter claimed *in combination with* technical features:

Table 15.3 Overview over Eligibility for a Business Method with Technical Features in Selected Countries

Jurisdiction	*EPO*	*DE*	*USA*	*CN*	*KR*	*JP*	*IN*
Eligibility for business + technical features	✓ if technically different from prior art	✓ if technically different from prior art	Risk of being refused as abstract idea	✓ if technically different from prior art	✓ if technically different from prior art	Mainly ✓ if in cooperation with hardware	⦸[25]

Whereas a pure business method implemented on a computer (e.g. an auction method where the inventiveness lies within an economic procedure) without any further technical effects:

Table 15.4 Overview over Eligibility for a Pure Business Method Without Technical Features in Selected Countries

Pure business	*CN*	*USA*	*JP*	*KR*	*EPO*	*DE*	*IN*
Eligibility	⦸	In general yes, but tends to be refused acc. to USC 35 §101	⦸	⦸	⦸	⦸	⦸

25. *Guidelines for Examination of Computer Related Inventions* (CRI), IPO (2016), available at http://www.ipindia.nic.in/writereaddata/Portal/IPOGuidelinesManuals/1_83_1_Guidelines-for-Examination-of-CRIs-19-2-2016.pdf (accessed 30 March 2017), *see* 4.5.2, p. 16.

§15.02 GENERAL RECOMMENDATIONS

The following recommendations are based on distinguishing between system software and application software. Furthermore, application software can relate to different sciences (as indicated in Chapter 2, §2.07[E]):

- 'Natural sciences (mathematics, computer and information sciences, physics, chemistry, biology, ...).
- Engineering and technology (civil engineering, electrical engineering, electronic engineering, mechanical engineering, information engineering, ...).
- Medical and health sciences.
- Agricultural sciences.
- Social sciences (psychology, economics and business, educational sciences, law, media and communications, ...).
- Humanities (history and archaeology, languages and literature, art, philosophy, ...)'.

A few hypothetical examples will be indicated below. Put simply, an invention in the broader sense can relate to the basic method and/or to a specific implementation in a programming language in combination with elements of the computer (such as interfaces, memories, registers or data structures).

[A] Application Software

There is the highest probability of patentability if the computer program is an implementation of new and inventive methods in traditional fields of technology.

It is assumed that patent eligibility exists when the software controls functionality of a system which is traditionally patentable in most countries. In other words, patentability will be affirmed if the invention describes a new and inventive method to control a system. The claim is usually worded as a method which is intended to be implemented as computer program.

A simplified hypothetical example in electro-mechanical engineering (application software relates to a traditionally patentable field) is given below:

A method for calculating an efficient direction for a moving lawn mower comprising the steps:

- *sending colour data from a colour sensor A to a control unit, sending speed data from sensor B to a control unit, sending previous movement direction data C, sending GPS data D ...*
- *processing the sensor data A, B, C, D according to the relationship .... and sending the movement direction data to unit X to cause the movement of the mower into the calculated direction.*

A lawn mower comprising ...

A computer readable data carrier comprising instructions for ...

Rule of thumb:

If the basic method is patentable then its implementation in software should be no problem.

From the perspective of a computer professional the use of the computer in a lawn mower is seen as an example of an 'embedded system' as the software is part of a device/system which is not a computer.

If the claim comprises a mathematical formula for the calculation of the direction of movement, it should be checked whether the requirements of a particular country might evaluate the mathematical formula as an abstract idea or a law of nature (as in the US, for example) or if the claim could be seen as a mathematical rule as such.

The drafting of a device claim has to take into account the respective level of abstraction. Means + function claims can be seen to lack clarity. If the description/specification is on a high level of abstraction (only means + function without the concrete elements of the lawn mower) lack of disclosure could be an objection.

In countries which require a technical effect, such technical effect has to be described in sufficient detail. In the example above, the effect may relate to the efficient movement of the mower over a particular area.

The formulation of a claim relating to the (assumed) computer program has to take into account the specifics of the respective country. Usually the method steps are repeated. In some countries a short version (referencing a method claim) is possible.

There is a lower probability of grant if the basic method is a well-known principle (e.g. in the US, building block of human ingenuity) or if such a method is excluded from patentability if claimed as such.

A simplified hypothetical example for a business method A is given below (pure business methods are excluded from patentability in many countries as business methods do not belong to traditional fields of the patent system, while application software belongs to a field outside of traditional fields of the patent system) – cf. example of calculation of weekly wages implemented in the Java programming language in Chapter 2, §2.07[D]:

A method for calculating the weekly wages for employees comprising the steps:

- *Read employee number,*
- *Read the pay rate,*
- *Read the hours worked,*
- *Calculate pay.*

If the description only shows implementation by computing means, the claim might be interpreted as an abstract idea in the US if the business method is well known (building block of human ingenuity). In countries that exclude business methods or mental acts as such, the claim might be disallowed (*see* the table 15.4 in Chapter 15, §15.01).

If generic computer elements (processor, memory, display, Internet, server, etc.) are added to the claim, the claim will presumably still not be eligible for patent protection because it will be regarded as an abstract idea. In countries with a technicality requirement, a claim with generic computer features in combination with a business method might be judged as technical but not as inventive (e.g. in Europe and Germany).

Care has to be taken if a mathematical formula is indicated in the claim. The claim could then be seen as a law of nature, and thus be excluded from patentability.

In countries requiring technical effect it is usually not sufficient to argue that the calculation is faster or can involve more data because of the computer, since this is normal when a computer is used.

There is a higher probability for patentability if the business method is combined with technological features of a real world system.

A simplified hypothetical example for business method B is given below (business method in combination with a traditional field of technology, where application software belongs to both a field outside of traditional fields of technology (payment) and also within a traditional field (petrol pumps)) – cf. example of petrol pump in Chapter 2, §2.07[D]:

Method to fill a vehicle with fuel and to pay for the fuel comprising the steps:

- *read the customer's bank account from the inserted card*
- *send the customer information to the bank for verification*
- *release the fuel hose, recognize the insertion of the fuel hose into the car's fuel tank ...*
- *create a signal A to indicate that the fuel hose is in the car's fuel tank*
- *sense the fuel, if the fuel does not match the required fuel of the vehicle do not allow the filling process; if the fuel is the correct type, open the valve*
- *...*
- *read the amount of fuel*
- *calculate the price*
- *encode the price and send the encoded signal to the server of the bank*
- *...*

Here, the payment might include steps to avoid fraud during transmission of data to and from the bank. The level of detail in the claim and in the description has to be high enough in order to avoid an objection based on an abstract idea, a mental act or a mathematical formula.

[B] System Software

System software controls the internal working of a computer (cf. example of real time operating system Chapter 2, §2.07[D]) or of a computer network. The term includes software for the development and testing of software, compilers or interpreters. Sometimes the term includes databases, web browsers or middleware (software for the connection of software).

A simplified hypothetical claim example:

A method for scheduling jobs in a computer for optimum assignment of resources of the computer to jobs, the process comprising:

- *allocating a priority to each job,*

- *assigning a resource to a job according to the highest priority for a predetermined time,*
- *reducing the priority of jobs that have been assigned to a resource,*
- *determining the job order based on the new priorities.*

Scheduling jobs (or processes) is part of the work of an operating system. Concerns exist relating to eligibility for patent protection in some countries which require an invention to be in a field of technology. Definition of technology is difficult and it is changing. If technology is understood in a more traditional way with a focus on hardware then there is a probability that processes inside of a computer are regarded as abstract and non-technical. The process given in the example above might be judged as non-technical since the scheduling does not, for example, change the physical or chemical state of a device or substance outside of the computer. Political reasons might influence the evaluation of such claims. Operating systems are an important field of open source activities. In view of some expert groups, operating systems should not be 'blocked' by patents. Furthermore, some concerns exist in finding the prior art since open source developers do not usually apply for patents. Thus, their solutions are usually not part of the patent documentation.

In countries that exclude computer programs as such from patentability, the claim might be considered in rare cases as a computer program. There might be the risk that the claim is seen in principle as a human activity or as a mental act.

[C] Summary

Since the appearance of the modern digital computer, the nature of computing has changed while certain fundamental principles remain. Miniaturization has resulted in devices and systems with software as the major element for the functionality of the system (e.g. a vehicle). Modern communication technology allows communication between computerized systems of all kinds. As a result, legal practice has become more liberal in many countries. Method claims are allowed with steps expressed in natural human language but in reality implemented as a computer program in a programming language. Likewise, apparatus claims are allowed with functional features which are implemented as computer program in reality. Concerns exist with respect to the possible breadth of such apparatus claims.

A more liberal approach can be observed in many countries over the years but at the same time the borderline between patentable and non-patentable subject matter remains blurred when processes of traditionally non-patentable areas are implemented as computer programs (aesthetic features, mental acts, etc.).

The 'computer program' claim format is allowed in many countries. However, differences exist in the formulation and interpretation of such claims. In some countries it is more reliable to formulate a claim relating to a data carrier comprising instructions which are an implementation of a claimed method.

Interpretation and use of fundamental terminology remains a source of confusion due to the rapid development of computing and its proliferation in many areas of science and technology. The computer program as a list of instructions in a programming language is not the subject of a patent claim. The program itself is hardly ever known to the patent office. The important element is usually the basic method (or algorithm) which is the basis for the development of software. While some computer professionals do not see a difference between an algorithm and a computer program, a difference may be discerned from the legal perspective. The code as an expression of an algorithm is protected by copyright, but the underlying algorithm is not. The latter might be subject to patent protection taking into account the requirements for patentable subject matter. Other means of protection such as design patents are not discussed here.

A major difficulty in the protection of software by patents remains the gap between legal language and the general language of computer professionals, which may not correspond. Moreover, a high level of abstraction is used in computer science and in addition a high level of abstraction is also aimed at in patent law for extending the scope of protection. This, in turn, may lead to very abstract claim language which may open up a risk of objections over lack of clarity. Therefore, care should be taken when using very abstract claim language.

Concerns are also expressed with respect to the 'one size fits all' principle which might not be suitable for the requirements of modern information technology. Implementation regulations and guidelines are supposed to provide guidance to patent professionals working in all areas of computing and converging fields. However, such general guidelines are very often formulated with a specific structure and using traditional technological terms that leave the reader with no possibility of clearly applying the guidance to the respective modern fields. Relevant information for software related applications are to be found in different parts of general guidelines. Some countries have created specific guidelines for software related patent applications, explaining the basic computing terms relevant to patent law.

International harmonization can be observed at least to some extent but patent practitioners have to take into account the specifics of the legal practice in the different countries.

§15.03 CHECKLIST

Table 15.5 Drafting Checklist

Part of the application	*Number*	*Checklist*
Claims	1	Did you use all available claim formats for independent claims if allowed by the national filing authority and/or at least prepare them as a fallback in the description?
	2	Did you evaluate the central *versus* unitary claim approach? (*See* Chapter 3, §3.04)
	3	Did you draft claims for protecting – if applicable – the virtual character of the software? (*See* Chapter 3, §3.03 and §3.04)

Part of the application	*Number*	*Checklist*
	4	Did you draft claims for protecting – if applicable – the distributed and downloadable character of the software?
	5	In particular, did you check whether it is possible to draft a signal and/or a computer program claim?
	6	Are there enough technical features in the claim to distinguish it from prior art (at least for jurisdictions which require technicality, such as EPO and Germany)?
	7	What actions should be patent protected: development environment, runtime environment, making of data carriers with software, ...?
	8	Is the clarity and conciseness requirement fulfilled, if applicable in the relevant jurisdiction?
	9	Did you avoid a result to be achieved language as far as possible? (*see* for example EPO Examination GL F-IV, 4.10)
	10	Did you provide a concrete technical implementation and not a mere abstract idea (for the USA, for example)?
Description	1	Have you properly and sufficiently defined the terms used within the application?
	2	Did you provide an explanation of how the software features interact or combine with hardware or technical features (for safeguarding the applicant's position in countries which require such an interaction, such as India or China)?
	3	Did you explain a further technical effect of the computer program when running on or loaded into a computer, going beyond the 'normal' physical interactions between the program (software) and the computer (hardware) on which it is run?
	4	Did you provide a basis in the description for defining the accessed functional modules at a lower level of abstraction?
Figures	1	Did you prepare a block diagram with structural elements for each independent product claim?
	2	Did you prepare a signalling, sequence or communication diagram, and/or a flow chart for each independent method claim?
	3	Did you check whether it is useful to prepare a system overview figure (e.g. for embedded systems)?

Index

D

E

F

G

H

I

R

S

www.ingramcontent.com/pod-product-compliance
Lightning Source LLC
LaVergne TN
LVHW020002031026
849161LV00023B/815
9789041152299